The Origins of the First World War:
Great Power Rivalry and German War Aims

The Origins of
the First World War

Great Power Rivalry and
German War Aims

edited by
H. W. KOCH

TAPLINGER PUBLISHING COMPANY
NEW YORK

First published in the United States in 1972 by
TAPLINGER PUBLISHING CO., INC.
New York, New York

Introduction, selection and editorial matter
copyright © 1972 by H. W. Koch
All rights reserved.
Printed in Great Britain

Library of Congress Catalog Card Number: 70–179661

ISBN 0–8008–6117–5

Contents

Preface

The purpose of this volume is to introduce readers who cannot easily read German to some of the main strands of the renewed argument over the origins of the First World War and Germany's war aims. Instead of selecting excerpts from articles or books, with one exception all articles have been reprinted in their entirety. The exception is the article by Fritz Fischer, the first part of which has been omitted since it discusses in great detail the objections of some of his German critics, a discussion so technical as well as polemical in nature that it would have required the complete reprinting of their articles as well. One might add here that the editor has on the whole not considered it to be his task to take sides in the argument. It is left to the reader to consider the arguments and make up his own mind.

Inevitably, a volume such as this can never replace reading Fritz Fischer's, Egmont Zechlin's or Gerhard Ritter's work, and those who wish to pursue the issues raised will have to go back to the originals. Only Ritter's work is now in the process of translation; a translation of Zechlin's is offered in this volume while Fischer's is available in an abbreviated translation. Given the original purpose of this volume, footnotes have been omitted while personalities with which the reader may not be familiar are adequately identified in the index.

With the exception of those articles which have previously been published in English, the German originals have been translated by the editor with the considerable assistance of Derek McKay of the London School of Economics to whose help I am heavily indebted. But here too there is one exception. Egmont Zechlin's contribution has been translated by Mr Heinz Norden. Still, whatever mistakes there are, are my own responsibility, as is the selection of the articles, which like all selections represents an uneasy compromise between what is desirable to do justice to the subject and what can actually be done, especially in view of the length of the two major contributions. Thus it is a pity that there has been no room to include some of the work of East European historians, but this short-coming is somewhat balanced by the circumstances that Fritz Fischer, for instance, appears to draw considerably on their research as well as to share some of their lines of argument. Consequently, the inclusion of work by F. Klein, A. Yerussaleminski or J. Kuczinsky, however desirable in principle, would in some respects have produced duplication.

H. W. Koch

Acknowledgements

I am grateful to Fritz Fischer, Imanuel Geiss, P. H. S. Hatton, Karl-Heinz Janssen, James Joll, and Egmont Zechlin for their permission to include their essays in this collection. I wish also to thank the following for permitting the use here of material originally published by them: _Past and Present_; Batsford Ltd., London; _Historische Zeitschrift_; _Journal of Contemporary History_; and _Zeitschrift für Politik_, Munich.

_H.W.K._

Introduction

When Leopold von Ranke published his *Historisch-Politische Zeitschrift* in Berlin between 1832 and 1836 he displayed on the one hand a penetrating understanding of the most refined intricacies of foreign policy and on the other a completely one-sided preconceived notion that the European order of 1815 represented the apex of man's political achievement, the ultimate form of political life for Europeans. He completely misjudged the strong currents and aims of the liberal movement in Europe, and he had no concept of the middle classes, let alone of the workers.

These are some of the essential weaknesses of Ranke as a historian; equally they are the weaknesses of a school of historians which has decisively influenced German historiography as a whole until very recently. Its main theme has been 'the State', ignoring or at least shunting into obscure sidings the new social and economic forces that came to the fore during the nineteenth century.

To defend Ranke's approach and also to vindicate him as an example to be emulated by future generations of historians, he has frequently been contrasted with Heinrich von Treitschke. Ranke, it is argued, consciously separated history and politics into separate autonomous entities, the latter not being allowed to intrude into the former. Treitschke in contrast used history to justify his political commitment – with rather disastrous long-term consequences. This alleged contrast is as artificial as the erroneous assumptions on which it rests. True, it was easier for Ranke than it was for Treitschke to aim at writing history 'as it actually happened' (an aim incidentally which he took more as a guide than a reality, knowing full well that no one would ever achieve it). His main work was not in the field of 'contemporary history', but nevertheless even for Ranke it proved impossible to separate the historian from the political animal. Nor did any of his disciples achieve this. Although Ranke escaped into pre-industrial epochs, his support for the Protestant territorial State against the Reich and for the cause of Frederick the Great against that of the Habsburgs are but two examples of Ranke's own inability to separate his own political commitment, the influence of day-to-day politics, from his professional work.

The difference between Ranke and Treitschke, considerable though it is, in many respects is one of degree only. Ranke thought he could separate history from politics and failed. Treitschke never even attempted it, nor did Droysen, Sybel or the neo-Rankeans. What all of them share is their overriding concern with political rather than social and economic history, with 'the State' rather than its society, with an implicit primacy of foreign over domestic policy.

Why should this be so? Given that Germany was in the front rank in the development of modern 'scientific' historical scholarship, nourished by the rich sources of Classical humanism, one is forced to ask how that scholarship could focus itself so narrowly. Any answer to this question is bound to be highly complex. But it ought to include the simple fact that during the nineteenth century and before, Britons and Frenchmen, for instance, could take their State for granted while Germans could not. National unity was achieved belatedly and only partially. Germany was and remained, as Helmuth Plessner put it, 'die verspätete Nation', the belated nation. From the very outset of unification the German nation was, as Bismarck rightly felt, fragile within and without. Hence the maintenance of an archaic but apparently stable social order harnessed to modern industrial techniques and also Germany's failure to produce a liberal industrial middle class on the British pattern which would spearhead liberal political reforms. Therefore, also, the readiness of virtually all sectors of German society, including its 'Socialist' component, to subject its interests to those of 'the State' and allow it to become both the preserver of the social and political *status quo* and the initiator of all change. The prevalent desire was for the absorption of all social conflicts by state institutions rather than their regulation within the political process. The forces of modernisation compromised with those of traditionalism, and socio-economic as well as political conflicts were absorbed at an institutional and ideological level.

A strong reflection of this is found in traditional German historiography with its typical emphasis on 'the State' – or strictly political issues – and the Hegelian 'world-historical individual'. The cataclysm of the First World War, the end of the Hohenzollern Empire and the birth of the Weimar Republic seemed to bring forth a new beginning, but the polemical extremes to which such scholars as the brilliant Eckart Kehr allowed their scholarship to be carried, and even more the endemic instability of the new Republic itself, made sure that at least within Germany the work of Kehr, Veit Valentin, Alfred Vagts, Hans Rosenberg or Arthur Rosenberg and others remained short-lived ventures. Hitler's rise put an end to all such endeavours and after 1945 it took almost a decade and a half for new methodological approaches to emerge.

Inevitably, the emergence of a new school of historiography implies the revision of the traditional historical picture. Perhaps any such revision would have stirred few minds other than those of the specialists had the subject-matter been something more remote than the origins of the First World War. Indeed, if we are looking for the causes of the failure of a new German historiography to establish itself after the First World War, we would have to add to the reasons Article 231 of the Versailles Treaty which was widely interpreted as saddling Germany with the sole 'guilt' for the outbreak of the First World War. This article not only ensured the 'primacy of foreign policy' in German historiography, but its interpretation incensed the German nation from Left to Right. After all, millions had fought in the war with the conviction of facing 'a world of enemies' who had 'encircled the Fatherland'.

Already during the first month of the war the German Foreign Office had indicated the 'guiding principles' of any future publication of official documents: German reaction towards the alleged Allied policy of encirclement; grandiose German war aims were to be denied. After the collapse of the German Empire, the Weimar Republic found itself faced by two tasks. Firstly, it had to discredit the policies of the Imperial government as much as it could; secondly, it had to prove the Allied indictment of the German government and the German nation wrong. This essentially was the twofold objective of the first German official post-war publication, *Die deutschen Dokumente zum Kriegsausbruch*, edited by Count Max Montgelas and Walter Schücking.

However, the apologetic tone which marks those five volumes soon disappeared in other official publications after the signature of the Versailles Treaty. The signature of Germany's plenipotentiaries was only the first dribble of ink of a veritable flood that was to be spent on the 'war-guilt question'. Convinced of the righteousness of its own cause, the German Foreign Office financed a vast campaign against this clause by supporting various bodies who publicly tried to repudiate Article 231. The most prominent and prolific member of some of these was Alfred von Wegerer, himself – unknown to most of the German public – an employee of the German Foreign Office. In his vast number of publications Wegerer primarily indicted Russia and France for unleashing the war, maintaining a somewhat more reserved and 'benevolent' attitude towards Great Britain. Much of his supporting evidence came from the Russian archives which the Bolsheviks, for a time at least, lavishly published. But the greatest documentary support for the vindication of German policy was derived from the publication, between 1922 and 1927, of large parts of the German diplomatic archives in *Die Grosse Politik der europäischen Kabinette 1871–1914*, edited by J. Lepsius, A. Mendelsohn-Bartholdy and F. Thimme. Some 15,889 documents were published in 40 volumes, arranged in 300 chapters. Like *Die deutschen Dokumente* the material published in this vast collection was almost exclusively diplomatic in nature, ignoring in the main military and economic aspects. Moreover, as in the case of similar publications by countries which emulated the German example, such as for instance Great Britain, France and Austria, ample grounds exist for suspecting a highly tendentious procedure in the selection of the documents to be published.

The German attempt to revise Versailles historiographically also received considerable support from historians outside Germany, notably in the United States where S. B. Fay's *The Origins of the First World War* proved a best-seller, one that was immediately translated into German. By comparison the conclusions of Bernadotte E. Schmitt (a compatriot of Fay) were hardly noticed, at least not in Germany. The last man to analyse the origins of the First World War in the inter-war years in considerable detail was the Italian journalist and politician, the former editor of the Milan *Corriere della Sera*, Senator Luigi Albertini. At first Albertini's massive three volumes had little influence upon German historiography in particular and the historiography of other countries in general. To begin with, the work was not completed before 1942, by which time the world had other worries than the First World War. The first complete English translation was not available before 1957. Furthermore, however detailed and meticulous a study Albertini's work may be, it is not free from case-pleading. He himself had been a leading advocate of Italy's intervention on the Allied side and inevitably his work is marked by his political preferences. Still, whether 're-visionist' or 'anti-revisionist', most of the historiography on the origins of the First World War is marked not only by its partisan nature but also by its purely political frame of reference in which social, economic and institutional questions are hardly posed, let alone answered. By and large, within and without Germany, the 'consensus' was established, aptly summarised by none other than Lloyd George himself, that all the nations of Europe had 'stumbled into the war'. This meant that Germany was no longer the party

carrying the sole guilt for the war and that it had not
entered the war premeditatedly. This 'consensus' even
survived the Second World War, and a Franco-German
historians' conference in the 1950s concluded that 'the
documents do not allow one to ascribe in 1914 to any
one government or people the conscious desire for a
European war'. Carefully phrased as it is, the statement
allows one to read it any way one wants.

By comparison with the 'war-guilt question' the
question of German war aims appears to have been a
purely secondary one. For the more extreme demands,
evidence was found which indicted the Pan-Germans,
and in general one cannot escape the impression that
the entire question was frequently evaded by historians like Hans Delbrück and Viktor Bredt, whose
conclusions culminated in blaming wholesale the
Third O.H.L. under Ludendorff with the responsibility for such traces of official annexationism as could be
found. Historians seemed to have settled all the issues,
so much so that one of them could conclude that 'the
history of the period 1914 to 1918 has been researched as
thoroughly as hardly any other epoch'.

Four years after this statement had been made, in
1959, the Hamburg historian Fritz Fischer published
an article in the *Historische Zeitschrift* whose thesis
was that German expansionist aims were pursued during the First World War not simply by fringe movements like the Pan-Germans or militarists like the
Army High Command under Ludendorff, but by
sectors and personalities who had previously been
classified as moderates like the Chancellor, Theobald
von Bethmann-Hollweg. Already at this stage the implicit thesis of Fischer's argument existed – influenced
perhaps by the more polemical writings of E. Ver-
meil, A. J. P. Taylor and Sir Lewis Namier – namely,
that there was a continuity in Germany's political and
economic aims from Wilhelm II to Adolf Hitler. At
that early stage, though, few but the initiated were
aware of the potential challenge which this argument
in Germany presented to established historiographical
orthodoxy.

Fischer's article concerned itself with Germany's war

aims in eastern Europe, and his views corresponded closely to those to Hans W. Gatzke who in 1950 published a brief study, *Germany's Drive to the West*, a study based mainly on printed materials, but new in the sense that it analysed the role of economic interest groups in the formulation of German war aims in the West. Gatzke's work was little noticed until Fritz Fischer's *Griff nach der Weltmacht*, published in 1961, drew attention to it.

Surprisingly enough, it was not the main body of Fischer's book, an exhaustive study of German war aims, which caused havoc among the historical profession inside and outside Germany, but his statement that Germany had accepted the risk of general European war during the July crisis. This was sufficient to upset current orthodoxy, and under the pressure of public controversy, instead of mellowing, Fischer's attitude hardened further, moving to somewhat extreme positions, especially in his most recent work *Krieg der Illusionen*, in which he puts forward the view that from 1911 the German Empire desired war, prepared for it and ultimately provoked it in 1914.

Fischer's views and those of his pupils, the most notable being Imanuel Geiss, were bound to be highly explosive in an atmosphere in which the problem of responsibility for the First World War was considered settled once and for all and in which not only the historical profession but the divided German nation to a greater or lesser extent was concerned in coming to terms with and explaining the recent phenomenon of National Socialism. But if it was part of Fischer's intention to challenge his colleagues, the challenge was taken up. Although the late Gerhard Ritter had long preached as well as practised a more critical approach to the history of Wilhelmine Germany than had hitherto been customary, particularly in his main work *Staatskunst und Kriegshandwerk* (translated into English by Heinz Norden and published by the University of Miami Press under the title *Sword and Sceptre*), Fischer's interpretation was too much for him. He was in a position to point out serious methodological and factual errors in Fischer's study of German war aims.

But for that matter Ritter also is not free from an occasional blunder.

Gerhard Ritter died in 1967, but opinions are still sharply divided not simply for and against Fischer but cover a wide spectrum which ranges between the two poles, a typical example being Egmont Zechlin. Even East German historians felt themselves compelled to take sides supporting Fischer and his pupils generally, but also pointing out that theirs is blinkered history because it ignores the fundamental readiness of the other European Powers to go to war.

Be that as it may, Fischer's work has opened new avenues methodologically for German historiography by abandoning the well-trodden paths of purely political history in favour of analysing sectional, economic and class interests and their bearing upon the formulation of German policy. German historians in the Federal Republic have discovered Karl Marx at last – with a vengeance perhaps – and allowed him to enter, if only through the back door. However, in view of the bitterness of animosity of response and counter-response caused by Fischer's work, one is compelled to add that it would be a pity if this also meant the total rejection of the high standards of professional ethics set by Leopold von Ranke.

In this selection of articles on the July crisis and Germany's war aims James Joll, who basically shares Fischer's viewpoint, outlines the debate as he sees it.

P. H. S. Hatton's contribution surveys the ground covered more fully in his article on Harcourt and Solf in the *European Studies Review*, 1 (April 1971). For reasons of space, this latter, along with other desirable material, has had to be omitted.

Imanuel Geiss adds his own interpretation of the background to the origin of the First World War which, as has been rightly pointed out, because of his own preconceived and strongly held notions, does not clarify the motivations of the other Great Powers and their readiness to accept war as an alternative to the political process. Geiss has frequently accused a previous generation of historians of selectivity and omission. True as this charge may be, L. C. F. Turner in an article published in the *Journal of Contemporary History* entitled 'Russian Mobilisation in 1914' supplies evidence that this charge holds true as well of Geiss, who appears particularly blind towards Russian and French policy during the crisis. Moreover, Geiss has argued elsewhere that to ask Russia in 1914 to cease supporting Serb nationalism and France to cease supporting Russia in such action would have been tantamount to asking the 'impossible of the two Great Powers', given the historical situation. Quite apart from the questionability of the argument as such, there is nothing which could not make it fit Austria–Hungary or Germany. Nor does it occur to Geiss that had Russia taken no action, Austria–Hungary, indecisive as it was in the conduct of its policy during the July crisis, would have been likely to have done nothing against the Serbs for lack of German support – unless, of course, Germany was prepared to unleash a war one way or the other and thus accept the onus of being the Power to make the first move. However, this was a step which Bethmann-Hollweg was unlikely to have taken because of his need of the support of Germany's Social Democrats. That support was only sure once Russia was mobilising.

Geiss's reinterpretation of the background to the July crisis is supported by Fritz Fischer's contribution 'World Policy, World Power and German War Aims'. Fischer interprets German policy during the July crisis as a product of its failure to expand politically and economically in south-eastern Europe during the preceding four years. He then goes on to argue his case of establishing a continuity between Germany's war aims and the pre-war aims of *Weltpolitik*, a continuity existing – within the frame of reference of the article – in the main in Germany's engagement in Austria-Hungary, the Balkans and Turkey.

Unfortunately, Gerhard Ritter has never criticised Fischer's work in its entirety but only isolated aspects of it, such as German pre-war policy or Fischer's treatment of the Chancellor, Bethmann-Hollweg. Ritter postulated a fundamental difference in aims between Bethmann-Hollweg and Ludendorff, between civil

power and the army. Fischer has argued that such a
difference is a purely artificial one which never existed.
Both politicians and army were agreed on the ends,
they only differed over the means. To present Ritter's
own interpretation would have required the reprinting not only of one but of several of his articles. This
was clearly impossible; hence one of Ritter's ablest
pupils, Karl-Heinz Janssen, provides a fair but also
critical summary and assessment of Ritter's position
and argument, an argument which is further elaborated upon by the late Klaus Epstein in his discussion of
'Gerhard Ritter and the First World War'.

Egmont Zechlin's contribution illustrates the point
made above that one cannot simply speak of for and
against the Fischer school in Germany. It would be an
unwarranted oversimplification to place Zechlin half-
way between Ritter and Fischer. After all, in the final
analysis, in spite of the feud between them Ritter had
found it necessary to adapt his own position as a result
of Fischer's work. Zechlin, however, appears to agree in
many respects with Fischer and attributes to German
policy during the July crisis a more active role than
German historians had been ready to allow before. He
emphasises Germany's readiness to accept the risk of a
general war, but making the very important distinction between a readiness to accept what may be
inevitable and the desire to provoke war to further
expansionist aims. The picture he presents is considerably more complex than Fischer's and devoid of oversimplification. Unlike Fischer as well as Ritter, Zechlin
sees the documents as bearing out the impression on
Germany's policy-makers of being subjected to an encirclement policy by the Powers of the Entente. This
policy Germany countered by a limited offensive
launched with a defensive aim. But once the traditional nineteenth-century pattern of limited Cabinet
warfare had been replaced by total war, Germany, in
Zechlin's view, had only one alternative, of wresting
from Great Britain its allies on the European mainland by speedily defeating them and fusing them into
an economic as well as political unit. *Mitteleuropa* was
the product of the breakdown of a Cabinet warfare

with limited aims, and its degeneration into hegem-
onical war was conducted both by the Central and
the Entente Powers. Egmont Zechlin's contribution also
points to the state of flux still existing in the current
research on this topic. Hence his final conclusions
will be found in his forthcoming book *Kriegsausbruch
1914 und Kriegszielproblem in der internationalen
Politik*.

'Can we be certain that Bethmann-Hollweg and his
colleagues were so different from other European statesmen in their almost unconscious assumption of the
Darwinian necessity and empirical morality of war?'
one reviewer asked in *The Times Literary Supplement*, and goes on: 'The mood suggests ... that the
German attitude was not wholly isolated from a
general European fever.' Actually, Imanuel Geiss has
argued that a specifically German ideology of the permanent struggle of the peoples lay at the base of German *Weltpolitik* which tried to justify Germany's bid
for World Power status 'philosophically'. Indeed, not
only Bethmann-Hollweg himself but also the diaries
and writings of his close confidant and adviser Kurt
Riezler provide sufficient evidence to demonstrate the
existence and general currency of Social Darwinian
premises on the eve of the First World War. Fritz
Fischer himself has frequently expressed surprise over
the extent to which the debate over his work has come
to centre around personalities rather than social and
institutional structures and intellectual currents. In
his most recent work *Krieg der Illusionen* he has devoted a few pages to them, arguing much the same case
as Geiss of a specifically German ideology.

James Joll in his 'Unspoken Assumptions' emphasises
the importance of intellectual currents and their influence upon policy-makers, using, for instance, Riezler's publications and fragments of his private papers
to speculate upon the 'Unspoken Assumptions' in Bethmann-Hollweg's mind. The editor's own contribution
questions the postulation of a specifically German ideology and looks at the 'Unspoken Assumptions' of
the period in a wider context, suggesting that Social

Darwinism was part of the intellectual fabric of western Europe and North America and pointing to the ultimate result of this ideology once both men and circumstances existed to carry it to its ultimate logical conclusion thirty years later.

1 The 1914 Debate Continues: Fritz Fischer and His Critics

James Joll

Two recent academic controversies, one in England and one in Germany, have aroused interest and repercussions far outside the university world in which they originated. Mr A. J. P. Taylor got into trouble for suggesting that Hitler did not plan the war that broke out in September 1939; Professor Fritz Fischer, of Hamburg University, has got into even worse trouble for saying that the German government did plan the war of 1914. While Mr Taylor's *Origins of the Second World War* has been subject to endless discussions in England and, as often with controversial works, has been, in part at least, accepted by many as a new orthodoxy, the stir provoked by Professor Fischer's *Griff nach der Weltmacht*, although it has been noted by British scholars such as Professor F. L. Carsten, has not yet been closely examined in this country. However, it is perhaps worth studying, not only because of the important new evidence which Professor Fischer has discovered about the origins and nature of the First World War but also because of the light which the reception of the book in Germany throws on certain fundamental attitudes and problems. Moreover, the book provokes reflections about historical method and even, it may be, about the way wars in general may start in a tense international situation dominated by an unrestricted arms race.

Professor Fischer's book was first published in 1961. It is a large detailed work, some 900 pages long, and is based on a vast collection of German government archives hitherto not available for study. While one might sometimes criticise the style and the construc-

tion of the work – it is perhaps over-long and, if anything, over-documented – no one can deny that it is
an important major work of scholarship which contains a mass of new evidence about Germany's
methods and goals in the First World War, and that it
will oblige other scholars of all nationalities to look
again at accepted versions of the policies and aims of
their own countries. Why, then, has a scholarly monograph with no great obvious appeal to the general
public and little stylistic attraction caused such an
outcry? It so scandalised some German historians that
one of the most respected of them [Gerhard Ritter]
wrote, 'I could not put the book down without feeling
deep melancholy: melancholy, and anxiety with regard to the coming generation. . . .'

To answer this, it is necessary to look at Professor
Fischer's main thesis and then to examine some of the
criticisms, both general and detailed, which have been
made against him. But even before doing this, it is
important for English readers to remind themselves
just how dominant a role the 'war-guilt question'
played in the study of contemporary history in Germany between the wars and how sensitive a point it
still is. Article 231 of the Treaty of Versailles laid
down that Germany accepted responsibility for the
war imposed 'by the aggression of Germany and her
allies'. This, quite apart from its political effects, was
to impose on German historians – and later on some
foreign historians too – the duty of assembling the
evidence to refute the view that Germany was responsible for the war. One of the most notable acts in this
connection was the German government's decision in
the summer of 1919 to publish a long series of volumes
of documents from the German Foreign Ministry
archives, *Die Grosse Politik der europäischen Kabinette*, an example which was followed by other major
belligerent Powers, and which was again adopted as a
precedent after the Second World War, thus providing historians with a wealth of material, though at the
same time provoking in some of them a suspicion that
there were still in the archives hidden secrets which

the publication of selected documents only served to conceal.

It might have been thought that, after the Second World War, the issue would have died, since even the Germans agreed that it was Hitler and the Nazi leaders who were responsible for the war and that the Nuremberg trials, whatever may be thought of them from a legal or political point of view, had at least served to clear up the question of war guilt for the Second World War once and for all. For the Germans this was extremely important: if the blame was put squarely on to Hitler, then the rest of his countrymen were absolved. Hitler and the Nazis, instead of being regarded, as they are by some historians, as a product of German society and German ideologies, could be treated as a unique phenomenon, a sort of inexplicable scourge inflicted on the German people from outside, and alone responsible for the disasters and horrors of the Third Reich. It is for this reason that many Germans resent any suggestion, such as that made by Mr Taylor in his *Origins of the Second World War*, that what Hitler was doing (at any rate up to 1939, which is when Taylor's book ends) was no different from what other German statesmen had wanted to do.

This brings one back to Professor Fischer, for, as he expressly states in his Introduction,

The book points beyond its own limits, in that it demonstrates certain ways of thought and formulation of aims for German policy in the First World War, which have continued to remain active. From this point of view it may also be a contribution to the problem of continuity in German history from the First to the Second World War.

It is this suggestion – and it is no more than that – which has particularly aroused many Germans to criticise Fischer, and started a controversy in which even the German government apparently intervened by trying to stop Professor Fischer from undertaking a lecture tour in the United States, while the President of the Bundestag accused him and his students of

being intellectual flagellants, and the editor of a respected newspaper denounced him for 'national maso-
chism' and suggested that he should resign from his
university chair.

Fischer's main thesis – perhaps over-emphasized by
the title 'Grasping at World Power' – is that Germany
was ready to resort to war in order to establish herself
as a *Weltmacht*, a Great Power, that is, which could
take its place along with the other World Powers, who
had established their position in the world before
Germany had achieved national unity. This idea of
achieving true Great Power status in a world balance
of power – a concept which Professor Ludwig Dehio,
although he has criticised some of Fischer's conclusions, had previously examined and developed in
some interesting essays – was easily turned into a plan
for organising the world, or part of it, in such a way
that it should be dominated by Germany and serve
German economic, cultural or strategic interests. Professor Fischer demonstrates, by a detailed examination
of the documents, first, that the German government,
if they did not actually want war in 1914, were at any
rate prepared to face the risk of it in pursuit of their
general aims, and that they systematically encouraged
their Austrian allies to provoke war with Serbia even
when they saw that it could not be localised; and
secondly, that, as soon as the war had started, they developed plans, which they had already previously discussed, for large-scale territorial annexations and for
the establishment of a German-controlled new order
in Europe.

This is a very crude summary of an argument that is
built up with great subtlety and detail in the early
chapters of the book, and it is these that have aroused
the most interest and provoked the most controversy.
Later chapters deal with the development of German
war aims as the circumstances of the war changed –
with the attempts to start subversive movements in
Russia and in the British Empire, with the proposals
for restoring a semblance of Polish independence or
for establishing a Flemish State in Belgium. The main
purpose of the later chapters is to show how, in spite

of the varying fortunes of the war and in spite of the
growing anxiety by 1917 about the nature and purpose of the war, the aims for which Germany continued to fight remained essentially those which had
already been set out in September 1914, in a memorandum by the Chancellor, Theobald von Bethmann-
Hollweg – a document the discovery of which forces us
to reconsider the nature of German policy in general
and the position of Bethmann-Hollweg in particular.
All this is easy for non-Germans to find plausible and
convincing; and, indeed, some of it is already familiar
through the work of Professor Hans Gatzke, for example, who has shown the extent of Germany's ambitions in western Europe in his book *Germany's Drive
to the West*, while in the East, the Bolshevik Revolution and the military collapse of Russia enabled the
German government by the Treaty of Brest-Litovsk to
put their war aims into practice, so that, instead of
being recorded in secret archives, Germany's aims
were there on the ground for all to see – though even
here Professor Fischer shows that the vast territorial
and political gains of March 1918 were considered by
many Germans in authority as only the beginning of
even more extensive conquests to serve Germany hegemony on the European continent. But for the Germans this apparent reopening of the war-guilt question is extremely painful.

The most striking section of Fischer's book – and it
has led many of his critics to overlook the interesting elaboration of his themes in later chapters – is the
early part in which he deals with the crisis of 1914 and
with the formulation of German aims in the first
weeks of the war, when it still looked as if a speedy
victory over the French, as foreseen by the German
military planners, might be possible. In the discussion
of this section of the book, some of Professor Fischer's
original intentions have perhaps been forgotten and
misunderstood. He is anxious to show that Germany's
plans for war and her aims once the war had begun
were the product of the social and economic situation
in Germany, so that the presuppositions of Germany's
leaders and the pressures to which they were subjected

were such that, in a sense, the personalities and decisions of individuals were of little importance and
their choices in fact strictly limited by the political,
social, economic and ideological climate within which
they were operating. The critics of Fischer's views,
however, have tended to concentrate on the personalities of the men whose actions were crucial to German
policy in the months of July and August 1914 – the
Kaiser, Bethmann-Hollweg (the Imperial Chancellor),
Gottlieb von Jagow (the State Secretary in the Foreign
Ministry) and Helmuth von Moltke (the Chief of the
General Staff). In particular, it is the new view of
Bethmann-Hollweg's character and purposes as it
emerges from the documents Professor Fischer has discovered that has upset people most. Indeed, it has, in
spite of Professor Fischer's expressed intentions,
turned the discussion largely into one about personalities. Once this is so, then the interpretation of
documents necessarily depends on the interpretation
of character; for the way in which one reads the
documents is determined by one's general view of the
nature and motives of the writer of the document, and
divergent views of a man's character will result in
differing interpretations of what he writes.

In Professor Fischer's view, Bethmann-Hollweg's
policy had been based on the assumption that British
neutrality in the war – a war which, on this view, he
regarded as inevitable – could best be secured by
making sure that the outbreak of war appeared to
have been provoked deliberately by Russia or by
France. Thus when, at the end of 1912, the German
government was collaborating with the British to keep
the Balkan War localised but when, at the same time,
they were preparing for new military and naval increases, Bethmann-Hollweg wrote that a war with
Russia in the Balkans would certainly involve France,
but that it was 'from many indications at least doubtful
whether England would actively intervene if Russia
and France appear directly as provoking the war'. For
Professor Fischer this is evidence of the continuity of
Bethmann-Hollweg's policies, and he suggests that the
Chancellor in 1912, as in 1914, was less concerned with

pursuing peace than with dividing Britain from
France and Russia and with keeping Britain neutral
by making sure that France and Russia appeared to
be in the wrong. This is one of several points at which
Professor Gerhard Ritter, the most formidable of
Fischer's critics, to whom we shall return later, chal-
lenges Fischer's interpretation and accuses him of mis-
reading the documents. He says that Bethmann-Hollweg in this particular report was making a purely
tactical point intended to calm down the Kaiser, who
was always ready to fly into a rage with the British,
and to try and make him resist the proposed naval
increases, which to the British appeared as German
provocation. If one reads the report in question dis-
passionately, it can, it seems to me, be taken either
way, and one's interpretation is not conditioned by
the document itself, or even entirely by the circumstances in which it was drafted, but rather by one's
view of Bethmann-Hollweg's character and policies as
a whole. A historian's view of a man's aims and motives is formed to a large extent by the documents, but
it necessarily also influences the way he reads them;
and it is unrealistic to expect Professor Fischer, who,
on his reading of the evidence, has formed one
opinion of Bethmann-Hollweg's political personality,
to agree with Professor Ritter, who, from the same
evidence, has come to a radically different conclusion.
Each, when interpreting a particular document, is
looking for support for a view already formed through
reading many other pieces of evidence.

Let us look, however, at Fischer's general view of
Bethmann-Hollweg and his policy. For Fischer, Bethmann-Hollweg is a typical product of the forces which
dominated German life at the beginning of the century, a period in which Fischer (following Ludwig
Dehio) sees the Germans convinced of their own
strength – politically, militarily and industrially – and
wanting desperately to be a World Power, to have a
vaguely defined and obscurely conceived world mission which would, in the world balance of power,
make up for the disadvantage under which Germany

suffered because of coming too late as a united nation on to the world scene. Bethmann-Hollweg was, Fischer shows convincingly, already before the war in touch with people who were specifically thinking in terms of a German-dominated *Mitteleuropa*, and to a large extent shared their thinking. Although he hoped for the possibility of achieving *Weltmacht ohne Krieg*, he was ready to accept the idea of war and to base his policy on the necessity of ensuring, if it came, that it was under conditions as favourable to Germany as possible. According to Fischer, Bethmann-Hollweg overestimated Germany's strength and, above all, maintained up to the final crisis an unfounded belief in the probability of Britain's neutrality. It is in the light of these general assumptions about Bethmann-Hollweg that Fischer interprets his conduct of affairs in the crisis of July 1914 and in the early weeks of the war.

It is here that the importance of Bethmann-Hollweg's Memorandum of 9 September 1914 lies, and it certainly forces us to reconsider the conventional picture of Bethmann-Hollweg as the liberal statesman (who reminded Lord Haldane of Abraham Lincoln), striving in vain to maintain peace against the machinations of the militarists. The Memorandum was sent by Bethmann-Hollweg from G.H.Q. in Koblenz to his deputy, Clemens Delbrück, the State Secretary of the Interior, in Berlin, just at the moment when the French counter-attack on the Marne was going to transform the course of the war, but before the outcome of the battle was known, so that the Germans still seemed to be faced with the problems that would confront them on achieving victory in the West. Bethmann-Hollweg laid down that the aim of the forthcoming peace settlement must be

> the security of the German Empire in the West and in the East for the foreseeable future. To this end, France must be so weakened that she cannot rise again as a Great Power, Russia must be pushed as far as possible from the German frontier, and her rule over non-Russian subject peoples must be broken.

Professor Fischer makes two important points about this document. Firstly, he shows in the subsequent chapters of his book that it in fact contains the minimum aims which some German leaders consistently attempted to pursue throughout the war: the reduction of France to a second-class Power by territorial annexations, the establishment of some form of long-term control over Belgium, the spread of German power eastwards, either by direct annexation or by the creation of a German satellite State in Poland, and the weakening of Russia by the encouragement of subversive movements of all kinds, while at the same time Germany would lay the basis of a new colonial empire by the acquisition of large areas of Central Africa. Secondly, Professor Fischer shows that this programme has strong similarities both with the ideas of a number of leading German industrialists for establishing a German-dominated, economically unified *Mitteleuropa*, and even with the more outspokenly annexationist demands of the Pan-German League, which had been drafted shortly before. Fischer shows convincingly that in fact Bethmann-Hollweg was in close contact with Walther Rathenau (the head of the great German electrical combine, the A.E.G., and one of the directors of the Berliner Handelsgesellschaft) – a neighbour and frequent visitor at Bethmann-Hollweg's country-house – and with Arthur von Gwinner of the Deutsche Bank, and there can, I think, be no doubt that their ideas directly influenced the formulation of war aims by Bethmann-Hollweg at a moment when he had every reason to expect an early peace.

For the Anglo-Saxon reader, there is perhaps nothing very surprising in all this: and some of it is already known – the paper on war aims which Rathenau sent to Bethmann-Hollweg on 7 September, for example, which expresses the necessity for controlling France in order to defeat England, and reiterates the importance of German supremacy in central Europe. But Fischer's exposition does suggest a consistency and continuity in German planning; in combination with his insistence that in July 1914 it was the Germans who were egging on the Austrians to

war, it makes the comfortable thesis difficult to maintain, that – to use the phrase coined by Lloyd George
– 'the nations slithered over the brink into the boiling
cauldron of war'.

Since it is Fischer's account of the period July–September 1914 on which his critics have largely concentrated, it is worth looking at what they say on this
point. One of the most widespread grounds for attacking Fischer is that he has dealt exclusively with German war aims and worked exclusively on German
documents. This seems to me a silly line of attack:
Fischer was writing a monograph on German war
aims and not a history of the war; he has shown
enormous industry in reading a vast quantity of documents and, apart from anything else, it just would not
be physically possible for one man to cope with the
material that would be involved in making an analysis on a similar scale of the policies of all the belligerent Powers. It is true that there were annexationist
and expansionist ideas to be found in the Allied camp
as well as on the German side; and this has in fact
been well known, at least since 1918 when the Russians published the details of the secret negotiations in
which the Tsarist government had been engaged with
Britain and France. Moreover, victorious Powers use
their victory to put their war aims into practice (as
Germany did at Brest-Litovsk), and we all know what
the Allies did with their victory, for better or for
worse. This does not mean that now that the British
archives are opened there will not be an interesting
study to be made of the development of British war
aims on the lines pioneered by Professor Fischer, and
it is to be hoped that this will soon be undertaken.

Some of the criticisms of Professor Fischer are more
serious. The most respected and the most formidable
of the older generation of German historians, Professor Gerhard Ritter, has not only suggested that
Fischer misinterprets documents but has also implied
that he has a political purpose in doing this. One
German newspaper, reporting the Congress of the
German Historical Association in Berlin in September
1964, at which the Fischer controversy was the main

attraction, wrote of Professor Ritter's 'short lesson on
exact work with historical sources and the citation of
false or incomplete quotations from the sources which
made not only Fischer but many other historians
blush'. My own reading of Ritter's published criticisms
of Fischer suggests that Fischer has no need to blush,
but it is true that Ritter has a view of the origins of
the First World War which is entirely different from
Fischer's. Professor Ritter is seventy-five years old, and
he himself tells us that he still has the manuscript of a
speech which he made in September 1914, when he was
a teacher in a secondary school, in which he warned
his pupils against premature rejoicing and against
misuse of power if Germany won the war. He is, that
is to say, a member of the generation which was
directly involved in the First World War and the
great surge of patriotic emotion of August 1914,
whereas Professor Fischer is a generation younger and
was still a child when the war began. Moreover, Professor Ritter is himself at present engaged on a major
work, *Staatskunst und Kriegshandwerk*, in which he
analyses with great learning and with a stylistic brilli-
ance which most German historians (or, indeed, historians of any nationality) lack, the problem of civil–
military relations and the concept of militarism, with
particular reference, of course, to Germany. A large
section of the second volume is devoted to the immediate origins of the First World War, and the third
volume to the development of Bethmann-Hollweg's
policies after the war began.

It is worth comparing the general picture which
emerges from Ritter's book with that which is to be
found in Fischer's *Griff nach der Weltmacht*, as this
illustrates the difference of interpretation which
underlies the current controversy. Owing to the publicity given to the argument – the fact that it was
prominently featured in the popular weekly *Der
Spiegel*, for example – and the personal bitterness
which some of Fischer's critics injected into it, it is
hard not to feel obliged to take sides with one or the
other party. But perhaps this would be a mistake, and
it may be that each book illuminates one aspect of

German behaviour in 1914, and that it is because German society and German ideology in the twentieth century were so ambivalent that they are hard to understand and lend themselves to different interpretations, not one of which is wholly adequate to explain the facts. For Professor Ritter, the German leaders, and especially Bethmann-Hollweg and Moltke, are the helpless and often anguished victims of circumstances, carried into war against their will by the inexorable unfolding of military plans which they did not devise and whose political consequences had never been properly foreseen. This view has been reinforced in the case of Bethmann-Hollweg by the extracts which Professor K. D. Erdmann, of the University of Kiel, has published from the diary of Kurt Riezler, Bethmann-Hollweg's personal assistant and a close friend.

'The Chancellor', Riezler noted on 27 July 1914, 'sees a doom greater than the power of man hanging over the situation in Europe and over our people.'

And Bethmann-Hollweg's son told Professor Egmont Zechlin (Fischer's colleague at Hamburg and one of his severest critics) that not long before the war the Chancellor said that there was no point in planting trees in the park of his country-house as the Russians would be there in a few years.

There is no doubt that Bethmann-Hollweg was wracked by doubts, hesitations and fears. There is equally no doubt that Helmuth von Moltke, the *Feldherr wider Willen*, was so haunted by his own inadequacy and so broken by his physical and neurotic weaknesses that he virtually collapsed as soon as the war started. Even the Kaiser, although I think Fischer is right in taking his violent racist outbursts seriously, had his moments of lucidity, responsibility and anxiety. It is quite true, as Professor Ritter emphasises both in *Staatskunst und Kriegshandwerk* and in his study of the Schlieffen Plan, that the military plans had irrevocable political consequences with which their authors had not been very much concerned and which their successors, and especially those responsible for foreign relations in 1914 – principally Bethmann-

Hollweg and Jagow – had to face. And yet, in the
light of the new evidence produced by Fischer, it is
hard to accept the picture of Germany's leaders as
helpless victims of a fate they were trying to avoid.

Professor Fischer's critics have, if they take this view
of the characters and motives of the rulers of Germany, still to explain away that September Memorandum and the speed with which the government
produced a statement of aims – a statement which is
certainly more understandable if it is taken as revealing the assumptions which underlay their actions
when they took the risk of war. One view that has
been suggested is that Bethmann-Hollweg, instead (as
Fischer says) of gambling unsuccessfully on Britain's
neutrality, expected England to enter the war but was
confident that the war would be a limited one or that
Britain could swiftly be persuaded by diplomatic
means to withdraw again. On this view, put forward
by Professor Zechlin, the September Memorandum is
not so much a statement of the ends for which Germany entered the war but a proposal of the means –
the economic organisation of Europe and the occupation of strategic points on the Channel coast – by
which Britain might be defeated. In the discussions
about Germany's position in the world before 1914,
Britain did perhaps occupy the largest place as being
the World Power with whom Germany would have to
reckon if she was to emerge as an Imperial nation with
wide overseas interests, and the Kaiser's almost para-
noiac outbursts against English encirclement are
characteristic of one strand of German thinking.
Moreover, in September 1914, Rathenau was pointing
out that, whatever the outcome of the battle in
France, Britain would remain Germany's principal
enemy. Nevertheless, it is hard to see the September
Memorandum just as a tactical statement of means
rather than a strategic programme of ends, just as it is
hard to believe that the war was purely a defensive
reflex on Germany's part, and an attempt to break the
circle of hostile Powers which she felt to be closing in
on her.

Professor Hans Herzfeld, the most generous as well

as the wisest of the historians who have commented at
length on Fischer's book, reproaches him for not doing
justice to the shifting political scene in German internal politics during the war – and for not giving
enough importance to those elements in Germany
which were trying to resist the more extreme annexationist aims of the military leaders and Pan-German
propagandists. There were undoubtedly some Germans who stood out against the prevailing mood, just
as there were some Germans who resisted the Nazis,
but in neither case did they have any influence on the
course of events, and their main historical importance
has been to give the Germans some slight comfort in
retrospect. Just how strong was the current against
which they were struggling is shown by an example
which Fischer quotes in an article in the *Historische
Zeitschrift* [see pp. 79–144 below] where he effectively
answers some of his critics and produces further
evidence in support of his views.

At the time of the sinking of the *Lusitania* in 1915,
Admiral von Truppel, a former Governor of Kiaochow, who was at the time working for the Hamburg–
America shipping line, predicted that the adoption
of unrestricted submarine warfare could lead to the
United States entering the war and to Germany's
downfall. Thereupon the Hamburg Chamber of Commerce protested to the Hamburg–America company
against the Admiral's views, and its President (Albert
Ballin, often regarded as a moderate in such matters)
assured the President of the Norddeutsche Bank that
the Admiral would be dismissed.

It is this climate of opinion that has to be taken
into account to understand how even high-minded
civil servants like Bethmann-Hollweg could go a long
way with their more extreme colleagues, and how
Griff nach der Weltmacht is not an unfair summary of
Germany's aims and motives in 1914.

History can be written in many different ways.
Some of those who have discussed Fischer's book have
quoted a dictum of the historian Hermann Oncken
that 'nuance is the soul of politics', and have suggested
that Fischer, by singling out one theme and following

it throughout his long work, has oversimplified the nature and evolution of German politics in the First World War. Fischer has answered this with the assertion that in certain circumstances 'nuance' is less important than *Wesen* – the essence or core of a political development.

Certainly, one of the effects of the salutary opening-up of the whole subject which Fischer's book has achieved has been to concentrate attention on the true nature of German policy in the First World War and to get away from the self-justifications and evasions into which, ever since 1919, the discussion has very easily slipped. Moreover, just as history can be written either as a history of nuances or as a history of main themes, so too government archives can be used in two different ways. Some historians – a good example is Gallagher and Robinson's *Africa and the Victorians* – when confronted with ministerial records are impressed by the confusion and the apparently accidental way in which vital decisions are taken. As a result, actions which have been thought of as acts of deliberate policy or part of a long-term plan can be shown to be the result of *ad hoc* administrative decisions or of some obscure precedent unearthed in the files. Officials, however, seldom make plain the underlying premises on which their decisions are based, and it is only by understanding these and the framework of ideas within which they are operating and the social and other pressures to which they are subject that the true grounds for their actions can be comprehended. This, it seems to me, is the justification of Fischer's method. By concentrating on a single theme and by following it through the enormous mass of archival material which he has used, he has contributed to our understanding not only of the actual causes and course of the First World War, but of the presuppositions, the *Weltanschauung*, and the intellectual, social and political limitations within which the leaders of Wilhelmine Germany were working.

It is this aspect of Fischer's work that accounts in part for the extreme hostility it has aroused in Germany. For the older generation of his critics, such as

Professor Ritter, Fischer must seem to be attacking
many of the values on which their lives have been
based. (It is significant that Professor Ritter is the
biographer of Carl Goerdeler, whose upright old-
fashioned Prussian conservative principles led him
into active opposition to Hitler and who embodied
many of the ideals of pre-1914 Germany.) If men like
Bethmann-Hollweg were carried so far in the same
direction as the extreme militarists like Ludendorff
and were powerless to resist them because they shared
some at least of their aims, then the presuppositions of
the whole generation of 1914 are called in question,
and there is more continuity between 1914 and 1933
or 1941 than many Germans would like to admit. The
reopening of the war-guilt controversy and the suggestion common to both Professor Fischer and Mr Taylor
that Hitler's aims were foreshadowed by the German
leaders of 1914 is bound to be disturbing, since it suggests that many other questions in German history are
still not settled. Germans have assumed, perhaps too
readily, that the truth about 1914 was known, that the
verdict of history had been passed and the Germans
acquitted. They have sometimes ignored those historians, such as Luigi Albertini, who have shown how
much blame the German government had to bear for
the First World War, and they have forgotten that
there is by no means uniformity among non-Germans
in absolving the Kaiser and his generals and ministers.
And if 1914 has to be thought of as an open question,
then the examination of the German past cannot stop
there, and the whole achievement of Bismarck must
be reassessed, and where, it might be thought, will this
process end?

It is understandable if Germans of the older generation, shaken by what they have experienced in their
own lifetime, are reluctant to see the apparent cer-
tainties of the past overthrown or at least challenged.
What is encouraging is that the younger generation
seem to have responded to Fischer's lead and to be
ready to look at the evidence in an unemotional and
dispassionate way. It seems that both at the Historical
Congress in Berlin in September 1964, as well as at the

International Historical Congress in Vienna in 1965,
some of the personal heat and animosity in the controversy was dying down, and it must be hoped that
the participants will see that, in Professor Hans Herzfeld's words,

> Only one thing is certain: that the value of Ger-
> man research – even at the cost of from time to time
> calling in question apparently firm conclusions –
> can only increase in the eyes of foreigners, if it
> avoids giving the impression of being based on un-
> thinking reaction from political motives.

What will remain is a lesson in historical method
which will influence historians outside Germany and
which doubtless some English historians will be ready
to apply now that the British archives for the First
World War are available for research.

2 Britain and Germany in 1914: The July Crisis and War Aims

P. H. S. Hatton

Professor Joll's article 'The 1914 Debate Continues' has done much to clarify the issues in the present controversy over Germany's war aims in the First World War. The way in which he explains how the emotional reaction of Professor Fischer's critics has caused a cruder version of that historian's argument to gain currency is particularly helpful; and his appeal to British historians to use the documents now available for research to elucidate the July crisis will surely be heeded. It should, however, be noted that the case in favour of Fischer's interpretation of German statesmen who welcomed war for the opportunity it offered to realise plans for expansion has not as yet been clearly proved. If, and only if, plans for German territorial acquisitions can be shown to have been in existence before 3 August 1914, has Professor Fischer really raised *eine neue Kriegsschuldfrage*. Till then his work must be classified as a thorough and extensive study of the development of German war aims, however much one may agree with Professor Joll on the need to take into account the unspoken premises in the minds of the German statesmen of 1914.

Once embarked upon a war, states in both alliance-groups thought in terms of what they might gain if the war was won. The documentation now available for the study of British policy in 1914 counsels caution in ante-dating such war-time plans, hopes and suggestions. The Colonial Office showed surprising speed [6.8.1914] in deciding that Germany's African colonies must be forfeit, if possible to Britain. If this were not feasible, they must go to France; they certainly must not fall to

From *Past and Present*, no. 36 (April 1967).

Belgium. Harcourt expressed determination that 'Belgian compensation must (and will) come in Europe (and in cash) not in German East Africa'. From this arose the desire in the Colonial Office that the German African colonies should be conquered by British forces alone. Foreign Office staff commented on 'the extraordinary jealousy of the Colonial Office' implied in its attempted refusal of all aid in Africa from Britain's allies. It would be rash to assume from this evidence, however, that the British government welcomed war in 1914 as an opportunity for imperialist expansion. A minute of the Imperial Defence Committee in January 1913 directed that 'in order to bring the greatest possible economic pressure on Germany it is essential that the Netherlands and Belgium should be compelled to declare at the outset to which side in the struggle they will adhere'. Asquith later amended this directive so that Belgium would be given the choice between closing her frontiers to Germany or suffering blockade by Britain. If one proceeds without due care, this might be construed as plans for a future violation of the neutrality of the Low Countries. The Belgian Minister in London certainly made representations to Grey after hearing rumours of such plans. Ramsay MacDonald's writing to Morel that he had been told of Grey's willingness to invade Belgium is probably based on similar rumours, but it would not do for the historian to make sweeping deductions from this, though MacDonald was convinced the charge was true. Similarly, the attempts to buy Italian neutrality with Austrian territory by October 1914 might be open to hostile interpretation as an aggressive policy of despoiling the Dual Monarchy. Research into the developing war aims of the allied powers has already started, and it is to be hoped that we will demand as certain proof of the Fischer thesis on Germany's aims before the outbreak of the war as we would in the case of Britain's.

There is a sense in which the examination of documents in British archives and private collections may help to illuminate, if not German war aims, at least the attitude of individual German ministers in the July crisis. This seems to be most likely in the case of Beth-

mann-Hollweg, whose role has been so much discussed
by German historians since Fischer's book: the manner
in which one interprets German documents on the July
crisis is frequently determined by one's judgements
about Bethmann's character and motives. Hitherto
the presentation in English books has tended to build
on the views derived from the German Embassy in London which presented the July crisis of 1914 – as the
crisis of 1911–12 – as one of a struggle for control of the
German government between Bethmann-Hollweg's
peace party and Tirpitz's war party. In this struggle,
the Embassy officials argued, the British government
could help the Chancellor to victory by a conciliatory
attitude in its policy towards Germany.

There are no official Cabinet minutes in existence
for July 1914, but the evidence we have – as, for example, from Asquith's memoirs – would indicate that
this view was accepted by the English government. It
certainly was so in March 1912, when Harcourt noted
Grey as having said at a Cabinet meeting on 16 March,
'so long as Bethmann-Hollweg is Chancellor we will co-
operate with Germany for the peace of Europe'. Harcourt himself, building on conversations with
Kühlmann, the German Chargé d'Affaires in London,
had helped to confirm Grey in this opinion, and on
Haldane the Colonial Secretary had impressed that 'we
could not sacrifice Hollweg to Tirpitz'. Jenkins is prepared to believe that on the morning of 4 August half
the Cabinet was ready to oppose the sending of an
ultimatum to Germany. This seems explicable only by
a belief in the need to support the German peace party.

It seems likely that Bethmann-Hollweg in 1914 was
pursuing a policy similar to that he had adopted ever
since late 1911, urging co-operation between himself
and Great Britain, pressing for concessions, and at times
exaggerating the warlike intentions of Tirpitz to gain
certain advantages. In this policy the close co-operation
between Solf, the Reichskolonialminister, Harcourt and
Kühlmann on African affairs was particularly useful
to him. Between March and May 1912 the negotiations
for the amendment of the 1898 agreement on the Portuguese colonies made rapid progress when in the hands

of Harcourt and Kühlmann. The francophiles of the
Foreign Office were suspicious and resentful since they
felt they were not adequately informed or consulted.
For his part Harcourt as late as January 1914 vehe-
mently objected to the use of the term 'triple entente'.
Solf, looking back on the pre-war years, described Germany's role in Africa as that of 'England's "junior
partner" ', and in April 1914 he endeavoured to reopen
negotiations with Britain on the partition of the
Congo: an overture which was overtaken by the outbreak of war. Bethmann-Hollweg probably overestimated the value of German contacts in ministerial circles
and it looks as if he assumed in July 1914 that Britain
and France would permit Austria to absorb or at least
humiliate Serbia. The Austrian Ambassador had asked
Grey as far back as 14 November 1912 what action
Britain would take if Austria attacked Serbia, and the
fact that he received no answer might have encouraged
an optimistic frame of mind. Such an interpretation
makes explicable Bethmann-Hollweg's ready acquies-
cence in Wilhelm II's pledge to Szögyény, the Austro-
Hungarian Ambassador, on 6 July, without recourse to
belief in his deliberately seeking war. Tirpitz in his
memoirs hints at the tactics here surmised. He claims
that the Chancellor's mistake was not to have settled
the crisis by diplomacy, once Serbia had replied favourably to the Austrian ultimatum, since in his opinion
'England, Russia, France and Italy had helped Austria
to a certain diplomatic success by pressure on Belgrade'.
Bethmann-Hollweg probably counted too much on the
characteristic of any alliance-system whereby allies who
wish to avoid war tend to coerce their more directly involved partner or partners into making adequate concessions. An example of his attempt to utilise this characteristic can be seen in the unsuccessful Halt on Belgrade plan which attempted to buy British pressure on
Russia against German pressure on Austria-Hungary.

In 1914 the German Chancellor's calculation proved
wrong because Poincaré was determined not to desert
Russia, and Grey was determined not to desert France,
regarding the suggestion that Britain and Germany
should secretly collaborate to solve the crisis as un-

thinkable disloyalty to Britain's ally. Thus Russia was
emboldened to stand firm and the pattern of the crises
of 1908–9 and 1912–13 was not repeated. Neither Germany nor the Western Powers dared to fail allies about
whose internal strength they had misgivings.

The German Embassy myth – which London accepted, in 1914 as in 1911–12 – of Tirpitz as the leader of
the war party, is in the process of being exploded. Tirpitz did not desire war, though he was not above using
war scares in order to justify his naval building programme. In his own memoirs he claimed to have been
against war in 1914, and Ritter has demonstrated that
Tirpitz in the July crisis was in favour of a diplomatic
solution and withdrew from earlier militant positions.
Tirpitz did not desire to send his fleet to almost certain
destruction nor to see it grow unseaworthy by being
blockaded in harbour. The most that the German fleet
on its own could achieve would be to immobilise the
fleet of Great Britain in northern waters; for a victory
to be gained the united Italian and Austrian fleets
would have to defeat that of France in the Mediterranean. In the British Cabinet discussions of 1912
which led to the adoption of the Entente naval disposi-
tions, Churchill and McKenna had argued that the
French fleet was strong enough to prevent the junction
of the Italian and Austrian fleets. Technically this
argument was not convincing, but it embodied their
shrewd disbelief in the possibility of any close co-
operation between the Italian and Austrian navies. The
printed documents for 1914 fail to reveal any pressure
by Tirpitz on the German Foreign Office to obtain
assurances of Italian naval help, a fact which would
seem to strengthen his later claim that he did not desire
an aggressive naval war in 1914.

Only further work in German and other archives, in
private as well as official papers, can hope to throw
light on the motives and policies of Bethmann-Hollweg and Tirpitz and to solve the remaining problems
connected with the July crisis and with the war aims of
all the belligerents. Professor Joll's appeal for such
work is most opportune. But care should be taken not
to assume too readily – as it seems to this writer that

Fischer has done – that specific national objectives expressed during the war presuppose more than vague aspirations before August 1914.

Note: The co-operation between the two Colonial Secretaries has been more fully explored in Mr Hatton's article 'Harcourt and Solf: The Search for an Anglo-German understanding through Africa 1912–1914', *European Studies Review*, 1 (April 1971).

Imanuel Geiss

Bismarck's Legacy

The events of July and early August 1914 cannot be properly understood without a knowledge of the historical background provided by the preceding decades of Imperialism. On the other hand, that background alone is not sufficient to explain the outbreak of the First World War. Two general historical factors proved to be decisive, and both were fused by a third to produce the explosion known as the First World War. Imperialism, with Wilhelmine *Weltpolitik* as its specifically German version, provided the general framework and the basic tensions: the principle of national self-determination constituted, with its revolutionary potential, a permanent but latent threat to the old dynastic empires and built-up tensions in south-east Europe. The determination of the German Empire – then the most powerful conservative force in the world after Tsarist Russia – to uphold the conservative and monarchic principles by any means against the rising flood of democracy, plus its *Weltpolitik*, made war inevitable.

Although the forces of national and revolutionary democracy were most active in south-east Europe just before the war, their roots go back to the French Revolution of 1789. Before 1914 the principle of national self-determination directly threatened the Ottoman Empire and caused the First Balkan War against Turkey, as a kind of war of national liberation. After the new Balkan nations had practically pushed Turkey out of Europe, the next target was inevitably Austria-Hungary, which, however, was closely allied to Germany. Although the German

Introductory chapter to the author's own selection of documents published in English by Batsford Ltd, London, under the title *July 1914* (1967).

Empire was a nation-State, it in fact included compact national minorities on its borders constituting about 10 per cent of its population: Frenchmen in Alsace and Lorraine; Walloons in Eupen-Malmédy; Danes in Schleswig; Poles in West Prussia, Posen and Upper Silesia. They led the more or less marginal existence of second-class citizens; they resented the arbitrary separation from their compatriots and their enforced inclusion in the German Reich. Thus, at least indirectly, even the German Empire was implicated in the rise of national self-determination.

The third factor which made the First World War inevitable in the form and at the time it did occur was the German Empire itself. It was important for two main reasons: firstly, its ambition to attain the status of 'a World Power beside other World Powers' (Erdmann), but without seeking an agreement with at least one of the World Powers already firmly established; and secondly, its self-proclaimed role as the great bulwark against revolution and democracy. It is significant that both factors, even if in a rather confused way, had played a dominant role in the revolution of 1848–9. While we shall probably never know whether a victory of liberal and democratic forces in Germany at that time would really have meant large-scale expansion of a newly founded empire, it is certain that Bismarck started his career by fighting both liberalism and democracy on the one hand, and expansion to at least a Greater German Empire, including Austria (with or without the non-German provinces), on the other. His Lesser German Empire founded in 1871 was a modest affair compared with the day-dreams of many a liberal Greater-German patriot. But it established Prussian predominance and was accomplished only by three wars in rapid succession. The victories of the Prussian armies – in 1870 over Bonapartist France, about to liberalise herself, and after Sedan over post-Bonapartist, democratic France who resisted German demands for annexations – in themselves introduced a new, disquieting element into the European scene. It was partly Bismarck's cunning diplomacy and Moltke's strategy of *Blitzkrieg*

(to use a fitting expression of a later period) that made
it possible for Bismarck to unite the Germans in the
face of misgivings in Europe.

The immediate effect of the re-establishment of the
Reich was to change profoundly the balance of power
in Europe. Since the late Middle Ages Europe had
been accustomed to weakness in its centre, in one form
or another. Either there existed a confused political
vacuum, created by the old Reich in its perennial
agony, or two great German Powers largely neutralised each other by their rivalries. The unification of a
majority of Germans in the 'Lesser' German Reich
under the leadership of Prussia helped to make the
new Germany 'into the greatest concentration of
power on the mainland in Europe'. Unification, rapid
industrialisation, military power and bureaucratic
efficiency were sufficient to raise even Bismarck's
'Lesser' Germany almost automatically into a position
of 'latent hegemony' over the Continent. Since then,
the future of Europe and the Reich depended on the
wisdom of Germany's political leaders, whether or not
they successfully resisted the temptation to convert
this latent hegemony into an open one.

Just as Frederick II of Prussia lay low after his conquest of Silesia, so did Bismarck after his successful
coups. He wanted to accustom Europe to the new
balance of power and to the emergence of Germany as
the potential leading Power in the centre of Europe.
Bismarck's 'peaceful' policy after 1871 thus finds a
very simple explanation. On the other hand, his new
caution, after nearly a decade of gambling, reckless-
ness and limited wars, probably also appealed to his
conservative instincts. He had been successful beyond
reasonable expectations, he did not want to run
the risk of losing everything by aiming at even
higher prizes. Bismarck's watchword that Germany was
'satiated' had two aims: to reassure Europe about
the danger of German hegemony, and to restrain
elements in Germany which were not satisfied with his
achievements. In the short run, Bismarck seemed to
have succeeded again, at least as long as he was
Chancellor. After 1871 he figures as the statesman of

moderation and peace. Yet, in the long run, he and his work became the victim of those elements with which he had co-operated and which he afterwards tried to moderate or channel. And after his fall we see him allying himself with those very elements which dreamt of expansionist schemes.

The real roots of Bismarck's triumph and of Germany's emergence as the leading Power on the Continent in 1871 had been Prussia's industrial preponderance over her more agrarian Austrian and French rivals. Soon after the foundation of the Second Reich heavy industry was developed beyond the immediate needs of an expanding economy. From the early 1890s onwards industrialists, in particular Krupp, pressed for fuller use to be made of the inflated capacity for steel production. The demands were translated into political agitation by the Navy League, which was one of the first modern pressure groups in Germany and inspired and largely financed by Krupp.

Similarly, the German economy expanded overseas and entered into conscious rivalry with British industry and finance, even though this was mitigated by short-term co-operation on such schemes as the Baghdad Railway. Soon after 1871 the pressure of foreign trade and increasing participation in world markets created the demand for a German share in world domination, or *Weltpolitik* as it was called. At least that was the explanation given, not by a Marxist but by Kurt Riezler, writing under a pseudonym shortly before the outbreak of the First World War. Bismarck, mainly for domestic reasons, had tried to give these expansionist elements a limited outlet by inaugurating German colonial policy in the early 1880s. Anti-British and anti-Russian economic policy (in order to satisfy agrarian interests) made Germany drift into a hopeless dilemma.

In spite of his sound insights into the dangers of open German hegemony, even Bismarck was unable to hold down for good the new demands for greater German power. After his fall, which was widely welcomed over practically the whole of Germany, Caprivi's cautious policy of consolidation stood on the

shoulders of Bismarck's peaceful policy of the post-
1871 period. Caprivi cared little for colonial and less
for naval ambitions, but concentrated his efforts
rather on strengthening Germany's position on the
Continent, especially vis-à-vis Russia – to the chagrin
of many German conservatives and patriots. In particular, the Zanzibar–Heligoland deal of 1890 provoked the anger of the new forces in Germany, and
Bismarck, now in enforced retirement, viciously denounced the very policy of restraint that he himself
had pursued for almost two decades. Out of this
agitation against the 'soft' Caprivi arose the Pan-
German League. For the period of Caprivi's Chancellorship, and again mainly for domestic reasons, Bismarck now openly allied himself with the incipient
Pan-German movement. Yet the old Bismarck apparently did not realise in his anger that he was supporting a cause which, in the long run, would endanger
his own work. Consequently, especially after his death
in 1898, Bismarck became the patron of a new wave of
German chauvinism, embracing all champions of German *Weltpolitik*.

German Weltpolitik

The new feeling was articulated for the first time in a
powerful and persuasive way by Max Weber. In his
famous Inaugural Lecture at Freiburg University in
1895, he pleaded for a new policy of striving for world
power:

> We must understand that the unification of Ger-
> many was a youthful folly, which the nation com-
> mitted in its declining days and which would have
> been better dispensed with because of its expense, if
> it should be the conclusion and not the starting-
> point for a German *Weltmachtpolitik*.

Max Weber's eloquent plea was immediately taken up
by Friedrich Naumann and by a vociferous group of
Liberal Imperialists, in constant rivalry with the more
conservative Pan-Germans in whose ranks Max Weber

had played a role as one of the founder-members.
Between them they provided the climate of public
opinion and the ideology for the actual change of
German foreign policy.

The emergence of the Pan-Germans and Liberal
Imperialists was one of the results of the new movement in German public opinion that clamoured for
Germany to play a bigger role in the world. It is not
surprising that the young Kaiser Wilhelm II, flamboy-
ant and constantly torn between cutting a figure as a
great Prince of Peace (*Friedenskaiser*) and a great
Warlord (*Oberster Kriegsherr*), should have been
among the first to voice the new sentiment, even if
only in the strictest privacy. As early as the summer of
1892 he revealed to his intimate friend and adviser
Count Eulenburg the 'fundamental principle' of his
policy: 'a sort of Napoleonic supremacy ... in the
peaceful sense'. In the Kaiser's versatile mind 'Napoleonic supremacy', albeit 'in the peaceful sense',
seemed perfectly compatible with his extraordinary
illusion that the Poles were craving to be 'liberated
from the Russian yoke' by the Germans: 'In the event
of a war with Russia the whole of Poland would revolt
and come over to my side with the express intention of
being annexed by me.'

Perhaps even more significant is a private memorandum composed in 1896 by Georg Alexander von
Müller, later Chief of the Imperial Naval Cabinet,
under the title *Zukunftspolitik*. Müller proceeded
from the assumption that world history was at present
characterised by a violent economic struggle, especially in Europe. While *Mitteleuropa* was becoming too
narrow, the 'free expansion of the nations living there
was limited by the existing distribution of the in-
habitable parts of the globe, in particular by England's world domination'. Out of the tensions 'war can
and, as many maintain, must arise'. According to
Müller there was common agreement in Germany
that the aim of such a war must be 'the destruction of
English world domination in order to acquire the
necessary colonies for the mid-European states in need
of expansion'. Apart from Germany, Austria–Hungary

and Italy were rated as such States 'in need of expansion', while Müller also considered the candidacy of
Scandinavia and Switzerland. But, 'In the necessity
and justification of expansion . . . Germany excels by
far.'

However, Müller, who had some liberal inclinations
(liberal, that is, by German standards), did not entirely agree with that common view, since Germany
would gain little from the destruction of the British
Empire. Instead he preferred an alliance with Britain
against Russia. As Britain for reasons of racial comity
would be Germany's 'natural ally', such an alliance
would also give the 'economic struggle an ideological
trait, the preservation of the Germanic race against
Slavs and Romans'. While the final result might be a
clash between the two powerful 'Germanic empires',
he preferred permanent co-operation between them in
the interest 'of the future struggle for the hegemony of
the Germanic race'. Müller clearly saw the two alternatives for Germany: 'Either to commit all the power
of the nation, recklessly, not even shirking a great war,
or else to limit ourselves to a continental Power.' He
was against both a feeble compromise and the attempt
to forge ahead against Britain.

The most interesting aspects of Müller's analysis
and recommendations are his testimony of how general the German desire in 1896 must have been for
expansion of the Reich – the realisation that the desired breakthrough to the status of World Power
would be possible only by war was, it seems, equally
widespread – and the emergence of a crude racism,
even in one of 'liberal' repute. The implication of the
new *Weltpolitik* – the Great War – was thus clearly
seen in Wilhelmine Germany, even before it was
launched. Although it would be of interest to
assemble all the evidence showing that Germany's
political élite understood this implication – before
and after the crucial decision to plunge into the
breakneck adventure of *Weltpolitik* – one more example must here suffice. Again, we quote not an extremist but a well-known moderate, the liberal-con-
servative historian and publicist Hans Delbrück, who,

as one of the few German 'critics of the Wilhelmine
era', was certainly not prone to extravagant pro-
nouncements. As early as 26 November 1899 he proclaimed in his *Preussische Jahrbücher*:

> We want to be a World Power and pursue
> colonial policy in the grand manner. That is cer-
> tain. Here there can be no step backward. The en-
> tire future of our people among the great nations
> depends on it. We can pursue this policy with Eng-
> land or without England. With England means in
> peace; against England means – through war.

Like Müller, Delbrück would have preferred the
former solution, but the government's *Weltpolitik* was
conducted not only without Britain, but even against
Britain. Müller and Delbrück differed from the main-
stream of political thought, as represented by the
Kaiser, the court and the navy, in their caution vis-à-
vis Britain. But all were agreed on the need for a
powerful German fleet as the most important instrument of *Weltpolitik*. Even before 1897 the navy
pressed for a more powerful battle fleet. After the
Kaiser had revealed to his intimate friend Eulenburg
his Napoleonic dream in 1892, Eulenburg persistently
pushed Bülow's candidacy as Foreign Secretary and
Chancellor, while Bülow was only too willing to
translate his Kaiser's ideas into action. Both were convinced that only a spectacular success in foreign policy
could restore and enhance the popularity of the
monarchy and establish the Kaiser's personal rule. Out
of all those dreams, sentiments, ambitions, cross-cur-
rents and pressures emerged German *Weltpolitik*. It
was apparently advocated for the first time at government level in July 1897 by the National Liberal Prussian Minister of Finance, Johannes von Miquel, as an
indispensable part of his new policy of 'Collection'
(*Sammlungspolitik*) – of rallying the well-to-do classes
around the throne against Social Democracy. At the
same time, the emphasis on foreign policy was to help
overcome serious differences between the industrial
and agrarian wings of Germany's wealthier classes and

to create a united front of the whole nation against
the world. Thus German *Weltpolitik* was partly created by a domestic policy, which aimed at diverting
the attention of the masses from social and political
problems at home by a dynamic expansion abroad. In
this the essentially demagogic slogan of *Weltpolitik*
proved only too successful. Through its 'national'
appeal it soon acquired a momentum of its own, and
finally domesticated the Catholic Centre Party, the
left-wing Liberals, and even the S.P.D. It gave rise to a
distinct political tradition that prevented even the
most sensible and strong-willed German statesman
from avoiding the collision course on which Germany
was set. If there is anything tragic about Bethmann-
Hollweg, as is nowadays often claimed, it lay in the
situation he inherited and was unable to affect, even if
this had been his genuine desire. By 1914 the Reich
had become victim of its own most valued slogan.

Bülow's arrival at the Foreign Ministry, the launching of Tirpitz's crash programme of naval armament
and Germany's seizure of·Kiaochow in 1897 all point
to the effective inauguration of German *Weltpolitik*.
The German navy, built not only 'for our commerce,
our security, our future', but also 'especially for the
person of our dear Kaiser', was understood by Britain
as a 'challenge to her naval supremacy'. Both Tirpitz's
concept of the *Risikoflotte*, designed to frighten Britain at least into neutrality, and the Battle of Jutland
in 1916 prove that British fears were not unfounded.
As late as February 1914 Jagow, the Secretary of State
at the Foreign Ministry, wrote to Lichnowsky, the
German Ambassador in London, on the question of
British neutrality in a future conflict:

> We have not built our fleet in vain, and in my
> opinion, people in England will seriously ask them-
> selves whether it will be just that simple and with-
> out danger to play the role of France's guardian
> angel against us.

German *Weltpolitik* pursued the tactics of claiming
equality with the established World Powers and demanded 'compensations' for any territorial or other

changes of the *status quo* anywhere on the globe. The
character of Germany's new course was thus one of
irritating vagueness, but it was clearly based on the
consciousness of growing power. German uncertainty
about the present status of Germany in the world and
her future role only increased confusion at home and
suspicion abroad. Whereas Max Weber in 1895 still
demanded a new *Weltmachtpolitik*, the Kaiser proclaimed that Germany had already become a 'World
Empire' (*Weltreich*) as early as 18 January 1896. No-
body doubted or disputed Germany's status as a great
continental Power. But it was increasingly hard to de-
fine her position in world politics.

The Effect of Weltpolitik on the Balance of Power

Germany's *Weltpolitik* had far-reaching effects. A less
obvious one was the change in the character of the
Triple Alliance. The Dual Alliance between Germany
and Austria had originally been concluded in 1879 as
a purely defensive treaty. The inclusion of Italy in
1882 did not alter that basic fact, although complications were introduced on account of Austro-Italian
rivalry. The new *Weltpolitik*, however, gradually
transformed the Triple Alliance into the basis for
German ambitions as a fledgeling World Power.
When Italy tried to do the same on a limited scale
with her Libyan war against Turkey in 1911 (a power
open to German influence), and when Austria tried to
use the Triple Alliance to support her own policy in
the Balkans, the Triple Alliance lost much of its defensive character and its superficially imposing unity
and power.

Even more startling was the effect on the other
Powers. In 1871 there was no system of alliance in
existence; in 1885, when the 'scramble for Africa' began, there existed only one alliance – the Triple Alliance; by 1907, however, the Triple Entente had
emerged. Among the first symptoms of the new development had been the Franco-Russian Alliance of
1892–4, which put an end to the isolation of France,

created by Bismarck's diplomacy after 1871. It also
ended for good the co-operation between the great
conservative Powers of the East, Russia, Germany and
Austria. Partly as a reaction to Germany's *Weltpolitik*,
her naval armament and her refusal to enter into a
loose arrangement with Britain, and partly as a
counter-move to the completion of the Trans-Siberian
Railway in 1902, Britain's foreign policy after the
Boer War was designed to end her erstwhile 'splendid
isolation'. The alliance with Japan in 1902 was followed in 1904 by the Entente Cordiale with France.
Although it was primarily an arrangement over
colonial questions, political co-operation between the
two Western Powers soon followed. In 1907, after the
Russo-Japanese War of 1904-5, Britain and Russia
concluded an even looser arrangement. The so-called
'Triple Entente' was, therefore, no solid alliance.
There was no formal treaty of alliance between all
three partners; there was only the treaty between
Russia and France. There were no formal and binding agreements for military co-operation between Britain and the other partners. The tensions between
Britain and Russia over Persia were a constant source
of friction between the two countries, even in early
July 1914. Neither the Triple Alliance nor the Triple
Entente were the monolithic power blocs they seemed
to be. But most contemporaries and participants in
the diplomatic negotiations at the time felt strongly
about the differences between the two groups. At least
Jagow, on 1 August 1914, attributed the deeper
reasons for the outbreak of war to 'this d—d system of
alliances', as he remarked in a conversation with Sir
Edward Goschen, the British Ambassador in Berlin.

Contrary to traditional German belief, the Triple
Entente was not conceived as an offensive alliance.
None of the three Powers pursued expansionist aims,
over which they would or could have gone to war:
British 'envy of the Germany economy' (*Handelsneid*),
French 'revanchism' and Russian 'Pan-Slavism' were,
and still are, grossly exaggerated in Germany. Alsace-
Lorraine was of course in the minds of many French-
men, but France would never have gone to war in

order to reconquer the two provinces, if only because
public opinion was on the whole pacific, as the German Ambassador in Paris stressed in detailed reports
from France. On the other hand, the French, in their
nouvel esprit, were no longer prepared to swallow
such a humiliation as having to sack Delcassé merely
to avert threats from Germany, as happened during
the first Moroccan crisis of 1905–6.

Russian 'Pan-Slavism' amounted to a vague feeling
of solidarity among all Slavs, and active, chauvinistic
Pan-Slavs in Russia were limited to small circles as,
again, the Kaiser and the Chancellor could have
learned from their top expert on the question, the
German Ambassador in St Petersburg. Tsarist Russia,
it is true, had her traditional ambitions for Constantinople. Yet there she encountered not only German
interest, but also British and French suspicions, which
by themselves would have been enough to neutralise
any Russian agression against Turkey. The Russians,
furthermore, faced a serious dilemma: 'a struggle for
Constantinople was not possible without a general
European war', as was pointed out in the famous
secret conference of 21 February–6 March 1914 in St
Petersburg, but in a general war military action
against Constantinople would be impossible, as all
forces would be needed on other fronts. Nor would an
isolated *coup* against Constantinople succeed because
it was bound to provoke a general war which the Russians knew they were too weak to wage on their own;
neither France nor Britain would come to their help
in a provoked war, let alone one provoked by the
seizure of Constantinople. This dilemma proved to be
insoluble, and in fact during the crisis of July 1914
Constantinople figured only in the back of the minds
of a few statesmen: Sazonov apparently wanted to
prevent the Germans from taking over in Constantinople once Serbia was crushed by Austria, while the
Austrians and Germans apparently feared Russia's expansion through the alliance with the south Slavs,
whose success would isolate the Central Powers from
Turkey. Constantinople was not a direct cause of war
in 1914.

48 *Imanuel Geiss*

The two most highly industrialised countries of
Europe – Britain and Germany – were each other's
best trading partners, and in Britain there was a
strong pro-German current, from the monarchy down
to a rather sentimental feeling of 'kith and kin' on the
part of the Left, who were most outspoken in their
opposition to entering the war on the side of Tsarist
Russia. Britain was also opposed to any offensive war
against Germany provoked by Russia or France and
would effectively have vetoed it.

There were, however, circles in Britain who were
disturbed and even frightened by the menace of the
German fleet, of Germany's vague, ill-defined demands, her pretensions and the ostentatious display of
her military and naval power. This group became
strong in the navy, the army and the Foreign Office.
The most detailed articulation of their misgivings is
to be found in Sir Eyre Crowe's famous memorandum
of 1 January 1907. His memorandum is, it seems, more
denounced as anti-German than actually read (at least
in Germany), perhaps on account of its length. In the
light of subsequent events and of our present knowledge, it proves to have been the most intelligent and
precise analysis of German *Weltpolitik* for a very long
time to come. Far from being crudely anti-German, it
was a balanced judgement of German intentions and
sought to find a rational explanation for the apparently irrational and bewildering manifestations of
German *Weltpolitik*. Crowe set it in historical perspective, in the same sort of way as many German historians, then and later, have traced the rise of little
Brandenburg into the mighty German Empire, via
Prussia. A close look at Crowe's memorandum is,
therefore, highly relevant in the present context, if
only because it was long considered in Germany as a
major factor contributing to war.

Crowe saw the rational core of German *Weltpolitik*
in the drive for equality of Germany overseas:

> Germany had won her place as one of the lead-
> ing, if not, in fact, the foremost Power on the Euro-
> pean continent. But over and beyond the European

Great Powers there seemed to stand the 'World Powers'. It was at once clear that Germany must become a 'World Power'.

The result was the inauguration of German colonial policy. Crowe's way of summing up political sentiment in Germany is worth quoting. In answering the question why Germans thought they must have colonies, a powerful fleet and coaling stations, he answers for the German mind:

> A healthy and powerful State like Germany, with its 60 million inhabitants, must expand, it cannot stand still, it must have territories to which its overflowing population can emigrate without giving up its nationality. . . . When it is objected that the world is now actually parcelled out among independent States, and that territory for colonization cannot be had except by taking it from the rightful possessor, the reply again is: 'We cannot enter into such considerations. Necessity has no law. The world belongs to the strong. A vigorous nation cannot allow its growth to be hampered by blind adherence to the *status quo*. . .'

After quoting some of the most revealing remarks of the Kaiser ('The trident must be in our hand', 'No question of world politics may be settled without the consent of the German Emperor', etc.), Crowe reached a provisional conclusion, which is more moderate than extreme:

> The significance of these individual utterances may easily be exaggerated. Taken together, their cumulative effect is to confirm the impression that Germany distinctly aims at playing on the world's political stage a much larger and much more dominant part than she finds allotted to herself under the present distribution of material power.

Crowe warned that it was not a matter of moralising, as examples of history showed. Again he revealed how well he knew the German mind:

No modern German would plead guilty to a mere lust of conquest for the sake of conquest. But the vague and undefined schemes of Teutonic expansion (*die Ausbreitung des deutschen Volkstums*) are but the expression of the deeply rooted feeling that Germany has established for herself ... the right to assert the primacy of German national ideas. And as it is an axiom of her political faith that right, in order that it may prevail, must be backed by force, the transition is easy to the belief that the 'good German sword', which plays so large a part in patriotic speeches, is there to solve any difficulties that may be in the way of establishing the reign of those ideas in a Germanized world.

Turning to the analysis of German *Weltpolitik* proper, Crowe made it clear that he was no anti-German, for he did not question 'that the mere existence and healthy activity of a powerful Germany is an undoubted blessing to the world'.

In spite of all English 'sympathy and appreciation of what is best in the German mind', created by 'intellectual and moral kinship', Crowe attached one condition to his welcoming an increase of Germany's influence and power in the world:

There must be respect for the individualities of other nations, equally valuable coadjutors, in their way, in the work of human progress, equally entitled to full elbow-room in which to contribute, in freedom, to the evolution of a higher civilization.

On the following page Crowe put the same argument in a different form:

So long, then, as Germany competes for an intellectual and moral leadership of the world in reliance on her own national advantages and energies England cannot but admire, applaud, and join in the race. If, on the other hand, Germany believes that greater relative preponderance of material power, wider extent of territory, inviolable front-

iers, and supremacy at sea are necessary and preliminary possesions without which any aspirations
to such leadership must end in failure, then England must expect that Germany will surely seek to
diminish the power of any rivals, to enhance her
own by extending her dominion, to hinder the co-
operation of other States, and ultimately to break
up and supplant the British Empire.

Crowe noted that, of course, German statesmen denied any such intentions. He pointed out that, even if
such assurances were sincere, they might be 'incapable
of fulfilment'. Furthermore, 'ambitious designs against
one's neighbours are not as a rule openly proclaimed'.
Crowe cautiously introduced the idea of what is now
called 'continuity' in German policy, by suggesting
'that a further development [of German policy] on
the same general lines would not constitute a break
with former traditions, and must be considered at
least as possible'. And he asked:

> Whether it would be right, or even prudent, for
> England to incur any sacrifice or see other, friendly,
> nations sacrificed merely in order to assist Germany
> in building up step by step the fabric of a universal
> preponderance, in the blind confidence that in the
> exercise of such preponderance Germany will confer
> unmixed benefits on the world at large, and pro-
> mote the welfare and happiness of all other peoples
> without doing injury to any one.

Crowe had his doubts. Again he stressed 'that a recognition of the dangers of the situation need not and
does not imply any hostility to Germany'; he was
ready to mete out to Germany the same as he expected
for England: 'Not to be wantonly hampered by facti-
tious opposition' when pursuing schemes which are not
harmful to third nations.

After a lengthy and detailed survey of the many
frictions between Germany and Britain, which Crowe
blamed on Germany's *Weltpolitik*, he returned to the
question of what German intentions could be. He saw
two possible explanations:

Either Germany is definitely aiming at a general political hegemony and maritime ascendancy, threatening the independence of her neighbours and ultimately the existence of England; or Germany, free from any such clear-cut ambition, and thinking for the present merely of using her legitimate position and influence as one of the leading Powers in the council of nations, is seeking to promote her foreign commerce, spread the benefits of German culture, extend the scope of her national energies, and create fresh German interests all over the world wherever and whenever a peaceful opportunity offers, leaving it to an uncertain future to decide whether the occurrence of great changes in the world may not some day assign to Germany a large share of direct political action over regions not now a part of her dominions, without that violation of the established rights of other countries which would be involved in any such action under existing political conditions.

And he added: 'In either case Germany would clearly be wise to build as powerful a navy as she can afford.' One might add today: the overall result would have been the same – the Great War. To meet either possibility Crowe recommended falling back on the traditional policy of the balance of power. This would not mean that Germany need be reduced to the rank of a weak Power, for

So long as Germany's action does not overstep the line of legitimate protection of existing rights she can always count upon the sympathy and good-will, and even the moral support, of England. Further, it would be neither just nor politic to ignore the claims to a healthy expansion which a vigorous and growing country like Germany has a natural right to assert in the field of legitimate endeavour.... It cannot be good policy for England to thwart such a process of development where it does not directly conflict either with British interests or with those of other nations to which England is bound by solemn treaty obligations. If Germany, within the limits imposed by these two conditions, finds the means peacefully and honourably to increase her trade and shipping, to gain coaling stations or other harbours, to acquire landing rights for cables, or to secure concessions for the employment of German capital or industries, she could never find England in her way. Nor is it for British Governments to oppose Germany's building as large a fleet as she may consider necessary or desirable for the defence of her national interests. . . .

Crowe summed up his policy, which could be called one of 'containment', in a remarkable passage:

It would be of real advantage if the determination not to bar Germany's legitimate and peaceful expansion, nor her schemes of naval development, were made as patent and pronounced as authoritatively as possible, provided care was taken at the same time to make it quite clear that this benevolent attitude will give way to determined opposition at the first sign of British or allied interest being adversely affected. This alone would probably do more to bring about lasting satisfactory relations with Germany than any other course.

But he warned of one road which would be disastrous:

That is the road paved with graceful British concessions – concessions made without any conviction either of their justice or of their being set off by equivalent counter-services. The vain hopes that in this manner Germany can be 'conciliated' and made more friendly must be definitely given up.

Crowe's memorandum can be regarded as the key document of British policy before 1914, which amounted to accepting the expansion of German influence and power in the world, as long as it was peaceful; provided, that is, that it did not violate vital British interests either directly or indirectly, nor tried

to upset the then existing balance of power in Europe
and in the world. Crowe was against a policy of concessions, merely to 'conciliate' (we would now say
'appease') Germany on her road to more power.
British policy of containing Germany could only lead
to collision if Germany were to bear out the worst
suspicions and fears of Crowe and his group.

No one who knows the course of German history
since Bismarck or the attitude of pre-1914 Germany
(as reflected both in the writings of the time and in
the minds of the present older generation) can doubt
that Crowe's assessment, on the whole, was to the
point, was just and fair. Even if Crowe had not read
Max Weber's Inaugural Lecture of 1895 and had not
known Müller's ideas on Germany's *Zukunftspolitik*,
even if one were to dismiss the Pan-Germans as repre-
senting the 'lunatic fringe' in German society (which
they certainly were not), he could not have known the
revealing German counterpart of his own analysis of
the situation and of the German mind, since it was
published only some years later.

Kurt Riezler is not a figure whose historical relevance can easily be ignored or belittled; he came from
a respectable, well-educated family, was the young but
influential adviser of the Chancellor, Bethmann-Hollweg, and had written two important books, couched
in the traditional (and often unreadable) jargon of
German philosophical idealism. His second book,
published under a pseudonym, appeared just before
the outbreak of the First World War and reflects the
position of the most liberal and peaceful wing of German patriotism. Nevertheless, in it Riezler gave expression to the widespread Social Darwinism of the
time and he seems certainly to have been influenced
by Max Weber, the greatest intellect of German
Liberal Imperialists. It is not surprising that for the
same reason Riezler, in spite of his criticism of the Pan-
Germans over details of policy, betrayed many affini-
ties with them over basic questions of German *Weltanschauung*. In many respects Riezler confirmed
Crowe's analysis of the German mind before 1914, as
did Müller's almost twenty years earlier.

For Riezler there was no question of a rational principle which would allow or make desirable the peaceful co-existence of nations, small and large. He not only fell back on a Hobbesian philosophy of war of all against all, but even proclaimed the theory that the eternal struggle – not for survival, but for obtaining world domination – was the supreme aim of all nations. If this was true of all nations, then it applied to the Germans:

> Ideally, every nation wants to grow, to expand, to rule and to subject [others] without end, wants to coalesce and to incorporate ever more [nations], wants to become an even more powerful unit, until the Universe has, under its own rule, become one organic unit.

In his next book, Riezler went as far as to use the precise term for this circumlocution – 'world domination' – as the supreme prize in the political struggle. It is logical that for Riezler enmity was the underlying principle governing the relations between nations, a principle which could only be temporarily modified by tactics and expediency. In his more popular book, he pleaded for the supremacy of German *Kultur* in the world by endorsing the Kaiser's view that the world should one day be healed by German ideas and methods. Like Max Weber, Riezler saw in Germany's economic expansion the impulse towards German *Weltpolitik*; he also saw in the foundation of the Reich by Bismarck in 1871 the basis for further political expansion:

> The young German Empire pushed out into the world. Its population grows annually by 800,000–900,000 people, and for these new masses food must be found, or, what amounts to the same, work.... The economic interest had to be followed by the political. The enormous potential and achievement of the rising nation pushed the young Empire into its *Weltpolitik* ... Germany's unification was, on

the one hand, a culmination of the national development, a fulfilment of national aspirations. On
the other hand, it was the beginning of a new
development, the germ for new, more far-reaching
aspirations. Just as in the strivings of the individual, so in the aspirations of the nations there is
neither culmination nor end. Parallel to the increasing interest in *Weltpolitik*, German nationalism orientated itself towards *Weltpolitik*. The demands of the German nation for power and prestige, not only in Europe, but throughout the world,
have increased rapidly.

But Riezler feared that Germany's territorial basis in
Europe for pursuing her *Weltpolitik* was too narrow.
He wanted to free the Reich from Bismarck's *cauche-
mar des coalitions* by making Germany so powerful
that, in the interest of her *Weltpolitik*, she would
have the chance of victory in 'any possible constellation', thus deterring any possible combination of
adversaries or rivals throughout the world. And Riezler concluded his analysis of German *Weltpolitik*,
which he took for granted:

Hemmed in by unfavourable frontiers, it [the
German nation] needs to display great power, so
long as it is obstructed in many ways from freely
pursuing its *Weltpolitik*. For the sake of freedom in
its world policy it must be guarded against any
eventuality. It cannot allow those spheres of activity
to be blocked which are still open for its world
policy. The attempt to contain this policy might be
temporarily successful, but in the long run it will
fail because of the nation's effective power and its
tremendous *élan vital*.

Riezler's philosophy amounted to a thinly disguised
claim to German world domination to be attained in
successive stages. His views, which were still the more
'moderate', 'soft' version of the prevalent German
Weltanschauung of the time, were bound to produce
war, once translated into practical policy. For on the

one hand, it was unlikely that the other Powers would passively allow Germany to advance towards world domination; on the other hand, Riezler apparently saw even a policy of containment as hostile obstruction, which would be brushed aside by Germany's 'effective power and its tremendous *élan vital*'.

The Growing Crisis

German *Weltpolitik*, the containment policy of the Entente and Germany's refusal to be contained made war inevitable. The elements of containment became apparent from the time of the Entente Cordiale of 1904. Germany's first political reaction of significance was the move against France over Morocco in 1905–6. It would have been a success but for German insistence on a fully fledged international conference to underscore the German diplomatic triumph, after Delcassé's fall under German pressure. The Bosnian crisis of 1908–9 brought another temporary victory for Germany, when Serbia was dropped by Russia under the veiled threat of German mobilisation against Russia. But Russian humiliation was such that a repetition of the same manœuvre was unlikely to be successful – as Prince Bülow, then German Chancellor, claims to have warned his Sovereign while taking his farewell after his dismissal in 1909.

The second crisis over Morocco in 1911 was in many ways a repetition of the first, but this time without the initial German success. The dispatch of the German gunboat *Panther* to Agadir produced anxieties in Britain, and British warnings, expressed by Lloyd George in his famous Guildhall speech, were prompter and clearer this time than ever before or after. When Italy and Austria refused to support Germany on her course of collision, Germany backed down with the help of a face-saving compromise, which gave her some additional territory in the Cameroons. The net effect of German endeavours was to weld together the Triple Entente, and to raise a new spirit of national defiance in France. Sir Edward Grey, the British

Foreign Secretary, and Paul Cambon, the French
Ambassador in London, exchanged their famous
letters in which they promised to co-ordinate the
foreign policy of their countries in future periods of
crisis, while arrangements for naval and military co-
operation between Britain and France were made in
the event of a German attack against France. The possibility of Germany's trying to breach Belgian neutrality was seriously considered and co-operation with
the Belgian General Staff sought for that contingency.

The effect of the German diplomatic defeat in the
second Moroccan crisis was even more dramatic in
Germany: German propaganda, from now on, loudly
proclaimed that the Reich was 'encircled' by the
Entente Powers, by a coalition of envious and mis-
chievous Powers, who were only waiting for their
chance to overwhelm the Central Powers. Probably
the first, at any rate the best-known, expression of the
new 'encirclement' complex had come a few years before from Field-Marshal Count Schlieffen, the prolific
ex-Chief of the Prussian General Staff. In his famous
article 'Der Krieg in der Gegenwart', written as early
as January 1909, we find most of the relevant clichés
gathered together: Britain envious of Germany's
economic and industrial progress, France thirsting for
revenge, Russia full of Slav resentment against the
Teuton, treacherous Italy lined up against Austria.
They had all built up powerful fortresses around un-
protected Germany and Austria-Hungary.

An endeavour is afoot to bring all these Powers
together for a concentrated attack on the Central
Powers. At the given moment, the drawbridges are
to be let down, the doors are to be opened and the
million-strong armies let loose, ravaging and destroying, across the Vosges, the Meuse, the Niemen,
the Bug and even the Isonzo and the Tyrolean
Alps. The danger seems gigantic.

These were not just the wild rantings of a frustrated
retired general, who had never had the chance of con-
ducting a great battle in actual warfare, but views

shared by many of the Wilhelmine Establishment.
Schlieffen's successor, General Moltke, to whom
Schlieffen had sent the manuscript of his article before
publication, warmly praised it. The Minister of War,
General Einem, had nothing against publication and
merely suggested that Schlieffen should discuss his
article before publication with the Foreign Ministry
(which he did not do). The Kaiser read the article
aloud to his commanding generals on 2 January 1909
and commented with a succinct 'Bravo'.

The naval equivalent of Schlieffen's hair-raising
nightmare has recently been well described by Jon-
athan Steinberg as the 'Copenhagen complex', the
almost obsessive fear of many Germans that the British fleet might attack the German fleet any day without warning, in order to cripple the unwelcome commercial and naval rival. Those fears arose even before
Weltpolitik, at a time when there was virtually no
German fleet in existence. The German fear of 'encirclement', as outlined above, was mistaken – and
there are reasons to doubt whether the German
leaders themselves believed in the 'fairy tale of encirclement' (H. Kantorowicz). In any case, at least
some of them seem to have realised that the Entente
Powers, with their sometimes conflicting aims (Persia,
Constantinople), had no aggressive intentions. In the
comparatively quiet pre-*Weltpolitik* and pre-Entente
days, in early December 1894, Holstein had countered
the argument that a successful war might help to
establish the Kaiser's personal rule by pointing out to
Eulenburg that there was 'little prospect just now of a
defensive war, for no one wants to do us any harm'.
The exact wording recurs just over one decade later:
one of the most capable and level-headed German
diplomats, Count Metternich, wrote to his government in 1905 during the first crisis over Morocco: 'If
we eliminate the problem of Morocco, our position in
the world will be completely unchallenged, for no one
wants to do us any harm.' In 1910 Alfred von Kiderlen-
Wächter, rated as one of the most brilliant German
Foreign Secretaries, went even further: 'If we do not
provoke the war, others will hardly do so.'

Schlieffen concluded his alarmist article of 1909 on
a more sober note, admitting that war might be delayed or, indeed, might not break out at all, as the
'enemies' were still hesitating. The Pan-Germans seem
to have shared the sentiment, even after the second
crisis over Morocco. In November 1913 one of their
leaders, the retired General Gebsattel, wrote in a
memorandum for the Kaiser and the Chancellor that
the Entente Powers were unlikely to take the initiative in starting a war (which Gebsattel fervently
hoped for in order to improve the domestic situation
in the Reich), since they would not dare to attack
Germany. In the early days of July 1914 there was no
talk in Berlin of an immediate danger of attack from
the other Powers. On the contrary, their present
peaceful intentions were given by the government as
arguments for the policy of localisation.

Those Germans who sincerely believed in the threat
constituted by 'encirclement' – and this was the overwhelming majority – clearly misunderstood the intentions of the Entente. But German public opinion by
now understood well enough that to become a World
Power within a short time, and in opposition to the
established Powers, could not be achieved without
conflict. The answer, however, was not drastically to
revise or forgo *Weltpolitik*, pursued now for half a
generation; rather the widespread German desire to
achieve the breakthrough must be intensified. In the
years before 1914 public opinion was characterised by
a strange mixture of pride in Germany's growing
power and gloom about the future, of the obsessive
will to push ahead with *Weltpolitik* and of Germany's
weltpolitische Angst.

The German Concept of a Preventive War

The only major modification of German foreign
policy was that introduced by Bethmann-Hollweg.
While armaments were increased in both the military
and naval sectors, German efforts were concentrated

on the Continent itself. At the same time, Berlin
sought to improve relations with London, hoping to
bring about by means of peripheral agreements not
involving concessions on German naval armaments –
such as the Baghdad Railway and the future of Portuguese colonies – an understanding with Britain that
would keep the latter neutral in a continental war.
Such a war was thought to be inevitable and imminent by many circles within Germany. Leading German geographers, especially Friedrich Ratzel, had
taught that growing populations needed growing territories, that industrialised countries needed *Ergänz-
ungsräume*, i.e. colonial or quasi-colonial territories
of lower population density. Eminent German historians had helped to implant the idea that Germany
in a changing world had either to stagnate and be
relegated to the status of a minor Power, or to promote herself to the status of a firmly established
World Power. They saw Germany as a fortress be-
sieged by enemies, and as they felt the ring around
Germany drawing closer and closer the idea of a sudden desperate charge out of the fortress became respectable.

The logical consequence was the concept of preventive war. Objectively, German fears were unfounded.
But the more Russia recovered her former military
strength after her defeat at the hands of Japan and
the revolution of 1904–5, the more urgently the idea
of preventive war was formulated in Germany. The
agitation of the Pan-Germans more or less openly
accused the Imperial government of cowardice for not
taking the plunge. General Bernhardi's widely read
book, which appeared in several impressions before
1914, spoke openly of the next war. It is true that the
group round Richard von Kühlmann, Secretary of
State in the Foreign Ministry in 1917–18, did plead
meekly for a *Weltpolitik* without war. But the Chancellor, Bethmann-Hollweg, although after 1945 credited with having subscribed to such a programme,
apparently could not and did not dare to come out in
the open with what was, by German standards, a near-
pacifist line: he was afraid of a new ouburst of Pan-

German agitation which might have endangered his
position. Ruedorffer's (Riezler's) book, which, until
recently, also belonged to those books that are more
often quoted than read, was equally far from advocating a peaceful German policy, as he was accused of
before 1945 and praised for since then in Germany.
He only warned of Pan-German impatience and
pleaded for a more temperate pursuit of *Weltpolitik*.

Traditional German historians have always angrily
denied the existence of the concept of preventive war
in Germany before 1914. There is, however, sufficient
evidence to support the view that it not only existed
but also exercised a strong influence on German
policy. It is natural that preventive war should have
found its keenest champions among the military,
whereas the government, following the post-1871
tradition of Bismarck, was reluctant. It is also significant that the concept of preventive war very soon included an attack through neutral Belgium. At the beginning of German *Weltpolitik*, in 1897, there existed
a plan – initiated by the Kaiser and seriously discussed
by the navy – to seize Antwerp by sea in a sudden
commando raid, without any declaration of war, and
to hold it until troops were marched through Belgium. For Antwerp was thought to be important for
mounting an invasion of Britain. The idea was
quietly dropped, not on moral grounds or because
international law would have been violated, but for
technical reasons. In the event, the seizure of Liège in
the first days of the First World War took the place of
a *coup* against Antwerp.

During the Russo-Japanese War at least part of the
German General Staff were for seizing the chance of a
preventive war against Russia, weakened by war and
revolution. Even if Count Schlieffen, Chief of the
General Staff, had not been a member of the war
party, at least junior officers on the General Staff were
vaguely for war, and Groener after 1919 proudly confessed that even after 1919 he supported the concept of
preventive war. General Einem, Prussian Minister of
War, boasts in his memoirs that he had supported the
Chancellor, Bülow, in his struggle against Delcassé,

hoping fervently then that the matter would be decided by the sword: 'Militarily, the situation then was more favourable for us than at any other moment.' Schlieffen's successor, Count Moltke, was of even softer metal than Schlieffen. But as 1914 approached he became more and more outspoken about the need for a war. Just before the peaceful settlement of the second Moroccan crisis he deplored the fact that the chance had been lost to seek a showdown with Britain:

> If we again slink out of this affair with our tail between our legs, if we cannot pull ourselves together to present demands which we are prepared to enforce by the sword, then I despair of the future of the German Reich. Then I shall resign. But first I shall ask that we abolish the army and put ourselves under the protectorate of Japan.

In the summer of 1911 Kiderlen-Wächter, Secretary of State in the Foreign Ministry, pursued a policy which his formal superior, the Chancellor, Bethmann-Hollweg, was not sure aimed at war or not. He could only find out by making Kiderlen-Wächter drink heavily one night. The Secretary, according to Riezler's diary, did not aim at war under all circumstances (and in fact did avoid war on that occasion), but even the comparatively mild Bethmann-Hollweg was then convinced that a war was necessary for the German nation. Apart from the Social Democrats and the left-wing Liberals, the parliamentary spokesmen of the German nation apparently were of the same opinion. For, in the great Reichstag debate after the settlement of the crisis, the Conservative and National Liberal parties were furious at the Chancellor because he had disappointed a nation which had been ready for war. It was on this occasion, on 9 November 1911, that August Bebel, the veteran leader of the S.P.D., gave his impressive warning of a general war and its revolutionising effects. But his warning was laughed at and went unheeded. One heckler in Parliament is recorded to have interrupted him with the words:

'After every war things are better!' Only a few months
later, on 2 February 1912, Spahn, the leader of the
Catholic Centre Party, construed in the Reichstag the
precise situation which was to lead to war in August
1914: Austria would attack Serbia, Russia would support Serbia. Spahn interpreted Russian assistance as
agression against Germany, so that the *casus foederis*
would arise for Germany as well.

After the second Moroccan crisis the disposition towards war in Germany only increased. The pre-war
diaries of Admiral Müller give the impression that
leading circles in Germany were obsessed with the inevitability of a great war, without admitting that they
themselves, by their own *Weltpolitik*, created the
essential conditions for it. During the crisis the Kaiser
had told Müller in an argument on whether the German navy was prepared for war or not:

> Its unpreparedness has always been objected to
> me in a moment of crisis. Now, in any case, is the
> moment for action. The people demand it. If the
> Chancellor and Kiderlen and Wermuth [Secretary
> of State for Finance] do not want to comply, they
> will be sacked. The Chancellor should inform him-
> self better of the mood of the people.

Admiral Müller himself was convinced that war
with Britain could not be avoided in the long run.
One of his reasons for preferring to see the showdown
postponed for the time being was that the Kiel Canal,
which would have allowed the free passage of German
capital ships from the Baltic to the North Sea, was still
under construction. The Canal was finished in June
1914.

During the First Balkan War the Kaiser suddenly
recognised Serbian aspirations and was for holding
back Austria against Serbia. But on 8 December 1912,
the Kaiser, Müller, Tirpitz and the Chiefs of the
General and the Naval Staffs held a kind of war
council. Prince Lichnowsky, the new German Ambassador in London, had reported a warning of Haldane's that, if Germany were to attack France, Britain

would have to come to the aid of France. The Kaiser
welcomed this declaration, because it clarified the
situation, and went on to outline the shape of things
to come:

> Austria had to act vigorously against the foreign
> Slavs [Serbs], because she would otherwise lose her
> power over the Serbs in the Austro-Hungarian
> Monarchy. If Russia were to support the Serbs
> [Sazonov's declaration: Russia would immediately
> invade Galicia, if Austria were to invade Serbia],
> war would be inevitable for us.... The Fleet, of
> course, would have to face the war against Britain.

The Kaiser's analysis, it should be noted, is the same
as that made by Spahn only ten months before.
Moltke's reaction to his Sovereign's expectations is
typical: 'In my opinion war is inevitable, and the
sooner the better.' But he advised that 'the popularity
of a war against Russia as outlined by the Kaiser,
should be better prepared' in the Press. The Kaiser
agreed and gave instructions accordingly. Admiral
Müller himself passed on the Imperial injunction to
the Chancellor, who had not even attended that important policy-making meeting: 'to enlighten the
people through the Press of the great national interest,
which would be at stake also for Germany, if a war
were to break out over the Austro-Serbian conflict'.
The reason is simple:

> The people must not be in the position of asking
> themselves only at the outbreak of a great European
> war, what are the interests that Germany would be
> fighting for. The people ought rather to be accus-
> tomed to the idea of such a war beforehand.

One week later the Chancellor too had apparently
'accustomed' himself 'to the idea of such a war', as the
Kaiser told Admiral Müller. He expressed his surprise
because Bethmann-Hollweg had said one year earlier
that he could never advise a war.
Again two weeks later the Kaiser related his con-

versation with the Belgian King Albert to Moltke and
Bethmann-Hollweg. When Wilhelm II and Albert
had met in Munich on 19 December 1912, Albert had
expressed anxieties over a possible threat to Belgian
neutrality, but the Kaiser assured him that 'his desire
was only to have the right flank safeguarded in the
case of war'. By now the Chancellor must have learned
of the German intention to march through Belgium at
the beginning of the war. For Moltke replied to the
Kaiser's account:

> He has to consider the situation. Our plan of
> deployment against France is based, as is well
> known (*bekanntlich*), on our advance through Bel-
> gium. Nothing could be changed in regard to the
> deployment.

The following year gave ample opportunity to
'accustom people to the idea of such a war'. The
centenary of the war of 1813 and the twenty-fifth
anniversary of the Kaiser's reign occasioned military
and academic ceremonies all over Germany during
1913, and was perhaps the emotional climax of Wilhelmine Germany before 1914. But in early 1913 the
German government did not yet want to risk a great
war. On 10 February, both Moltke and Bethmann-
Hollweg warned their respective Austrian counter-
parts in separate letters of the danger of making war
with Serbia at the present moment over the Albanian
question. Moltke expressed his conviction 'that a
European war is bound to come sooner or later, in
which the issue will be one of a struggle between Ger-
mandom and Slavdom', and he proclaimed: 'To prepare themselves for that contingency is the duty of all
States which are the champions of Germanic ideas and
culture (*Geisteskultur*).' But he warned Conrad von
Hötzendorf, the Austrian Chief of Staff, that the great
war 'necessitates the readiness of the people to make
sacrifices, and popular enthusiasm', and therefore he
was against provoking war with Serbia, especially after
Serbia had gone back on her Albanian demands. Now,
Moltke wrote, it would be difficult for Germany to

'find an effective slogan' for a great war. At the same time, he told the Austrian Military Attaché in Berlin: 'When starting a world war one has to think very carefully.'

In his letter to Berchtold, the Austrian Minister of Foreign Affairs, the Chancellor raised two other points which became relevant in the crisis of July 1914: Russian intervention in the case of Austria attacking Serbia, and British neutrality:

> After analysing the situation objectively, one has to conclude that, considering her traditional relations with the Balkan States, it will be nearly impossible for Russia passively to watch military action by Austria against Serbia without a tremendous loss of face. The exponents of a pacific orientation, whom we can see no doubt in Messrs Kokovzov and Sazonov, would be simply swept away by the indignation of public opinion, if they were to try to resist it. The consequences of Russian intervention, however, are obvious. They would result in a warlike conflict of the Triple Alliance – probably without enthusiastic support by Italy – against the Triple Entente, and Germany would have to bear the full brunt of the French and British attack.

Bethmann-Hollweg hoped instead for a 'reorientation of British policy' – in other words, for a drifting apart or even disintegration of the Triple Entente, which would automatically improve prospects for the Triple Alliance:

> The British attitude [in the Balkan crisis] is only one of several symptoms which suggest that the Entente has passed its climax and that we may look forward to a reorientation of British policy if we succeed in emerging from this crisis without conflicts. These are, of course, developments which are just beginning and which will take some time to bear fruit. But to precipitate a violent solution – even if some interests of the Austrian–Hungarian Monarchy were to demand one – at the very moment when we seem to have the chance, if only a

remote one, to have the conflict under conditions
much more favourable for us, would be, in my
opinion, a mistake of incalculable consequences.

Only seventeen months later the 'much more favourable conditions' for the showdown seemed to have
arrived: the treaties over the Baghdad Railway and
over the future of the Portuguese colonies as a further
step towards the creation of a German *Mittelafrika*,
and the visit of a British naval squadron to Kiel in
June 1914, seemed to inaugurate a new phase of
Anglo-German co-operation and to offer the chance of
eventual British neutrality in a continental war. If
neutrality were not to be had, at least the Kiel Canal
had been completed by now.

Meanwhile, the diplomatic crisis over the Second
Balkan War provoked new outbursts of warlike sentiment behind the scenes in Germany. During the
spectacular ceremony at Leipzig, when the great
monument in memory of the Battle of Leipzig in 1813
was unveiled, the Kaiser told the Austrian Chief of
Staff, Baron Conrad, that he supported Austria
against the Serbs:

> I am with you there. The others [i.e. the other
> Powers] are not prepared, they will not do anything
> against it. Within a few days you must be in Bel-
> grade. I was always a partisan of peace; but this has
> its limits. I have read much about war and know
> what it means. But finally a situation arises in
> which a Great Power can no longer just look on,
> but must draw the sword.

About the same time, the Kaiser commented on
Berchtold's appreciation of German support for an
Austrian *démarche* in Belgrade and the hope expressed that the Serbs would give in forthwith, so that
extreme measures would be unnecessary, with the
words: 'This would be very regrettable! Now or
never! For once things down there have to be put
right and calm restored!' The Kaiser's patience was
apparently wearing thin, and he voiced some senti-

ments which were to reappear in July 1914 – even the
magic formula of 'Now or never!' While the government did not dare openly to embrace the course of
'*Weltpolitik* and no war', in late 1913 they came
under pressure from the Pan-Germans, this time
mainly for reasons of domestic policy. The elections of
1912 had made the S.P.D. the strongest party in the
Reichstag; the policy of *Weltpolitik* for diverting the
attention of the masses from the Socialists had apparently failed. (In fact it had only superficially failed
because the S.P.D. in the process had become largely
nationalist in their turn, as not only the war in 1914
was to show.) This is why some circles now returned to
the old idea of a *coup* against Reichstag and Constitution. After legislation for a massive expansion of the
army had been passed by the Reichstag in the summer
of 1913, the Pan-Germans stepped up their campaign
against the Chancellor.

In October 1913 their leaders sent an important
memorandum to the Crown Prince, whose Pan-German sympathies were notorious; he passed it on to the
Kaiser in mid-November, at the peak of the crisis over
the Zabern incident. The memorandum suggested the
abolition of the Constitution, the suppression of freedom of the Press and discriminatory legislation aimed
at the Jews; and it accused the government of wanting
to preserve peace at any price. Even an unsuccessful
war would be preferable to a 'long and cowardly
peace'. Since the other Powers would hardly attack
Germany, the Reich had to take the initiative. While
Bethmann-Hollweg, in a long letter to the Kaiser, rejected all the concrete proposals of the Pan-Germans,
he revealed that he did not differ basically from them
on some points, but differed rather on tactics and emphasis. He merely maintained that what counted was
to be successful: a *coup* against the Reichstag would
fail, because it would start a civil war which in its
turn would lead to war with foreign Powers. The
Chancellor also rejected the charge of wanting to
preserve peace at any price. He could envisage only
two cases in which he would advocate war: if the
'honour and dignity of Germany were to be affected

by another nation', which had not happened so far,
according to Bethmann-Hollweg, and if he could 'envisage vital aims for the nation' which 'could not be
accomplished without war'. As examples he quoted
Bismarck's wars: 'In order to accomplish such tasks
and aims Bismarck wanted, and made, the wars of
1864, 1866 and 1870.'

One such 'vital aim' for Germany was to achieve the
status of a World Power on an equal footing with the
others. It was Riezler who formulated this in 1914, a
few weeks before the outbreak of war. Although the
geographical basis was apparently too narrow for such
a course, he insisted that

> *Weltpolitik* must nevertheless be pursued ...
> German policy must escape the *circulus vitiosus*. It
> cannot opt for a purely continental policy. The task
> which arises out of the situation is the essential
> problem of the foreign policy of the German Reich.
> Everything that happens can be interpreted as an
> attempt at its solution.

And what was the supreme task of German policy? To
make the Reich stronger than any combination of possible enemies. Such a *Lebensaufgabe*, to quote Bethmann-Hollweg, was, of course, impossible without
war: of this others besides Riezler were well aware.
Again, the final logic points to preventive action, before the potential enemies were strong enough to prevent German expansion, which would sweep away the
barriers of containment.

The tensions with Russia over the mission of the
German General Liman von Sanders to Turkey had
hardly abated when Moltke was pressing more urgently than ever before for an early war. He was especially worried about the military recovery of Russia. On
12 May 1914 he spoke to Conrad at Carlsbad about
the possibility of war. According to Conrad he said
that 'any delay meant a lessening of our chances; we
could not compete with Russia in masses'. The same
obsession with Russian armaments was revealed a few
days later by a conversation between Jagow and

Moltke, on either 20 May or 3 June 1914, when both
travelled in Moltke's car from Potsdam to Berlin.
Moltke feared that Russia would have built up maximum armaments in two or three years and thought no
other way was left but to 'wage a preventive war in
order to beat the enemy while we still have some
chance of winning'. Moltke, therefore, advised Jagow
'to orientate our policy at the early provocation of a
war'. Jagow refused, pointing to the steady improvement of Germany's economic situation, but after the
war he admitted that he himself 'never condemned in
principle and *a limine* the idea of the preventive war'.
In his view even Bismarck's wars had been preventive.
It is perhaps as a consequence of this conversation
between Moltke and Jagow that Bethmann-Hollweg
spoke with the Bavarian Minister in Berlin, Count
Lerchenfeld, early in June 1914, about 'the preventive
war demanded by many generals'. When Lerchenfeld
objected that the right moment had passed already,
the Chancellor agreed, but added:

> There are circles in the Reich who expect of a
> war an improvement in the domestic situation in
> Germany – in a conservative direction. He, the
> Chancellor, however, thought that on the contrary a
> world war with its incalculable consequences would
> strengthen tremendously the power of Social Demo-
> cracy, because they preached peace, and would
> topple many a throne.

In spite of his correct insight into the consequences of
a world war, Bethmann-Hollweg was either too weak
or too inconsistent to translate his theoretically sound
judgement into practical politics. Apparently he was
the prisoner of the tradition of *Weltpolitik*, now
nearly two decades old, of some of his own ideas and
of his surroundings: he himself was no longer in
principle against a war, and he was ready to fight one
to accomplish the great, vitally important aims of the
nation. Riezler had pointed to one such vital aim –
the need to broaden the basis for pursuing the *Weltpolitik*. Moltke pressed for an early preventive war,

and Jagow was not against it in principle. The Pan-
Germans and most political parties accused him of
cowardice, while the Kaiser oscillated.

The Kaiser's person was an additional reason for
Jagow's hesitation to risk a preventive war, because he
thought Wilhelm II would not have the strength to
see a great war right through. A similar view had been
expressed by Tschirschky, the German Ambassador in
Vienna, a few months earlier. When, on 16 March
1914, Conrad suggested an early war against Russia,
Tschirschky objected: 'Two important people are
against it, your Archduke Franz Ferdinand and my
Kaiser.' Tschirschky added that only under compul-
sion of a *fait accompli* would they resolve to go to war.

On 28 June 1914, one of the two obstacles to war
had been removed – Archduke Franz Ferdinand. His
murder provided Berlin with the chance to 'find an
effective slogan' in Germany for a great war, for which
the German nation had been psychologically and
materially prepared since at least December 1912. The
showdown came at a time when the German 'chance
... to have the conflict under conditions much more
favourable' than in February 1913 seemed to be
brighter than ever before.

Austria–Hungary and Serbia: The Assassination of Archduke Franz Ferdinand

The spark which set off the First World War sprang
from the apparently only secondary field of tension
between Serbia and Austria–Hungary. In reality there
lay concealed beneath this the secular conflict between
the dynastic, supranational, conservative idea of State
and the modern national revolutionary and national
democratic principle of self-government, which in its
many different forms has determined the course of
world history from the French Revolution down to
the present day – a conflict which opens up perspectives of a universal historical nature far beyond and
above the mere consideration of the question of 'war
guilt'.

The Danube Monarchy had had to contend with the problem of the emergent nations, in one form or another, throughout the nineteenth century. As the successor to the Holy Roman Empire of the German nation on southern European soil, the Habsburg Monarchy had never been able to come to terms with a modern world of heterogeneous nationalities all agitating for emancipation. As far back as 1859, in circumstances strikingly similar to those which led to the First World War in 1914, she had been defeated by a national revolutionary movement allied with a European Great Power – the then emergent Italy, which could count upon active support from France under Napoleon III. Then, to be sure, Austria had only lost the greater part of her Italian possessions, but the loss left behind an incurable resentment against the liberal, national revolutionary Italy of the Risorgimento. At least as important as this was the Austrian quest for a substitute for Venetia and Lombardy. Almost two decades later the Danube Monarchy found itself in occupation of Bosnia-Hercegovina, which only intensified the underlying problem. With the occupation and annexation respectively of these two south Slav provinces (in 1878 and 1908), the Danube Monarchy incorporated the political explosive which was to cause its destruction in 1918. Yet it was the south Slav nationalists, above all, who were struck by the example of Piedmont and the need to win the support of a Great Power in the struggle against Austria. The same combination as in 1859 – a national revolutionary movement inside Austria and its support by an already existing national State, receiving help in turn from a Great Power – led in 1914–18 to the collapse of the Danube Monarchy.

Since the almost total elimination of the Italian element after the war of 1859, the Danube Monarchy found itself confronted with the nationalist movements of the Slavs, mainly south Slavs and Czechs. After the defeat in 1866 in the internal war for German hegemony, the Habsburgs could only prevent the secession of the Magyars by allowing them to share power with the Germans who had, in effect, had a

monopoly of power up till then. For the Hungarians,
and more especially the powerful and self-assertive
Magyar aristocracy, it was in the interest of survival to
keep down the south Slavs. The reorganisation of the
Imperial State into the Dual Monarchy by means of
the Compromise of 1867 (which had to be endorsed
and modified every ten years in laborious negotiations) gave the Magyar aristocracy a kind of veto over
Vienna. Even the threat of withdrawal from the Imperial Alliance would have been enough to block any
kind of federal or democratic reform which could have
undermined the dualism of Austrians and Magyars
or even granted to the Slav nationalities complete
equality of rights.

For decades Austria-Hungary had been content
with a system of 'muddling through' which had led to
a state of complete political paralysis. As a result of
her anachronistic construction and concomitant stagnation, she had from the turn of the century drifted
helplessly into the maelstrom of the Slav nationalist
movement. After the overthrow of the Obrenović
dynasty in 1903 the Serbs constituted the most dynamic element in the Balkans and, as such, the greatest
threat to the Danube Monarchy; for the immediate
aims of unification of the Serbs with Montenegro,
parts of Macedonia and ultimately the south Slav
provinces of the Danube Monarchy, Bosnia and Hercegovina, would inevitably result in the addition of
Dalmatia, Croatia and Slovenia to an enlarged south
Slav national State. The realisation of the national
right of self-determination for south Slavs (whether of
the Greater Serbian, Centralist or south Slav Federalist variety) thus constituted a threat to the Dual
Monarchy if she failed to remodel herself in time into
a federalist and democratic structure. The leading
Austro-Hungarian statesmen were fully aware of the
basic problem; thus Conrad von Hötzendorf wrote to
the heir apparent, Archduke Franz Ferdinand, on 14
December 1912:

The unification of the south Slav race is one of
the powerful national movements which can neither

be ignored nor kept down. The question can only be, whether that unification will take place within the boundaries of the Monarchy – that is at the expense of Serbia's independence – or under Serbia's leadership at the expense of the Monarchy. The cost to the Monarchy would be the loss of its south Slav provinces and thus of almost its entire coastline. The loss of territory and prestige would relegate the Monarchy to the status of a small Power.

With his realistic analysis Conrad unwittingly anticipated the end of the Danube Monarchy, for it proved incapable of creating the necessary basis for a constructive solution; and the development of Serbia from 1903 onwards had already progressed too far for it still to be possible to compel a unification of the south Slavs with the increasingly self-assertive Serbs within the framework of the Danube Monarchy. The ruling class of Austria-Hungary, notoriously unable to adapt their conservative, dynastic régime to the exigencies of modern times, abandoned themselves to a chivalrous mood of decline: if their traditional positions of power could no longer be assured by political means, there was a wish at least to 'go down with honour'. For the ruling class, still adhering to their feudal modes of thought, this was only conceivable in a war, which it was hoped – against all reason – would somehow succeed in prolonging an existence which had long since become questionable.

The most influential exponent of this fatalistic conception of war was Conrad. He hoped to save the Danube Monarchy by a preventive war, at one moment against Italy, which although officially a member of the Triple Alliance sympathised with the south Slavs, and at the next against national democratic and national revolutionary Serbia herself.

Austria-Hungary had already on two occasions demonstrated her hostility to the expansion of Serbia and had even partially mobilised her army in the annexation crisis of 1908–9 and the Balkan wars of 1912–13. The tense atmosphere was shattered by the shots at Sarajevo on 28 June 1914. Several factors combined to make the outrage possible.

Franz Ferdinand, the heir apparent, had the reputa-
tion of wanting to reconstruct the Dual Monarchy
into a Triadism, with the south Slav nationalities as
the third pillar, thereby saving the situation and taking the wind out of the sails of south Slav nationalism.
In the light of this the choice of the heir apparent as
the victim of the assassination was certainly no coincidence, the less so since Franz Ferdinand made his
entry into Sarajevo at the close of the manœuvres in
Bosnia on 28 June, the anniversary of the Battle of
Kosovo in 1389.

The second factor was the south Slav movement
emanating from Serbia. Earlier German and Austrian
interpretations which take the guilt or complicity of
the Serbian government as their point of departure do
not stand up to examination. Still less tenable, if only
because the murder was the most extreme and violent
expression of south Slav nationalism, is the monstrous
theory of collective guilt which attempts to pin the
responsibility for the outrage of Sarajevo on to the
Serbian people as a whole. Rather it would seem
necessary to show careful discrimination: the outrage
of Sarajevo was by no means the work of the Serbian
government; in any case, the latter did not have
enough knowledge of the plans to take preventive
measures in time. On the contrary, Sarajevo was
planned and organised by the extreme wing of Serbian nationalism, the secret society 'Death or Unification', better known under the name of the 'Black
Hand'. This consisted of an association of nationalist
officers, officials and intellectuals. In the summer of
1914 the 'Black Hand' was locked in a struggle with
the Serbian government, which may have led to the
fall of the head of the society, Colonel Dimitriević-
Apix, Chief of the Military Secret Service.

In this tense situation the outrage resembled an
attempt to plunge the more prudent government of
the Old Radicals, under Nikola Pašić, headlong into
the alternative of either submitting to the Austrians,
with the subsequent risk of an armed revolution such
as was frequently feared in the July crisis, or postpon-

ing its more cautious programme for the liberation of the south Slav provinces and taking on a war with Austria-Hungary instead.

Recent research has shown that Pašić had certainly heard rumours of arms smuggling over the frontier into Bosnia and that he consequently demanded an inquiry. Dimitriević-Apix, however, while conceding in a long written report to Pašić that the pistols emanated from army stores, claimed that they were only employed for the protection of his Secret Service agents in Bosnia. Despite this deliberate deception by Apix, Pašić did not allow matters to rest there and issued an order to the frontier authorities to prevent arms smuggling and the illicit entry of young men. In view of this, Apix attempted to call off the whole undertaking. Like the Norodna Odbrana, whose agent heard of the planned attempt, Apix tried at the last moment to put a stop to the outrage through his contact man with the group of conspirators in Sarajevo. The conspirators, however, with Gavrilo Princip at their head, refused to abandon their plan for assassinating the Archduke.

At this point a third factor comes into play: the perpetrators all came from Bosnia itself and were thus Austro-Hungarian subjects. They were much less blind and willing tools of the 'Black Hand' than has up till now generally been accepted in Germany and Austria. Princip and his circle of friends belonged to the national revolutionary movement among young intellectuals, students and schoolchildren, commonly known as 'Young Bosnia'. In contrast to the more exclusively Pan-Serbian ideas of the 'Black Hand', they stood for a south Slav, federal solution on the basis of equality for all south Slav groups. The idea of an attempt on the life of Franz Ferdinand in Sarajevo originated in 'Young Bosnian' circles, and merely happened to fit in with similar, but as yet uncrystallised ideas of the 'Black Hand' which finally took over the practical preparations for the attempt (such as procuring the weapons and equipment, training the accomplices, and helping them over the frontier). At the decisive point in the crisis, when Apix tried hard to pre-

vent the outrage, it was Princip's firm determination
to carry out the attempt at all costs that prevailed. In
the last analysis, the murder at Sarajevo was thus
primarily the deed of Princip himself and can only
indirectly be charged to the 'Black Hand', and virtually not at all to the Serbian government (let alone
the Serbian people).

In a deeper sense the ultimate responsibility falls on
the ruling class in Austria-Hungary, less because it
sent Franz Ferdinand into an 'alley of bomb-throwers'
than on account of its inability to satisfy the legitimate struggle of their various nationalities for freedom, equality and social justice (a motive which is
generally overlooked in the wholesale condemnation
by Germany and Austria of the conspirators of Sarajevo). By their rigid adherence to outdated political
and social conceptions, the traditional Powers left no
room for the political agitations of the young south
Slav intelligentsia who, in their desperation, were finally driven to the crime of political murder. No historical account seeking to do justice to the complicated
events of July and August 1914 can any longer afford
to ignore this important aspect, neglected for so long
in Germany and Austria. It becomes clear that the
Austrian and German governments were in fact mistaken in their assumptions about the background to
the outrage.

Sarajevo was the dramatic culmination of the conflict between the Danube Monarchy and the south
Slav national movement which had been smouldering
for so long. Everything now depended on how Austria-
Hungary would react. The manner of her reaction
could give rise to a confrontation with Russia, and
create the constellation which would make world war
inevitable, a constellation so accurately predicted by
Spahn in February 1912, by Bethmann-Hollweg in
February 1913 and by the Kaiser in October 1913.

4 World Policy, World Power and German War Aims

Fritz Fischer

The slogans which Wilhelm II proclaimed vociferously and which Bülow adopted without resistance, though in a somewhat smoother form, were world policy as the task, world power as the aim and naval construction as the instrument. The broad mass of the nation, especially its intellectual and economic upper strata, welcomed them on the whole very approvingly in the belief that it would be possible to secure for ever Germany's position as a World Power equal in rights and strength to England. Behind this belief was the conviction that the nation's unparalleled industrial advance, the industrialisation which was permanently dependent on the supply of raw materials from abroad, the development of overseas trade, and also the supplying and feeding of the growing population at home, could not be guaranteed unless it attained a position [of power] which was not limited to European frontiers. The intoxicating energy and speed of the boom caused them to overestimate the strength of the Empire's position in Europe. The uncertainties of the latter were fatally obscured by the deep-rooted Imperialist tension with England on the one hand and with France and Russia on the other. (Herzfeld)

This judgement made by Hans Herzfeld in 1952 about Germany's position at the start of her Imperialist era proper, which was signalled by the appointment of Bülow and Tirpitz to crucial offices in 1897, can be affirmed without any reservation in 1963. Its

From the *Historische Zeitschrift*, CXCIX (Oct. 1964).

author, however, apparently no longer believes it to be right; otherwise one could not understand the premise of his criticism of my position, which he set out expressly by questioning the validity of my assertion that there was an 'active and conscious German striving for world power'. But it appears entirely inconceivable that these aims of the German Empire at the start of the First World War should no longer have been in its political consciousness and should no longer have been seen as the object of German policy!

That this was not the case is shown – among many other statements from the period at the outbreak of the war – by the avowal of the editor of the *Preussische Jahrbücher*, a representative of the Wilhelmine era, the historian Hans Delbrück in his book *Bismarcks Erbe* ('The Bismarckian Inheritance'), which appeared in 1915:

> Bismarck's inheritance has been preserved … but it was only properly fulfilled the moment, as peace could no longer be preserved, we went to war, with as much confidence as he did, to defend first of all our very existence and thenceforward to be a World Power like ourselves among the other World Powers.

Ausgekreist

In 1896 the same Hans Delbrück, in complete agreement with the ideas of Gustav Schmoller, Otto Hintze, Erich Marcks and Max Weber – you need only think of Weber's Inaugural Lecture of 1894* – formulated the 'German mission' in its classic form:

> In the next decades vast tracts of land in very different parts of the world will be distributed. The nation which goes away empty-handed will lose its place in the next generation from the ranks of those Great Powers which will coin the human spirit. Did we found the German Empire to see it disappear under our grandchildren?

* Fischer's error: the date is 1895—Ed.

For twelve years under Bülow, Germany believed she could reach the objectives of 1897–8. But when the balance-sheet was drawn up at Bülow's departure (July 1909), it turned out that Germany was *ausgekreist*, had achieved none of her aims. In fact, even her European position itself seemed to be threatened, whereas under Bismarck her hegemony had been generally accepted.

Those World Powers already established, France, England, Russia and America, could block the impetuous pressure of a Germany aware of its very late appearance. To the same degree as they had acquired vast tracts of the earth since the 1860s and 1870s, they were also more successful at the turn of the century in getting what they wanted than the new competitor. In view of the possibilities for expansion, what else did the Entente of 1904 and the Russian–English understanding of 1907 signify than the exclusion of Germany from the major show-places of spheres of influence throughout the world, first in Egypt and Morocco and then in Persia, Afghanistan and Tibet; at the same time they also meant that Germany's rising industrial production met considerable handicaps in other areas, while the other Powers were successfully extending their influence, Japan in Korea and China, America in Cuba, Puerto Rico, the Philippines, Panama, Nicaragua and Mexico, England in South Africa and many other places round the world, France in Africa and south-east Asia, and Russia in East and Central Asia.

And what had Germany achieved in the twelve years of world policy? The lease of Kiaochow in 1897 for ninety-nine years, causing a great deal of friction with England, Russia and Japan; then in 1899, after England's withdrawal, two Samoan islands as sovereign possessions (an acquisition which went back to Bismarck's time), through their partition between Germany and America, which in fact left much ill-feeling in America, and which together with Britain's simultaneous withdrawal from the Caribbean helped prepare England's approach to America; then the purchase of some of Spain's legacy in the Pacific in 1899, the Palau Islands, the Carolines and the Mariana Islands – really a very paltry acquisition, though Bülow, announcing the completion of their purchase to the Kaiser, said that this gain '[will] prompt the people and the navy to follow Your Majesty further along the way leading to world power, greatness and eternal glory'. Similarly, when the Samoan islands, which have already been mentioned, were acquired, Bülow had justified it in a report lasting for several hours before the German Kolonialrat on the grounds of how it raised 'Germany's prestige in the world'.

These were the only German acquisitions overseas up to 1911, in fact to 1914 if we ignore the slight enlargement of the German Cameroons, even though the years 1897–8 had been the start for 'the struggle for world power and naval construction', marked by the passage of Tirpitz's two Navy Laws through the Reichstag in 1898 and 1900 by the use of all the means of modern mass persuasion.

World Policy and 'Interests'

Where and how did Germany try to gain influence and acquisitions in the subsequent seventeen years? Already since the 1880s in South Africa, from which Germany began to withdraw at the end of the 1890s after fierce friction with England (the Kruger Telegram of 1896); in the Congo and Central Africa in order to gain the territory of Katanga with its rich mineral deposits and to establish a connection with German East Africa or to make sure of part of the Portuguese colonies for herself; in Morocco and Egypt; in East Asia and the Pacific; in South America – Chile, Brazil, Argentina, Venezuela and Mexico.

Everywhere Germany's presence implied conflict, even though till the beginning of the century the fronts were by no means clear-cut. And for a long time also perhaps Anglo-French antagonism and the friction between England and Russia hid the tensions produced by Germany's rise and pretensions, which in fact finally caused the close *rapprochement* of those Powers.

Already in 1898 the attempt to acquire at least a part of the Philippines had failed. The near collision of the German overseas squadron and the American war fleet off Manila caused by this left resentment in the United States which was never to be forgotten. This reappeared through the Venezuelan affair, in which the Disconto-Gesellschaft, an active associate the Great Venezuelan Railway Company, got the Empire to defend its investments by armed intervention. Although the blockade was carried out jointly with England and Italy, public opinion in the United States was excited primarily against Germany, and Theodore Roosevelt's use of the American fleet was celebrated as a victory of the President over the Kaiser. Around 1902 Wilhelm II tried to acquire a naval base in Mexico in Lower California, but met Japanese and American resistance. In President Diaz (1874–1910) the Kaiser had an admiring friend who looked to the German State as a model and who expected economic aid and help in military training – in Diaz's reception hall for foreign diplomats hung a portrait of Kaiser Wilhelm II. After Diaz's death as a result of the conflict in and over Mexico, Paul Hintze, the last German Ambassador there before the war, produced the idea, as did Arthur Zimmermann, who actually tried to put it into effect in 1917 as Secretary of State (the Zimmermann Telegram), of drawing Mexico on to the side of the Central Powers and of co-operating with Japan (Moltke was already thinking about this in August 1914) in a war against the United States, if she entered the war against Germany.

Or in the Far East where before and after the acquisition of Kiaochow and a sphere of influence in Shantung the China-Syndikat of the major German banks also tried to gain influence in central China by building railways, acquiring mining companies, building factories and founding trading settlements, once again in the fiercest rivalry with England, an action which led to political friction with England, Russia, America and Japan. Attempts were made to acquire further

bases in Polynesia besides the South Seas possessions.
These bases were above all intended as telegraph
stations which would open up the Pacific area and be
independent of the agencies of communication of the
Great Powers.

Turkey, and the Balkan bridge to it, was the principal point of Germany's economic commitment and of
her political prestige. According to Arthur von Gwinner, Director of the Deutsche Bank and initiator and
supporter of the Baghdad Railway enterprise, here
Krupp and Creusot, both backed by their 'respective
governments and high finance', were fighting for a
market for their war materials and for political influence. In a classic manner Gwinner outlined the activity of Germany's foreign missions. They arranged
foreign business transactions on behalf of German industry (most telegrams of the representatives of important German firms were communicated or passed
to them by the Foreign Office), above all on behalf of
the armaments industry, such as the supply of guns,
rifles, munitions and warships, of electric and telegraphic equipment (A.E.G. for high-power current
and Siemens for weak current). All these transactions
were always carried out in sharp competition with
nations who in the long run had the greater capacity
for playing off the dominance and monetary resources
of their markets against the isolated Berlin one.

The outstanding rise of the German economy produced at the same time the shortage of capital. As
Helfferich, Director of the Deutsche Bank and specialist in Balkan and Turkish questions, stressed to the
Greek Prime Minister, Venizelos, on 27 January 1914,
Germany felt on an equal footing with America in the
modernity of her economy, even superior to America;
moreover, as he said, 'German capitalist circles'
differed from the French: 'In France state stock is preferred above all, while in Germany an additional industrial flavour is liked.' But German industrialisation had consumed vast investments, which were no
longer available in the race for spheres of influence;
this was directly contrary to France, which could
employ enough investment-seeking capital politically,

because she was less developed economically.

After glancing at the Central African policy of Chancellor Bethmann-Hollweg and his relations with England, this problem will have to be explored in a field crucial for the German economy and policy, the Balkans and Turkey during the years 1912–14. This examination is chiefly based on material previously unpublished, which is of decisive importance for an assessment of German policy immediately before the First World War, although it cannot be treated fully here.

The Difficult and the Easy Way: Morocco, Central Africa and England

In the renewal of the discussions of German war aims in the First World War the personality of the German Chancellor, Bethmann-Hollweg, and an assessment of his policy, have again come to the forefront of historical interest, especially by my critics. When a personality is singled out so sharply, it is necessary to look more closely at the turning-point which Bethmann-Hollweg's appointment signified in relation to Bülow's time, which began under the banner of 'world policy' and led Germany to isolation.

Against such an interpretation Bethmann-Hollweg himself could be cited as a witness, not only because he had been suggested to the Emperor as his successor by Bülow himself, but also because after Bethmann-Hollweg had been in office for half a year, he – obviously to answer objections to his conduct of foreign policy – ordered his Foreign Office staff to draw up a memorandum which demonstrates that since he had taken office there had been no departing from the hitherto accepted policy prescribed by his predecessor, *especially not in the sense of a greater subservience to countries abroad*' (author's italics). In detail the Imperial Chancellor, among other things, wanted especially the following points pursued:

England: continuation of spinning the thread of understanding begun by my predecessor over sev-

eral African questions, willingness for further
understandings of this kind. Any modification of
our Navy Law excluded.

This means that Bethmann-Hollweg considered his
policy as a continuation of the dual policy of Bülow,
especially in relation to England. On the one hand 'to
try for an understanding' over colonial questions; but
on the other hand to remain unyielding on the question of naval armament.

We have to consider briefly in this general setting
(before turning to German policy in the Balkans and
Turkey) Bethmann-Hollweg's and Kiderlen-Wächter's
German policy in North and Central Africa, where
also private economic interests went hand in hand
with Imperial policy. Kiderlen-Wächter (for many
years German Ambassador to Rumania, who had impressed the Kaiser by his reports, which were as saga-
cious as they were amusing) appears to have followed
the harder line, but he could not have acted without
the countenance of the Imperial Chancellor, Bethmann-Hollweg; Jagow, whose keynote was an anti-
Slav one, later assumed a more flexible attitude to England, a mixture of patience and toughness – because
of the ultimate aims of 'world policy'.

At the same time as the Bosnian crisis of 1908–9 and
the *Daily Telegraph* affair, which blighted Bülow's
last months as Imperial Chancellor, the Imperial
government – entirely because of the Balkan danger –
managed to reach a compromise with France over
Morocco, where the Germans together with the pre-
tender, Mulai Hafid, had been pursuing a policy
which was risky and in the end condemned to failure.
In the form of an interpretation of the Algeciras Act
(February 1909), Germany acknowledged France's
political position in the land of the Sherif and France
in return acknowledged Germany's economic interests
there. The most significant aspect of this treaty, which
was both highly equivocal and is still in need of further interpretation, was the governmental support for
co-operation between German and French interests in
Africa. A project for a Franco-German plantation and

settlement company in the border territory of the German Cameroons and French Congo, in the Ngoko-Sangha, put forward by the National Liberal Deputy, Dr Semmler from Hamburg, and the Editor in chief of *Les Temps*, Tardieu, was pursued through the active good offices of the German Embassy in Paris, especially by the Counsellor of the Embassy, van der Lancken, with the occasional support of the Ministers Caillaux and Pichon, although under rising distrust and opposition from the French Parliament. Careful examination of the documents in fact shows that this project amounted to nothing more than an attempt at personal gain, at least on the part of the French company, which largely on that account did not have the support of the French Chamber, and because of which all the hopes of the Germans to gain a foothold in the French Congo came to nothing. A similar fate was suffered by the project for a German–French Central African railway, which should have gone through the South and North Cameroons and the French Congo to the Belgian Congo.

Certainly the idea of a continental bloc played a part in all this, as Bethmann-Hollweg at the same time tried for a *détente* with Russia (after the war crisis of 1909), shown by the evidence at Potsdam (November 1910) and in the Russo-German agreement of 19 August 1911, in which Germany expressed disinterest in Persia and Russia agreed to the extension of the Baghdad Railway (the construction had stagnated for some time), but which was a disappointment to both sides – as, for example, in the founding of a German bank in Teheran which failed through Russian opposition.

The disappointments in the form of the abortive Franco-German co-operation shown above and the lack of success in such indirect ways of acquiring economic spheres of interest led to the idea of 1911 of making political capital out of France's action in Morocco, which according to the German interpretation violated the Algeciras Act (and thus restored freedom of action to Germany), in obtaining a consolidated possession in Central Africa through a de-

mand for compensation. (The compensation offers of
France of 7 May and 20–21 June were thought too
little.) By exaggerating the interest of Mannesmann
Brothers and some unimportant Hamburg trading-
posts on the west Moroccan coast, for the protection of
which the Foreign Office allegedly sent the gunboat
Panther to Agadir, and by stirring up, through the co-
operation of the Foreign Office with the Pan-German
League, public excitement at the same time, the Secretary of State, Kiderlen-Wächter, was fully conscious
that Germany's goal of the French Congo in return for
giving France a free hand in Morocco could only be
reached by taking all risks, including the risk of war.
In July 1911 his policy could be sure of the support of
the overwhelming part of the German Press, but he
did not receive the Kaiser's consent. In fact the '*Panther*'s leap' had only been forced on the Kaiser by the
repeated threat of resignation.

Furthermore, it can be left quite open whether the
primary aim of Bethmann-Hollweg's and Kiderlen-
Wächter's policy was not so much Central Africa as
(repeating the first Morocco crisis) the breaking-up of
France's military alliance with Russia and her Entente
with England: the objective was no less than this –
after all what would France have been without her
Entente? She would have become a junior partner of
Germany, a position which perhaps could have been
eased through her membership in *Mitteleuropa*.

After hard negotiations, which were several times
broken off, in the compromise reached at last, Germany was ceded strips of territory which gave her
access to the Congo and Ubangi (4 November 1911). It
was the result of both nations' backing down, France
because she had not received the complete support by
treaty from England (despite the Mansion House
speech) and also because Russia was still not ready for
war; Germany because the Kaiser especially shrank
from the prospect of a war on three fronts for which
Germany was as yet not ready militarily or economically.

Considering the nation's high expectations, the re-
percussion of this failure in Germany was of decisive

importance for the future attitudes of the ruling classes, the military, navy, heavy industry and National Liberal bourgeoisie. Already during the negotiations of the summer and autumn of 1911, the mood of the Pan-German League, disappointed over the delays, had changed into outspoken hatred of England when she covered the French position. But also the excessive excitement and disappointment turned against its own government, not least against the person of the Kaiser himself. All this hate against England exploded in the Reichstag speech in November 1911, against which the Chancellor, Bethmann-Hollweg's – another instance of 'resistance'! -- mollifying speech was unable to prevail, a speech he made because he did not want to break the thread with England, since she was the only country willing to try for an agreement with Germany.

The bitterness whipped up in the German people against the English continued and formed the background to the Supplementary Naval Law of May 1912 (practically a third Naval Law, which was to run until 1920). Under the determining influence of Tirpitz and the forces rallied behind him, this was submitted to the Reichstag on the day of Haldane's arrival, and supported, despite English wishes, by the Kaiser. The Reichstag passed it, although the nationalist parties there did not find it far-reaching enough. At the same time the War Ministry prepared to reinforce the army by nearly exhausting the limits of conscription (the first reinforcement since 1891), which led to the first increase in the army in 1912 (from 1 October 1912 an increase from 595,000 to 622,000 men). Under the impact of the excitement on both sides of the Channel, Bethmann-Hollweg, on the advice of Kühlmann, the Chargé d'Affaires in London, and with the help of Ballin and Cassel, tried through the Haldane mission (February 1912) to bring about a *détente* and reach an agreement between England and Germany, which was aimed at the same time at loosening England's ties with France and Russia. This attempt at a *détente* was of course distinctly limited by the barrier erected in the form of Tirpitz's Supplementary Naval Law.

Bethmann-Hollweg himself saw very clearly the contradiction between the attempted *détente* and the Supplementary Naval Law. Writing on 10 April 1912 to the former German Ambassador in Constantinople, Freiherr von Marschall, asking him to take on the post of Ambassador to London (after the Kaiser had decided to recall Metternich in June–July), he declared that 'the task of achieving a political agreement with England at the same time as passing the Supplementary Naval Law produced a bellicose atmosphere which made it tantamount to squaring the circle'. Because of this 'the talks now begun' (subsequent to the Haldane mission) would 'not lead to a settlement for the moment'. But because he considers the pivot of our policy now and in the future 'the state of our relations with England', he desired 'the deployment of our ablest people' in London, despite his regret at having to entrust, at the present time, 'our Near Eastern policy' to someone else.

Bethmann-Hollweg hoped through a neutrality formula, which would have neutralised England in case of 'warlike developments' on the Continent and in this way have paralysed the Entente, to obtain some relief for Germany on the Continent and at the same time achieve her colonial aims in Central Africa which had failed because of France. A settlement with England over the Afro-Turkish question would have allowed Germany to pursue the construction of the Baghdad Railway to Basra, in return for which England would have had her sphere of influence in Kuwait and on the Persian Gulf guaranteed. Beyond this, Germany – in return for renouncing prospecting rights along the Baghdad Railway beyond Baghdad – would have gained a half of each of the Portuguese colonies of Angola and Mozambique.

From the spring of 1914 the Congo question was again added as a subject for discussion to the negotiations between Germany and England over the Baghdad Railway and the Persian Gulf as well as the partition of the Portuguese colonies.

In his reports of 9 December 1912 and 11 March 1913 over the Congo negotiations with the British government, the German Ambassador in London, Metternich, had reported English territorial claims in the north-eastern Belgian Congo. These definitely affected German interests, since the Imperial Colonial Office and extensive economic circles desired at some future date to establish via the northern Congo a connection between the Cameroons and German East Africa (including Portuguese East Africa) and then to get hold of the valuable mines in Katanga for Germany alone or to exploit them together with England.

As a result on 20 April 1914 the Secretary of State at the Imperial Colonial Office, Solf, suggested to Jagow, Secretary of State at the Foreign Office, that they should take up the negotiations once more on the basis of these reports – in this way to include a third subject in discussions for a commercial entente. Accordingly England's claims, which were not clearly defined, should be limited to Upper Katanga, while Germany would make certain of securing for herself among other things the valuable territory to the west of Uganda. On 23 April 1914 Kühlmann answered Solf's proposals: as a result of soundings made to the British government England wanted to fix latitude 10° South as the limit of her claims in Katanga. Consequently, the important mineral area somewhat to the north of Elisabethville should be divided between England and Germany.

At about this time the Benguela Railway, Katanga's main link with the Atlantic, with the harbour of the same name in Portuguese West Africa (Angola), was already up to 60 per cent controlled by the Deutsche Bank in association with Belgian capital, after the original owners, the English firm of Williams and Company, had since 1908 got into increasing financial difficulties. Although the Deutsche Bank could not obtain an Imperial guarantee for it, it had taken on this commitment at the wish of the Chancellor, Bethmann-Hollweg, as a *quid pro quo* for receiving an Imperial guarantee of 3 per cent for the Baghdad Railway loan. It was Solf who got Bethmann-Hollweg to get the Deutsche Bank to invest in the enterprise.

This was part of a policy of *pénétration pacifique* (as

practised by France in Morocco and by England in
Egypt and elsewhere) which Germany practised in the
Portuguese colonies, hoping ultimately to obtain them
in part or in their entirety. Parallel to West Africa the
Deutsche Bank also took over a great part of the
Nyasaland Company's concessions in Portuguese East
Africa.

While the neutrality agreement in a form satisfactory to Germany could not be obtained, especially because Germany was not prepared to make a cut in the
Supplementary Naval Law (after all it was not Tirpitz's but Germany's fleet), the negotiations over colonial and Near-Eastern agreements which had already
started in the summer of 1911 continued from February 1912 till July 1914 and seemed with their positive
result – at least in the opinion of Bethmann-Hollweg
and the Kaiser – to have produced a very intimate relationship between Germany and England. But it
should be remembered that these territorial and economic agreements had no effect, as they were not ratified and, as was the case with the Portuguese partition
plan, were clogged with many reservations.

Bethmann-Hollweg's effort to reach agreement with
England, manifested in these months-long overseas
negotiations between private interests and state
organs, culminated in the co-operation between England and Germany during the two Balkan Wars and
gained further depth during the London Conference
of Ambassadors from November 1912 onwards. This
co-operation enabled the localisation of these conflicts
and prevented (at too early a date) complications between Austria-Hungary which could have extended
the localised conflict into a general war.

If, as a result of the Anglo-German co-operation, the
outbreak of the expected Austro-Serbian, and consequently an Austro-Russian and general war, was
avoided, the Balkans and Turkey were none the less
in another way theatres for economic-political quarrels among the conflicting Great Powers. In these
quarrels in the year and a half before the outbreak of
the First World War the German government (the
Kaiser, Bethmann-Hollweg, Jagow, Zimmermann, Ber-

gen, Wangenheim) and those leading men of the
economy closely connected with them (Krupp, Gwinner, Helfferich) felt more and more strongly the limits
of Germany's effective military-political range and
economic-financial power. German imperialism had
reached a dead-end.

Bulgaria: Loans Policy in the Struggle for the Balkans

An example of this situation and the increasing difficulties of German policy was the arranging of the Bulgarian loan of 1913–14 of 500 million leva, which
could only be carried out with the greatest difficulty
on the Berlin market under the management of the
Disconto-Gesellschaft. Despite pressure from the German Ambassador in Sofia, Michahelles, the intervention of Krupp, who was pushing the loan for his own
interest, pressure from the Hamburg houses of M. M.
Warburg and Schröder and Company, and from the
Berliner Handelsgesellschaft under Fürstenberg, who
had advocated a loan for Bulgaria because of the tobacco monopoly offered as security by Bulgaria (parallel with the tobacco monopoly offered as security for
the Serbian loan), the negotiating of the loan seemed
about to come to grief because of the shortage of
money on the Berlin market and because of the resistance caused by this from the Deutsche Bank, which
wanted and required the existing reserve of the capital market to negotiate a new Baghdad Railway loan,
and also because of the resistance of the Disconto-
Gesellschaft, which was preparing the market for the
negotiating of a Rumanian loan. That the loan did
not fail was due to the political events of May and
June 1914, as well as the personal relationship of
Krupp, Baron von Schröder and Max Warburg with
the Foreign Office and Imperial government and the
possibility of concluding a commercial treaty with
Bulgaria, which made it appear desirable and necessary to enter into a politico-economic partnership with
Bulgaria, which since the end of the Second Balkan

War was trying to revise the effects of the Peace of
Bucharest, especially to regain the northern part of
the Dobrudja from Rumania, through acceding to the
Triple Alliance.

In contrast with Germany after the Second Balkan
War, Austria-Hungary was seeking close relations with
Bulgaria to counterbalance the enlargement of Serbia
as the nucleus of a Slav empire, and at the same time,
as Melchior, a member of the Warburg banking house
and representative in the negotiations for the loan, reported, to 'lock out' Germany from Bulgaria and the
eastern Balkans. Under these auspices the conclusion
of the negotiations with Bulgaria meant a necessary
settlement with Bulgaria after the desertion of Rumania, the beginning of an attempt to block Austrian
ambitions, and also an attempt to frustrate the intentions of the Anglo-American tobacco trust, which was
also after a monopoly of Bulgarian tobacco. The Bulgarian loan was at last settled through the political
intervention of the German Ambassador and with
the Disconto-Gesellschaft stepping into the breach left
by the Fürstenberg–Warburg–Schröder consortium,
which was too weak to affect it. The Disconto-Gesellschaft's change of position was determined by the
threat of the Rumanian loan slipping into Franco-
American-English hands.

Despite being repeatedly urged by the Under-Secretary of State, Zimmermann, as well as by the Prussian
Ministry of Commerce, the Deutsche Bank held aloof
from the new policy towards Bulgaria, although it remained active in the German interest in the Balkans.
The representatives of Germany's interest in Turkey
feared that the German market would be even more
strained through the loan to Bulgaria than it had
already been through the economic crisis of 1913. But
as the Deutsche Bank as well as the Disconto-Gesellschaft and the Dresdner Bank were forced to establish
markets and commercial financing for those branches
of industry connected with them, it seemed doubly
necessary through the crisis for the Deutsche Bank to
keep hold of the Turkish market, especially the
Asiatic Turkish one, and to prevent its falling into

Anglo-French hands. The Baghdad Railway – Gwinner stressed to Wilhelm II that it was not ·a commercial undertaking but a political one, since it would reflect the position of the German Empire, its prestige in the world, its financial power and economic expansion – needed new sums for the construction of the line to Baghdad and beyond in addition to the money already invested for its rapid construction. The Berlin money market had to be kept liquid for this.

Moreover, after the end of the Second Balkan War which changed the Bulgarian–Turkish border, the Deutsche Bank actively intervened in Germany's Balkan policy by the repurchase of the European Orient Railway shares from Austria. The Deutsche Bank in the 1890s had taken up these shares of the Hirsch–Rothschild railway construction going back to the eighties. But as the Bank's commitments in the Baghdad Railway began to grow, these had been transferred to Austria, and until 1912 the Bank had withdrawn from the lines in the Balkans outside Turkey. When the enlarged Serbia after the Second Balkan War wanted to nationalise those lines inside her own territory, the attempt was made with French help to internationalise all the lines.

With the support of the Imperial government the Deutsche Bank, in opposition to the Franco-Austrian co-operation, demanded from Austria the return of those shares sold to them, so that they could make good with these securities the danger to their influence on the Balkan lines, which were a bridge to their chief undertaking, the Baghdad Railway.

Austria, however, tried to come to an arrangement with France, in order to obtain the aid of the Paris money market to realise not only her own railway aims but also for Austria to build a community of interests between Albania, Serbia and Bulgaria, which would express itself, as the Austrian Ambassador, Szögyény, put it, in a 'community of tariff interests'. In this case Austria-Hungary, as later in the war, was trying to save at least part of the Balkans from its economically stronger German ally.

Greece: Dynastic Policy versus Financial Power

Unlike in Bulgaria, where political objectives could
be developed with the help of a loans policy, Germany
was unable to draw Greece into her Balkan bloc.
Although the German Ambassador, Count Quadt, de-
tected in Venizelos a leaning towards help from German capital, since he felt that they were too dependent on French capital, the German Foreign Office had to
say resignedly that a loan for Greece as well could not
be raised on the German money market. The German
Ambassador in Athens, Count Quadt, actually believed firmly that the only proper course for Greece
was 'to attempt a close union with Rumania and one
with Turkey, which was showing new life to some extent in Asia at least. . . . I believe that we should encourage Greece in this way of strengthening herself
and eventually to give her the chance of keeping herself, as before, independent from France and the
Triple Entente by granting her a loan.' But the
Foreign Office adviser Rosenberg could only remark
on this: 'Considering the burdens on the money
market and the danger of fragmenting our financial
strength, it does not seem right at the moment to influence our banks officially.' Consequently in December 1913 France gave Greece a loan of 500 million
francs, in two instalments of 250 million, which
Venizelos negotiated in Paris. In return for this loan
France acquired a monopoly of arms supplies, the
building of the link line from Larissa to the Orient
Railway and the construction of the harbour at Salo-
nica, which Greece had recently gained. On the order
of his government the German Ambassador made
futile protests to King Constantine at the exclusion of
German industry from the Greek market, which that
loan resulted in. As well as this, Germany failed to get
the expected contract for building two dreadnoughts.
To Germany's mortification the contract went to England instead.

In another sphere as well, tied very closely to the
supply of arms, the Germans were outdone by the

French. Although King George of Greece had promised, in 1908 at Corfu on Wilhelm II's insistence, to
accept German military instructors into the country,
the Venizelos government had then called in a French
military mission under Major Eydoux; this was caused
not least by Germany's attitude in the Crete question,
which because of her consideration for a friendly
Turkey was more reserved than that of the so-called
protective Powers (*Schutzmächte*), which included
Italy as well. The immediate effect was that Greece
then ordered telegraphic equipment for the fleet, not
from Siemens in Berlin as intended, but from Marconi
in Italy; the Germans did not even get a share in this
project with the Italians. It seemed that Wilhelm II's
policy here, resting entirely on the dynastic connection, proved as barren as in Rumania. The same was
the case after the murder of King George in May 1913,
when William's brother-in-law, Constantine, took the
throne, who was strongly influenced by his energetic
Prussian-minded wife. His enthusiasm aroused by
Constantine's ability as a military leader in the First
Balkan War, Wilhelm II sent him a congratulatory
telegram; originally the Kaiser had actually wanted to
award the 'Pour le mérite' to the Turkish commander,
Muktar Pasha, as well as to Constantine, as he had
done with Nogi and Stössel, the two opposing commanders in the Russo-Japanese War, since he believed
it had made an excellent impression. The Kaiser further explicitly explained to Constantine the reason for
his enthusiasm: the King, supported by his military
glory, could now at last confront his Parliament. He
also made him, as he had made King Charles of
Rumania before, a Prussian Field-Marshal in December 1913 during a visit to Berlin, just at the time that
Venizelos was taking up the 500 million franc loan
from France.

On being given this honour, Constantine gave a
speech to the German generals at Potsdam, where he
appeared to denigrate the French military instructors
in comparison with the Prussian General Staff school
(represented by himself and the officers in his headquarters). This speech caused a political crisis in

Athens and resentment in the Parisian Press. In the
Reichstag Bethmann-Hollweg defended King Constantine's expressions against criticisms of the affair.
He claimed that these remarks had above all destroyed the widely believed story that German arms
and German military instructors had been beaten in
the Balkan wars.

In the first half of 1914 Germany tried in vain to
bring Greece and Turkey together over the islands
question, which had led both Powers to the brink of
war, and thus to draw Greece into a combination of
Turkey, Bulgaria and the Triple Alliance. The Greek
Prime Minister only went along with it ostensibly. In
fact Greece was tied to France both financially and
through the military mission. Because of this King
Constantine had to reject Wilhelm II's urgent appeal
to enter the war on Germany's side in August 1914.

Rumania: The Great Disappointment

Wilhelm II's efforts over Greece were always clung to
rather dubiously as a kind of private policy: many
people feared that new naval plans and ideas about
naval bases in the Aegean, at Valona, Mersina or
Adana, took second place to his liking for his summer
seat, the Achilleion on Corfu, and for archaeology.
More promising were German efforts over Rumania,
which had belonged to the Triple Alliance formally
since the 1880s and had even renewed the alliance
with Austria in 1912. In Rumania as well Wilhelm II
tried to use the dynastic-military connection, through
the visit of a delegation of officers to Bucharest to
celebrate King Charles's fiftieth anniversary as a member of a Prussian dragoon regiment or through the
mission of Prince Eitel Friedrich. In contrast to the
inscrutable but purposeful policy of Ion Bratianu
and Take Ionescu, these gestures of a late monarchical style could achieve nothing. At the same time, besides the financial—economic problems the Greater
Rumania movement had appeared, directed against
Hungary. It had gained strength since the Balkan

wars. Germany had been pressing the Hungarian Prime Minister, Tisza, without any success for suitable reforms. Wilhelm II in a public telegram of congratulation to Charles praised the conclusion of the Peace of Bucharest in August 1913, in which he played a part himself by advising Charles of Rumania to give Kavalla to Greece despite Bulgaria's wishes, as a 'definitive' solution of the Balkan problem. But relations were always uncertain, especially after the Tsar's visit to Charles in Constanta in June 1914, even though Wilhelm II became suspicious over this gradually rather than immediately. In Rumania also King Charles could not get his country to take part in the war. Wilhelm II in July 1914, overestimating the possibility, still believed he could influence him. In fact Charles could hardly keep his country neutral after the set-back on the Marne, the Austrian defeats in Galicia and the Russian advance over the Carpathians. King Charles died at the end of 1914, possibly with the help of his pro-English sister-in-law Maria von Coburg. The country was only kept neutral with some difficulty till 1916 by the German successes of the spring of 1915 and very frequent German financial interventions.

That Rumania did not join the First World War on Germany's side was of great consequence, as the Germans considered Rumania – as was the case with Turkey – an outpost of their economic commitment in the Balkans and Near East. From the 1880s the Disconto-Gesellschaft, and later the Deutsche Bank as well, had invested large amounts of capital first in railways, in the redemption (*Ablösung*) of the Strousberg railway enterprises, then in oil. The security for this was partly the receipts from the Orient Railway and partly toll receipts, mining rights and rights to use harbours, such as Constanta. In sharp competition with Anglo-Dutch and American companies, and less so with Russian ones, in the oil business, the Disconto-Gesellschaft and the Deutsche Bank (in competition with each other) set up a subsidiary banking and production investment system (Steaua Romana and Banca Generala). But the Disconto-Gesellschaft com-

panies, because their bore-holes were less rich, were
forced increasingly to join with the Anglo-American
trusts. On the other hand, the Deutsche Bank through
reinsuring itself with the Russians was able to form an
independent pool, the primary aim of which was to set
up an oil monopoly in Germany, having created a
German bank-holding company as the exclusive sup-
plier for the German market. The very keen rivalry
between Salomonson (Disconto-Gesellschaft), who was
backed by Deterding and Rockefeller (i.e. Shell and
Esso), and Gwinner (Deutsche Bank), who was affili-
ated with producers in Baku, was not settled before
the world war, but the Deutsche Bank had nearly
gained a monopoly in oil because of the intimate relations of Gwinner and Helfferich with Wilhelm II.

At the same time since the 1890s Rumania had increasingly become the scene of very keen competition between Schneider-Creusot and Krupp, who were both
trying to capture for themselves the supplying of arms
to the Rumanian army. In all the years after 1890,
and especially after 1905, the Kaiser acted as the energetic champion of Krupp's interests, and the danger,
as it seemed in 1906, that a large order for howitzers
and field-pieces might go from Krupp to Schneider-
Creusot moved Wilhelm II to write such irritated
marginal notes as 'blackguards!' He ordered Ham-
merstein, the German Military Attaché in Bucharest,
to communicate this: 'they [the howitzers and field-
pieces] must definitely be ordered from us in Germany, else I shall clear out of Rumania, throw her
officers out of my army and break off relations!' The
Foreign Office was used to bring this threat of serious
consequences immediately home to the Rumanian
government like an order through the German Ambassador.

The arms business again meant a serious commitment of international financial power to negotiating
loans for Rumania, which at the height of the Balkan
crisis attached itself more firmly to the French side.
The Disconto-Gesellschaft (Salomonson) and Bleich-
röder tried to neutralise them through new loans,
which were floated by a very serious straining of re-

sources, as was the case with the two German loans to
Rumania of the spring and late autumn of 1913. The
French banking groups which had taken about a third
part of the state loans of 1905, 1908 and 1910 for political motives refused to take any part in the loan of 150
million francs in the spring of 1913, which would have
made it feasible for Rumania to rearm for the Second
Balkan War. The loan of 250 million francs in the
autumn went only to Germany, because the French felt
their economic influence in Rumania was so secure that
they overreached themselves and demanded from the
Rumanian government in return for the loan the
assurance that all the larger state orders during the
next two years should go to France. The Prime Minister, Marghiloman, rejected this demand and turned
to the Germans again, but they could only meet his
request for financial aid with difficulty.

But the shipping orders promised to the Schichau
shipyard went to the Italians. While France's 'treating
Rumania indulgently as never before' marked imperceptibly her enlistment to the Triple Entente as
well, the visit of the Tsar in June 1914 already mentioned gave the outward sign. Neither the intense
activity of Krupp and the Rheinische Metallwaren-
fabrik which reinforced Krupp on the munitions side,
and of Mauser-Rottweil and the Deutsche Bank, nor
Wilhelm II's efforts with Charles and the Crown
Prince, Ferdinand, and those of the Foreign Office
with Rumanian politicians, especially with such conservatives as Carp, could stop Rumania from following her economic interests (the greater resources of the
French money market) and her national aspirations
(in Transylvania) and approaching the Entente.

The Balkan Crisis, Serbia and Both Balkan Leagues

After the Greeks, despite the pro-German inclinations
of King Constantine, had come to depend heavily
on France through the 500 million franc loan obtained
by Venizelos in Paris in December 1913, a third
Balkan League took definite shape because a certain

rapprochement occurred between Greece and Rumania, the two chief gainers from the Second Balkan War and the two States most interested in preserving the *status quo* of the Peace of Bucharest of August 1913. This combination was strengthened, although there was no formal alliance, by the new Rumanian Foreign Minister, Take Ionescu, who had replaced the more conservative Majörescu, during a five-day visit to Athens, and who on the wish of the Turkish Minister of the Interior, Talaat Bey, intervened and mediated an agreement between Greece and Turkey who had been close to war over the islands question, especially over Mytilene and Chios. It was made clear here that Rumania would not intervene in a Turkish–Greek naval war (such a war could only in fact have been carried out once both Greece and Turkey had received their two dreadnoughts, which were on order from England – a good example of how war and business are interrelated), but would intervene by an attack on Bulgaria if Bulgaria allowed Turkish troops to land in Dedeagach or if, as a result of a Turkish victory, Bulgaria accepted Kavalla for herself, which would have meant a breach of the Peace of Bucharest.

This combination becomes more interesting with the inclusion of Serbia into this group of two, which at the beginning had been praised in the newspapers on both sides as a coalition of the Greco-Latin civilisation against the Slavs. Serbo-Greek hostility was mainly due to the frontier demarcation of the newly-created State of Albania. Rumania contributed to reducing the tension, helped by the fact that the new state's ruler, the Prince of Wied, was nephew to the Rumanian Queen. Belief in a revived Balkan League was strengthened when Venizelos and Pašić (the moderate yet decidedly Greater Serbia-minded Premier of Serbia) visited St Petersburg, and had joint talks in Bucharest with Take Ionescu.

The settlement created by Rumania between Greece and Serbia led the three Powers to their frequently declared aim of bringing Turkey as well into their group of three, which an isolated Bulgaria would have had to join whether she liked it or not.

Of those countries mentioned above, Serbia for quite a long time had already been largely dependent on the French money market: as late as January 1914 she received a 250 million franc loan from France. Greece had just become dependent on the same. The Turks, whose financial administration, the Ottoman debt, was for the most part under Anglo-French control and which contained three times as much French investment as German, received a French loan of 500 millions in the spring of 1914. Although the Rumanians had received a French loan as late as October 1913, in her economic life the German banks, as has been shown, were in sharp competition in the oil interests with Anglo-Dutch-American capital.

Besides these financial connections it was very important that two of the above States were becoming increasingly opposed to Austria-Hungary through *irredenta* questions: Rumania because of Transylvania, and Serbia because of Bosnia and Hercegovina (and Croatia and Slovenia as well), which the Serbs had only allowed to be annexed in March 1909 under German pressure.

The difficulties of Germany's position in the Balkans were further added to by her diplomatic and economic activity in Serbia, Rumania and Bulgaria conflicting with that of her ally, Austria-Hungary. Already during the Bosnian crisis of 1908 when the Germans in their 'shining armour' had defended the Danubian Monarchy against Russia, they had taken over the economic position which Austria had previously held, thus causing strong complaints by Austria-Hungary. The import statistics of the Balkan States show very plainly how far the Germans had driven Austria out of this market.

In the years from 1901 to 1905 the German and Austrian share of the total imports of Rumania were still almost equal with 27.1 and 28.5 per cent. But in 1913 the Austrian share had dropped to 23.4 per cent and the German had risen to 40.3 per cent. The example of Serbia is still more pronounced. While Austria-Hungary in 1884 held the leading position with 62·4 per cent of Serbia's total imports and Germany had only 14·9 per cent, by 1910 the proportions had nearly reversed themselves: the Austrian share had dropped to 19 per cent and the German had risen to 41·3 per cent.

The predominance of the Berlin trading company (Berliner Handelsgesellschaft) which had considered Serbia its own domain since the 1890s and had compelled Serbia to form a combined tobacco and salt tariff monopoly as security for its loans caused great alarm in Austro-Hungarian business circles, since their chief territorial market was the Balkans and it would have to remain so, given the needs and resources of the Dual Monarchy. To defend themselves from German pressure in Serbia, as was the case in Bulgaria, Austria-Hungary approached the French money market. French capital was to participate in the project for the 'internationalisation' of the new Serbian railways. An Austro-French company was planned by the two railway magnates, the French Vitali and the Austrian Adler, who were to raise the money, while an Austro-French-Serbian company intended to run the administration of the lines. At the same time this was meant to neutralise the Serbian demands for the nationalisation of the lines with material antidotes. In the face of these dangers mentioned above, the Imperial government's policy in the Balkans increasingly hesitated between seizing the Balkans as its own direct sphere of interest and conceding a predominant influence there to the Austro-Hungarian Monarchy. Austro-German relations were increasingly blighted by this.

This conflict of interests within the Triple Alliance was encouraged further at the beginning of 1913 and again at the beginning of 1914 when Serbia, which had already expanded considerably through the Balkan wars, seemed on the point of further expansion by aiming at union with Montenegro. If this happened, Austria wanted to respond by annexing the Lovčen and by handing over Montenegro's coastal strip with the harbour of Antivari to Albania (here Austria-Hungary was already marking out what was to be one

of her principal war aims in 1914–18), to shut out the
new Serbia from the Adriatic, which it had reached in
1913. For her part Italy, who had just renewed the
Triple Alliance at the end of 1912, certainly did not
want to allow such an increase in Austro-Hungarian
power on the Adriatic. San Giuliano declared to the
German Ambassador, Flotow, that if Austria-Hungary
acted in this way Italy would have grounds for war.
Only one compensation would cause Italy not to go to
war: the cession of the Trentino.

Germany had already seen serious dangers in the
difficulties which had arisen between the members of
the Triple Alliance, Austria-Hungary and Italy, in
their quasi-condominium over Albania (it seemed very
reminiscent of the Schleswig-Holstein situation of
1864–6), and tried with all kinds of diplomatic influence to prevent Austria from acting on her own and to
make her come to some understanding with Italy on
this question for the sake of holding the Triple Alliance together. It was not only very important to Germany to keep Italy in the Triple Alliance because of
the pressure on France, but also because of Wilhelm
II's belief that the united fleets of Austria-Hungary
and Italy together with his hopes for united fleets of
Greece and Turkey would be equal to the Franco-
Russian fleet (he does not seem to have thought of
England as an opponent in the Mediterranean in the
spring of 1914!). That the Kaiser and Tirpitz had new
naval plans and ideas for naval stations in Asia Minor
is known because of remarks of Wangenheim and of
the Chancellor, who was afraid of such plans because
of Anglo-German relations.

The dubious element in the Balkans in the period between the Second Balkan War and the World War, and
in the new power relationships and their repercussions
upon the Great Powers, lies in the fact that Germany
also had plans for Balkan leagues, though with different combinations (the Kaiser was especially thinking
of Greece and Turkey, while the Ambassador in Constantinople, Wangenheim, and following him the
Foreign Office, were thinking of Turkey and Bulgaria),
which could check the Rumanian–Russian alliance,

which the Ambassador believed in existence. Serbia could also have been fitted into this combination. The Germans, as shown, were highly active economically in Serbia and believed that Serbia should be pulled into the Triple Alliance by the Austrians through trade treaties and a customs union.

Ostensibly German intentions seem identical with the plans of Ionescu Pašić and Venizelos. The last appeared to demonstrate by a visit to Berlin in December 1913 the new connection between Greece and Rumania as an approach to the Triple Alliance – possibly not without some cynicism. But in fact because French money and Russian diplomacy were very much at the bottom of them, these combinations were not only a threat to Austria-Hungary, especially in the case of Serbia and Rumania, but also in the last resort no less a threat to German policy in the Balkans and the East. Kaiser Wilhelm II built up all his combinations primarily on the monarchs, in Athens, Bucharest and then in Sofia. But these rulers did not have the same position in their States as the Prussian King, and he seriously underestimated these rulers' dependence on the attitudes of their Parliaments and their national aspirations. Consequently the Germans, by sticking to what were also foreign dynasties, were putting themselves against the strongest movements of the time. They continued with this approach in their aims during the First World War in setting up a chain of satellite monarchies – in Finland, Courland, Lithuania, Poland, etc.

These parallel but completely different plans for Balkan leagues, apart from the influence of the Entente, demonstrate also an active striving for independence for these nations and States, a striving for freedom from dependence on the Great Powers. Even the Turks were affected by this. During the war Wangenheim said that the 'Osmanisation of Turkey' (as he put it), which he noticed to be especially strong, had already been established before the war – the Young Turk revolution of 1908 was a product of it. The particular economic situation was still more important for Germany's acute situation in the autumn

of 1913 and the spring of 1914 than the resistance
from the currents of time, which were working against
Germany. Above all, Germany could no longer meet
the demands of those States for state loans nor attach
them to her by economic penetration. Economic concessions were in fact given in return for loans. Instead,
Germany saw the financially stronger rivals of the Entente overtake her, above all France and England and
already behind them – often already mentioned ex-
plictly in the documents – the United States.

The Crisis in the Near East: Turkey moves towards the Triple Entente

After the second Morocco crisis the German Foreign
Office hoped to ease the strained relations with England through a 'global *entente*' which would have
brought the Germans some consolidation in Central
Africa through a simultaneous agreement with England and France, as the German Chargé d'Affaires in
London, Kühlmann, was proposing, and which would
have given her at the same time a free hand in the
Balkans against Russia.

The Baghdad Railway question was bound up with
others – the questions of the irrigation of Mesopotamia and of oil – which together with the agreement
between the Anglo-Persian Oil Company and the
Deutsche Bank–Shell group came up again in 1914
and formed the core of the London negotiations for
agreement between Germany and England. Ballin
and Wönckhaus were also demanding a solution of
the questions of navigation and of the ports in the
Shatt El-Arab. There was also the question over mining in Heraclea, where Hugo Stinnes saw German
heavy industry's 'essential' interest.

The London negotiations showed that because of
Germany's lack of capital, German interests in Turkey
as well as in the Balkans were forced to come to terms
with the other Imperial Powers. The coveted guarantee for the new Baghdad Railway loan could only be
secured though a tariff increase, which in turn could

only be obtained through the agreement of England and France in the Turkish financial administration, and this agreement would have to be bought by Germany through concessions to both Powers. This problem became even more serious, since Germany believed not only because of the economic crisis of 1913 that she was increasingly dependent on markets but also that in line with her economic development since 1880, she could not give up her claim to a position of world power, which she desired for herself and fully affirmed, but on the contrary must push towards further expansion.

Those European Powers who were rivals in Turkey had already discussed, in the 1880s and 1890s, plans for partitioning the Ottoman Empire. But not least through the German military missions and the Baghdad Railway, Turkey had become somewhat stronger; this, however, was followed by serious upheavals in the form of the Young Turk revolution, and in the Balkan and Libyan wars. When, in May 1913, before her temporary recovery in the Second Balkan War, Turkey's weakness was especially apparent, Wilhelm II believed that everything indicated that Russia, England and France intended a partition of Turkey. On a report about Russian troops gathering in north Persia the Kaiser wrote: 'Preparations for the partition of Turkey: it is apparently more imminent than was believed. In Palestine and Syria a life-and-death struggle between England and France has already broken out underhand. Therefore pay attention! Let us ensure that the partition shall not be carried out without us. I want Mesopotamia, Alexandretta, Mersina. The sensible Turks are already expecting this fate patiently.' In these reflections, as we know from Bethmann-Hollweg, the Kaiser was influenced by reports made personally to him from Professor Moritz, the Director of the Oriental Seminar in Berlin. The Kaiser worried the Imperial Chancellor by wanting ships sent to Alexandretta and Mersina to enforce German claims. According to one of the Kaiser's memoranda it was very important 'to have definite objectives in this event [the partition], instead of

warning the Turks, which the present Turkish
government does not deserve and would never be
acted on anyway'.

The Kaiser (and in this he was entirely at one with
his Chancellor, Bethmann-Hollweg) associated in his
own mind these partition plans with co-operation
with England, such as had been experienced for six
months at the London Conference of Ambassadors,
and with attempts to reach agreement with England
on the basis of common interests (since 1911, in fact,
the Baghdad Railway and colonial agreements had
been negotiated). It was in this light that the Emperor
commented on an article in the *Daily News* on the
occasion of Lord Morley's visit to Berlin on 15 May
1913, which expressed the view that European peace
would be safe if England and Germany worked together:

> Splendid! This signifies introspection and con-
> version. I could not wish for a better ... merciless
> judgement upon the policy of great adventures and
> Ententes of my uncle Edward VII! In the long run
> a policy directed against Germans with Slavs and
> Gauls is absolutely unworkable for the Anglo-
> Saxons! We shall find one another in Asia Minor,
> either for the sake of Turkey (perhaps on the basis
> of the Cyprus Treaty, the *status quo* and defence of
> Turkish territory from Russo-Bulgarian aspirations)
> or at her expense!

The 'principal question' for the Kaiser was England's position 'with the French against the Germans
or as a neutral'. How far the Kaiser was thinking in
line with Houston Stewart Chamberlain's categories is
shown by his remark about the London Conference of
Ambassadors: 'Chapter 2 of the Barbarian migration
is now closed. Chapter 3 now opens with the fight of
the Germans against the Russo-French for existence.
No conference can settle this because it is not a political but a racial question. . . . It is the question of to be
or not to be for the German race in Europe.'

Also in the Liman von Sanders crisis England's

position in a possible future war with Russia and
France was the German Imperial government's chief
consideration.

When, on 22 October 1913, the Russian Foreign
Minister, Sazonov, was in Berlin, Wilhelm II believed
it right that he should not tell him about the impending dispatch of General Liman von Sanders to Turkey. He believed this although the treaty concluded
between the Imperial government and the Turkish
government on 28 October 1913 contained the extraordinary innovation that Liman von Sanders should
not only be the head of an enlarged military mission
of German instructing officers but should also be the
general commanding the First Army Corps in Constantinople. This arrangement caused a sensation and
was felt in St Petersburg especially to be a provocation.

Because the three Entente Powers closed ranks
against this arrangement, the Germans had to give
way in the end, although this was cloaked by the
appointment of Liman as a Turkish Marshal. The
most interesting point in the Liman von Sanders
crisis, however, was the belief of the Imperial government and especially of the Kaiser that they could play
off England's special position on the Bosphorus (the
English Admiral Limpus's position as commander of
the Turkish fleet) against her Entente allies to isolate
Russia (and France). So on 18 December 1913, when
Zimmermann wrote to Wilhelm II, he received the
Kaiser's full support in believing that 'His Majesty's
gracious directives would be complied with, if we
made a point of undermining as far as possible the
understanding between Russia and England over this
question and on the same grounds further play on the
Dardanelles question and the English Admiral's command in the Bosphorus'.

It was because of their intention to detach the English from their allies and bring them towards the
Germans that the Foreign Office held back over the
Anglo-Turkish Dock Treaty of October 1913, which
gave the English practically a monopoly of all Turkish shipbuilding, repairing, equipping and so on. The
Foreign Office's position here seems to have been dic-

tated entirely by political calculations, because German economic interests demanded loudly that the
German government should intervene with the Turkish against this treaty. Krupp raised strong objections
against this treaty several times. He did this first officially and then through his intimate friend, 'dear
Diego' von Bergen, Referent in the Foreign Office,
whose significant role in German policy from 1914 to
1918, especially in revolutionising Russia, I have
shown in my *Griff nach der Weltmacht*. Wangenheim,
Ambassador in Turkey, counselled his government
that they should point out resolutely in London 'that
we could not acknowledge any interpretation of the
Dock Treaty which excluded us from any competition
in Turkish shipbuilding'. And Günther, the second
Director of the Anatolian Railway and thereby Helfferich's and Gwinner's representative in Constantinople,
telegraphed angrily to Helfferich, who passed it on
immediately to Zimmermann:

> By this [the Ismed Dock Treaty] our base in
> Turkey and maritime Constantinople is brought
> under English control and it will be said that the
> Baghdad Railway starts in an English arsenal and
> ends in an English net, the Persian Gulf. In our
> authoritative quarters they do not seem completely
> to grasp the consequence. . . .

He gave urgent warning against allowing a *fait accompli*. As well as Krupp, the Deutsche Bank stood out
against indulging the English too much, since the
question of its own existence was bound up with it,
because a Baghdad Railway hedged in by the English
would cause any loan negotiations in Germany to be
illusory. In the same way Albert Ballin, Director of
the Hamburg–America line, stood out against indulging the English, because it would injure German
maritime interests in the Persian Gulf.

It is therefore all the more important that the Imperial Chancellor, Bethmann-Hollweg, decided himself
out of political considerations not to upset England,
but by accepting the Dock Treaty to provide a further

element in building a German–English understanding, which would serve to isolate England and to break up the Triple Entente. Wilhelm II made this calculation quite on his own, as is shown by his marginal notes to reports from Pourtalès, for example that on 18 December 1913.

The Kaiser sketched out expressly the route which German policy should follow (20 December 1913). Wilhelm II wrote about a report from Wangenheim that England's relations with Russia were strained because of the Ismed Dock Treaty, which the Russians were taking worse than the Liman von Sanders episode:

> Marvellous! Consequently the Triple Entente has to submit to English interests! And it is important for Germany that we should not make her angry through a quarrel with us!

The Kaiser was impressed and took notice of the warning given by the *Daily Graphic* that England should not out of consideration for the Entente allow herself to be dragged into opposition to the German military mission, but on the contrary should try to maintain good relations with Berlin. He went on in fact to say that he believed:

> London's interests are more secured through co-operation with Berlin than through working with the Entente Powers! In German that means that the Entente does not correspond to English interests. Ergo it is no longer attractive.

Even England's final co-operation with France and Russia in the Liman von Sanders question did not end German hope of England's breaking away from the Entente.

This very careful demeanour in Germany's relations with England was matched by an, at least initially, tough attitude to Russia, which only stopped when it came up against a common *démarche* of the three Entente Powers.

The Kaiser wrote a revealing marginal note (not printed in *Die Grosse Politik*!) to the report in which Zimmermann proposed that the German Ambassador should talk to Giers, Russian Ambassador in Constantinople, and should promise to keep German influence in Turkey in line with Russian wishes (the transfer of the First Army Corps to the provinces). In this note Wilhelm observed:

> As they [the instructions to Wangenheim] are herein drafted, no! They will have to be considerably altered! They look like a capitulation on our part to Russia! I am no longer in the mood to bargain with Russian wishes at the cost of my army and of Turkey. My officials forget that they have three million bayonets and a dozen ships of the line at their disposal! ! !

Also in the marginal notes to Pourtalès's reports over the Russian position in the crisis (where apparently the Kaiser was thinking about Russia's backing down in March 1909) can be found the hope of being able to bring the English out of the Entente:

> Once again Russia, as so often before, has tried one of her several attempts at bluff at our cost and through her allies. Naturally we will not allow ourselves nor the allies as well to be taken in by it! Turkey's prestige will increase as the result of any great Russian disgrace!

A similar conviction is shown by the Kaiser's marginal note to the assertion by the Russian newspaper *Retch* that the Entente would hold fast and united: 'Bluff! You have no idea at all! When the English have refused point-blank the union will come to an end!' Even after the settlement of the international conflict over Liman von Sanders, his role and activity remained a weight on German–Turkish relations and on Germany's whole Oriental policy. Conflicts arose over Liman, which give very revealing insights into the motives and impulses behind Germany's whole

policy and at the same time into the apparently insoluble difficulties resulting from it.

Liman has been described as 'passionate and ambitious' (Pourtalès) and 'conceited and suspicious' (Gerhard von Mutius). His behaviour and interminable
quarrels over protocol in claiming to have precedence
at dinners over the Turkish Minister of War and
Foreign Minister (on the Prussian pattern) put Enver
Pasha out of sorts. Enver Pasha had just been
appointed Minister of War at thirty-one and Germany
was later to control Turkey through him. By this
action Liman greatly endangered not only the activity
of the military mission but Germany's whole policy.
There was one event which was highly significant for
the structure of the German Empire: without consulting or notifying the Imperial civil government (Ambassador, Foreign Office, Imperial Chancellor) Liman
made a Bavarian lieutenant-colonel, Kübel, on 1
March 1914, Chief of the Railway Department in the
Turkish General Staff. This led to a conflict which
completely shook Germany's whole policy in Turkey.

During a journey of inspection of German and
Turkish General Staff officers and representatives of
the Anatolian Railway, this man clashed violently
with the first Director of the line, Huguenin. In
accordance with his instructions he demanded from
him the extension of the railway network within half
a year for military deployment. According to the estimates of the Deutsche Bank, the financial backer of
the undertaking, these structural changes would have
needed at least 100 million marks. But no security in
Turkish assets or custom receipts was, nor could be,
available, because everything, even the future receipts
of graveyards – there were long negotiations over this,
which in the end failed because of Turkish national
feeling – and the wealth of the museum, had already
been pledged to the German and French consortia.
But the Deutsche Bank, to finance the speedy continuation of the railway, had already lent very great
sums in the last loans to the limits of its resources, and
to get security for a new loan had negotiated with the
Great Powers for an increase in Turkish tariff rates

from 3 per cent to 4 or 5 per cent, negotiations which had passed over the German government. In this conflict between the 'Anatolians' Helfferich and Gwinner and the banking groups and authorities dependent on them in Turkey, and the military mission, the Ambassador, Wangenheim, passionately sided with the Baghdad Railway and appealed to the Imperial Chancellor on 12 May 1914 to enforce the authority of policy over the short-sightedness and wilfulness of the military. The Ambassador said that the Baghdad Railway

is the mainstay of our Oriental policy which H.M. the Kaiser began. A threat to the Baghdad could not only lead to an economic Panama but could also have incalculable effects for us politically. The military mission is not an end in itself, but only an expedient for our Baghdad Railway policy. [Jagow altered this in the report for the Kaiser to 'Eastern policy'.] Because of that it is indispensable that the activity of the military mission be subordinated to our political interests.

This event – the Near Eastern equivalent of Zabern – was so irritating and dangerous for the German Empire's whole policy that Bethmann-Hollweg tried to force the Kaiser to a decision by presenting a long immediate petition on 20 May 1914 – this was two months before the effecting of the German–Turkish alliance at the end of the July crisis. The Chancellor tried to make the Kaiser realise that Liman von Sanders did not seem to grasp:

That his mission is not an end in itself, but only a means to an end. Germany's interest in the strengthening of the Turkish army stands and falls with our political influence at the Golden Horn. We are only interested in the success of the reform work if, and for as long as, Turkey remains on our side. If we fail to keep Turkish support, any increased battle-worthiness of their army would merely be a gain for our enemies. We have no

reason to sharpen the Turkish sabre for France or
Russia. . . .

These conflicts in question at the moment could
'cause irreparable damage to our position in the Ottoman Empire' and the Kaiser should therefore interpose his authority.

The Kaiser's marginal notes to this immediate petition of the Chancellor reveal at a stroke the situation
which the Empire was in with its Oriental policy at the
end of May 1914. Referring to German influence in
Turkey the Kaiser said:

> It is absolutely nothing compared with earlier!
> Turkey no longer intends to stick with us. She is
> trailing in the Russo-French wake, where money is
> thrown about, and is feeding us solely with words.

Wilhelm II was referring here to the large French
loan to Turkey, and brings out the outstanding significance of the lack of German financial resources for
German foreign policy:

> We cannot! [keep Turkey on our side] because
> we have no money! They are no longer on our
> side!

The Kaiser already saw the Turks in the Entente
camp, who were ready to give her not only money but
also support in her fight with Greece over the islands:

> While she amuses us with phrases and fine-sound-
> ing words and a few Turkish princes, she is joining
> Russia and the Triple Entente for anti-Greek aims.
> We are in fact sharpening Turkish weapons for
> them.

The 'dishonesty' and 'hollowness' of the Turks expressed itself in that they 'even' wanted 'to buy
cruisers immediately from us now to use against
Athens!' Through this Wilhelm II's policy for a
Greek–Turkish agreement was wrecked, and at a time

when German officers were trying 'to bring some order
– without <u>money</u> naturally [underlined by the
Kaiser] – into this ragged army'. Wilhelm II threatened:

> I will no longer stand for it. If the Turks want to
> make war on the Greeks over the islands, I will
> withdraw the officer mission!
> <u>Turkey is beyond help, and of no further value!</u>
> She may as well go to pieces in the arms of the
> Triple Entente! Wilhelm I.R. [Underlining by the
> Kaiser.]

It was not only French capital which the Germans
could no longer compete with and the Entente's
policy which threatened Germany's position in Turkey, but also the political situation within the Ottoman Empire. The Kaiser said that the Young Turk
government would 'tell a pack of lies' to the Ambassador, whereas Liman, 'with the army, has to deal with
facts'. The Young Turk government was approaching
the Entente and was 'lying, untrustworthy, empty,
conceited and venal'.

Even if the Kaiser's lofty phrases put things too
dramatically, it none the less by and large corresponded to the state of things and above all to the
view of things held by the German Imperial government. How greatly in fact Germany's economic and
consequent political position in the East was threatened in the spring of 1914 is shown, as already said, by
Germany's being unable to supply a sufficient state
loan to Turkey, which had to be issued on the Paris
market with enormous concessions to France to Germany's obvious disadvantage, such as railway concessions (as the Arghana–Bitlis–Van railway line) which
came up against the Anatolian Railway, and harbour
concessions in Jaffa, Haifa, Tripoli (Asia Minor) and
Heraclea on the Black Sea which endangered Hugo
Stinnes's plans. The impossibility of Germany's furn-
ishing such a loan was shown by Jagow's attempted
bluff to obstruct the Franco-Turkish loan negotiations. Writing to Wangenheim on 15 March 1914

Jagow reported a conversation with the French Ambassador, Cambon. According to him he had told
Cambon that if the negotiations for the Franco-Turkish loan were not completed soon, he would be unable
to resist much longer the pressure from German financial circles for a Turkish loan which he had held out
against till then from loyalty to France. Jagow went
on to say:

> This bluff does not seem to have failed to impress
> the French Ambassador because he told me that he
> wanted to communicate it to Paris. To be realistic I
> do not think it would be possible to meet Turkish
> financial needs in Germany.

This threat to Germany's political and economic
position in Turkey can be seen above all, however, in
the domestic German struggle between the two most
important German exporters to Turkey, a struggle
which probably ran parallel with the one above. On
the one hand was Krupp in alliance with the Dresdner
Bank (headed by Eugen Gutmann), which was the
Deutsche Bank's keenest competitor, and on the other
was the Deutsche Bank itself. Krupp and his ally the
Rhenish metal and armaments factory (Rheinische
Metall und Waffenfabrik), whose board included
Paasche, the Vice-President of the Reichstag, to stop
themselves being driven from the Turkish market by
Schneider-Creusot – look at the conditions about all
arms to be supplied by France which was attached to
the French loan to Greece! – wanted a 120 million
franc loan for Germany to be negotiated on the Berlin
market which would pay for their arms supplies to
Turkey.

The Directors of the Deutsche Bank, Helfferich and
Gwinner, fought this by addressing a string of forceful
petitions to the Foreign Office which they definitely
hoped the Kaiser would see. These Directors were
already having to negotiate on the Berlin money
market a badly needed loan of 250 million francs for
the Deutsche Bank for the extension of the Baghdad
Railway, and they therefore pointed out that from

their long experience of the Berlin market it was impossible to raise two such loans for Turkey because of
the difficulty over securities.

Since the 1860s there had been a tradition at the
Berliner Platz of reserving the resources of the Berlin
market for the floating of loans by one of the biggest
banking groups. The Deutsche Bank was all the more
dependent on the state of the market at the Berliner
Platz being favourable to it, because not only was it
facing competition from Krupp who hoped to force
through loans for Turkey and Bulgaria with the
Dresdner Bank on the one hand and the Berliner
Handelsgesellschaft and Warburg on the other, but
also the Foreign Office on political grounds was pushing forward for agreement with England, thereby endangering the security and the sale of Baghdad Railway securities.

Because of this, as Helfferich wrote to Zimmermann
(by hand on 29 May 1914), there was a danger of the
Deutsche Bank's collapse with incalculable consequences for German economic life and for German
policy.

> As things are going, everything is at stake over
> Baghdad. Not one of our Board of Directors can
> take the responsibility of going any further with the
> advances for the construction of the Baghdad Rail-
> way without the certain prospects of a Baghdad
> loan in the very near future. If the market is ruined
> for us by a Bulgarian or Turkish armaments loan
> we will have to shut up shop!

The bankers could not have expressed more clearly
and openly the bankruptcy threatening this great
company. Helfferich and Kankowski, the third Director of the Bank, threatened the Foreign Office with
stopping the construction of the Railway, which
would wreck German prestige in Turkey, unless the
Empire supported and forced through an issue of the
Baghdad Railway loan under monopoly conditions.

In fact the loan for Baghdad was floated by the
Deutsche Bank alone. Krupp got his share for the

industrial firms connected with him, which meant that
the Dresdner Bank had to withdraw. But after the
Baghdad Railway loan was negotiated, a way was
found for issuing one for Bulgaria – on political
grounds – though with some difficulty and, what is
more, through the Disconto-Gesellschaft.

German Imperialism therefore was faced by a basic
dilemma. If the armaments business could no longer
find finance, German industry – an over-extended,
heavy industry, dependent on exports – would lose its
selling markets; but if investment facilities could not
be found for the undertaking of the Baghdad Railway
which would be under construction for many years,
not only would German prestige suffer but also
directly from this German political influence in Turkey
and with it Germany's position in the East would be
in danger.

The Kaiser's friend Gwinner wrote on 13 June 1914,
two weeks before Sarajevo:

> We felt we had to undertake this sacrifice [i.e. of
> making large uncovered loans for continuing and
> accelerating the construction] because everything
> depends on showing our strength to the Powers un-
> friendly to the Railway, and because a halt in the
> further construction, which would have been right
> from a purely financial and business point of view,
> would have been interpreted by our enemies as
> showing that German financial resources were in-
> adequate to carry through this great enterprise and
> that Germany would therefore have to accept any
> conditions in the dispute over Turkish railway
> questions.

In June 1914, therefore, not only was Germany's
bridge to the East, the Balkans, in danger, but also the
object of German political and economic expansion in
the East, Turkey itself, was in very great danger. Thus
the moment had come, which Wilhelm II had already
pointed out in 1907 as the critical point in relations
with France, when he minuted a report over the
threatening French rivalry in the East:

Envy, nothing but envy; everyone is envious of us. But the French especially must be left in no doubt that they should not dare to rely on the Entente with Britain to amuse themselves by trying to supplant us in the East. These are vital interests which must be defended at all cost. If need be I will fight for them.

The Revival of the 'Mitteleuropa' Policy

The impasse which German imperialism had reached in 1913 was accurately expressed in Rathenau's resigned and blunt observation: 'The time of great gains has been missed for Germany.' But according to Rathenau they were all the more necessary for her because, as 'the most populous, richest and most industrialised country of Europe, with the most powerful army', Germany had a legitimate moral claim to an equal part of the earth as that of her neighbours. Rathenau saw 'a last possibility' of making up for Germany's lost opportunities in 'going after a central European customs union, which willingly or unwillingly, sooner or later, the States of Western Europe would join', i.e. Belgium and France and in the end England as well. 'The object should be to create an economic union which would equal, perhaps be superior to, the American.'

Behind these ideas was the thinking which had been formulated for the first time by the Tübingen political economist and former Austrian Minister of Commerce, Albert Schäffle: 'The British Empire and *Mitteleuropa*. . . . This European–German world ought to resist American–Russian exploitation in this way.' To this should be added Wilhelm II's statement a few months before the outbreak of the First World War in the spring of 1914, which, when taken with those of the spring of 1912, shows how strongly Germany was already conscious in her policy and economy of the world power of the United States. When disturbances had broken out again in Mexico in 1913–14 and it was thought that Germany ought to inter-

vene there, together with England and France, the
German Ambassador in Washington, Count Bernstorff, on being asked for his opinion, said that Wilson's policy had shown 'that Europe is not united and
strong enough to resist American policy in the Western Hemisphere', and he forecast Europe's withdrawal
from Mexico. The Kaiser minuted this with:

> England has left Europe magnificently in the
> lurch and discredited it. She ought to defend
> Europe's interests in Mexico together with the
> Continent and in this way smash the Monroe Doc-
> trine.

In this situation of 1913–14 can be seen the consideration for England and wooing of her as well as the
anti-American bias.

The *Mitteleuropa* concept makes it clear that Germany's striving for world power, which by 1912–13
seemed no longer to have any realisable objectives in
the world – unless very restricted ones in a working
association with England in Turkey and possibly in a
partition of the Portuguese colonies – was moving
demonstrably towards a European hegemony, at least
in the economic sphere, a hegemony which, according
to Rathenau, had been Germany's for a short time
under Bismarck but which had not been sufficiently
strengthened and which had been taken from her. For
Germany the strengthening of her position in Europe
had become a question of existence. According to him
the power of civilised States (*Kulturstaaten*) depended
on their economic power, and Germany's raw-material
basis was too narrow. Germany was dependent on 'the
charity of the world market', as long as it did not control sufficient sources of raw materials and safe markets. To ensure Germany's basis for life in the present
and in the future, they needed *Mitteleuropa* and its
complementary, Central Africa:

> It would be impossible in a generation to feed
> and employ a hundred million Germans from the
> product of half a million square kilometres of our

home ground and plot in Africa, and we do not
want to depend on the charity of the world market.
We need territory on the globe ... in future partitions we must get hold of the necessary territory,
until we are as satisfied as our neighbours.

Ideas like these came up in the Kaiser's talks with
Rathenau, as for example one evening at Admiral
Hollman's house, two days after Haldane's visit to
Berlin, on 13 February 1912. Starting from his good
relations with Alfred de Rothschild ('My highly respected friend') and the City of London, as well as his
friendly relations with George V, the Kaiser developed
his ideas to Rathenau. 'His plan is for a United States
of Europe against America.... This would not dis-
please the English. Five States (including France)
would be able to do something.' It must remain open
whether Rathenau had fired the Kaiser with his ideas
or the other way round. What is certain is that
Rathenau in the July of the same year, on 25 July
1912, while a guest of Bethmann-Hollweg on his estate
at Hohenfinow – the two had had neighbouring
estates since Rathenau had acquired Schloss Fürsten-
walde and visited each other often – had put these
ideas to the Chancellor and had met with Bethmann-
Hollweg's basic agreement, as he expressly noted.
Rathenau's report of it was:

> I developed my ideas: 1. Economics. Customs
> union with Austria, Switzerland, Italy, Belgium, the
> Netherlands, etc., with closer association at the same
> time. 2. Foreign Policy. The key to it: the German–
> French conflict, which lets all nations grow fat.
> Key: England. Today disarmament is impossible.
> Start by increasing tension – although dangerous –
> also ruin England's position in the Mediterranean.
> Then alliance. Purpose: Central Africa, Asia Minor.

(A third topic of conversation was the reform of the
franchise in Prussia and the general democratisation,
which Bethmann-Hollweg showed great interest in as
well as the then Under-Secretary in the Imperial
Chancellery, Wahnschaffe.)

All the general points of German world policy appear in this conversation: *Mitteleuropa*, Central Africa and Asia Minor. The last two were the remainders of the, at that time virtually shattered, aspirations for world power outside Europe; the first point indicates a new solution in the form of a concentration on the extension of the European basis, a solution which came to be more and more the centre of Rathenau's political ideas. But above all, here, in July 1912, are the two principal aims in Europe and Africa which appeared two years later in 1914 in Bethmann-Hollweg's September programme: *Mitteleuropa* and Central Africa.

In this conversation there also figured a further fundamental idea of Rathenau: these aims could only be realised through an understanding with England, and better still through an alliance with England. As we have seen, an alliance with England did not really correspond fully with Bethmann-Hollweg's wishes, since he really wanted a small colonial agreement with her to keep her neutral, but not an alliance which would have robbed Germany of freedom of action. But Rathenau believed that they could get an alliance through further pressure on England, either through standing by the Supplementary Naval Law, or through diplomatic activity in the Mediterranean, possibly in Egypt, or Turkey, but more probably in Greece where the Kaiser had recently had high hopes. This policy was based on the assumption and aim that the English were ready to surrender the Entente with France and Russia and that this would make possible a complete reshuffle of the relations between the European Powers. Rathenau believed that this was not utopian but a possibility, since England would better be able to defend herself economically against America through a connection with Germany. Because of this he demanded publicly from England her making possible and acknowledging Germany's future position on the Continent in the sense of the *Mitteleuropa* plan (25 December 1913). On the first day of Christmas 1913 in the same article in which he demanded the creation of *Mitteleuropa*, he warned Eng-

land: 'There is a serious, definite, particular concern
growing up in the civilised States about helping us
out of a problem which, if unsolved, must become a
lasting danger to Europe.' With that he put England
into the position of deciding over European peace:
France did not come into the question because of her
complete dependence on England. Indirectly, the
island empire was loaded with responsibility for a possible outbreak of war. Here, in December 1913, the
Mitteleuropa project was being offered in the sense of
a peaceful partnership with England – but a year
later, immediately after the outbreak of war when
England had joined Germany's continental adversaries, it became an anti-English war aim.

Bethmann-Hollweg took up these ideas of Rathenau, together with the Central Africa and Baghdad
Railway ideas of Kühlmann. the originator of the
pamphlet *World Policy without War* (1914). They
were the kernel of his concept of political war aims
with which he opposed the stringent annexationist
aims of the Pan-Germans. He did not consider indirect
rule to be the only way, but in general he adhered to
this programme till his fall and then passed it on to
Kühlmann.

But it should be noted here that the German
Mitteleuropa plans have absolutely nothing in common with the plans of the fifties and sixties of this
century. In 1914 *Mitteleuropa* was seen essentially as a
form of mastery and a confirmation of Germany's
hegemony on the Continent and as a foundation for
her as a World Power alongside the other World
Powers, since the control of the main arteries of traffic
in all directions and of the most industrialised part of
the world, that is Europe, would make the German
Empire equal to the powerful countries of America,
Russia and the British Empire, in extent of territory,
in size of population and resources.

These were not considerations made after the event,
but ideas expressed at the time by the men who pursued this *Mitteleuropa* policy. There were many officials in the Prussian and Imperial higher bureaucracy
who belonged to Schmoller's school. He had origin-

ated the doctrine of the 'three world empires', which
the Germans should confront with *Mitteleuropa* as a
fourth. Characteristic of his ideas was this observation
made by him in 1890:

> Whoever is far-sighted enough to realise that the
> course of twentieth-century world history will be
> determined by the competition between the Rus-
> sian, English and American and possibly Chinese
> world empires and by their aspirations to make all
> the other smaller States dependent on them, will
> also see in a *Mitteleuropa* customs union the seed of
> something which can save not only the political
> independence of those States from destruction but
> also Europe's superior, old culture itself.

Schmoller's lecture of January 1900 on 'The Economic Future of Germany and the Navy Bill' showed
that this *Mitteleuropa* customs union had to be led by
Germany. Schmoller said then:

> Just as Frederick the Great assembled the other
> German States to prevent Austrian annexionist
> aims, so the German Empire today must act as the
> focal point of a coalition of States, which can be of
> some weight among the world empires, and which
> can tip the scales in the great struggles among them,
> especially in the final, decisive fight between Eng-
> land and Russia. But that will only be possible with
> a stronger fleet than we have today.

He then continued:

> We should win over the small and middling States
> because they will see that we are not threatening
> them, that we are ready to guarantee their posses-
> sions and perhaps even their colonies, if they will
> make a peaceful economic alliance with us.

Mende's* request for a definition of the words 'world
power' seems naïve considering the crushing wealth of
self-evidence, as does Engels's* asking why only Ger-

* Critics of Fischer—Ed.

many 'grasped' at world power: the Germans believed
that the others were already World Powers.

While Bethmann-Hollweg, Rathenau and their
circle of friends were discussing *Mitteleuropa* plans on
the plane of high policy in Hohenfinow and Berlin,
other things were happening which merit attention in
connection with this.

There had been private *Mitteleuropa* economic
societies for a decade in Germany, Austria, Hungary
and Belgium – discussions were in train in France as
well – which were composed of political economists
and Members of Parliament and which were encouraged by their respective governments. Their aim,
which was discussed in several congresses, was to
achieve the facilitating of monetary and commerical
exchange and of passport and customs clearance matters. While the official announcement of its establishment in 1904 expressly rejected the pursuit of political
aims, the chief founder and for many years the Chairman of the German Society, the Leipzig political
economist Julius Wolf, had already pointed out at its
founding what they ought to achieve by the consolidation of the economic base of the Triple Alliance.
Although he declared officially that a customs union
'under today's conditions' would be utopian, he none
the less saw the work of the society in aiming to prepare the way for a *Mitteleuropa* customs union, above
all between Germany and Austria-Hungary, and he
judged the work of the society as a service in 'preparation for great eventualities', as he put it. The members
of the society were drawn from the crucial sectors of
the Germany economy and from four of the parties
which supported the Empire, the Conservatives, the
Reich Party, the National Liberals and the Centre.

One of the most important representatives of business, the National Liberal Reichstag Deputy and
Privy Councillor, Professor Doctor Paasche, who was
later Vice-President of the Reichstag, resigned from
the society in 1911 because he was dissatisfied with its
cautious, temporising policy. In September 1913 he
founded the German–Austro-Hungarian Economic
Association which immediately separated itself from

the other bilateral economic unions by its announcing
officially that its object was to remove the protective-
tariff policy existing between the two countries. In
April 1914, despite Article 11 of the Peace of Frankfurt which had given France perpetual tariff preference, Paasche demanded that they should at least
provide customs-policy exceptions towards Austria-
Hungary, if they were not allowed to carry a customs
union 'for the present'. After the outbreak of war this
society took the initiative sooner and more intensively
than the *Mitteleuropa* economic societies in the question of an economic merger between Germany and
Austria-Hungary.

The Armaments Race and the National Euphoria in Germany, 1911–14

The Balkan wars and the shock which they administered to Germany's position in Europe, as well as the
previous defeat of her friend Turkey in North Africa
by Italy, a member of the Triple Alliance, caused a
general armaments race between Germany and the
Entente Powers. In Germany as a result of the Bills of
December 1912 the large increase in the army was
accepted in the spring of 1913 (the Army Bill was
moved in the Reichstag on 7 April 1913), but France
answered this, even before it became law, by the introduction of three-year service, thereby largely nullify-
ing its effect. (It is therefore really incomprehensible
how Gerhard Ritter can call this increase in the army
Bethmann-Hollweg's greatest feat of statesmanship!)
This increase in the army was effected with the help of
agitation from the National Defence League (*Wehrverein*) which General Keim founded in 1912 and
which soon had more members than the Navy League
in which Keim had agitated before. It was significant
for his stand in this armaments policy that Bethmann-
Hollweg, although warning of the perils of exaggerating the Slav danger in the Press and of overrating
the slogan of the struggle of Slavs and Teutons
(which, however, the Kaiser was continually mouth-

ing), justified this Bill by the danger of 'Pan-Slavism' which had been increased by the changes in the Balkans. This was possibly done with an eye to the Social Democrats, who were anti-Tsarist, but in any case it was likely to cause Russia to increase her armaments. Moreover, this speech was quite in line with Bethmann-Hollweg's indulgent policy towards England. It corresponded with a remark of Moltke to Conrad on 10 February 1913: 'But the Slavs must attack first.'

France and Russia were rearming. As the Russians increased their army with French financial help, and as a result of this recovery in military strength after the humiliation of their defeat by Japan in 1904–5 and the humiliation of March 1909, Germany was faced by the pressure of a coalition which some years ahead would be superior to the Central Powers – they reckoned this would be the case in 1916 or 1917. Thus the army increase of 132,000 men approved by the Reichstag even before the Second Balkan War was of limited value for Germany's military strength because only 72,000 men could be conscripted by October 1913 (and so be deployable in the autumn of 1914).

That first upsurge of national emotion in Germany in July and August and again in November 1911 resulting from the diplomatic defeat in the so-called second Morocco crisis is excitement which must be judged to be an expression of isolation in foreign policy as much as a permanent claim to a position as a World Power. It was answered domestically in the Reichstag election of January 1912, in which the Social Democrats scored a great victory (34·8 per cent of the votes cast) and became the strongest party in the German Reichstag with 110 Deputies.

This victory for Social Democracy was at the same time a threat to the internal political structure of Prussia-Germany, where the outcome of financial reform had been provocatively the reverse of those simultaneous changes which had strengthened British domestic politics. This victory had given a strong domestic political impetus to the vote, producing co-operation between Social Democracy and the Liberal Left. Moreover, because of domestic developments in

the southern German States, it was no longer a Social
Democracy which could have been suppressed by force
as a revolutionary party, such as the Kaiser had
written about in his famous New Year Letter of 1906
under the 'lit Christmas tree' to Bülow:

> First shoot the Socialists, behead them and make
> them harmless, if need be through a bloodbath.
> And then war abroad. But not before this has been
> done and not *a tempo*.

This was in the same letter in which he had connected
their embarking on a possible war with an alliance
with Turkey and the revolutionising of the Islamic
world! The Conservatives and Pan-Germans in 1912
believed that there was a danger of creeping democratisation if the Chancellor, because of foreign policy
dangers, gave way to the influence of Social Democracy in such fields as the Prussian franchise, or to the
trade unions in social-political questions, which the
majority of industrialists feared as greatly as the
agricultural worker. In fact a controlling group of
Ebert, Scheidemann, Noske, Heine and Frank had
taken over the Social Democrats in this election, who
appeared more acquiescent towards the Empire's military and foreign policy in the hope of political concessions and reforms at home. Bethmann-Hollweg had
especially assumed office with the job of assimilating
Social Democracy into the State. August 1914 showed
the result of this development, although no serious
political reforms had yet come about because of the
resistance of the conservatives, above all of the Prussian Minister of the Interior, von Loebell, and Bethmann-Hollweg's own very cautious political position
at home. Although Bethmann-Hollweg was on the
whole liberal, he could only be called a conservative
liberal who was on no account trying to change the
Prussian–German government system fundamentally.
It was exactly against the pliable, patient, expectant
Social Democrats that the German Crown Prince
directed his plan for a *coup d'état* in November 1913,
which we will discuss below.

The growing nervousness and the accelerated nationalist upsurge in the winter of 1912–13 after the outbreak of the Second Balkan War are manifested in the army increases, in the domestic events connected with it, and in the change in the popular mood. Distrusting the Chancellor, Bethmann-Hollweg, and afraid that the army increase planned in the winter of 1912–13 would be too low, the National Liberals on 9 February 1913 held the meeting of their Central Committee in Berlin. In the main speech of Bassermann, their Chairman, there cropped up once again, as in the speeches of November 1911, disappointment over the outcome of the Morocco crisis: 'Other countries get territory; we get a new Army Bill.' Some days previously Tirpitz had told the Estimates Committee, with the approval of the Progressives and Centre (on 6–7 February 1913), that a German–English naval ratio of 10 to 16 was satisfactory for finding a basis for German agreement with England. But Bassermann made a stand against this: 'A Great Power should not tie itself down.' He declared that Germany could do too much conciliating England and not champion Austrian interests in the Balkans enough. With Bismarck and Bülow they had been able to accept that the government would demand what was necessary, but with Bethmann-Hollweg it was otherwise. Bassermann revealed that he had spoken to some high-ranking officers (Ludendorff) who were demanding that general conscription be used, and he produced some detailed demands himself (the formation of cavalry divisions in peacetime, improvement of the horse team, filling up the third battalions, etc.). The national revolution – such as the majority of the Reichstag, in 1914–17 and beyond to the end of the war, was to identify itself with – was raising its head. The parties could and had to demand more if the government itself was too weak: this was the sense of his speech.

In the debate Prince Schönaich-Carolath, who stood out for an agreement and community of interests with England, was isolated. Stresemann and an Africa specialist, Arning (post-war Headmaster of the Witzenhausen Colonial School), demanded that the

National Liberal Party, which had supported the creation of the Empire, should also be a party for the expansion of the Empire. They discussed the question of a partition of Turkey – see the Kaiser's similar expressions – as well as the creation of a coloured army on the French pattern. Time and time again the debate referred back to the people's distrust of the Imperial government's lack of initiative in foreign affairs. In reporting the debate, those National Liberal newspapers edited by Arthur Dix, a pupil of Schmoller, said on 16 February 1913: 'Bismarck is not dead, Bismarck is alive, but not in the government, in the people.'

An extremely revealing letter from the same Bassermann to Schiffer of 5 June 1914 shows that the Conservatives were even more distrustful of the Chancellor, who had quite unjustly lavished honours on them. Indeed they despised him, as he said, on the grounds of both domestic and foreign policy. This shows the 'pressure', which my critics put forward so frequently, and which I in no way dispute, which Bethmann-Hollweg was under and which limited his freedom of action so considerably. There can be no dispute about the Conservatives and National Liberals having been the strongest political forces in Germany before 1914.

A few weeks after this demonstration by the National Liberals, in April 1913, preliminary negotiations were held with party representatives. These were secret meetings; in them the Chancellor and the Secretary of State, Jagow, with representatives of the military departments, justified the Army Bill. To get them to vote in favour, Jagow spoke of the coming 'world war'. These words often turn up, as for example in the letter already cited from Bassermann to Schiffer of 5 June 1914, which contains the half-resigned observation that 'We are drifting towards world war.' This was three weeks before Sarajevo.

In these preliminary negotiations with the party leaders over the large increase in the army for 1913 it was already plain that if a war broke out with Russia over the conflict in the Balkans, it would be fought in

the first phase by an offensive aimed at a decision in
the West, since the representatives for the army only
put forward as justification for the Bill a military plan
about the deployment of troops in the West (the
Schlieffen plan). Because of this, some of the Social
Democratic negotiators, who really wanted to fight the
Russians, not the Western democracies, dared to ask if
this would mean the violation of Belgian neutrality.
Bethmann-Hollweg answered evasively – in good
faith. Twice before, in 1910 and 1912, the Imperial
government had assured Belgium that in the case of
conflict with France they would observe Belgian neutrality, and at the end of 1913 the Kaiser asked King
Albert if Belgium would allow the Germans to march
through.

A day after the speech by Bassermann, which we
have quoted, to the National Liberal Central Committee, which in fact was made at the time of greatest
tension in the Austro-Serbian conflict over a possible
increase in the size of Serbia and her reaching the
Adriatic, Moltke wrote that letter to Conrad which
has often been cited and which according to Gerhard
Ritter's ideas is to be taken as evidence of the German Chief of Staff's basic love of peace. Certainly
Moltke (and this letter was certainly written only in
agreement with Bethmann-Hollweg) warned Conrad
(and therefore the Austrian government as well) of the
undesirability of a preventive war against Serbia at
that point in time, and this certainly led to disappointment in Austria, which had carried out a costly
mobilisation. But this letter said nothing more than
that a war of nations (which Moltke judged an Austro-
Serb conflict would lead to!) would require the whole
strength, both material and moral, of their peoples
and that this would therefore have to be mobilised (10
February 1913):

Politics and conduct of war are surely closely cor-
related. I still believe that a European war must
come sooner or later and then it will be in the long
run a struggle between Teutons and Slavs. It is the
duty of all States who are the standard-bearers of

Germanic spiritual culture to prepare themselves
for it. But the Slavs must attack first. Those who can
see this struggle coming will be clear that it needs
the concentration of all forces, the use of all possibilities, but above all complete understanding by
the people for the world-historic development.

A few days later the same Moltke, on 19 February
1913, told the Austro-Hungarian Military Attaché in
Berlin: 'One should think very hard about beginning
a world war'; and the Kaiser told the Austro-Hungarian Ambassador:

It would be difficult to make the German people
see the need for war: they will not understand the
'Durazzo' question [later 'Diakova', a small place on
the Albanian–Montenegrin border, was often mentioned in the same sense! – Author]. Consequently
we must not go over the edge for the sake of a few
Albanian towns.

The Kaiser, whose influence is shown on every page
of the official documents (it cannot be made light of
simply because it was not very constitutional), had
already, in November 1912, just after the outbreak of
the First Balkan War, which German–English co-
operation was still able to localise, ordered that his
own people should be mobilised, through the use of
propaganda, to be ready for the great war which could
grow out of an Austro-Serb conflict's becoming an
Austro-Russian one. 'The everlasting stress on peace',
Wilhelm telegraphed to Kiderlen-Wächter from
Rominten, 'at every opportunity – aptly or inaptly –
during the forty-three years of peace, has produced a
downright eunuchised outlook among the leading
statesmen and diplomats of Europe.' War between
Turkey and the Balkan States was coming, and it
would therefore be 'better', the Kaiser continued, if 'it
happens now – when it would not suit Russia and
France – because both of them are not ready to take us
on, than later when they would be ready.' The people
had to be informed 'before it happened', through the

'activity of the Press', about the interests it would have to fight for and in this way be made 'familiar with the idea of such a war'.

And just that happened at the numerous celebrations held in 1913. In March at the centenary of the start of the 'War of Liberation' the Chancellor read an appeal 'To the people'; in June there were parades and speeches on the occasion of the Kaiser's Silver Jubilee; there was the commemoration of Lützow's death; there was the gathering of the German Princes in the Hall of Liberty at Kelheim; and finally there was the imposing mass demonstration at the unveiling of the memorial to the Battle of the Nations in Leipzig, in October 1913, with the Kaiser present – a demonstration which had a thoroughly Pan-German character and in comparison with which the meeting of the youth movement, at the Hoher Meissner, which has so frequently been invoked with its vague and aimless idealism, was politically ineffective, although this idealism inspired these schoolboys and students half a year later to volunteer for the war and to sacrifice and devote themselves to it.

Some weeks later in November 1913 the German Crown Prince demanded that a strong line should be taken against the Social Democrats. This step showed how the ultra-conservative and Pan-German circles which the Crown Prince was intimately connected with had become worried by the growth of Social Democracy. The Chancellor took this attempt very seriously, as was shown by the thirty-or-so-page answer which he drafted by hand to justify why he believed such action was then unfeasible. In all this should be remembered that the Pan-Germans' indignation against the Kaiser because of his backing-down in 1905 –6 and in 1911 went so far that they were toying with the idea of his deposition and the succession of the Crown Prince – a threat which must have been especially in the Kaiser's mind in July 1914, more so as the Kaiserin also was leaning towards the Crown Prince's views.

At the unveiling of the Battle of the Nations monument in Leipzig, Wilhelm II had met Conrad and had

let himself be won over (on 18 October 1913) to his
programme for action:

> I am with you there. The others [i.e. the other
> Powers] are not prepared, they will not do anything
> against it. Within a few days you must be in Bel-
> grade. I was always a partisan of peace; but this has
> its limits. I have read much about war and know
> what it means. But finally a situation arises in
> which a Great Power can no longer just look on,
> but must draw the sword.

The strong anti-Serb attitude which he expressed
then, he kept to during the following months as well.
It must have been in this sense that, on 1 January
1914, the Kaiser, in his traditional speech to his commanding generals, let fall words which made it
appear that he expected that a decision for war would
be made in 1914. A statement with this meaning has
come to us from two different places. The commanding general at Strassburg, General Deimling, at the
official dinner for the Kaiser's birthday on 27 January
1914, announced that the war would come that year.
On the same day the commanding general of the
Rhine Army Corps at Koblenz, General Tülff von
Tschepe und Weidenbach, at the traditional reception for officers said word for word: 'Gentlemen, I
have to inform you that it will break out this year. Be
ready for it. I have it from His Majesty's own lips.'
Communications like those could not have taken
place in both places without express instructions. In
whatever way the pronouncement should be interpreted or whatever was its meaning – at least to increase their readiness for a war which was seen as unavoidable – it was a sign of the degree of anxiety
which the Kaiser's thoughts had reached. He – almost
using the same words as Moltke and Jagow – saw the
approach of the struggle between Slavs and Teutons,
in which he knew the French would be on the side of
the Slavs (see also his similar pronouncement made in
November 1912), and the only undecided question
was whether the Anglo-Saxons would support the

French and the Slavs or the Teutons indirectly
through neutrality.

One should take this frame of mind together with
all the factors described in the preceding paragraphs
of this inquiry, especially those we have just discussed:
the German domestic situation; the widespread conviction that war was unavoidable and furthermore
that a preventive war was necessary; the anxiety
about being outstripped by the growing military
strength of Russia and France; the tense nationality problem in and around Austria-Hungary and her
obvious weakness; the crisis in German policies and
economic advance in the Balkans and Turkey faced
by financial competition from France; the emergence
of the concept of *Mitteleuropa* as a counterpoise to
America and Russia, which would have included
France, Belgium, Holland, etc.; and finally, the hope,
desired but always questionable, of being able to
keep England neutral in the event of a great war
breaking out on the Continent. In this light, Wilhelm
II's forecast of 8 June 1914 becomes comprehensible:
'The third chapter in the Balkan War is coming soon,
which we will all take part in. This is why the Russians
and French are making colossal preparations for war.'
And his order to the Imperial Chancellor 'to clarify
relations with England'.

The latter was attempted by intensifying negotiations with England over the colonial and the Baghdad Railway questions (as has been shown) and finally,
after the news had become certain of an Anglo-Russian understanding over a naval convention, the sending of Albert Ballin during the July crisis itself to
London, where he may perhaps also have discussed co-
operation with England against America. It was attempted ultimately by Bethmann-Hollweg's entire
British policy during the July crisis, and even more
finally by his offer to England on the night of 29–30
July, which already expressed their future war aims
against Belgium as well as against France. If England
would stay neutral, Germany would assure her 'that in
case of a victorious war in Europe we would not aspire
to any territorial increase at France's expense in

Europe'. A corresponding promise over French colonies, which the English Ambassador inquired about,
was not given. In the same way, 'provided that Belgium does not join against us', Germany would preserve Belgian integrity. Moltke repeated the same idea
on 2 August, when the situation had already become
very black, in an instruction to the Foreign Office,
which showed very plainly still that originally only a
continental war with France and Russia was being
counted on:

> If England should make her neutrality in the
> German–Austrian–Russian–French war dependent
> on a German assurance 'that she would act leniently
> in the event of victory over France', this assurance
> can be given unconditionally in a very concrete
> form. There is no question of our destroying
> France, only beating her. English neutrality is so
> important to us that we can make this concession to
> her unconditionally.

Although Moltke spoke here in fact of a 'mere' defeat
of France, this would have meant for all practical
purposes – as has already been shown above – detach-
ing France from her alliance with Russia and the
Entente with England and making her politically and
economically dependent on Germany, although this
might have been made more acceptable through the
Mitteleuropa programme. But this would have threatened England extremely since it would have ensured
the basis for a German hegemony on the Continent.
From 1912 the English had made it plain that they
would not allow the overthrow of France. But Germany none the less had tried right up to the end to
keep England neutral through concessions on secondary questions.
  That English neutrality was still regarded as open
on the same 2 August 1914 was brought out by one of
the Kaiser's marginal comments to a newspaper report
that the English fleet was protecting France's North
Sea coast 'through the tying down of our fleets'.

This is the help of one ally to another, instead of a position of neutrality. Since England is preventing my fleet's co-operating with my army against the enemy already at war with me [this comment moreover is positive evidence of their thinking of co-operation between the army and fleet, which has often been disputed], this state of affairs cannot continue! England must show her true colours unconditionally! And at once, ONE WAY OR THE OTHER!

Only first the suspected and then clearly apparent opposition from England led not only to the hurried concluding of an alliance with the Turks, who in the middle of June had still been thought unfit to be allied with, but also to the programme of revolution, which was intended to cause revolts in Egypt and India as well as in the Dominion of South Africa, and to Moltke's demands to attempt to get Persia and Turkey, Sweden and Norway to go to war with Russia, and finally to the invitation to Japan 'to satisfy now her entire Far Eastern claims, preferably by war against the Russians while they were tied up in the war in Europe'. This extension of the war programme demonstrates the overestimation of Germany's domestic and foreign resources.

The July Crisis and German War Aims

Once the Imperial German government had taken the risk of continental war against France and Russia by not merely promising to support Austria-Hungary against Serbia and protect her from Russia during any warlike action but also by pushing its ally into it — contrary to Gerhard Ritter, I look upon the July crisis from the angle that it developed specifically from the entire intellectual, political and economic position of the Empire in Europe, not from a standpoint fixed by after-the-event apologies determined by war experience and the 'war-guilt question' — Bethmann-Hollweg believed that he could rely on a dependable tie with England. The Ministry of War and the General Staff had concluded their military preparations for the war, while the French and Russians still did not seem to have reached their full strength which would have been considered a threat to Germany, while economic developments were still undecided or retrograde.

It is with this whole situation in mind that the decisions taken by the Imperial German government in July 1914, eight days after the murder at Sarajevo, must be understood. Two representatives of German business, from heavy industry and banking, Krupp von Bohlen und Halbach and Karl Helfferich, who were both (with Arthur von Gwinner) close friends of the Kaiser and of the Chancellor as well – Krupp actually was closer to the Kaiser and the military – knew early on in the middle of July the decisions taken by the Kaiser and Chancellor on 5–6 July. They recognised their full magnitude and acted accordingly: they protracted outstanding armaments orders for abroad and 'no longer put back the shrinking gold resources into circulation'. In the middle of July when Helfferich discussed in Berlin with the Krupp director and long-serving representative of Krupp's in the Balkans, Dr Mühlon, the supply of war material to Bulgaria and Turkey, Helfferich justified his momentary hesitation on the question of credit by his knowledge that 'Vienna . . . in eight days time would give an ultimatum to Serbia which would be very sharp and with quite a short time limit' and would demand 'immediate satisfaction' if Austria-Hungary were not to declare war on Serbia. Helfferich added 'that the Kaiser had expressed himself determinedly for this action. This time there was no hesitation.'

As Mühlon knew Helfferich's 'especially trusted relations with the leading men, who must know what is going on', he communicated his information on his return to his chief, Krupp von Bohlen und Halbach, who made this reply:

He had been with the Kaiser himself this day. The Kaiser had also spoken to him about the discussion with the Austrians and the outcome, but he described the thing as being so secret that he would

not once have dared to tell his Directors about it. . . .
The situation is in fact very serious. The Kaiser has
declared to him that he will declare war at once, if
Russia mobilises. This time they would see that he
would not fall back. The Kaiser's repeated stressing
that in this case no one would be able to reproach
him again with irresolution had an almost comic
effect.

The Kaiser's repeated protestation that he would
not fall back this time, which appeared 'almost comic' to
Krupp, can only be understood if taken together with
similar protestations from the side of the military,
such as that of Moltke during the July crisis of 1911:

> If we again slink out of this affair with our tail
> between our legs, if we cannot pull ourselves to-
> gether to present demands which we are prepared to
> enforce by the sword, then I despair of the future of
> the German Reich. Then I shall resign.

It also has to be taken together with the Pan-German
threats to depose the Kaiser if he showed weakness
again and to replace him with the Crown Prince,
threats which must have reached the Kaiser's ears.

The Kaiser, the German military leaders and the
Foreign Office insisted in the July crisis that Austria
should immediately begin hostilities against Serbia.
They agreed with the Austrian ultimatum to Serbia,
which was so sharp that there was the greatest probability that it had to lead to war between the two
countries. In this way they consciously risked a continental war of Austria-Hungary and Germany against
Russia and France. What was crucial in the July crisis
was that besides the Kaiser, the military and the
Foreign Office, the formally responsible statesman, the
Imperial Chancellor, Bethmann-Hollweg, also decided
himself to take the tough line and to run that risk on
5–6 July. When the Kaiser threatened to show weakness again, Bethmann-Hollweg even disregarded him,
as appears from the fact that Wilhelm's proposal for
moderation ('Halt in Belgrade') was not passed on
properly and in good time to Vienna. Similarly, the

Chancellor rejected or delayed all English attempts
at mediation or forwarded them to Vienna without
stressing them enough. If Bethmann-Hollweg believed
that in doing this he could 'localise' (contrary to all
previous assumptions such as Moltke's) an Austro-
Hungarian punitive war against Serbia, the minor
Slav State, whose integrity the Tsarist Empire's prestige was tied to, and accepted that Russia 'is only
bluffing', which the military and part of the Foreign
Office professed to believe, although Bethmann-Hollweg's closest friends and advisers, the bankers, did not
believe it, this is all secondary to the principal decision. That he none the less took it appears plainly
from the notes in the diary of his private secretary,
Kurt Riezler, which have not been published up to
now but which show that Bethmann-Hollweg was certainly 'ready for war' in the July crisis.

To understand this decision, all the facts mentioned
have to be valued as prerequisites for this political decision (*Willensbildung*), not least just those affecting
the Empire's economic commitment in Austria-Hungary, the Balkans and Turkey, and the crisis which it
had become involved in through it. To lay bare and
to understand this development, especially its economic factors which led to the situation which developed after Sarajevo into the July crisis's origin, has
been the purpose of this examination. And above all
to answer the question why and how the Imperial
government acted the way it did in the July crisis and
why the country approved the decision and followed
it enthusiastically. There can be no talk of any accidental 'stumbling into war'. Bethmann-Hollweg's
actions at the beginning and at the height of the crisis
were not ruled by destiny or a fateful tragedy, but
were a conscious political decision. It appears that the
interpretation put forward by a politician extremely
favourable to the Empire and later in the war the
chief apostle of the *Mitteleuropa* ideas in Austria,
Baernreither, in his diary in an entry for December
1914, got to the heart of the matter, when he said:

    Seckendorff confirms what has been clear to me

for a very long time. Germany was afraid that we would refuse to go along with them if war broke out over a question not directly concerning us. At Algeciras we were only second, later not even that. In the Morocco crisis we did not stand firmly by Germany. But war had to come, as things had developed, because of the mistakes of German and Austro-Hungarian diplomacy. So after the Sarajevo murder Germany seized the chance and grasped the opportunity which had arisen on the Austrian side. That is the history of the war.

Baernreither saw his interpretation of the July crisis confirmed through a talk with the Berlin East European historian and leader-writer for the *Kreuzzeitung*, the later German National Deputy, Otto Hoetzsch, in November 1915: according to Baernreither's entry, 'the German Kaiser sailed to Norway then [after 5 July 1914] certain that war would break out. All of it was organised very skilfully by Germany and the moment used very quickly with the sure intention of making a war which had become inevitable in the last years with the definite accompaniment of Austria.'

A week later Baernreither had this interpretation confirmed by Hoetzsch's Berlin colleague, the political scientist, Jastrow.

Arthur Gwinner, the Director of the Deutsche Bank, took the same line in a conversation at the end of August 1914 over the July crisis with the Under-Secretary of State at the Admiralty, Capelle, when he expressed very clearly the state of mind prepared to run the risk of war, especially in the Foreign Office, as well as bringing out the uncertainty about their Austrian ally: 'Lichnowsky [the German Ambassador in London] was not told that they wanted here [in the Wilhelmstrasse] to push it to the point of war.' When Capelle asked who had been doing the pushing, Gwinner answered: 'Herr von Stumm in the Foreign Office.' Because Capelle seemed to have doubts, he went on: 'Perhaps it was a whole group. They worked at it systematically, first of all to have Austria engaged in it firmly so that they could be sure of her. But

the whole action in Serbia from the first was begun in
such a way that the conflict was unavoidable.'

The historian, Karl Alexander von Müller, had the
same idea. In the spring of 1915 he was asked together
with Riezler to write an apology for July 1914 for the
Chancellor. After examining the documents and consulting Riezler, who explained Bethmann-Hollweg's
calculations during the July days, Müller turned
down the request, but without omitting to note down
the next night the pith of his conversation. Müller
wrote:

> If they wanted again to risk a diplomatic trial of
> strength with the Dual Alliance, only a south-east-
> ern question could be considered, that is one in
> which Austria had an interest as principal and in
> which Germany stood behind her.

Although the aims formulated immediately after
the outbreak of the war were doubtless sharper in
their form and more naked in their wants because of
being made on the high tide of apparent military
success, none the less in them appeared again the old
aims of world policy and those worked for in the economic sphere in relation to Belgium and France. This
is the one central significance of the September programme of Bethmann-Hollweg for the peace negotiations with France, which I analysed originally and
which a great number of other people interested in it
have done since. The secondary significance of it lies
in that in this German programme aims and conditions for the realisation of these aims were expressed
which German policy previously had amounted to,
although the specific war situation had produced
modifications. The description of German war aims
should not begin from the verdict of 'boundless and
extravagant demands' (Hölzle), but Germany's war
aims policy has to be analysed as a product of German
claims to world power, that is the claims to be or become one of the great World Powers. If in this process
associations, which are unpleasant for a national view
of German history, become clear, this has nothing to
do with the historian's task.

Cabinet versus Economic Warfare in Germany:
Policy and Strategy during the Early Months of
the First World War

Egmont Zechlin

Just after the second Morocco crisis had been settled
by the Morocco–Congo treaty, the German Chancellor, Theobald von Bethmann-Hollweg, on 16 November 1911 wrote a confidential letter to Carl von Weizsäcker, Premier of Württemberg, in which he defended his foreign policy against Pan-German and
conservative charges of unpardonable softness. He
acknowledged that some aspects of the Morocco agreement fell short of perfection, but expressly denied
having pursued a military conflict for the attainment
of limited colonial interests. His argument ran:

> Had I ... allowed the war stage to be reached, we
> should now be somewhere in France, while the
> major part of our fleet would lie at the bottom of
> the North Sea and Hamburg and Bremen would be
> blockaded or under bombardment. The German
> people might then well have asked me why? Why
> all this – for the fictitious sovereignty of the Sultan
> of Morocco, for a piece of the Sudan or the Congo,
> for the Mannesmann brothers? And they would
> have had every right to string me up from the next
> tree.

It is true that the Chancellor was ready, if necessary,
'to take to the sword for the honour of the nation', as
he noted down during these very days; but he was
ready to act only 'in full awareness that any political
act by a Great Power could pose the fateful challenge
of war or peace'. Hence it was his 'duty so to conduct

From the *Historische Zeitschrift*, CXCIX (Oct. 1964).

the affairs of state as to avoid a war that could be avoided, that did not involve Germany's honour'.

In March 1912, when the British threatened to strengthen their North Sea fleet, and Wilhelm II proposed to answer with a threat of war, Bethmann-Hollweg used the same argument to justify his request to be allowed to resign. He said that to provoke war when neither German honour nor German vital interests were at stake would be a crime against Germany's destiny, even if Germany could reasonably anticipate full victory. In November 1913 he conceded to the Pan-German critics of his Morocco policy that German foreign policy should be boldly conducted; 'but to begin rattling the sabre at every diplomatic crisis, even when Germany's honour, security and future are not under threat, is more than rash – it is criminal'.

Bethmann-Hollweg was mouthing no empty phrases to soothe his critics when he said he stood ready to wage war for Germany's 'honour' or 'vital interests'; nor was his aversion to sabre-rattling at the slightest sign of diplomatic trouble based on a kind of philosophical pacifism. As he put it himself, he was motivated by thoroughly practical considerations. Bethmann-Hollweg had a very clear picture of himself as the responsible head of a great European Power, and he knew that this role required a successful policy, based on national interest and implying an unlimited willingness to apply pressure tactics against other Great Powers, for the attainment of Germany's claims – if necessary to the brink of general war. Such a policy, of course, meant nothing more nor less than the resolve to stick out the crisis to the end, by accepting the risk of war. In his diary Kurt Riezler, kindred spirit and conversational partner to Bethmann-Hollweg, has testified to the Chancellor's willingness to use such pressure tactics in the second Morocco crisis; but following a discussion on 30 July 1911, he also noted down the limits to the risk of escalation that were set in the calculation: 'He does not aim at war as the only solution.'

The Chancellor, on the other hand, did not share

the illusions of the conservatives. In the pre-war period they had repeatedly advocated preventive war, as a means of buttressing their domestic power; and on the eve of war, in July 1914, they fully expected that the impending passage at arms would strengthen the traditional patriarchal order. Bethmann-Hollweg, for his part, is on record as early as November 1911 as criticising his Pan-German and conservative opponents for 'thoughtlessly toying with war'. He told the Württemberg Premier, Weizsäcker, why. Among other things, it delayed almost indefinitely any hope for a sound domestic situation. Two years later he issued a stern warning to the Crown Prince, one of the severest critics of his foreign and domestic policies. In any future war undertaken without compelling reason the Hohenzollern crown as well as the future of Germany would be at stake. In July 1914 Riezler noted down the Chancellor's fears that 'any war, no matter how it may end, will mean the overturn of everything we know'. Bethmann-Hollweg was well aware of the instability and the unresolved stresses inherent in the Prusso-German constitutional system. Hence for domestic reasons alone he might have been expected to pursue a policy of peace at any price, to spare the German monarchy the extreme stress of modern mass war. The purported German pursuit of world power, often the subject of public discussion in pre-war Germany, likewise exerted no influence on the Chancellor's decisions during the July crisis, any more than did the clamour of the big trade associations.

In the spring of 1914, however, there were intimations of a trend that loomed as a direct threat to Germany's vital interests and future security.

As recently as November 1912 Moltke, the German Chief of Staff, had assessed the military balance of power in Europe in such a way as to justify the fullest confidence in Germany's ability to face whatever the future might have to offer; but when Russian rearmament began in the summer of 1913, and especially after details of the Russian army and navy programmes became known in the spring of 1914, estimates of the chances of military success had become

increasingly pessimistic within the German General
Staff. A crucial element in this respect was the view
that even drastic increases in German military manpower could not in the long run redress the balance,
since Germany would not be able to match Russia
man for man. An added factor was that Austria, the
only ally on whom Germany could rely, seemed to be
growing perceptibly feebler in a military sense, on
account of her unresolved nationality problems, thus
endangering German plans for a two-front strategy
which contemplated a powerful Austrian relief offensive in the East. There was more and more doubt,
moreover, whether Italy and Rumania could still be
considered dependable allies.

Chief Quartermaster Count Waldersee summed up
this pessimistic prognosis in a memorandum which he
transmitted to Moltke on 18 May 1914. Unless Germany were willing to have peace at any price, he concluded, it would be utterly irresponsible, before the
judgement of history, to fail to do anything and everything possible to avert a crisis. Sharing the views of his
deputy, the Chief of Staff confronted the Chancellor
with this gloomy estimate of Germany's military and
political prospects before the month was over. At the
same time he unburdened himself to Jagow, the
Foreign Minister. He said that he was depressed by
the outlook for the future. Within two or three years
Russia would have completed her arms programme.
When that happened Germany, now still about evenly
matched with her potential enemies, would no longer
be able to stand up to their military superiority.
Hence in Moltke's view there was nothing left but 'to
wage a preventive war, in order to defeat the enemy,
while we still have some chance to endure the
struggle'. He advised Jagow to adjust German policy
to the prospect of bringing about a war soon.

There can be no doubt that the judgement and
advice of the Chief of Staff, the highest military
authority in the land, left a deep impression upon the
politicians and upon Wilhelm II. One visitor who had
a long talk with the Kaiser about the overall situation
found him deeply troubled. He thought that the great

Russian arms and railway construction programmes meant that Russia was preparing for a war that might break out in 1916. He had actually considered whether it were not better to strike rather than wait. Bethmann-Hollweg's close associate Kurt Riezler has preserved remarks the Chancellor made about the July crisis, showing how deeply he was influenced by Russian developments in his likewise gloomy overall estimate of Germany's situation and thus presumably in his decisions at the time. Those developments betokened a shift in the balance of power. 'The future belongs to Russia', Riezler quotes the Chancellor on 7 July. 'She keeps growing and growing, bearing down on us like a nightmare.' Two weeks later he was even more outspoken. 'Within a matter of a few years we shall no longer be able to fend off Russia's growing claims and immense dynamism, especially if the present European constellation endures.' This was precisely Moltke's view, presented only a few weeks earlier to Jagow and possibly Bethmann-Hollweg himself.

Paris and London too were worried over the fact that a major increment in Russian power impended, indeed was already partly underway. It is all the more remarkable that there were voices, especially among British diplomats and generals – who could certainly not be credited with outspokenly pro-German sentiments – that judged Germany's situation in the face of this anticipated growth by one of the Entente partners in much the same way as Bethmann-Hollweg and Moltke. As early as March, for example, Sir Arthur Nicolson, the Permanent Under-Secretary in the Foreign Office, calculated 'that ... Germany does fear the possibility, or even the probability that before long she will find herself in an isolated and critical position, unless she steers an entirely different course to that which she has hitherto followed'. George Buchanan, the British Ambassador in St Petersburg, related German expectations of a worsening of German political power in Europe directly to the irresistible growth of Russian military strength. Germany, he wrote to Nicolson on 18 March 1914, far from improv-

ing her military position by her most recent Defence
Bill, would be far worse off in three years' time. 'Will
she bring in another Army Bill? If she does, Russia
will go one better; and in this race for armaments she
can always outdistance Germany.' Buchanan summed
up this military dilemma as bluntly as Moltke himself: 'Can Germany afford to wait till Russia becomes
the dominant factor in Europe or will she strike while
victory is still within her grasp?' The same thought
occurred spontaneously also to Sir Henry Wilson,
Chief of the Operations Division of the British General Staff, when he read a report on the Russian army
programme: 'It is easy to understand now why Germany is anxious about the future and why she may
think that it is a case of now or never.'

In the light of such an astonishing coincidence between these theoretical views and Berlin's concrete
analysis of the situation, there seems to have been
ample justice to German fears that the impending
expansion of Russian power would bring incisive
changes in Europe's still stable power structure, to
Germany's disadvantage. It is particularly noteworthy
that even in Britain resort to preventive war was
viewed as a policy that might commend itself to
Germany. This fact should pave the way for a rather
less prejudiced view of Moltke's fateful counsel and
Bethmann-Hollweg's grave decisions in the July crisis.
It is true, nevertheless, that sympathetic appreciation
of the German position stopped at the point where
Russian military expansion impinged on the interests
of the other countries concerned. In the last three
months before the outbreak of war, the British
Foreign Office, in the matter of its Russian policy, was
sharply confronted with Britain's own security needs,
compelling it to yield to the pressure for intensifying
the Anglo-Russian Entente.

The German government, however, interpreted
precisely this development as a second ominous indi-
cation that the balance of power had begun to shift
inexorably and that Germany's position as a Great
Power was growing more and more critical. During the
month of May the German Foreign Ministry received

unimpeachable documentary evidence, from within the Russian Embassy in London itself, that of late Russia, strongly supported by her French ally, was pressing Britain to elaborate the Entente treaty of 1907. The British Foreign Office, it was shown, had expressed willingness to meet these Russian importunities by agreeing to a bilateral naval convention on the model of the Anglo-French military agreement of 1912.

The German Foreign Ministry already had the full text of the exchanges between Grey and Cambon in 1912, confirming the talks that had been held by the British and French General Staffs and Admiralties. It must have been influenced in some measure by the apparent existence of far-reaching plans for military co-operation by the two countries in the event of war. It is true that both governments had expressly reserved the right to decide when and whether these military clauses were to come into effect; but Berlin is unlikely to have found this reassuring, for the two countries were pledged to consultation in the event that either should have substantial grounds for anticipating an unprovoked attack on the part of a third Power. It would almost certainly not always be possible to establish unequivocally which side was guilty and which innocent. The Wilhelmstrasse felt, moreover, that the combination of a military agreement with a pledge of consultation might well give rise to a moral obligation to provide assistance.

The intelligence from London confirmed that Grey had advised the Russian Foreign Minister in May 1914 that Britain had no objections to an agreement between the Russian and British Admiralties along the lines of the exchange between himself and Cambon. In Berlin this was bound to create fears that Germany would henceforth be confronted not only with even closer Anglo-French solidarity than had been experienced in the two Morocco crises, but with the crushing superiority, at the outset of any conflict, of a united three-Power bloc. These fears were undoubtedly enhanced by information from the same London source that Sazonov was strongly pressing for further strengthening and elaboration of the so-called Triple Entente, and even for its conversion, if possible, into a new Triple Alliance.

Grey had firmly rejected the idea of an alliance and was fond of describing the 1912 agreement with France as non-political and having purely technical military functions; but it was no secret to the German Foreign Ministry that Russia by no means viewed the projected naval convention in that light. Benckendorff, the Russian Ambassador in London, assured his Foreign Minister that once it was concluded

> we shall, I believe, have attained our main goal, to put something tangible in the place of the basically theoretical and peaceful notions that have prevailed hitherto.... I question whether there could be any stronger guarantee of common military operations in wartime than the spirit of this Entente, as it now stands revealed, reinforced by the existing military agreements.

Sazonov himself was highly gratified at British willingness to begin negotiating an agreement between Russia and Britain without delay. In a 'top secret' letter of 28 May he told Benckendorff – and thus almost immediately the German government as well – that he not only welcomed the military opportunities opened up by the projected convention, but also attributed great importance to it in a general political sense.

> We view such an agreement as a major step forward in bringing Britain more closely into the Franco-Russian alliance and an effective means for deepening appreciation of common British and Russian interests. We are convinced that it will exert a favourable influence on all matters touching those common interests.

In Berlin these words were bound to be read as signalling an immediately impending power shift.

It goes without saying that the German Foreign Ministry tried at once to throw a spanner into the contemplated naval convention. The secret intentions of the British and Russian governments were publicised in the *Berliner Tageblatt* and the *Tag*, in the hope of mobilising anti-alliance forces in Britain against the Foreign Office. Grey himself was to be intimidated by the threat of incisive counter-measures; but little was achieved beyond a prompt Russian disavowal and a question in the House of Commons, which Grey, in Jagow's view, answered by somewhat tortuously denying the stories in the German Press. Theodor Wolff of the *Berliner Tageblatt* was further importuned by the German Foreign Ministry, which wired him not to allow himself to be swerved; but the main effort to dissuade the British government shifted to the diplomatic sphere.

On 15 June Jagow called on the British Ambassador, Goschen, opening the discussion with an apparently plausible piece of dissembling in respect of the main object of his visit, the naval convention. He 'confessed' that Sir Edward Grey's statement in the House of Commons had greatly relieved him and 'that his mind was now completely at rest'. This tactical trick was intended to make his further remarks appear in London, not as an immediate massive threat that would commit Germany and incisively compromise Anglo-German relations, but as no more than a plain-spoken diplomatic warning.

'If the rumour had been true,' Jagow went on, 'he thought the consequences would have been most serious. Anglo-German relations would have, of course, lost that pleasant cordiality which he was glad to say characterised them at the present moment, but an even worse result would have been that there would at once have been a revival of the armament fever in Germany.' In view of Germany's geographical situation, facing France and giant Russia 'virtually alone', the German navy, if following the conclusion of an Anglo-Russian naval convention it would now have to take into account the British fleet as well, would understandably demand every sacrifice to meet such an emergency. Jagow admitted that probably none of the Entente Powers really wanted to attack

Germany; but it must be borne in mind that more
aggressive political parties might quite quickly gain
the upper hand in both Russia and France. The following day, 16 June, choosing the same tactics, Bethmann-Hollweg put it more concretely. An Anglo-Russian naval convention, he said, would 'greatly encourage Russian and French chauvinism'.

This directive to Lichnowsky, the German Ambassador in London, drafted by the Chancellor himself,
was intended to confront Grey even more emphatically with the estimate of the situation obtruding itself
upon the German Foreign Ministry in May and June
1914, and to warn him equally emphatically against
pursuing a policy that could only serve to strengthen
the already 'bellicose tendencies of the Russian militarist party'. It was probably true that Russia did not
immediately plan war against Germany,

> though we are very much constrained to take into
> account, in our political dispositions, that of all of
> Europe's Great Powers Russia is the most likely to
> be inclined to run the risk of a military adven-
> ture. . . . On the other hand, one can scarcely blame
> Russia for wanting to be much better armed, so that
> in any new eruption of a Balkan crisis she can cut a
> stronger figure than the last time round. Whether it
> will come to a European conflagration in such an
> event will depend exclusively on the attitude of
> Germany and Britain.

War could be avoided only if both countries jointly
accepted the role of guarantors of peace in Europe.
'Otherwise the torch of war is likely to be lit by any
inconsequential conflict of interest between Russia
and Austria.'

The 'inconsequential conflict' that was here hypo-
thetically postulated was actually triggered off unexpectedly by the assassination in Sarajevo – at least it
was inconsequential at the outset. Barely two weeks
earlier the Chancellor, feeling that the foreign situation represented a growing threat to Germany, tested
the British Foreign Office for the last time. His pur-

pose was to establish whether Britain was still prepared, possibly at the expense of Entente interests, to preserve enough freedom of action to provide a politically feasible basis for a possible Anglo-German solidarity of interests. In the event of an Austro-Russian conflict in the Balkans, he said, neither Germany nor England would be prevented – the one by the Triple Alliance, the other by her Entente obligations – from presenting a common front in that part of the world as guarantors of peace in Europe 'so long as we pursue this goal from the beginning under a common design'. Bethmann-Hollweg emphasised the passage just quoted, suggesting that he was indeed looking for enduring and effective co-operation with Britain. At the same time he suggested that an Anglo-Russian naval agreement would ineluctably prejudice any joint Anglo-German action to guarantee peace. This threat, by contrast, already points clearly to the decision the Germans were to take in the July crisis, namely to sabotage in so far as possible British mediation and thus destroy one of the most important elements conducive to the preservation of peace among the Great Powers.

Sir Edward Grey continued to deny that an Anglo-Russian naval convention was in preparation and changed his tune only on 9 July when he admitted in general terms that talks had taken place from time to time among British, French and Russian naval and military authorities. In a political sense the British Foreign Secretary's insincerity weighed less heavily in the balance than the fact that the time turned out to be too short for talks between Berlin and London to eventuate on the substance of Bethmann-Hollweg's directive of 16 June. The Wilhelmstrasse probably discounted as mere cynicism or political naïveté Grey's repeated assurances that Britain, despite military talks and agreements with her Entente partners, always retained freedom of political action in the event of a conflict. In any event, the German Foreign Office was convinced that this response left no door open to an Anglo-German understanding as a basis for long-term security.

Grey was doubtless quite sincere in insisting that Britain's freedom of action in the field of foreign affairs was not seriously curtailed, but his interpretation was also doubtless too narrow. Clinging to the literal text of the written agreements, he was underestimating the political substance and thus the crucial effect of both the actual military convention with France and the proposed naval agreement with Russia. He never fully appreciated the German concern that the growth of the Entente heralded a significant power shift in Germany's disfavour. Grey's artful foreign policy structure, seeking a compromise between isolationism and a policy of alliances in order to gain the advantages of both at the same time, was too unstable to vouchsafe an enduring political balance of power in Europe. The fact that the Russian Foreign Minister Sazonov was able, in June 1914, to exploit the British dilemma in the direction of persuading the British Foreign Office to adopt a more conciliatory attitude and to speed up negotiations on a naval pact is concrete evidence that the Ententes had only provisional character. A point had been reached at which Grey, in the interests of the security of the British Empire, could no longer close his mind to the political advantages of the alliance Russia was so generously offering. It must remain a moot point whether he was in any position, during the few remaining unquiet weeks before the outbreak of the war, to admit to himself the full gravity of the step he had taken, a step that heralded nothing less than the collapse of his whole foreign policy approach. Beyond doubt, however, it was no mere cynical gesture when he asked the Russian Ambassador on 8 July to see to it that the Russian government did everything in its power to reassure Germany and advise her that the naval talks held no threat to the Reich. This was part of a sincere endeavour to sustain German willingness to co-operate in the maintenance of peace, even at a critical juncture; but it does suggest that the main reason why Grey failed to comprehend Bethmann-Hollweg's concern was that he overestimated his own freedom of action in matters of foreign policy, under the impact of the rapidly rising Russian power potential and the increasing dynamism of Tsarist foreign policy.

It is true that German naval policy had from the beginning scarcely left the British Foreign Office any reasonable alternative to setting its sights for an entente. Hence any efforts aimed at a more or less close political alliance between Britain and Germany were bound to lack credibility in advance. Bethmann-Hollweg understandably viewed Tirpitz as the man chiefly responsible for the failure to reach an understanding with Britain, and thus for the quandary that ultimately, in July 1914, persuaded him that he must withdraw Germany's prior willingness to preserve the peace by a common effort, as had been done during the Balkan wars. The Chancellor did not believe that the way out of the political dilemma, in which Germany's *de facto* isolation seemed to be foreshadowed, lay in bilateral negotiations with Britain over local problems, even when such problems were of some importance. Actually, an acceptable agreement on the Baghdad Railway question had almost been reached and talks about the Portuguese colonies were proceeding satisfactorily; but on 6 June 1914 Bethmann-Hollweg told Ernst Bassermann, leader of the National Liberal Party, that relations with Britain had not improved of late. News about the Anglo-Russian naval convention was bound to revive painful memories in the Chancellor. As the price for British friendship, Germany would have had to forgo building a powerful navy of her own. 'It would be idle today,' he said, 'to consider whether we might have found this possible.'

In the face of a situation judged as growing more and more dangerous for Germany, Bethmann-Hollweg, as has already been said, also lacked the patience for the still feasible policy of settling conflicts of interest by direct negotiation. Yet after the news of the impending Anglo-Russian naval convention Germany seemed farther removed than ever from the readjustment of existing power groupings which she regarded as necessary. On the contrary, that very threat made such a readjustment more and more unlikely, especially with Russia growing stronger day by day. It was this conclusion that ultimately provided the impetus for the German decisions taken in the July crisis.

Ever since it had had knowledge of the Grey–Cambon exchange of 1912 and of the putative substance of the projected Anglo-French naval pact, the German Foreign Ministry had counted on Britain entering any war that might break out between Germany and the Franco-Russian Dual Alliance – though, understandably, it still hoped that in the end Britain might remain neutral. On 6 July, when by his assent he gave constitutional sanction to the 'blank cheque' to Austria, Bethmann-Hollweg had a long evening talk with Kurt Riezler on German foreign policy in which, significantly enough, he emphasised the grave implications of the looming agreement between Russia and Britain. 'Secret intelligence about the Anglo-Russian naval negotiations raises the serious prospect that in the event of war the British might try for a landing in Pomerania.' Within the frame of reference of Germany's political 'encirclement', which he felt to be more and more menacing, the Chancellor regarded the new naval agreement as 'the last link in the chain'. These developments weighed heavily in the balance for Bethmann-Hollweg, especially since Russia was growing stronger and stronger while Germany's only dependable ally, Austria, was growing weaker, almost certainly incapable of taking the field for the German cause, as he put it. 'The Entente is quite aware that we are as a result completely paralysed.'

Two quite separate but mutually reinforcing elements thus influenced the German view of the situation: Anglo-Russian relations and the growing military strength of the Tsarist Empire; and to the Chancellor they signalled an intolerable threat to German power, the beginning of an existential crisis. It was at this precise juncture, when his fears had solidified into an utterly devastating impression, that

the assassination in Sarajevo set off another Austro-
Serbian conflict.

The assassination did indeed signal an immediate
threat to the freedom of action of the Central Powers
in south-east Europe, both in the political and economic spheres. The Greater Serbian and Pan-Slav
nationalist movement not only laid claim to the Serbs,
Croats and Slovenes within the Habsburg Empire but
also served as an outpost of Russian Pan-Slavism,
which used it as an ideological pretext for Russian
expansionism. Serbia was the cornerstone of a political
structure which Russian diplomacy was trying to put
together, under Russian leadership but with French
assistance. From the minutes of a Cabinet meeting
that took place in St Petersburg on 21 February 1914,
we learn that this policy was deemed to be essential
against the possibility that it might become necessary
to seize the Straits in the near future. As Foreign
Minister Jagow put it on 18 July 1914, indirectly
Germany too could not allow Russian dominance in
the Balkans to become thoroughly stabilised.

It was in the face of this threatening shift in the
balance of power against the Central Powers that
Austria, on 5–6 July, got assurances of German backing
for a war against Serbia. Certainly much more was envisaged than a mere punitive expedition in retaliation
for the assassination, as shown by the aims enumerated in a handwritten letter by Emperor Franz-Joseph
to the Kaiser. Serbia was to be isolated and reduced in
size and eliminated as a fulcrum of Pan-Slav policy
and as a political power factor in the Balkans; and
before the day in point, 6 July, had drawn to a close,
Bethmann-Hollweg had given his associate Kurt Riezler some notes showing that as far as the Chancellor's
intimate circle was concerned Germany's 'blank
cheque' was intended to be more than a response to
Austria's chronic difficulties, rendered more acute by
the assassination of 28 June. It was a reaction to the
precarious developments within the European constellation which the Chancellor had been watching with
growing concern since May.

The Kaiser and Bethmann-Hollweg expressly stated

that Germany's blank cheque would apply even if
Russia intervened in the war against Serbia, i.e. if
there were 'serious European complications'. In making these pledges the Chancellor was well aware that
such a policy represented a naked challenge to Russia.
Yet what he had written to Berchtold in February
1913 was truer than ever, in view of Russia's growing
military strength and self-confidence. Because of its
traditional ties to the Balkan states, Russia would find
it virtually impossible to stand by idly if Austria com-
menced hostilities against Serbia. To do nothing
would risk an immense loss in prestige. Bethmann-
Hollweg was not engaging in empty dramatics when
he confided to Riezler on 6 July that in his view any
action against Serbia might well lead to a world war.

By taking advantage of the Austro-Serbian conflict,
the German Foreign Ministry placed the Tsarist Empire in a serious predicament. Unless Austria was re-
strained, Russia would either have to capitulate or use
its military might to counter the challenge by the
Central Powers represented by the threatened subjugation of Serbia. Bethmann-Hollweg calculated that
even if Russia shrank back and war was avoided,
Germany might score a political success, in that the
Entente might be disrupted. Riezler noted in his diary
on 6 July 1914: 'Should there be no war – i.e. if the
Tsar does not want war or a frightened France advises
him to keep the peace – we would still stand a chance of
manœuvring the Entente apart over such an action.'

Indeed, the Foreign Ministry, at the Chancellor's behest, tried hard to move things in this direction. For
one thing, Bethmann-Hollweg gave orders from
Hohenfinow that for the ensuing weeks the German
Press should as much as possible avoid any anti-French
animus; and the German Embassy in Paris was instructed to promote a policy of non-intervention in
the Serbian question in the French Press. By 16 July
the Chancellor actually struck an optimistic note. 'We
have reason to assume and certainly must hope,' he
wrote Count Rödern, Secretary of State for Alsace-
Lorraine in a private letter (actually drafted by
Riezler), 'that France, currently weighed down with

problems, will do all it can to keep Russia from inter-
vening. If we succeed in keeping France itself quiet,
let alone in getting the French to exhort St Petersburg
to keep the peace, this would be bound to have an
effect on the Franco-Russian alliance favourable to
us.'

When Vienna's rejection of the Serbian reply note
made it clear beyond any doubt that this design had
not succeeded – in other words, that no wedge could
be driven between the two allies by prevailing on
France to restrain Russia – Bethmann-Hollweg un-
hesitatingly got set for the alternative solution to the
crisis, war. Russia on its part showed from 26 July on
that it was totally unwilling to tolerate any Austrian
occupation of Serbian territory.

Austria in turn was resolved not to be deterred from
invading Serbia, even in the face of Russian military
pressure; and it was at this juncture that the German
leadership insisted on maintaining its challenge to
Russia, by consistently boycotting British mediation
efforts and obstinately refusing to engage in any
serious effort to restrain Austria from military action.
Even the Kaiser was outmanœuvred when he accepted
the Serbian reply note in principle and concluded
that there was no further reason for war. The Foreign
Ministry then found pretexts for the assertion that the
Tsarist Empire would have to accept full responsibility if a general war grew out of a conflict between
Vienna and Belgrade that might have been originally
localised.

The Chancellor unswervingly stuck to his design,
even in the face of pressure from the military; until
Russia took the expected and crucial step of ordering
general mobilisation. It was that step, and that step
alone, to which Bethmann-Hollweg looked for support,
especially before German public opinion, for the theory
of 'surprise attack'. This was to justify, at home and
abroad, German mobilisation as a necessary response.

In February 1918 Bethmann-Hollweg had a confidential talk with Conrad Haussmann, a Reichstag
Deputy of the Progressive People's Party. In the course
of this discussion, speaking of German policy at the

outbreak of the war, he admitted that Germany
shared the blame to a considerable extent. When
Haussmann challenged him directly, he went even
further. 'Heavens, yes,' he said, 'in a certain sense it
was a preventive war.' In close correspondence with
the motives we have tried to lay bare, he gave the
reasons that had helped persuade him to risk a
preventive strike. There was, first of all, the military
judgement that two years thence Germany would
have not been able to stand up to a war that was
bound to come sooner or later. Less directly, he hinted
at the conclusion that there was no longer any hope of
realising a politically durable understanding with
Britain. In the face of these developments in power
politics, the Chancellor felt that even July 1914 could
no longer be regarded as the best timing for a passage
at arms, as the Foreign Ministry opportunistically kept
insisting to Austria, in order to encourage that
country to move against Serbia. It was merely the
'least unfavourable time'.

By getting Russia to declare general mobilisation,
which meant taking the first and almost irrevocable
step towards world war, Bethmann-Hollweg and his
closest associates at the top succeeded in overcoming
the internal conflicts within a badly divided Germany.
It was Bethmann-Hollweg – with the help of three or
four intimates in the Foreign Ministry – who set the
course of German policy in the July crisis. He did so
both in actual fact and in the constitutional sense. It
is true that he needed the Kaiser's consent, but under
the constitution he and not the Kaiser was responsible
for German policy. Overcoming social and political
counterforces, Bethmann-Hollweg did manage to influence, indeed to change the course of history in a
unique way that will probably never be repeated.
This was an event that is of outstanding interest to
scholars and historians, amply justifying and even
demanding that his plans and calculations, and the
motives behind them, be fully described and analysed.

Thus he exploited the dynamism of a defensive war
that seemed to have been forced upon Germany – 'for
when that happens the whole nation will sense the

danger and rise as one man'. He was convinced that only if this happened would there be a chance of victory. There is a curious contradiction here, however, since he was equally certain that 'war will destroy the world as we know it' – the very argument he had used against the critics of his foreign policy in the years before. In the light of this unresolved discrepancy between the unanswerable case for a preventive strike, fuelled by the hope that a nation united in struggle could achieve victory, and fear of cultural decadence and political revolution, Bethmann-Hollweg's option for war appears as the result of a classical conflict rather than of a hard-headed Imperialist calculation – a 'leap into the dark, into this gravest duty', as he himself characterised it in mid-July 1914.

Considered on its own, the decision identifies the Chancellor as a statesman whose views on Germany's destiny did not materially differ from the general national consensus. He opted for war as a means for preserving Germany's power and status as a Great Power, with rights equal to those of other Great Powers, thus falling in with the indisputable expectations of the 'Fatherland', which would have rejected as traitorous and dishonourable any failure to resort to this ultimate recourse. Bethmann-Hollweg was convinced that he was not responsible for the dilemma into which an ill-starred and aimless foreign policy had manœuvred Germany in the summer of 1914; but he had no alternative to offer – except his fear that his successor would be even worse than his predecessor.

Two critical questions of fundamental importance may be directed to these ideas and this policy. First, how can this obsession with the maintenance of Germany's status as a Great Power and consequent freedom of action in the pursuit of isolated 'interests' be reconciled with the risks of a great European war that was likely to include Britain? And second, what persuaded the leading group centred on Bethmann-Hollweg that Germany could successfully wage war even against a Grand Coalition?

Both these questions will be examined in the following for the early months of the war, when the

realities of world war invalidated the very premises
and foundations of pre-war political notions and
categories, which nevertheless continued to serve as
the criteria for assessing the situation.

Bethmann-Hollweg on the Origins of the War

The moral issue of blame and responsibility for the
outbreak of the war has profoundly preoccupied the
European public as well as historians. Even when
there is a disposition to picture German policy in
terms of value standards that differ from those of the
actors in the events, the question at issue may be usefully explored in an effort to gain a perspective of the
historical problem concerned with the limitations
of contemporary political outlook and to mark the
frontiers beyond which freedom of action ceases. We
are in a fortunate position in this respect, since the
'philosopher of Hohenfinow' (Bethmann-Hollweg) repeatedly and self-critically revealed the basic outlines
of his policy, reproaching both himself and the Cabinets of Europe for the narrowness of their views on
the political world order. This happened in the first
instance in a long letter of 17 January 1918, addressed
to Prince Max of Baden, whom Bethmann-Hollweg
counselled on whether and in what circumstances he
should accept a summons to the Chancellorship. At
the time, January 1918, Germany seemed to have once
more regained the military initiative by the peace
negotiations at Brest-Litovsk; President Wilson was
proclaiming new ideas for a democratic world order
in his Fourteen Points; and mass strikes in Austria-
Hungary (14–20 January) gave another hint of the revolutionary repercussions of the war.

Bethmann-Hollweg advised the Prince not to allow
himself to be worn down in the struggle with the
military powers, but to take over the affairs of state
only at the moment of 'great crisis', when the situation
at home and abroad had reached the acute stage.

Against this contingency – the stage just before defeat and revolution, when the power of the Supreme

Army Command (*Oberste Heeresleitung* – O.H.L.)
would have been weakened – Bethmann-Hollweg developed the basic outlines of his political *Weltanschauung*, intended as a testament for his successor.

The experience of the World War formed the point
of departure for his reflection:

> Ever since I have been no more than a spectator, I
> am gripped day by day more deeply than before by
> the awesome grandeur of what we have undergone,
> by the sublime splendour of man's heroism and the
> sombre depth of his delusions, through which we
> are passing. This, the most stupendous revolution
> ever to shake the globe, cannot end, the nations can-
> not 'atone' before God and the world for all the
> horror they have done, unless mankind turns away
> resolutely from the conditions that conjured up this
> war and seeks to create something new in their
> place.

In the light of this ethically and politically radical
view, Bethmann-Hollweg deplored profoundly as
untrue the excuse put forward by Chancellor
Michaelis, namely that the war had been 'caused by a
conjunction of unfortunate circumstances'. The real
causes were 'Imperialism, nationalism and economic
materialism, which in broad outline have governed
the policies of all the nations during the past generation', setting goals 'that could be pursued by each nation
only at the cost of a general collision'.

In this letter to Prince Max of Baden, Bethmann-
Hollweg was still putting his main emphasis on 'a
general disposition towards war in the world ... how
else explain the senseless and impassioned zeal which
allowed countries like Italy, Rumania and even
America, not originally involved in the war, no rest
until they too had immersed themselves in the bloodbath?' Charging himself and other pre-war politicians
with having accepted war rather than working for
peace, the Chancellor justified the peace policy of the
Social Democratic Party (S.P.D.): 'Many had more or
less of an inkling of this development; but basically

only the Social Democrats openly pointed towards it,
and only they worked against the war with conviction.
The other parties fell more or less under the spell of
Imperialism.' He demanded that the consequences be
drawn and that 'government should be in greater
agreement with the true will of the people'.

Political trends, as he saw it, would even so power-
fully tend in that direction, even at the cost of revolution.

> So great is the force of this challenge, and so
> widely will the ethical ideas on which it rests spread
> after this bloodbath, that it is bound to prevail,
> even against the will of the chauvinists and re-
> actionaries who will survive, though their future
> power will dwindle in the precise degree of their
> present savage demeanour. I am utterly convinced
> that this will happen, the more so since peace is un-
> likely to come until the war-weary masses will force
> it in one way or another and since these very masses
> will discern the full burdens and dimensions of the
> war only after peace has been concluded.

This may not reflect with complete authenticity
what were the Chancellor's thoughts and ideas in
1914, but nevertheless it can be shown to bear a close
relation to the issue of greatest relevance to our further presentation. In 1914 as in 1918 the Chancellor
thought himself free of any passion for war, and he
rejected the view that governments – more specifically
the German government – were responsible for the
hatred that developed among the nations of Europe.
It was precisely these passions and these hatreds that
destroyed all his political calculations, and he was
gripped by the 'awesome grandeur' of shining heroism
and the 'sombre depth of human delusions', even
though or precisely because he had foreseen and
feared the possibility of the war bringing about revolutionary change.

In his *Betrachtungen zum Weltkriege* Bethmann-
Hollweg, as a contribution to a historical understanding of his policies, analysed the limitations of his political ideas more unambiguously than in the references

to a general disposition towards war that are found in his letter to Prince Max of Baden. For himself and his critics he tried to answer the question why German policy had not been so conducted as to avoid a confrontation with the 'fateful question' in the first place. It seemed to him, he said, that 'there is a widespread overestimate of the degree of freedom of decision left to us in the last decade. Germany too was not immune to the dreams of power that dominated the world.' He felt that one must:

> face the brutal fact that Cabinet policy was not determined by great humanitarian ideals and accept that statesmanship can and desires to do no more than allow the realisation of its aspirations to be dependent on the fortunes of war.... Politics had simply not yet won its way to the conviction that changing world conditions compelled the nations to revise their attitude to war. Ignoring the fact that in the existing power constellation any major shift among the Great Powers of Europe was bound to involve the whole world, those Powers had their eyes fixed only on the growth of their own power. By common tradition, moreover, war was not only the appropriate expression of national power but believed to carry the power of moral regeneration. These ideas continued to proliferate despite the fact that total mobilisation of whole nations and the sinister inventions of science had turned what was once a chivalrous test of strength into insensate butchery, bound in the long run to destroy all moral feeling. Cabinets simply did not accept any collective responsibility for all mankind.

Despite these admissions, which bear the stamp of the bitter experiences of the World War, and represent a considerable measure of public self-criticism and basically betoken a political and moral deference to new forces, Bethmann-Hollweg continued to justify his policies *in toto* in his memoirs. 'To take the view that Russia could not possibly have tolerated frustration of her Balkan plans' and that this was foreseeable; and that Germany 'therefore should not have supported Austria in her aggressive actions against Serbia, would have meant to accept self-emasculation for Germany'. To have accepted the disintegration of Austria-Hungary would have placed Germany in a state of dependency on Russia. The Russians, he wrote, mindful of the absolute dominance Nicholas I had exercised over a recalcitrant Germany, could then have 'set the day at their pleasure when they might see fit to expunge Germany from the circle of Great Powers'. Such a 'capitulation' had seemed to him impossible.

The force with which this 'Great Power' concept had manifested itself as a basic value and premise of the political universe, independent of everyday political pragmatism, is shown by the fact that precisely in the context of such searching reflections there should have been a reaffirmation of a policy based on self-interest for the preservation of Great-Power status, together with a rejection of such essential limitations as 'self-emasculation' and 'capitulation'.

On 23 July 1914, during the impassioned debate on the German goal of enhancing Austria's status as a Great Power, Prince Lichnowsky, taking a pragmatic oppositional stand, had asked Jagow: 'What would you say if Britain or Russia were to encourage the French to revitalise their badly depleted prestige by engaging in a dynamic and dangerous foreign policy?' Once again this question documents the fact that there was no possible reconciliation between a formal approach based on the principle of all or nothing and the requirements of pragmatic politics. After the fact, Bethmann-Hollweg viewed this essential limitation in German political thinking as a basic fault, especially in his policy towards Britain: 'We considered only ways of dealing with immediate issues, ignoring the impending changes in the international power structure.' Germany was in peril and he lacked the necessary patience to unravel the larger issues.

Ideas of Limited Warfare

From the limitations in political thinking, distilled from the German Chancellor's interpretation, important perspectives may be gained for the question: On the basis of what ideas and calculations could a war against a continental and even more a Grand Coalition seem acceptable, despite full insight into the ramifications of European power politics? Was there the firm expectation that the war would have to be fought to the bitter end, that is until there would be no further military resistance from the Russian giant and from Britain, protected by her navy and the seas?

Discussion of this crucial problem has left no trace, either in the diplomatic exchanges of the July crisis or in Bethmann-Hollweg's confidential talks with Riezler. Every ounce of attention and energy was preempted by the primary tactical task of steering the developing crisis in such a way that the war guilt should fall on Russia. Yet the decision in favour of this course of action was not an act of sheer desperation, despite what he felt to be an extremely grave emergency; and with all his agitation over the immensity of the risk of a European conflagration, Bethmann-Hollweg did tacitly assume that there was a chance of military success. Hence it may be taken for granted that he had a more or less clear idea where this chance lay.

The burden of our case, which we shall find confirmed in the ensuing account of German policy and strategy following the outbreak of war and the reactions to its military and political realities, is that Bethmann-Hollweg sought the military confrontation for the attainment of a defensive goal, the preservation of Germany's status as a Great Power. He was not after a struggle for world dominion and was not, therefore, interested in fighting the war to the total military defeat of the enemy. True, Berlin did realise that a war among the Great Powers might seriously shake the balance of Europe, ultimately replacing it and its self-regulating power mechanism with the alto-

gether different law-enforcement system of predominance by military victory; but it was hoped that successful advances by the German armies in the early phases
of a war would serve to bring about an effective corrective to the pre-war shift of power, which was felt to
be such a grave threat; and again that Germany's
enemies, fearful of a war for predominance with its
incalculable consequences to the tested balance of
power structure, would shrink from pursuing any war
to the bitter end. Such a war, limited in purpose and
intensity, was accounted the ultimate permissible political weapon.

   This rational approach to war exerted its influence
particularly on the evaluation of Britain's possible
role in a military confrontation. Even the last-minute
offer of 29 July – or rather Bethmann-Hollweg's
spontaneous reaction to the no longer expected and
supposedly trustworthy news that Britain would remain neutral after all, for a price Germany would be
glad to pay – must be seen from this point of view.
Britain was to be reassured on the extent of German
ambitions and persuaded that her entry into the war
was unnecessary, since Germany was prepared to
respect the main British concern, maintenance of the
balance of Europe. This was to be achieved by preserving France's integrity as a Great Power, respecting
Dutch neutrality, renouncing control over Belgium
after completion of military passage through that
country, and afterwards establishing an Anglo-German
condominium over Europe.

   The German Foreign Ministry had reason to anticipate that British neutrality would impose a severe
strain on the Entente and possibly even call its continuance after the war into question – which would
have meant an incisive shift of power in Germany's
favour; but given British assurances of neutrality,
Germany was basically prepared, on the very eve of
the war, to forgo one of the most essential belligerent
rights, the right of a free hand in concluding peace.
Even though this would have been done only for the
quid pro quo of British neutrality, it represented an
unusually sweeping concession within the framework

of traditional Great Power thinking; and it becomes understandable only in the light of a German intention not to use the war to achieve a position of predominance. The idea was that Britain would, however, accept changes in the *status quo* short of the achievement of such a position.

There was a basic error in this type of mechanistic thinking. A guarantee given by a Power, to the effect that it will voluntarily maintain a balance of power in the event it is victorious, represents a contradiction in itself. Only the self-regulating mechanism of a balance of power itself – or so it was generally felt – could offer a sufficient guarantee, certainly not avowals of self-imposed moderation, no matter how sincere, backed only by the word of a Cabinet. It is questionable whether the Germans and the British meant the same thing when they spoke of a balance of power; nor was there any reason for a tacit assumption that they could without difficulty reach agreement on a model of a balance of power that would satisfactorily meet the interests of both countries.

The Chancellor, following the brief interlude on 29 July, regretfully saw his expectations confirmed by Britain's entry into the war. He was not disconcerted, however, for he thought that the successful early border battles might offer the British impressive evidence of German power; and he hoped further that this shift in power would persuade Britain to acknowledge the German successes, pragmatically honouring them by assenting to limited corrections in the pre-war distribution of power. The basic criticism of the notion of a limited war in which Britain would remain neutral, as set forth above, can now be stated in more concrete terms as it is applied to a war that included Britain. It was quite unrealistic to expect that any power shift in favour of Germany and satisfying her need for security as a Great Power would have been, no matter what its nature, compatible with the British concept of a balance of power. Except possibly in the unlikely case of a political and military *rapprochement* between the two nations – which would indeed have had an almost revolutionary effect on the

distribution of power in Europe, Bethmann-Hollweg
would have been theoretically in a position to prevent the British Foreign Office from viewing any
German-engineered change in the *status quo* on principle as heralding the danger of German predominance on the Continent.

What ultimately crushed Bethmann-Hollweg's hopes
for a limited war was the realisation that Britain had
always been predisposed to regard any such military
confrontation as a war for predominance; and this
brought to the fore his earlier pessimistic intimations
that the war would bring on a complete upheaval of the
existing order. Both the Chancellor and Kurt Riezler –
according to his testimony of October 1915 – began
to fear that 'Britain's tragic error was forcing us to
strain our every resource, involving us in world-wide
problems, compelling us to reach for world power
against our will'. As long ago as 1948 Ludwig Dehio, a
German historian, classes the great war between the two
power blocs among the European struggles for predominance; and indeed, the British determination to force
Germany to her knees did objectively turn the war into
such a struggle on the Napoleonic model. In the final
days of August and the first week of September 1914,
this realisation crucially changed Bethmann-Hollweg's
judgement of the war situation and of the likelihood
that the war would secure German power in the peace
settlement to come. The responsibility which he accepted with his decisions in the July crisis is defined by
the fact that even then and before he was far from blind
to the possible danger that the war might tend in such
a direction. Still, what seems to have made it easier for
him to accept that responsibility was the hope that the
course of the war might remain subject to rational
Cabinet control rather than governments being swept
into a merciless war of annihilation by popular hatreds.
Yet here lay the real risk of his policy in the July crisis,
as he well knew.

Bethmann-Hollweg and those in the leadership who
thought like him were free of what Dehio calls *hege-
moniale Dämonisierung*, the demoniac drift towards a
struggle for predominance, already latently effective

in peacetime, but celebrating its triumph only in war. Throughout the war they were constrained to sober judgement and avoidance of self-deception by fear of the threat to the German leadership from defeat and a realisation that German power was severely limited by the general political situation, German dependence on the world market and Britain's ability to impose a blockade. Hence the Chancellor deeply deplored the brazen braggadocio of most German politicians, to say nothing of the great mass of the people, who from August 1914 onward indulged themselves in ecstatic dreams of vast German annexations that would indeed establish *Deutschland über Alles*. Yet Bethmann-Hollweg himself, to unite the people, had seen fit to make a plausible case for the myth of 'unprovoked enemy attack' in the July crisis, thus contributing his share in letting loose powerful aggressive impulses and lending a veneer of moral justification to any and all demands to be imposed on the 'ruthless' enemy. During the war he wanted to replace these dangerous illusions with hard-headed confidence in victory, by enlightening the people on the actual distribution of power and the prospects for the future as he saw them; but he no longer found himself able to accomplish this. Indeed, to buttress his own position at home, Bethmann-Hollweg repeatedly had to pay hostages to the people's unrealistic dreams of victory and to the hate-inspired annexationists. The German government was probably in a worse position than the Entente Cabinets to put into effect the German Chancellor's goal that belligerents must retain sufficient freedom of action to make pragmatic decisions at any time on the question of ending the war.

Unexpected Decay of International Law

In the narrower sense the war as an instrument of diplomacy seemed no more than an interlude rather than an incisively new element. When it was over, traditional Great-Power politics would be resumed, under circumstances more favourable to German

ambitions. The Germans certainly expected that during and after the war the traditional European community of nations, governed by international law,
would survive and continue its unrestrained jockeying
for power. Such, at least, were the views held by the
leading government officials, inured to orderly and
legalistic thinking. They included the Chancellor
himself and his deputy, the Minister of the Interior,
Delbrück.

The formal declarations of war, the public admis-
sion that the invasion of Belgium represented a
breach of international law for which restitution was
pledged, must be viewed in this light. In the face of
the military contingencies forced upon Germany by
her central position and of the resultant violations of
international law, they were efforts to keep the war
from getting out of control, to keep it under the
thumb of Cabinet policy. Behind all this there was
also the notion that the situation was quite exceptional, arising only because Germany was threatened
by a Grand Coalition. This notion clearly betokens
the completely self-centred thinking that then prevailed in Germany. The Germans simply could not
see themselves as a threat to other Powers.

The German political authorities were zealous in
their observance of the Hague Convention, especially
the protection of private property, and they resolutely
set their face against precipitate action. In consequence they were particularly dismayed and disappointed by the quick decay of international law in the
private sector. In choosing her economic weapons,
Britain went far beyond prevailing notions of international law in her interference with private rights.

For example, all debts owed by British subjects to
citizens of the Central Powers were declared null and
void and their payment was treated as treason. Legal
protection before British courts was revoked, even in
the case of prize courts, an institution created specifically for wartime purposes. Even neutrals were no
longer able to cash notes bearing a German endorse-
ment. British joint-stock companies were forbidden to
pay dividends to enemy aliens, and this applied even

to neutral concerns in Britain. German enterprises were forced into liquidation and the yield was applied to obligations owed to British subjects. German patents were declared invalid, prompting the President of the Reichsbank, Havenstein, to remark that 'the theft of intellectual property is now officially sanctioned and promoted'. For a while there was even a regulation under which Britons were forbidden to have any business contacts with neutral companies in which Germans had an interest.

All these measures confronted Bethmann-Hollweg with a new situation. They shook the very foundations of his political views of a war that would be curbed and directed by reasoned Cabinet policy and traditional European public morality. In a broader sense they also pulled the rug out from under his efforts to limit and localise the confrontation. After the war, under the impact of its revolutionary momentum, he concluded that 'the World War has utterly destroyed what we once regarded as public morality'.

The Hague Convention and the Example of Longwy–Briey

In this connection the treatment of the Longwy–Briey ore basin is highly instructive. Quite early on, this region entered into German annexationist planning against the day of peace; but Bethmann-Hollweg and his deputy rejected any intervention in its private ownership relations as a violation of the Hague Convention. When the Kaiser ordered the pits and smelters of Longwy–Briey seized, the Chancellor saw to it that the running of these works was suitably modified to bring it within the Hague Convention.

To this end the Chancellor, without consulting the Kaiser, made his own rules as he went along, putting them to the local officials – in this case the Governors of Metz and Lorraine – in the form of 'recommendations'. He promptly called to their attention that 'in the seizure of the French mines and steelworks decreed

by His Majesty the inviolability of private property
should be observed, as laid down under international
law by the Hague Convention'. What Bethmann-
Hollweg was doing was to exploit the military occupation of the ore basin, decreed by the Kaiser, for purposes of putting into effect his own ideas of politics
and international law. There was no appeal from the
Kaiser's order that Longwy and Briey were to be
administered as a single unit; but following protests
by the Reich Office of the Interior against the military
character of this administration, the Lorraine bureaucracy co-operated in bringing it under the jurisdiction
of that Office, which was an even more determined
upholder of national and international law.

The German industrialist Thyssen had an interest
in the Longwy–Briey mines, as did other German
steelmen; and to compensate for the loss of French
plants, he wanted authority to exploit the Longwy–
Briey pits during the war. To this end, he submitted
three separate petitions, on 21 and 28 August and 5
September, capping the campaign with a personal
visit to Headquarters some time between 9 and 12
September, made possible through the good offices of
the Centrist Deputy, Erzberger. All these efforts were
fruitless. Bethmann-Hollweg kept invoking the principle that private property was inviolable under international law in wartime. By manœuvring officialdom
in Prussia and Lorraine and taking advantage of fac-
tionalism within the steel and coal industries, he succeeded in isolating and frustrating Thyssen completely.

The Governor of Metz held a meeting with repre-
sentatives of the entire industry of the Lower Rhine,
Lorraine and the Saar region, to which Bethmann-
Hollweg dispatched his personal delegate, the envoy
Stumm. Against Thyssen's protests, it was there de-
cided 'that war-induced difficulties in importing
foreign iron ore did not justify exploitation of the
French pits on behalf of the German steel industry.
The view was held that existing stockpiles and the
German iron-ore mines in Lorraine and on the Lahn
river were entirely sufficient to meet greatly reduced

German needs during the war. The primary goal should be to put German pits back into operation.'

On the basis of the Chancellor's directives, the meeting worked out seizure methods that would not violate the rights of the French private owners. These measures amounted to no more than a kind of protective custody, to maintain the productive capacity of plant, by keeping the mines from becoming flooded, for example.

Bethmann-Hollweg instructed the Under-Secretary, Zimmermann, to investigate the claims against the French government put forward by such as Thyssen and Kirdorf and to see whether they might be considered at the peace table. 'It goes without saying,' he said, 'that the form of indemnification envisaged by Messrs Thyssen and Kirdorf is out of the question. . . . If the Briey region should fall to Germany at the peace table, it would certainly be desirable that the French pits and property-owners were expropriated, but in that event the German government would assume legal ownership, with the right to dispose of the properties.' Before doing so, Bethmann-Hollweg proposed to transfer the properties from French to German government ownership. Petitions and visits and even the acceptance of suggestions did not imply that the government was susceptible to influence. Government officials had considerable power and independence, and conflicting views among the industrialists concerned offered further scope for manœuvre. The government's financial interest in disposing of such properties should not be underestimated as a motive to the adoption of an independent policy.

This distinction between a wartime and a peacetime policy for the ore region of Longwy–Briey was more than merely a matter of sound administration, a tactical move on behalf of the government's financial interest as against that of private industry. This whole policy question and especially the Imperial seizure decree represented a major political event at the critical juncture from August to October 1914, touching the Chancellor's political strategy in an important point.

The Problem of Keeping the War within Diplomatic Bounds

The goal of this policy was to avoid prolonging the war by engaging in no more than the absolute minimum of military operations, since anything more than that was likely to institutionalise it and limit the scope for negotiation. The course of events was to be held at the diplomatic level of Cabinet policy, making possible the kind of pressure tactics that had proved successful in diplomatic crises. Military successes – rather than grand and final victory – were to lay the groundwork for what it was hoped would be a favourable issue to the great struggle. Prior to his departure for Headquarters the Chancellor, in his discussions with the Prussian Cabinet, avoided using the term 'victory' in a military sense, concluding with the hope that by the time of his return the German army and navy might have won peace on good terms. It was in line with such considerations that Bethmann-Hollweg laid down his policy in August 1914.

First, of course, came the deployment phase, together with a continuation of efforts initiated during the July crisis to gain diplomatic backing and the support of allies. Next it was necessary to await the great initial clash of the land armies, the resort to the 'fortunes of war'. These early battles would settle the basis for further political initiative – whether this was to be the defeat or outmanœuvring of the army, possibly followed by massive invasion; or whether the army might fight through to operational freedom and security from disastrous collapse, thus regaining scope for political action.

Actually, such security seemed to have been provided by the German victories in the border battles in Lorraine, 20–22 August, and then the great initial successes of the German flanking wing, reaching their climax between 24 and 27 August. In the East, on the other hand, the disastrous consequences that followed when the initiative was lost were brought home to the whole nation; but fortunately for Germany, Hindenburg's clear-cut victory at Tannenberg on 30 August 1914 brought significant relief.

Poland and the Question of Inducements for Italy

During the early months of the war relations with Russia and the closely associated Polish question were noted in only a general way on the German side, without receiving any methodical analysis. The problems of limiting and mastering the war in the West were very much to the fore. There was always a latent realisation that in one way or another Russian 'preponderance' represented a threat, but in these weeks the advocates of a German policy oriented towards the East remained in the background. During the ceaseless talks about the problems in the West, Jagow did repeatedly admonish that the East must not be neglected and that Russia would have to be pushed back and separated from Germany by several buffer States; but this stereotyped formula was about all, and nothing eventuated in practice. The whole Russian problem was simply postponed, with some general phrases, such as are to be found in the September Memorandum, for example.

Considerable signs of activity began to develop in this political vacuum, however, once the military had given the impetus. The idea of encouraging an insurrection in Poland and, in a somewhat contradictory way, throughout the Russian minority regions, was considered in its political and military implications, but turned out to be quite at odds with strategic border security and with the Polish policy in Germany's eastern provinces envisaged by conservative Prussian interests. Various official agencies busied themselves with such problems, in a totally unco-ordinated way, for example the Polish and Ukrainian Section of the Deputy General Staff; certain Foreign Ministry specialists disposed to use revolution as a political weapon; the conservative citadels within the Ministries of the Interior of both Prussia and the Reich; and lastly some of the regional authorities in the

eastern provinces. The idea of fomenting rebellion,
however, was never able to develop any political momentum, because it was outweighed by military fears
that such an effort might get out of control, and above
all because Austria was disinclined to use such a
double-edged sword.

The question of what would prove politically wise
and feasible in practice had to wait until the Russian
question once again asserted itself in political calculations. This took place in an effective way only when
German political and military strategy was re-
examined in November 1914 and underwent an eastward shift under the dual aspect of possibly seeking a
military decision or a separate peace in the East.

Even before then, however, both the German
government and the O.H.L. were compelled to take a
closer look at the Polish question, in the light of
political and military actualities. For all three embattled powers that had once partitioned Poland the
occupation of Polish territory by Germany and Austria posed immediate political problems that could
not be left entirely to a future peace settlement.
Directly after the outbreak of war Austria approached
Germany with a clear-cut request that the reorganisation of Poland be tackled even before Russia had been
decisively defeated. The aim was to prepare for the
integration of Russian Poland with Galicia by establishing an Austrian administration in even those
Polish areas occupied by German troops. Moltke and
Bethmann-Hollweg were opposed to freezing a political solution to the Polish problem so early in the war.
'Let us kill the bear before we divide his pelt,' they
said.

The German Ambassador in Vienna was directed to
explain that Germany could not immediately accept
the Austrian proposals, but would first have to
examine the question thoroughly. The matter was put
more plainly to Tschirschky personally. Germany
wished to use delaying tactics, he was told, to avoid
any premature conflict with Austria. Such Austrian
pretensions, the Chancellor added, were bound to
affect and even collide with German interests. The

fate of Poland would have to be left to later agreement. Bethmann-Hollweg was emphasising, in other words, that he was not currently concerned with the Polish question.

This rebuff did not banish the political claims of Austria from the official exchanges, for Vienna continued to put them forward; but the German Chancellor did manage to keep open all of his options for solving the Polish problem at some future date.

As early as August 1914 the whole Polish question, which Austria had raised, became linked to the broader question of limiting the war. This was when the idea of compensatory territorial gains was extended to Austro-Italian relations. The Germans saw a possibility, first set down in an exchange between Wahnschaffe and Rechenberg, that the so-called 'Austrian solution' of the Polish question – excluding north Poland, however – might offer a way of providing Austria with satisfactory compensation for the cession of South Tyrol to Italy, which seemed essential to ensure Italian neutrality. Although this was the primary goal, Germany herself was nevertheless unwilling to be left empty-handed in this general territorial bargaining. The dialogue between Wahnschaffe and Rechenberg went into more and more detail, including serious discussion of possible exchanges of Silesian territory on either side of the Austro-German border. Here was the beginning of what later on, when the question of Italian entry into the war on the enemy side grew critical, was called the 'Silesian offer'. The Prussian Cabinet then authorised Bethmann-Hollweg to cede parts of Silesia, conquered as long ago as Frederick the Great, to Austria, if that were necessary as a last resort to persuade that country to meet the Italian demands.

Rechenberg, former Consul-General in Warsaw and Governor of East Africa, expanded this whole elaborate structure of territorial swops into a broader political concept in his correspondence with Wahnschaffe, who was Bethmann-Hollweg's Under-Secretary at the Reich Chancellery. Since Germany, although she bore the main burden of the war, stood to gain only meagre

territorial increments in Polish and Austrian Silesia,
compared with the vastly greater gains that would fall
to Austria, Rechenberg, on 27 August, proposed that
this discrepancy be made up for by economic advantages. While forgoing territorial gains in the East, he
wrote, Germany would have to insist on compensatory
trading privileges. In so far as possible, Germany, Austria and Poland should become a single trade area.
This need not be done immediately, but should be
tackled when existing commercial agreements ran out.
The document in question was first presented at
Supreme Headquarters on 3 September. Bethmann-
Hollweg read it only on 11 September, although it
had been sent to him a second time two days earlier.

Here, then, we find one of the sources of the *Mitteleuropa* notion, later to blend with other sources, as
will be shown. It is noteworthy that this concept, relating more particularly to east-central Europe and
the idea of territorial compensation, was not based on
questions of economic structure. Rechenberg was thus
moving in the direction of the traditional notion of a
customs union, which had been mooted between
Prussia and Austria ever since the middle of the nineteenth century.

The Main Problem: Ending the War in the West

The core of Germany's problem in limiting the war
and keeping it under control was the strategy to be
pursued against France and Britain. Bethmann-Hollweg and Jagow had realised fully from the early days
of August 1914 on that Germany lacked the military
means for vanquishing Britain. The Chancellor
looked on the German navy even in wartime as no
more than a means of applying diplomatic pressure
against the peace negotiations to come. It had to be
conserved to that end and its losses must be mini-
mised. Bethmann-Hollweg never tired of making this
clear to the German naval authorities. As early as 6
August 1914 he told the Chief of the Admiralty that it
was 'absolutely necessary that we still have a large fleet

by the time peace is concluded'. To his mind the only
way of ending the war swiftly and in a way satisfactory
to Germany lay in limiting it. To achieve this three
things seemed to him necessary:

(1) Prompt strategic victory over the French armies
    in the field.
(2) French willingness to sign a separate peace after
    defeat, without fighting on to the bitter end.
(3) As a corollary, the Anglo-German confrontation
    must not be allowed to harden into a hopeless
    war situation by major combat action. A gentle-
    men's agreement between Britain and Germany
    on this point would be the prerequisite for what
    was hoped would be British realisation that their
    Empire stood to gain in power by virtue of Ger-
    man military successes. At the same time, this
    might form the beginning of a change in Anglo-
    German relations such as they were in the pre-
    war period.

Avoidance of a 'People's War' in France

Bethmann-Hollweg's first premise also underlay the
strategic concept of the German General Staff. Hopes
that it would be met had reached their climax by 27
August 1914, and remained high until the strategic retreat after the Battle of the Marne, despite increasing
doubts that the border battles would be sufficient.
Following consolidation of the German front in September, hopes soared again with the decision to launch
the offensive in Flanders on 18 October 1914; but
when the attack on Ypres bogged down and was
broken off a month later, the earlier hopes finally gave
way to the reasoned view of a stalemate in the West.
    Mindful of the complete military defeat of the
French army in 1870 and the capture of Paris, Bethmann-Hollweg was thoroughly aware that even the
greatest military successes were extremely doubtful
political assets. If they were to be fully exploited, they
had to be carefully buttressed in the political sphere.
    The military successes in the West must not be im-

perilled by a people's war in France and the refusal of
the French government to make peace. In the discussions among leading politicians during morning walks
and rides, and in the political consultations in the improvised Headquarters offices, first in Koblenz and
after 30 August in Luxemburg, there was frequent
mention of the possibility that the French army be
offered an alliance directly after its defeat and that
France be spared, so that she 'would fight on our side'.

This was a notion of the Kaiser's, among others,
which he discussed with Tirpitz, and which Tirpitz in
turn discussed with Bethmann-Hollweg, Jagow and
the Chief of the Admiralty, Pohl. Along similar lines,
the carving-up of Belgium and the apportionment to
France of Belgian industrial regions were discussed as
possible ways of compensating France for the contemplated annexation by Germany of French industrial
areas. In the brief time from 19 August to 27 August,
when the military situation began to change, such
considerations, however, never gave rise to a serious
plan, let alone a possible offer of negotiations to the
French government – even though Delbrück, the
Minister of the Interior, as late as 20 October did discuss this solution with Bethmann-Hollweg, as a way of
compensating France for the loss of Briey and Longwy
and relieving the Belgian situation.

More significant were Bethmann-Hollweg's consistent efforts not to provoke the French people, especially the propertied classes, to continue resistance to
Germany in the wake of further advances and the possible strategic defeat of the French army, which they
might be motivated to do by an open German threat
to private property, heralded by out-of-hand expro-
priations in Longwy–Briey. Such political motives are
apparent in the drafts of a proclamation to the French
people prepared by close associates of Bethmann-Hollweg.

These drafts were written at a relatively late date,
around 6 September 1914, and they also display quite
prominently, if not decisively, an element rather at
odds with the policy described, namely a claim to
north France as an operational base against Britain,

against the eventuality that the French government might refuse a separate understanding with Germany despite a strategic defeat; but while this new element overlies the older motivations, the idea of sparing and respecting France remained intact.

The three drafts are by Riezler, the Chancellor's secretary, Mutius, his cousin, and Radowitz, and their common point of departure is the statement that Germany actually regarded the current confrontation with France as unnecessary and regretted having been forced into it by the Triple Alliance's coalition policy. Even at the last moment Germany would have been willing to respect the integrity of French territory, had Britain offered a guarantee of French neutrality. All three drafts studiously avoid any offensive locutions or victorious crowing; and in two of them (by Mutius and Radowitz) the valour of the French armies is singled out for praise and German victory described as a chivalrous issue achieved with neither hate nor passion. There was to be not the slightest reflection on French honour, lest that provoke irrational consequences. Similarly, care was taken to avoid provoking a conflict between government and people, although there was mention of the French government's ambiguous attitude in this 'unnecessary' war and of its ties and its dependence, especially on Britain.

Clearly, what was to be avoided was the kind of loss of legitimate authority capable of negotiating peace that had caused Bismarck such trouble when the French Imperial government fell in 1870 – in fact anything causing domestic chaos that might in turn lead to a revolutionary people's war. The French government, after all, had already left the capital and withdrawn to Bordeaux. The Germans were preaching their own maxim that the foremost duty of citizens was to maintain law and order. A guarantee was given that the exactions of war and occupation would be kept to a minimum and the urgent request was voiced that 'everyone should quietly pursue his occupation and resume his work' (Riezler). Radowitz went furthest in concretising the Kaiser's 'order' to officers and men, who were asked to ensure normal economic life,

and he emphasised that private property would be in-
violate; but as against these pledges all three drafts
included a warning that all civilian resistance and
every hostile act would be answered with the utmost
severity. Another major limitation was that German
troops 'would have to stay as long as your allies continue the war and keep your leaders from concluding
a just peace with me' (Radowitz); or as Riezler put it
in an enlightening formulation, 'in holding the
northern part of your country under occupation, I
await the moment when Britain will permit your
government to make peace'.

Various possibilities of war and peace are discussed
and proposed side by side in the several drafts. They
display an uncertainty in political thinking that became more noticeable in the days between the original
German advance and the failure of the offensive on
the Marne, heralding a hesitant reorientation in ideas
of limited war as a political instrument, now that the
realities of war had begun to destroy the hopes enter-
tained during the July crisis and the early weeks of
August. This uncertainty is shown in Radowitz's contradictory formulation, already noted, to the effect
that the Germans would continue to hold French territory as long as the Allies wished to continue the war
and prevent the French government from concluding
peace with Wilhelm II. The first condition could relate only to a general peace, the second, on the other
hand, only to a prior separate peace. Riezler, however,
seemed to count on the French government remaining
largely paralysed because of its ties to Britain, despite
any generous proclamations the Germans might issue
on the occasion of victory. He thought that a state of
latent war, at least, would continue.

The British Interest in Peace Taken into Account on the German Side

In the light of Britain's growing ties with Russia and
France, Bethmann-Hollweg had feared British entry
into the war; but he could never bring himself to be-

lieve that Britain had good reason for such a step, which he viewed as incompatible with British interest in maintaining a balance of power. He concluded that Sir Edward Grey, the British Foreign Secretary, had not foreseen the extent of British entanglement. The step had therefore been taken against Britain's own interest, and questions of honour and other imponderables had played an important part in it.

He hoped accordingly that superior political wisdom would soon prevail, influencing Britain in the direction of seeking a way out of the war as fast as possible. When Prince Lichnowsky, the German Ambassador in London, arrived back home, his report to the Chancellor on 8 August 1914, ran along similar lines.

Bethmann-Hollweg felt that the most important piece of supporting evidence was the fact that the German armoured cruiser *Goeben* had managed to break out of the Strait of Messina despite enemy naval superiority. To attribute this *coup* to a blunder on the part of the British admiral in command seemed so unlikely that Bethmann-Hollweg and the German Chief of the Admiralty were inclined to conclude that Britain was unwilling to strike any 'heavy blows' against Germany.

To encourage this supposed policy, the Chancellor urged that no military action be initiated against Britain, despite the existing state of war. He opposed the sallies by light fleet units ordered by the Kaiser and sought to prevent not only the commitment of the battle fleet proper, but for the time being even the use of German U-boats against British troop transports in the Channel. The response from the Chief of the Admiralty, Pohl, was that even if the conjecture concerning the *Goeben* were correct, Germany could not simply 'cease waging war'.

Yet this was precisely what the Chancellor wanted. In a telephone conversation with Pohl, he tried again to enlist the admiral in his campaign to dissuade the Kaiser from the operational orders: 'My conscience leaves me no peace. Upon mature reflection I think it probable that Britain is holding back in order not to tip the balance in favour of prolonging the war. It would be extremely desirable if we followed suit, to afford an opportunity for Britain to bring about peace.' Pohl responded by citing the inexorable logic of war. The scheduled operations could not possibly be called off and such considerations must not be allowed to keep Germany from the vigorous pursuit of the war: 'It is Britain that has declared war on us and she must bear the consequences.' Pohl went on to point out that his influence and Bethmann-Hollweg's did not go beyond a certain point. Orders to limit hostilities could issue only from the Kaiser, and this could scarcely be achieved at this time. Despite his agitation, the Chancellor gave up. Matters would have to take their course, he said, since he himself could certainly not secure such orders from the Kaiser.

It was thus that Bethmann-Hollweg came face to face with the logic of war, with realities that could not be undone but 'must take their course'. Here were the sombre and incalculable forces that had thrown him into such turmoil when he had taken the seemingly unavoidable plunge into war in the July crisis, quite devoid of the exaltation that had then taken hold of the German people. Yet for a transitional period he still clung to his hopes and the concept based on them. He tried to 'freeze' the Anglo-German war and for the time being saw no need for contemplating effective new means in the war against a sea Power.

This attitude is betokened, for example, in his refusal to denounce British seizures of ships bound for Holland with cargoes of grain as flagrant violations of international law. Even more telling is the argument he used in a meeting with Tirpitz, Jagow and Pohl on 19 August, when Tirpitz proposed that as much territory as possible be occupied in the West, so that Germany might hold 'hostages' with which to exert political pressure on Britain. 'Even if we are successful in the West,' the Chancellor said, 'we shall presumably have to detach ourselves eastward at a later date, unless we were to abandon Austria. The occupation in France must be limited.' Tirpitz had his notes of this talk countersigned by Pohl and wished to use them to warn the Kaiser against Bethmann-Hollweg's 'misguided' policy towards Britain, but Admiral Müller, Chief of the Imperial Naval Cabinet, rejected such a private initiative as unconstitutional. Admiral Capelle, Under-Secretary in the Reich Naval Office, thought that direct representations to the Chancellor would be unwise, since Bethmann-Hollweg was likely to turn the issue into a jurisdictional dispute.

Tirpitz went back to the fray in another talk the next day. His immediate concern was the military and political defence of Tsingtao, threatened by a Japanese ultimatum. Jagow expressed doubts that Germany could vanquish Britain and said that the East and the Polish question must not be lost sight of and that a buffer State must be created to relieve the Russian pressure, while Bethmann-Hollweg considered whether a mutual assistance pact with France might be attainable. Tirpitz insisted that all such considerations must take second place. He was convinced that without *Lebensraum* overseas Germany would decline to the insignificant status of a land-locked nation. 'No matter how great our power on the Continent, without world stature our status as a World Power would be at an end. Commerce and industry, the essential sources of our economic power, would never recover.'

Close on the heels of the outbreak of war, Tirpitz was here giving an almost classic definition of the concept of world power (*Weltmacht*). The assertion of commerce and industry with their markets and raw-material sources, the maintenance or restoration of 'world stature' and the regeneration of 'World Power status', since an export-intensive Germany was dependent upon access to world markets – all these are used synonymously in Tirpitz's formulation. The war had destroyed Germany's world stature. As the Reichsbank President, Havenstein, had said and the Minister of the Interior, Delbrück, had foreseen even before the war, Germany had turned overnight into a closed mercantile State on the classic economic model.

A critical question is posed here: What was the feasible and possible course? Restoration of assured

access to world markets or, alternatively, the creation
of a great inland continental market? A particularly
knotty point was whether the interior market should
be built up only for the war period or for the time
afterwards as well; and a particular point of dispute
between Bethmann-Hollweg and Tirpitz was what
was meant by 'assured' access to world markets and
how it was to be achieved. In view of Germany's industrial structure, the ultimate basic decision was in
favour of the world market. At the same time, however, the factual situation exerted its ineluctable influence in the direction of building up the home
market for the war period. In these deliberations the
statesmen were more inclined to think within a long-
term context than the economic pragmatists, who were
concerned with the immediate future of their enterprises.

The Danger of Britain Taking a 'Hard' Line
(27 August 1914)

A week later, military events in the West forced Bethmann-Hollweg to re-examine his policy towards
Britain. His expectations that it might be possible to
limit the commitment dwindled day by day. By 27
August 1914 it had become clear that Britain had involved herself on the Continent with great momentum through the unforeseen fighting power of her
Expeditionary Force. By that day the conviction had
spread beyond the General Staff at Headquarters that
the successes of the third week of August had not
decided the campaign in a manner that could be
viewed as providing sufficient military and political
guarantees of German power in the time to come. By
means of a skilful strategic retreat, the enemy armies
had avoided encirclement without suffering critical
losses and demoralisation; and this meant that the
Germans would have to fight further battles and possibly undertake a protracted siege of Paris and the
time-consuming pacification of the country. This related most conspicuously to the British army, which

had prevented the crucial envelopment of the
northern flank.

That same day, again in discussion with Tirpitz,
Bethmann-Hollweg, still reiterating the commonplace
that 'the difficulties in concluding peace lie in
Britain', stated for the first time that 'British obstinacy
must not be underestimated' – on the contrary, 'it
must be put very high'. Hence 'anything we can do to
damage the British would be of the greatest importance'. Here is the essential point of a reorientation.

Tirpitz took advantage of the occasion to discuss a
possible threat to Britain from the direction of the
coast of northern France. He had already discussed
this with the Quartermaster-General; and in a talk
with Moltke, the Chief of the Admiralty, Pohl, had
developed 'far-reaching perspectives' in this connection, looking towards exerting pressure on Britain.
Bethmann-Hollweg allowed Tirpitz to outline the elements of his occupation plans, but as always in these
days put him on the defensive by reiterating a request
that the Suez Canal be blocked by ships. Tirpitz could
not promise such a thing, since it was 'technically difficult', and his militant stance thus lost plausibility.

Yet the discussion was a significant sign of a change
in course, based on the now evident fact that the British were resolved to fight to the limit; and henceforth
opinion began to change in the direction of coming to
grips with this new fact, although the older alternative continued to be a subject of discussion.

Political considerations concerned with the significance of the British policy of maintaining a balance of
power, however, were not the only element entering
into the controversy over the proper policy to be
adopted towards Britain; nor was the idea of exerting
political and strategic pressure by means of 'hostages'
and occupied territory. Bethmann-Hollweg's initial
hope that the Anglo-German war would 'swiftly roar
past, like a thunder-storm' was not based purely on
abstract political ideas; nor were German calculations
upset by the striking power of the British Expeditionary Force alone.

German Pre-war Concepts of Economic Warfare

Behind the whole dilemma stood a basic uncertainty
on the crucial question as to who was the principal
sufferer from the destruction of world-wide economic
ties. Was it Germany, which had lost her world
markets and international stature, but still had access
to a great interior market as well as to the neutral
nations of Europe? Or was it Britain, with all her sea-
lanes intact, but shut out from her most important
market, the European continent, having no sizeable
domestic market of her own, and far more dependent
on food imports?

Political considerations continued to be regarded as
critical; but there was the added economic calculation
that the war would end when economic interests required it. This aspect was emphasised especially by
those who thought primarily in economic terms, which
was expected to be the case in Britain. In Germany,
on the other hand, the economic balance-sheet was not
deemed to be a proper motivation for the German
government to break off the war.

These basic considerations, especially the comparative economic capacity of Britain and Germany in
wartime, were not discussed prior to the World War.
The economic consequences of war were studied only
in respect of the ability to stand up to it. The possibility that a war might have to be broken off because
it 'did not pay' was disregarded. There was a discussion of the general problem, under the heading of
'economic mobilisation', fostered at the beginning of
1912 by the Minister of the Interior, Delbrück, who
was impressed with the danger points in Europe, but
it never went beyond the theoretical stage. There was
a bitter jurisdictional quarrel until a decision of the
Chancellor forced the Minister of Finance to make
available funds from the general budget as of July
1915 for the purpose of at least compiling statistics on
food grains.

In a way the fact of the war was taken for granted
and political considerations of whether it could be end-

ed or have been avoided were submerged in the over-
lapping technical and ministerial consultations on
economic mobilisation. There were in fact certain
preparations on the financial side – for example the
provision of loan funds, to avoid a credit and economic squeeze when war broke out – but this work was
entirely limited to technical contingencies inside Germany. There was a reassuring conviction that Germany's house was in order, allowing for a reliable assessment of economic and political contingencies in
the event of war. Comparisons with the economic resources of possible enemies seemed uncalled for; and
when such information was no longer obtainable during the war, scraps of intelligence were interpreted as
symptoms of basic crisis that gave rise to soaring hopes.

These pre-war discussions nevertheless did lay the
groundwork for certain general views on the economic
consequences of a major European war. The basic
conclusion was that the wars of the nineteenth century
provided no reliable guide. It was necessary to go back
to the Napoleonic period. The 'fearsome burdens' of
that time, in the words of Delbrück, could be borne
only by a country essentially based on agriculture, the
people being fed by the products of their own soil. In
the wars of unification in the later nineteenth century,
on the other hand, no serious difficulties had been experienced, because the issue had been so swiftly settled, while there had still been no interruption in the
supply of foods and raw materials. The structure of
the economy, moreover, had been quite different then
from what it was now. Both German industry and
agriculture were now much more interdependent with
the economies of other countries than had been the
case in 1870. Delbrück concluded that there must be
great and justified concern about the economic effects
of a three-front war – he was already including
Britain! – which would reduce Germany from a
country reaching out on every side to the status of a
closed economic region.

The essential elements of this view were the emphasis on the export-minded structure of the German
economy, on the danger of a conflict with the Triple

Entente, which had become obvious in 1911 and 1912, and particularly on a long-range blockade of the Channel and of the Mediterranean at Gibraltar, which would tend to isolate Germany from the world market.

Hence the focus shifted to the question of a 'reckoning', of forcible intervention into this complex network, with incalculable consequences. This was underlined in the memorandum which the Chief of Staff, Moltke, contributed to the consultations on economic mobilisation. The challenge was here met but imperfectly, note being taken only of possible regulation of the use of domestic output. Radical debarment from the world market was indeed foreseen, since the projection went far beyond the immediately plausible closure of the North Sea and the Mediterranean. There were no illusions that imports might come by way of the smaller neutral Powers, since the enemy controlling the sea would prevent this through political and economic pressures.

Yet there was a persistent expectation that a great neutral Power might not bow to such pressures, thus greatly easing the German dilemma, though the experts remained sceptical on this point. In this connection it was the American merchant marine that appeared as the gateway to the world market. The United States, it was thought, would not allow her markets to be foreclosed – on the contrary, she would seek to exploit her opportunities.

In a committee meeting on 21 November 1912, the German Foreign Ministry expressed itself in highly optimistic terms about this possibility; and the following day the argument was taken up by the Reich Office of the Interior, which was in charge of economic policy. The trouble was that the United States did not have enough bottoms of her own; and there was talk that she might recruit neutral merchantmen to sail under the American flag, which Britain would presumably be inclined to treat with greater respect than the flags of the smaller neutrals.

But the hopes which the experts staked on this American solution soon collapsed, when the repre-

sentative of the Reich Naval Office indicated that
Britain and France would certainly block the Channel
at Dover and Calais and exercise priority options in
the purchase of food imports from overseas, while the
United States, presumably interested only in making
money, would offer no objections. The assembled experts accepted this estimate of the situation, which
turned out to be only too true later on.

Unfortunately, expert opinion does not seem to
have had any effect on the formulation of national
policy. Although Delbrück himself ended this particular analysis with an exclamation-mark, he reverted to
the earlier hopes that there was a community of interest betwen Germany and America. They appeared
in his concluding memorandum of 28 August 1913,
which carried all the more weight, since by that time
there were already contracts with companies in Rot-
terdam for shipments under the American flag of
grain and feed, the only types of commodities ordin-
arily considered.

In August 1914 the predominant German view was
that in the long run, at least, America would not
allow herself to be pushed out of the German market
and that her considerable economic and political
power was bound to leave Germany with a certain
freedom of action. This was not the central issue,
however, but rather a symptom of how the question of
who would be hardest hit was viewed. The Germans
apparently thought that their country, with its large
domestic market (including Austria), the Baltic Sea as
a communication area, and a possible community of
interest with a great overseas Power, was less vulnerable than the British Empire, which was far more dependent on uninterrupted world trade. Tirpitz expressed himself along such lines to Jagow and Bethmann-Hollweg on 19 August 1914, despite the fore-
casts of his own experts. On 11 September he noted
that during the month of August Britain had lost 49
per cent of her trade and commerce – adding directly,
however, that this was likely to strengthen British
militancy. Lichnowsky gave a diametrically opposite
interpretation of the situation. He told Capelle,

Under-Secretary in the Reich Naval Office, that
Britain was so deeply concerned with her trade with
Germany that for this reason alone she would want to
see the war ended within a reasonable time.

A representative statement of the German view of
the economic changes brought about by the war was
given by the Reichsbank President, Havenstein, to the
Board of Directors of the Reichsbank on 25 September
1914. Havenstein concluded that the world economy
had virtually collapsed. The major stock exchanges
had ceased to function, there was a complete failure of
the market and of quotations in foreign exchange and
an equally complete cessation of international settlements. All countries had had to revert to a closed
economy and all had been severely hit, being forced to
seek new economic ties. The only saving grace was
that Germany's chief economic enemy had been
damaged at least as much as Germany herself in this
world-wide process of financial disintegration, and
especially by the credit squeeze, which only Germany,
in contrast to other lands, and especially Britain, had
been able to surmount smoothly and without a mora-
torium. Havenstein did not underestimate the resources of the modern world, but he did cite the com-
plexities of modern economies in arriving at rather
optimistic political and economic conclusions. In his
view, organisational and financial problems had more
importance in the modern world than such natural
advantages as control of the seaways, which could not
make up for the world-wide economic decay. Staking
his hopes in the natural economic self-interest especially of America, Havenstein thought that Germany
could expect much of her remaining international
connections, despite the evidence of the early weeks of
the war. 'The Baltic seaway is open,' he said, 'and it
is to be hoped that we shall be able to arrange a reasonably regular and adequate substitute for imports
and exports by the land route via Austria and such
neutral countries as Switzerland, Italy and Holland,
and thence further in American vessels.' Germany
could count on the likelihood that the United States,
which had a vital interest in the German and Aus-

trian markets for cotton and copper, would vigorously seek somehow to open up a way to them.

There is much evidence to show that during the first month of the war Bethmann-Hollweg thought along similar lines. Apart from the political consequences they drew from it, those two antipodes, the ex-Ambassador, Lichnowsky, and the Minister of the Navy, Tirpitz, were agreed on this estimate of the situation, Lichnowsky being actually closer to the Chancellor's political views in holding that considerations of sheer economic expediency were bound to persuade Britain to break off the war. Bethmann-Hollweg held talks with both of them during August. Like Havenstein, moreover, he still counted on imports through the intermediary of neutral grain-traders as late as 29 August 1914, sending Delbrück suggestions to that end. These crossed the Minister's own proposals for the administrative regulation of such problems.

Bethmann-Hollweg's Change of Course

During the last days of August 1914 the strong fight put up by the British Expeditionary Force increased the Chancellor's fears that he would not be able to count on any British willingness to make peace, but that, on the contrary, the war would have to be fought to an end. Among his closest advisers faith was destroyed in the validity of calculations based on the assumption that British economic interest required a brief war; nor did similar calculations based on supposed American vital economic interest seem any more realistic.

A critical process of political and military reorientation now set in. The Chancellor feared, among other things, that his political opponents might turn out to have been right in insisting that British blockade-measures were not intended purely as methods of naval warfare, but stemmed from political motives of economic warfare. Between 27 August and 9 September 1914, it was decided to consider the possibility

that Germany would have to face the most stubborn
opposition in the economic sphere, far transcending
the war as such. By 5 September Pohl was convinced
that the Chancellor had changed course and even
Tirpitz, who refused to believe in such a possibility,
thought that a political 'breakthrough' was likely to
take place at Headquarters, perhaps quite soon.

During these days the British government provided
the Chancellor with several demonstrations of their
resolve that seemed quite unmistakable. On 5 September they published the agreement that bound the
Allies not to make a separate peace; and violating all
the rules of diplomatic etiquette, they deliberately
broke off the last personal ties with moderates within
the German government by making public in a biased
and insulting version the private talks between Bethmann-Hollweg and the British Ambassador in connection with the transmission of the declaration of war.
In this account Goschen figures as a detached and em-
barrassed witness of a scene in which Bethmann-Hollweg completely lost his composure. Actually, the
Ambassador himself was reduced to tears by the
Chancellor's high-minded distress and had to ask leave
to withdraw to the antechamber so as to regain his
own composure before the Chancellery staff. This
publication, which included the German neutrality
proposal, took place on 31 August and became known
at Headquarters on 4 September.

On that same day another piece of news transpired
at Headquarters, causing further indignation and
seriously troubling the Chancellor. Japan was said to
be dispatching troops to the European theatre of war.
Bethmann-Hollweg now gave up his protests against
exacerbating the war against Britain by arbitrary German military action. He summoned the Chief of the
Admiralty and questioned him on how the Trans-
Siberian Railway might be bombed, the Suez Canal
blocked and unrest fomented in India and Egypt.

Other realisations seemed to have strengthened his
fears during these days that it was useless to count on
British willingness to engage in talks. Three prominent German businessmen are known to have held

views of the prospects of economic warfare at this time
that differed widely from prevailing opinion. They
were Gwinner, Director of the Deutsche Bank, Ballin,
Director of the Hamburg–America Line, and Rathenau, Director of the Allgemeine Elektrizitäts-Gesell-
schaft (A.E.G.). They shared the view that in terms of
economic policy time was on the side of the British
and that the United States had a solidarity of interests
with Britain.

On 22 August Gwinner told the Under-Secretary in
the Reich Naval Office of his dissent from Lichnowsky's view that British interest in the German market
would persuade that country to seek peace soon
enough to affect the length of the war. Gwinner did
agree with one element in the more optimistic estimate of the situation, namely that the structure of the
British economy was even more sensitive and vulnerable than the German; but he pointed out that
Britain had her back free and the cables at her disposal. She was methodically working for the destruction of German world trade and that would gradually
give rise to a war boom.

This theme was varied by Ballin in a letter of 30
August to Admiral Müller, Chief of the Imperial
Naval Cabinet, which Müller passed on to Tirpitz
and Pohl on 2 September. The vast machinery of the
world's economy had been brought to a standstill, he
wrote. The network extending all over the civilised
world had been cut and the contacts broken. Britain
was now trying to start up the great engine again,
without Germany. He hoped she would not succeed,
despite the trump cards she held; but he conceded
that the United States, by means of emergency legislation breaking hitherto untouchable taboos, was preparing to usurp Germany's place in world trade with a
merchant navy bought up helter-skelter.

Lastly, Rathenau, in a letter of 7 September requested by the Chancellor, attacked the whole economic optimism of German public opinion as erroneous. Germans preferred looking at the map to looking
at the globe, and this was why it was generally
thought that Britain would fare worse than Germany

in the course of the war – firstly, because she was a
mercantile nation only moderately industrialised;
secondly, because of the loss of her continental
markets; and thirdly, because America would rebel
against the European blockade. It was true that
Britain would lose her continental markets, but in return only Britain and America would be left to supply
world demand. They would divide these vast regions
among themselves and thus grow more and more
closely linked. After an initial crisis, the British
economy would experience a vigorous boom, while
Germany could expect the opposite. There was no real
parallelism between German and British economic
handicaps, and as soon as this was known Britain
would be encouraged to prolong the war.

All three business leaders maintained good personal
relations with the Chancellor. They were in correspondence with him or in personal contact at Headquarters; and it must be assumed that even before 11
September, when he read Rathenau's letter, Bethmann-Hollweg was aware of these pregnant economic
analyses that emphasised Britain's interest in prolonging the war and that were so greatly at odds with German public opinion.

The crucial turning-point came on 4 September. On
the day before, a letter of 28 August from Rathenau
had been submitted to the Chancellor. Rathenau
asked that timely thought be given to the future peace
with France, which should be tackled only after a most
serious effort concerned with Britain, but which should
at the same time – and here was the crucial political
element – be part and parcel of an approach by which
Britain's carefully calculated end-game might be
thwarted without risk to the German navy.

Rathenau outlined three steps: French-oriented
economic warfare, the technical details of which he
was preparing in collaboration with the Deputy Minister of War, under whom he was running the Military
Raw-Materials Section; the counterpoise of a central
European customs union centred on Austria, which he
had proposed for the second time in a memorandum
directly after the outbreak of war; and financial agree-

ments with the major continental Powers concerning the capital market, which might result in the financial isolation of Britain and the United States – Britain being already isolated and committed to finance world trade, while America might thus be severely handicapped in building up a war industry.

On the basis of this letter the Chancellor had Mutius, on 4 September, ask Rathenau to make a more detailed presentation of his plans, in the hope that this might result in suggestions on how to control the problems arising from the protracted war that now threatened. The Chancellor emphasised that European disunity and internal enmity in the post-war period had to be taken into account – at least for a number of years.

A strategic defeat of the French army and the occupation of north France, including the Channel coast and Paris, might offer scope for a more active policy. Such a calculation called for peace to be concluded with the French government as a basis. In the more probable case that France's allies would prevent her from concluding a 'just' peace, occupation without legal sanction would have to suffice. The only strategic security in such an event would be that the French armies would have lost their operational momentum, though without becoming fully neutralised, as would have been true in the case of an armistice.

Rathenau's Concept and German Pre-war Economic Policy

For Bethmann-Hollweg the politically crucial point in Rathenau's very sketchy suggestions of 28 August was that the industrialist's views on a customs union – previously known to the Chancellor – were now strongly linked to an anti-British strategy. Rathenau was here influenced by his experiences in the War Ministry's Military Raw-Materials Section. His thinking was probably determined by the military situation in those days; for on 28 August the role of the British Expeditionary Force in severely shattering German strategic hopes became clear. It was surely no accident that Rathenau put the Chancellor's main strategic point at the heart of his alternative: the German navy must not be sacrificed. Presumably Rathenau knew by 28 August how much store the Chancellor set by the navy and an end to the war with Britain. His plans certainly met Bethmann-Hollweg's own thoughts half-way, for Rathenau was attacking aspects of German public opinion similar to those about which the Chancellor had recently become disillusioned.

Mutius,* if no one else, must have pointed out, in his letter of September, the part in Rathenau's plan that had found the strongest response. We know Rathenau's first memorandum on a customs union with Austria – in continuation of his pre-war thinking – only from Delbrück's detailed criticism; but in Rathenau's letter requested by the Chancellor – and Mutius is bound to have commented on this request – the central European customs union as a weapon directed at Britain is at the very heart of the presentation.

Looking at Rathenau's concept, which actually goes back to pre-war times, one sees much in support of the view that he made the suddenly risen concern with the British threat of economic warfare the vehicle of his earlier plan, rejected both in peace and war by the executive bureaucracy in power. He was taking advantage of an opportunity to engage the Chancellor's interest. In so nimble and almost capricious a mind as Rathenau's, one factor was almost certainly his growing familiarity with the new situation. Founder and Head of the Military Raw-Materials Section, he became the creator of the German nitrate industry, which from the spring of 1915 on saved the country from disastrous munitions shortages. Here was a possible way of putting over after all an economic policy that had failed to draw interest in the pre-war period.

The first time that Rathenau brought his plan for a central European economic union to Bethmann-Holl-

* Gerhard von Mutius, close friend of Bethmann-Hollweg and Counsellor of the German Embassy at Constantinople.

weg's attention was during a visit to Hohenfinow, the Chancellor's country estate, on 25 July 1912. The actual occasion for the talk was the Chancellor's Russian visit in July 1912, which afforded him some reassurance for the state of current relations with that country and gave him reason to entertain hopes that a *modus vivendi* might be achieved, but which nevertheless conjured up sombre perspectives for the long run. Three days before Rathenau's visit, Bethmann-Hollweg had written to the Prussian representative in Karlsruhe. Russia's wealth in natural resources and brute manpower, he wrote, was nothing for Germany to be afraid of. At the same time, in the light of 'our softness engendered by our advanced civilisation', neither should it be underestimated. Yet during a talk in these days with Flotow, later to be Ambassador in Rome, he had cast an eye over the grounds of his estate at Hohenfinow and wondered aloud whether there was any sense in reforestation, since the Russians were bound to arrive within a few years.

It was against such a background that Rathenau developed his concept of a customs union with Austria and the smaller countries of western Europe. He appreciated the dangers of a political offensive, but he was willing to stretch the situation a bit further, only to bring about a sudden turn when tension was at its highest, by concluding an alliance with the Western Powers. The key, to his mind, was settlement of the conflict between France and Germany, which 're-dounded to the advantage of all the other nations'. Britain, in turn, was the key to that settlement. The goals must be Central Africa and Asia Minor. The inexorable logic of any Western reorientation, however, called for progress in the direction of parliamentary government. Bethmann-Hollweg expressed general agreement but ignored the relevant questions of foreign and economic policy. Concerned with the home front, he asked Rathenau to offer proposals for electoral reform in Prussia. Rathenau declined.

The discussion must be seen in the context of German concern with the Russian menace and the difficulties in the way of any Franco-German *rapproche-*

ment following the Morocco crisis and the failure of
the Haldane mission, which certainly provided possible arguments militating against Rathenau's ideas.
Russia's industrial growth might make it advisable to
maintain access to that huge market as well as to the
West. Any incisive domestic reorientation opened up
the whole question of the basic structure of the German Reich. The talk between Bethmann-Hollweg and
Rathenau was a friendly affair among neighbouring
estate-owners. It is fair to suggest that both men were
brilliantly toying with ideas rather than considering
them seriously.

It was Rathenau's lot during the ensuing period to
have to listen again and again to almost stereotyped
assertions of Germany's internationally oriented economic policy and agricultural protectionism, as against
his ideas of a circumscribed central European economic realm. In 1912, 1913 and 1914, on the floor of the
Reichstag, Germany's need for access to the huge
markets available to the British and Russian Empires
was sharply emphasised.

As late as 18 January 1914, a joint statement by the
Chancellor, the Minister of the Interior (who had
taken the initiative in the matter) and all other
government agencies in the economic sphere, reiterated that there was no reason for basic changes in the
tariff and trade policy pursued by Germany. The 1902
Tariff had stood up well and there was no reason for
Germany to take the initiative in revising trade relations by serving notice of termination of the tariff
treaties of 1906. Delbrück told the Reichstag that by
and large the existing situation met all the needs of
the German economy.

This continuation of traditional German tariff and
trade policy conflicts with the view that there is a
direct and inexorable line leading from Rathenau's
pre-war *Mitteleuropa* notions – intended to secure a
position of dominance for Germany – Bethmann-
Hollweg's own policy in the July crisis and the reap-
pearance, in the September Memorandum, of what is
often taken to be the same *Mitteleuropa* project.
There were many continuities in the transition from

peace to war, the most important being that Germany's status as a Great Power was taken for granted, before and after; but German war aims were by no means identical with the goals of German pre-war *Weltpolitik*; nor is there any validity to the theory that the Germans wanted to advance to a new position of power through the war, their own borders having become too constricted in the light of the steadily growing pressure of economic growth and the accompanying hunger for prestige.

Quite apart from that, one would have to examine whether Germany's increasing participation in the internationalisation of industry and communications throughout the world – and especially in France – amounted to an invitation to 'direct political action', since this could only endanger the gains. The American Ambassador put such reflections to Gwinner in August. As reported by the German banker, the American said that in another twenty-five years, with things going the way they were, Germany would be completely invulnerable. Now she was staking everything on a single card. Gerard was unable to understand how the Kaiser could have reached such a decision. Commenting on this analysis to the Under-Secretary, Capelle, Gwinner, rather than using economic arguments, said he had been unable to make the American understand that technical considerations of mobilisation, deployment and similar elements put an unacceptable premium on delay in a political and military crisis. Gwinner was actually quite critical of Germany's policy at the outbreak of war and levelled charges of war-mongering. The sole motive that occurred to him was the restoration of 'Austrian prestige'.

Reflections on new economic approaches did exert some influence on policy, but there were no firm decisions, first because of the opposition of the experts and then because the military situation changed. These ideas stemmed primarily from the actual experience of economic warfare, which – it was projected – would extend into the post-war period; but in another way – for example, in Rechenberg's calculations – they grew out of the failure of German nationality policy, which

made the old political instrument of territorial compensation appear shop-worn.

American Peace Mediation (5–20 September 1914)

Before analysing the September Memorandum and
going into its political and tactical history, it seems
wise to consider a diplomatic initiative that was running separately, the first American effort to mediate
peace, falling into the period from 4 September to 19
September and extraordinarily illuminating, and also
affording us insight into the problem of the extent to
which the Germans were really willing to make peace.
At the same time it will give us some idea of the ideological world of the Allies and the United States.

Even before Britain had transmitted her declaration of war in Berlin, President Wilson had decided to
offer the five major European Powers his good offices
as mediator, with reference to the Hague Convention.
This was done on 4 August 1914, in identical personal
messages to the Heads of State of the belligerent
nations. In deliberate violation of the principle of
secret diplomacy, this step was made public a few days
later in the *New York Times*, a practice to be followed
on all subsequent occasions, probably for the purpose
of exerting a certain moral pressure on the European
Powers. On this occasion, the Powers unanimously rejected mediation as premature and suggested that it
be tried at a more favourable juncture.

At a Washington dinner on 5 September, the former American diplomat Oscar Strauss asked the German Ambassador, Count Bernstorff, whether the
Kaiser, in Bernstorff's view, was likely to be receptive
to another mediation proposal by the President. Bernstorff admitted that he had no instructions on this
point, but he did say that he thought Germany would
accept mediation, if her enemies likewise displayed
such willingness. Strauss reported this to the Secretary
of State, Bryan, early the next morning, a Sunday.
Bryan, with the President's approval and Bernstorff's
permission, decided to pass on the conversation to

Berlin and also to consult the British and French
Ambassadors in Washington. The American Ambassador in Berlin, Gerard, was wired instructions on 7
September to report the talk to the German government and reiterate the President's willingness to
address a mediation offer to the Allies as well, if the
German reply were favourable. The goal was to con-
vene a conference of the belligerent nations in Washington, at ambassadorial level. Bernstorff, subject to
constant pressure from the American side, which he
did not wish to evade, did from the beginning mention a stricture: the Germans would not be willing to
accept an armistice with its attendant loss of momentum for the German armies. Both the British and German Ambassadors recommended that their Foreign
Ministers not reject the American offer outright, with
a view to public opinion in the United States.

Gerard now added proposals of his own to the
mediation initiative, for which Bernstorff, in his remarks to Strauss, had given the original impetus – he
was under the mistaken impression that it stemmed
directly from Wilson. The American Ambassador was
overwhelmed by Germany's military successes in the
West and the East – the Battle of Tannenberg: 'Germany is walking through the French, English and
Russian armies as if they were paper hoops.' He was
deeply impressed by the way the German people had
rallied in August and by the order and discipline they
had displayed. He found it almost inconceivable that
1,200,000 volunteers should have enrolled in a few
days – 'this of course in addition to the millions
already on the army lists.... This will give you an
idea of the spirit of the people.' Gerard already
counted on the capture of Paris, the occupation of the
Channel coast and the initiation of Zeppelin air raids
on London. It was under the impress of such considerations that he spontaneously reiterated American
willingness to mediate to Zimmermann, the Acting
Under-Secretary in the German Foreign Ministry. He
was sure that Germany would demand cession of all
French colonies, if she were victorious in France. This
conviction apparently went back to a talk Gerard had

had with Gwinner, Director of the Deutsche Bank, in
mid-August, when the American had mentioned the
possibility of peace on the basis of the *status quo*. The
banker demurred, pointing to the German successes
in France. When the American pursued the point,
Gwinner, with what was probably deliberate exag-
geration, said on the spur of the moment that he was
thinking of a war indemnity of 3 million dollars and
cession of the French colonies.

Gwinner could scarcely have anticipated the effect
on the American of his improvised reply, intended to
apply solely to France. Gerard was under the impression that what the German told him represented official policy, which he was bound to find corroborated
in the British White Paper that probably came to his
notice in early September. Here he could read that
Bethmann-Hollweg had specifically exempted the
French colonies when, on 29 July, he had offered to
respect the territorial integrity of France, if Britain
would guarantee French neutrality. Gerard probably
thought he would get a good reception by adding a
proposal of his own in discharging his commission of
informing the German government in writing of the
content of the Strauss–Bernstorff conversation and reiterating the readiness of the American President to
serve as a mediator. What he proposed to Zimmermann was that Germany, when Paris had been taken,
might well make peace with France on the basis of a
war indemnity and the acquisition of the French
colonies; and that she could then accept American
mediation to initiate peace negotiations with Britain
and Russia.

It is not clear precisely what persuaded the American Ambassador to take this step, which went far beyond his instructions. Apparently he thought that the
German march through the Allied 'paper hoops' and
possible German annexation of the French colonies
inevitably touched the very heart of American security
interests, making it necessary for America to exert
some influence on German ideas of what the peace
should be like. Gwinner was a man strongly oriented
towards Europe, and his casual remark to Gerard was

almost certainly intended to apply only to the French colonies in Africa; but France also had islands and bases close to the Atlantic coast of America and above all in the Pacific, where the French possessions represented a sizeable power factor.

Early on in the war, the United States was concerned not only with the events in Europe but the possible involvement of the Pacific area. An attempt to neutralise the Pacific having failed, the American government faced the rising danger that Japanese entry in the war might trigger off decisive power shifts in Asia. The open-door policy and American interests in China seemed in imminent danger from Japanese advances in the Pacific, made on British sufferance, especially the attack on Kiaochow. Culminating in the notorious Twenty-one Points, the Japanese offensive did indeed open up more big holes in Chinese sovereignty, marking the beginning of the crucial final phase in the century of the Chinese Revolution; for when the Great Powers, committed in Europe, failed to afford the expected protection, the intellectual and nationalist movement on 4 May 1919 was set off. Impressed by the display of superior German power, Gerard, in contrast to his government in Washington, associated Japanese expansionism with the repercussions that might follow the destruction of the German power base in the Pacific. The extraordinary spirit in Berlin that wrung such admiration from Gerard persuaded him that Germany would never forget the Japanese attack on Kiaochow nor fail to revenge it. The key to this situation would be a German attempt upon the French position in the Pacific, and since that would affect United States interests, that country must interpose in time.

Actually, while the German government fumed over Japanese behaviour in the Pacific area, it did not dream of such sweeping maritime perspectives. It was Britain after all that held dominion of the seas. If that were ever to be changed, the issue would be settled in Europe. At best the Germans anticipated that their power might be so enhanced at the end of the war that Britain might guarantee them unimpeded access to Africa.

Zimmermann did tell Gerard that success for the American mediation effort would be more likely if the British could be persuaded to influence the Japanese to change their policy. By and large he rejected Gerard's special pleas at this first talk and responded only cursorily to the American memorandum, transmitted on 8 September, which contained the mediation proposal on the basis of Bernstorff's talks. For Zimmermann the crucial point was that the peace terms Gerard had in mind related only to France, providing no approach to peace with Germany's true enemies, Britain and Russia. Even when Gerard handed him the memorandum, he pointed out that a peace treaty along Gerard's lines – i.e. relating only to France and the French colonies – would in no way meet German security needs and that a 'day of reckoning' with Russia and Britain was inevitable. The German people would fail to comprehend any American mediation effort on the basis outlined by Gerard. From sheer self-preservation, the German government would not be able to take up the Ambassador's suggestion, well intentioned as it undoubtedly was. In the face of such massive opposition Gerard abandoned his private and unauthorised plan for a separate Franco-German peace. The Germans were clearly not prepared to accept his premises, namely that Russian mobilisation and the British blockade would continue. Henceforth he concentrated on Wilson's memorandum, which was to restore a direct line with Britain.

Bethmann-Hollweg ordered the American memorandum to be answered verbally on 12 September. He expressed appreciation for the offer but pointed out that a German victory over France would not solve Germany's security problem, since she would still be facing Russia and Britain. The Triple Alliance, moreover, had agreed by treaty not to make peace separately. The British Prime Minister, the London *Times* and British diplomats were all insisting that Britain would fight on doggedly and expected to win, the longer the war lasted. What America would have to do first was to persuade Germany's enemies to listen to peace proposals. Germany could accept only a peace that held out the prospect of being enduring. If Germany accepted the American mediation offer, her enemies were bound to interpret it as a sign of weakness, while the German people would simply not understand. In the face of the hardships they had suffered they wanted guarantees of security and tranquillity.

Gerard chose to interpret the note as 'an opening to mediation' and passed on its text to Washington with encouraging comments. By the time it got there on 16 September, the British reply was already six days old, the American Ambassador in London, Walter Hines Page, having transmitted an 'informal' reply from Sir Edward Grey, as well as some additional remarks, marked 'strictly confidential'. At the very beginning of his declaration, Grey described German war guilt and the violation of Belgian neutrality as 'grievous and irreparable. . . . No peace can be concluded that will permit the continuance or the recurrence of an armed brute power in Central Europe which violates treaties to make war and in making war assaults the continuity of civilization.' The crucial official demand was that 'any terms that England will agree to must provide for an end of militarist power and for reparations to make amends to Belgium'.

In his 'inviolably secret' supplement intended for Wilson, Grey thus defined his demands: The British people regard the German Emperor and the system of government that he stands for as they regarded Napoleon, a world pest and an enemy of civilisation, and hence there can be no permanent peace till he and his system are utterly overthrown. This certainly betokened a firm resolve to fight on, but Grey reinforced his rejection of the mediation offer by suggesting that the Allies would be agreed that any German peace proposal was bound to be nothing more than propaganda. Page read this as a threat of rejection of the United States as a mediator in any situation later on, if it involved offers on Germany's behalf which Britain considered inadequate. It is not surprising that, compared with this blunt language on the part of Grey, the State Department looked on Bethmann-Hollweg's reply as expressing acceptance. The reservoir of goodwill towards Britain that nevertheless continued to exist in Washington may be gauged from the fact that neither Wilson nor Bryan were deterred from their mediation efforts by the tone taken in the British reply.

Two days later, on 18 September, House and Bryan, encouraged by Bethmann-Hollweg's note, at the directive of President Wilson and with the approval of Bernstorff tried to lay the groundwork for a secret ambassadorial conference in New York, to include France, Britain and Germany. On that day, at a meeting in Bernstorff's New York apartment, of which supposedly only Bernstorff and the President knew, House managed to extract agreement for preliminary negotiations from the British Ambassador, Spring-Rice. House envisaged as a basis for these negotiations discussions on the restoration of Belgium and a general disarmament pact. He thought that this was indeed the minimum basis and he anticipated German agreement.

On 20 September House met Spring-Rice in New York. House said that Britain stood in danger of losing American sympathies. The United States was not prepared to accept the entire elimination of Germany; she wanted restoration of the balance of Europe rather than destruction. Invited to talk with Bernstoff, Spring-Rice let loose a tirade against his 'enemy' colleague. He said such a meeting was completely out of the question, since Britain was bound by treaty not to engage in separate peace negotiations. House vainly put forward once again his major argument. American policy, he said, sought to prevent 'that either Germany or Russia would gain a great preponderance'. In the long run, however, the British attitude prevailed, for given the choice between German and Russian predominance, House too thought Germany by far the greater evil. A German victory would mean 'the unspeakable tyranny of militarism for generations. . . . Fundamentally, the Germans are playing a role that is against their natural instincts and inclinations, and it shows how perverted men may become by habit and environment. Germany's success will ultimately mean trouble for us.' This was scarcely the mediating voice House adopted towards Wilson on 22 August 1914.

The words of Grey and House on the subject of peace mediation once more make plain the dilemma confronting Bethmann-Hollweg's policy. Faced with the choice between a compromise peace and war to the bitter end – the latter line being loudly proclaimed by Germany's enemies – he had no alternative but to accept the same course.

One question, however, must be asked with every emphasis in respect of German policy in the pre-war period and the early weeks of the war. How could matters have reached a point where a neutral mediator could speak of Germany in such fashion?

The British and the German attitudes in the mediation effort supplemented each other in a curious way. Grey during these weeks was afraid that Germany might assume continental dominance in the style of Napoleon; and his answer was war to the end, even to the elimination of the German political system and its representatives; and the German government, without having a true inkling of how radical this position was, got set for it by preparing for a 'continental blockade'.

Yet even if a readiness to conclude a compromise peace were assumed, the chances of success would have had to be assessed as very low. Even ignoring for the moment the call for the overthrow of the Kaiser, the unconditional British demand for the restoration of Belgium clearly provided no common basis for negotiation, even had the Germans forgone their claims for an indemnity and their minimum terms of changing Belgium's status as a nation and its use as a territorial hostage – let alone the much broader possibilities of German influence in Belgium, which Bethmann-Hollweg still thought negotiable.

Yet the demand for the elimination of militarism seems to have weighed even more heavily. Even when it was taken to mean sweeping disarmament – which was the way House viewed it – rather than to include

the abolition of conscription, the General Staff, heavy
weapons and the battle fleet (actually accomplished at
Versailles), there can be not the slightest doubt that
any intervention in the Prussian–German military
system was thought totally unacceptable in Germany.
By a remarkable coincidence 19 September, the day on
which House was trying to lay the groundwork for
talks between Bernstorff and Spring-Rice on disarmament questions, also saw Bethmann-Hollweg emphasise
to his deputy, Delbrück, that if the Social Democratic
Party really wanted a domestic reorientation, it would
have to accept the Prussian conscription system,
which it had pilloried as 'militarism'. He thought that
this would be relatively easy, since surely the war had
taught the Social Democrats the bitter lesson that any
international disarmament and security system was
beyond reach. Among the factors that militated
against mediation was the great upsurge in nationalist
sentiment that had swept the country in August.

It is a moot point whether during this brief period
from 5 to 19 September mediation might have succeeded on some other basis. Zimmermann and Bethmann-Hollweg had said that any German government
prepared to accept peace without demanding security
guarantees from Britain and Russia as well would be
swept out of office by aroused public opinion; and
they had in mind that there was no hint of such
guarantees in the American offer. Yet the dynamics of
the embattled Entente probably precluded any compromise that would not have been considered unsatis-
factory and unacceptable in advance and on principle,
measured against the political concepts of the German
government and the expectations of the German
public. Thus the events surrounding the American
mediation offer of September 1914 merely serve to
highlight the incompatibility of the respective points
of view, thus setting the scene for a war to the bitter
end, which was precisely what the German Chancellor
had wanted to avoid.

The Political and Tactical History of the September Memorandum

On 6 September 1914, proclamations to the French populace were being drafted in Germany, against the eventuality of the French armies being defeated in the field. On 8 September Riezler was working on the covering letter for a document entitled 'Preliminary Notes on an Approach to Peace', often described as the 'September Memorandum'.

Both efforts were part of a single event and they display parallels in thinking. The covering letter of 8 September must have been prepared after the text of the Memorandum itself was typed, hence the talks that led to the formulation of the Memorandum must have taken place between 6 and 8 September. There is a strong likelihood that the Memorandum was written at the same time as the proclamations, on 6 September.

Apparently a number of people were consulted, at the Chancellor's request. There is evidence that Tirpitz was asked for his views on war aims in the West and that he was familiarised with the thinking that went into the Memorandum. He too was pressing for a customs union with Austria, but he rejected as illusory the whole precautionary enterprise of a separate peace with France: 'The point is', he said, 'we shall never get Britain to agree to a peace in which we would compensate ourselves. The whole idea of a separate peace with France is impossible.' In a sense the request to Rathenau may also be considered as part of the preparatory work for the Memorandum, although his reply was not yet on hand when it was written. Apart from talking with his associates, Bethmann-Hollweg himself apparently made no written notes in preparation for the Memorandum. The men closest to him had already spent several days coming to grips with ideas of economic warfare, *Mitteleuropa* and how to exert pressure on Britain, and he seems first to have asked them to prepare an outline, before he began to concern himself thoroughly with all the relevant ques-

tions. He spent 11 September methodically examining
the question of a customs union. He read Rathenau's
letter of 7 September, studied Rechenberg's letter to
Wahnschaffe of 27 August and the next day took note
of Delbrück's refutation of Rathenau's plans. It was
only then that he embarked on a real discussion with
Delbrück, his deputy and the Minister chiefly concerned, in his letter of 16 September, which crossed
Delbrück's letter of 13 September, and which Delbrück answered on 19 September.

This chronology is highly illuminating in assessing
the Memorandum's background and significance.
Since 8 September the attention given to this whole
question had been lagging more and more, and there
was a considerable loss of momentum. This is in
marked contrast to the way in which news and
opinion tumbled over each other between 4 and 6
September. The last remnants of this precipitate haste
are seen in the technical and logical errors that dot
the text of the September Memorandum.

This was the political situation that prevailed:
After 27 August, Bethmann-Hollweg was constrained
to review his policy in respect of Britain, as we have
already seen. There was more and more bad news. On
the military side there were the British Expeditionary
Force and the Japanese landings, on the diplomatic
front the barrier to a separate peace and Goschen's
lack of discretion, and lastly in the economic sphere
the danger that a boom in Britain might prolong the
war. An added element of urgency was the anticipa-
tion of a great strategic success. Bethmann-Hollweg
committed himself firmly to a policy of fighting
Britain with every means available and of exploiting
the military situation in France, preferably by efforts
in the direction of a separate peace, but, if that were
not possible, by occupation.

His change of policy was also useful to him on the
domestic scene, for the maintenance of his position at
Headquarters and the restoration of his political prestige, which had suffered by British entry into the war.
He was under constant attack from his opponents,
who kept probing for a crucial point at which they

might discredit the Chancellor and undermine his standing with the Kaiser. Being in constant social contact with Bethmann-Hollweg, they were sensitive to the slightest nuances in his speech and went after him, hammer and tongs. Tirpitz actually visited him on 6 September, in an attempt to launch a new effort that might mark his downfall. Indeed, the September Memorandum may have started as a counter-manœuvre. Tirpitz's plot was supported by the National Liberal Deputy, Paasche, leader of the Reichstag moderates, who announced a sweeping Supplementary Naval Bill, which the Chancellor opposed as 'premature'. Omission of the Social Democrats in this effort proved to be a political blunder of the first order by the Chancellor's enemies. Bethmann-Hollweg instantly went into action with the National Unity Front and made himself indispensable to the Kaiser for the maintenance of good relations with the Social Democratic Party. Tirpitz promptly realised the error. In a Prussian Cabinet meeting on 15 August 1914, Bethmann-Hollweg had actually succeeded in committing Tirpitz to a statement on co-operation with the Social Democrats by accepting some of Tirpitz's argumentation intended to counteract Conservative disquiet over the new situation.

Annexationist circles in Berlin were beginning their agitation at this time, and the Chancellor's reaction to this worrisome news affords further insight into the background and motivation of the September Memorandum. On 29 August the Under-Secretary, Zimmermann, had reported on a newspaper article by General Keim, President of the National Defence League (*Wehrverein*) and Council Member of the Pan-German League. From local observation and the opinion of propaganda experts, this was only one head of a hydra, to be followed by others that would grow back. To meet the threat, Zimmermann inquired what exactly were 'the positive goals of German policy in West and East'. In his reply, sent to Press Chief Hamann the very same day, at the Chancellor's instruction, Riezler said that things were still in a state of flux with respect to the war-aims question. In Beth-

mann-Hollweg's view it was still too early to take decisions, since prompt peace with France was improbable
and there was considerable uncertainty whether Germany would be able to dictate peace terms to Britain.
This restraint was in sharp contrast to powerful sentiment for outright and totally unrealistic annexations
that was rampant at Headquarters and in the ranks as
well. Riezler said that the goal of the war was to
secure Germany for an indefinite time to come both in
the East and the West, by weakening her enemies. This
formulation was taken over almost word for word in
the opening sentence of the September Memorandum.
Annexations, Riezler went on, would scarcely serve
that end. They might indeed become a source of German weakness. As for weakening Germany's enemies,
this might be done economically and financially, by
trade pacts, etc. Riezler concluded on a note that
shows that the debate within the Chancellor's circle
had not yet crystallised. 'In the face of the difficulties
posed, the different views and the confused situation,'
he said, 'no wonder the people here are not yet sure
what they will ultimately want.'

Tenor and content of this letter coincide with
directives that Bethmann-Hollweg transmitted to the
Foreign Ministry in Berlin two days later, on 31
August, as guidelines for the Press. He remarked that
only the first chapter of the war had been concluded
so far, that heavy, large-scale fighting still impended
in France and, more importantly, that the course of
the war with Britain was as yet quite uncertain. Giving his directive an optimistic tinge, he said that while
there was justified confidence that the war would ultimately end victoriously, public opinion must display
great patience and be prepared for severe and protracted hardships and even reverses. Hence any discussion of possible territorial gains, whether in Europe or
the colonies, seemed quite out of place. 'The primary
goal must be security against further war in the foreseeable future. The Press should be indoctrinated in
that direction.'

This formulation about security against wars to
come henceforth became a stereotype in official com-

munications and the Chancellor's speeches. It was sufficiently vague and ambiguous to serve as a tactical weapon without offering the gathering annexationist movement any needless provocation. In his letter of 29 August, Kurt Riezler had already spoken disparagingly of annexationist sentiment not only in the ranks but at Headquarters as well. Some of his diary entries also display this opposition to the military who seemed to compete in their annexationist demands with 'victory-drunk' public opinion. On 4 September he noted:

> If Europe fails to find some enduring form of commonalty on this occasion, it will mark the downfall of the Continent. Yet how is it to be accomplished? The soldiers with their blind faith in the steam-roller and their antiquated annexationist goals are doing hair-raising things in an economic sense. They first destroy cities and then try to impose indemnities.

On one occasion – 22 August – Bethmann-Hollweg had already dissociated himself from such plans of unrestrained greed by remarking wryly to Moltke: 'L'appétit vient en mangeant.' This military appetite was indeed taken up in the September Memorandum, which, however, managed to neutralise annexationism in a political sense at the same time.

On 5 September, with preparations for consultations on war aims (in which Rathenau and Tirpitz were included) still proceeding, along with work on a proclamation to the French people, Joffre's plan of attack for the following day was leaked to the General Staff by an indiscretion. It was the very plan that was put into effect to mark the beginning of the Battle of the Marne. The proclamation to the French people was forgotten – no further drafts were prepared, nor any final version. Estimates of the military situation grew increasingly pessimistic, and with them grew the need for codifying the changed policy course, as a preliminary outline of the peace to come. In meeting this domestic necessity Bethmann-Hollweg actually

allowed his opponents to collaborate with his associates, as he told Delbrück. The covering letter includes
the crucial qualification that these notes were to be
considered 'preliminary', since the war was as yet far
from decided and it looked as though Britain might
succeed in holding her allies to a fight to the last.

Analysis of the September Memorandum

The fact that there were differences of view in the war-
aims debate at Headquarters is reflected in the differences between the covering letter and the September
Memorandum itself. Taking the whole background
into account, the letter emphasises reorganisation of
economic conditions in central Europe, while the
Memorandum, possibly bearing the stamp of Bethmann-Hollweg's influence to a lesser degree, mentions
the establishment of a European economic union only
as one among other goals in an overall armistice
scheme that had to meet military requirements. Thus
two rather different concepts appear side by side in
the Memorandum, with no effort to conceal their
rivalry.

Under 'General Goal of the War' we read: 'Security
for the German Reich in East and West for the foreseeable future. To this end France must be weakened
to the point where she cannot rise again as a major
power, while Russia must be pushed away from the
German border, her sway over the non-Russian
peoples broken.' The weakening of France was to be
accomplished financially by war indemnities and
economically by the loss of mineral deposits; and she
was to be made economically dependent on Germany
through a bilateral trade pact. It is this Point 1 (together with Points 2 and 3, concerning Belgium and
Luxembourg) that fails to square with Point 4, providing for a central European economic union that
was to embrace western Europe as well and stabilise
German predominance in central Europe in quite
another way.

It was Delbrück who put his finger on the heart of

this contradiction. 'One may well doubt,' he wrote, 'whether it is wise to bleed a country white when one wishes to incorporate it into one's own economic sphere. Annexation of the ore basin of Briey may well become unnecessary if France and Germany were to become a single economic area, to say nothing of other measures.'

On the premise that Britain was the main enemy, both possibilities discussed at Headquarters evidently got into the Memorandum side by side; and this dual approach seems to have survived in a later memorandum by Gwinner, undated but entering channels on 15 November. 'Further elaboration of peace terms,' he wrote, 'will depend on whether German policy proposes to exhaust France completely or work for reconciliation with the French.'

As against this clear-cut paradox in the goals formulated in the Memorandum, its immediate purpose – to lay the basis for a strategy against Britain by creating another Napoleonic 'continental blockade' – was expressed only covertly in the text. A trade pact with France was to 'eliminate British trade in France'. French Flanders with the ports of Dunkirk, Calais and Boulogne was to be separated from France and given to Belgium on condition that Germany would enjoy the right to occupy all ports of military importance. Thus the military did tip their hand. Indeed, as though to give *ex post facto* sanction to the change of course relating to the new estimate of Britain's attitude and justify falling in with Tirpitz's militant policy, the September Memorandum submitted to the arbitrament of the generals: 'It will be up to the appropriate authorities to evaluate the military value of this position vis-à-vis Britain.'

This view of the Memorandum as a first effort to assemble material on the use of all possible weapons in a fight to the end against Britain is confirmed in a letter that Lieutenant-General Graevenitz, the Württemberg military plenipotentiary at Headquarters, wrote to his Prime Minister, Weizsäcker, on 5 September 1914, at the very time, in other words, when Bethmann-Hollweg, under the impress of the strong line taken by the British, felt compelled to revise his British strategy. Summarising his talks with leading politicians and officers, Graevenitz reported to Stuttgart that 'the Chancellor, like everyone else, proceeds on the basis that Britain and Japan must be vanquished. Clear heads realise, however, that our current naval resources are not sufficient for that purpose and that we must yet build the greater part of our fleet, with French and Belgian funds.' In drawing the balance from his talks and adding his own conclusion, he suggested that Germany would have to familiarise herself with the idea of an intermediate peace, following the complete subjugation of France. It was precisely against such an eventuality that the September Memorandum was to provide a first basis for discussion. The starting-point was that such a preliminary peace with France must provide Germany with the means for further military and economic warfare against Britain. The main accent would lie in western Europe, especially the Channel coast, whence the war must be carried to Britain by means of an economic offensive, a counter-blockade on land, along Napoleonic lines.

France as a War Base

An important commentary by Rechenberg clearly shows that all this related primarily to the war as it then stood and the as yet unvanquished main enemy, Britain. This was further corroborated in Rathenau's argumentation of 7 September – the letter was actually read only on 11 September – in which his suggestions of 28 August were developed in detail.

The Chancellor's deputy, Delbrück, had assigned Rechenberg to work on the whole complex of the September Memorandum, as the best available man. Actually, apart from the overworked Ministerial Director, Müller, under whose jurisdiction the subject lay, there was no high-level official in any of the government departments concerned who was receptive to the *Mitteleuropa* idea. Only Schönebeck, one of

Delbrück's advisers, had joined the ranks by October.

Between 13 and 18 September Rechenberg noted down key elements for his first general report on the September Memorandum to the officials concerned. The reason that they are preserved among the Chancellery files is that the Under-Secretary, Wahnschaffe, wanted them for information. Most prominent among these notes are technical details concerning customs and tariffs, etc. The life of the proposed customs union was put at ten years, with possible revision and extension at the end of that time. Rechenberg discussed the voting ratio within the 'Delegation', the central customs union authority in charge of administration, control and review, which was to be 9:6:5 or possibly 9:7:6 for Germany, Austria and France – Germany, in other words, might have been outvoted by the other two Powers. The proposed procedure was first to reach an agreement with Austria and then to impose the organisation on France and Belgium.

Crucial in the present context are the military clauses, which were no longer to be deferred until after the war. Point 17 provided for the razing of French fortifications in the north and east and a prohibition of their rebuilding. Germany was to have the right to occupy the Channel and western ports, possibly until the war with Britain was ended. The French army was to be demobilised and moved to the south. Point 18 applied similar treatment to Belgium. The remaining clauses dealt with other details, notably colonial questions.

Point 17 with its premise that ending the war with Britain remained a problem still to be solved formed the particular point of departure for Rathenau's proposals, embodied in his letter of 7 September. The effect of this letter did not reach beyond Bethmann-Hollweg at Headquarters. Its influence was exerted by way of the Chancellery in Berlin and the Under-Secretary, Wahnschaffe, to whom Rathenau sent a copy. Rechenberg in Berlin also took note of the Memorandum: and since Rechenberg had been entrusted with his current mission, Rathenau had been in constant touch with him. As he told Mutius with con-

siderable satisfaction on 10 October, the day Antwerp
fell to the Germans, he believed that something useful might eventuate. Rathenau once again explained
his reasoning to the Chancellor's intimate. He did
not think that peace would come soon; and since a
German invasion of Britain was scarcely feasible,
careful calculation justified the confident conclusion
that Germany would retain a position of superior
strength, even if the war were protracted. Bethmann-
Hollweg read this letter too and thus accepted the
collaboration between Rathenau and Rechenberg in
Berlin.

Rathenau's letter of 7 September was based on two
assumptions: contrary to the general expectation, he
did not believe that the subjugation of France would
cause Britain to seek peace but that the war would
drag on; and secondly, again against expectation and
as already mentioned, he felt that economic developments would favour Britain and America, because of
the growth of the overseas markets. Accordingly,
Rathenau's proposals were based on the idea of peace
with France along the lines of the Peace of Nikolsburg
with Austria in 1866. Central Europe would be unified under German leadership, on the one hand in
opposition to Britain and America, on the other hand
politically and economically strengthened against
Russia. The time was propitious, since the unex-
ampled subjugation of France by the armies of Germany represented a conspicuous climax that would
provide a suitable psychological background for such
sweeping events. Britain's further treatment would be
guided by the following considerations:

(1) Systematic demoralisation of enemy cities by
     means of overwhelming air power, on a far larger
     scale than heretofore. (In a technical sense this
     was still illusory and represented an overestimate
     of the new Zeppelin and aeroplane weapons sys-
     tems – but it did foreshadow the air war of the
     future!)
(2) Utilisation of the western ports of France to
     breach the Atlantic blockade.

(3) Posing a threat to the British position in the Mediterranean, especially in Egypt, Suez and Gibraltar.

(4) Most important of all, the economic integration and emancipation of Central Europe. (The importance of a continental customs union was, of course, self-evident in this connection.)

Following military confrontation on the Continent, the war with Britain would continue in the form of protracted economic warfare; and it did not seem possible to offer any clear predictions on how this would run and end; but in well-informed leading circles it was generally held that Britain could not be forced to her knees by military means. In the perspective of such a long and indecisive struggle, the line between war aims and the means to attain them grew blurred. Even in Rathenau's plan, 'war measures' merge imperceptibly into the notion of *Mitteleuropa* as the 'final goal'. When Bethmann-Hollweg spoke of basically reorganising the economic situation in central Europe he certainly was not thinking solely of temporary measures intended only for the duration of the war.

It would be a mistake to view the September Memorandum purely in terms of a strategic war-aims programme. In a permanent economic struggle with Britain, fluctuating for ever between war and armistice, it would be impossible, in retrospect, to distinguish sharply between intermediate and final goals, and indeed between war aims as such and the means chosen to attain them. Hence one should not underestimate the power shift in Europe that would have been inevitably associated with any central European economic organisation dependent on Germany. Such a thing would very likely have replaced the traditional balance of power with German predominance. Just how that position could have been secured by a European guarantee in the post-war period was an open problem; for the German government were aware that Germany lacked the power to force Britain to tolerate German preponderance in Europe. The struggle with Britain over German predominance in Europe thus

almost inevitably grew into an Imperialist tug-of-war
on a world-wide scale.

Yet there was no continuity at government level between the pre-war and wartime desire of the Germans
to reshape the relations of power in Europe, centred
on the *Mitteleuropa* idea, as Fritz Fischer maintains
in *Weltmacht oder Niedergang*. Rathenau's *Mitteleuropa* plans may have been adapted to wartime contingencies straight from his pre-war concept, but at
government level such plans were a direct response to
the challenge posed by Britain's evident willingness to
fight to the limit, forcing Germany to consider every
resource at her disposal on the Continent to counter
the threat. The moment it became clear beyond
doubt that there would be a protracted economic
struggle with Britain, *Mitteleuropa* took on the
character of a carefully considered project, though still
tentative and non-committal, because it was based on
the anticipated subjugation of France. In the light of
his fight against the annexationists, Bethmann-Hollweg may have welcomed the plan, if only because it
seemed a likely means – or so Rathenau, at least,
thought – for channelling German public opinion and
its exaggerated expectations when peace did come.

In August Bethmann-Hollweg had aimed his hopes
and efforts in the direction of limiting the war and
keeping it under control; but he had not been able to
rule out the possibility that it might unexpectedly expand into the economic sphere, thereby effecting a
fundamental alteration in the existing field of force.
Early in the month Rathenau had voiced fears to the
Chancellor that the war might disastrously affect German markets outside Europe and that a search must
therefore be made for possible substitutes on the Continent. It was against this background that Bethmann-
Hollweg first engaged in talks with Delbrück on an
economic programme that contemplated a central
European customs union, the emphasis being placed
on Austria, in keeping with Rathenau's memorandum; but no directives were issued at that time and the
departmental consultations on economic policies to be
pursued at the end of the war never got beyond the

hypothetical stage. It was only the September Memorandum, with Bethmann-Hollweg's covering letter, that gave the departmental chiefs a basis for concrete discussion of a central European economic union, to their surprise.

These hesitant consultations on economic reorientation after the war were paralleled at Headquarters, first in Koblenz and then in Luxembourg, by preliminary discussions on economic guarantees for postwar Germany. It was on 21 August that the idea of a central European economic union first entered this debate. Riezler noted: 'In the evening a long discussion on Poland and the possibility of loosely integrating other countries with Germany – a central European system of differential tariffs, a Greater Germany with Belgium, Holland and Poland as immediate and Austria as a more distant protectorate.' Even before Rechenberg had presented his more limited eastern *Mitteleuropa* concept to the government, the Polish question had here already provided the impetus for a far-reaching examination of the idea of an interdependent central European economic system. True, it is not known to what extent Bethmann-Hollweg took part in these talks nor whether he thought the idea meaningful and feasible at this early date. The discussions among the politicians, at any rate, testify to uncertainty and irresolute improvisation rather than faith in victory and sweeping programmes of conquest. Quite evidently there was no consistent and practical picture of just how Germany's position could be made 'secure' after the war; and at this early stage of discussion the Chancellor did nothing to develop such a programme and a consensus around it. Otherwise Delbrück, in his memorandum to the Chancellor of 3 September, could scarcely have challenged Rathenau's proposal so forthrightly. It did not contain a single new thought, Delbrück wrote. It was merely a one-sided presentation in a new guise of a problem that had ceaselessly preoccupied the statesmen of the two great empires for more than sixty years.

In these first controversial discussions the dominant element was not yet the aggressive turn against Britain with the idea of including western Europe and especially the Channel coast. This came to the fore – and drew Bethmann-Hollweg's attention – only after Rathenau's suggestion in his letter of 28 August. It was then that the realities of economic warfare with Britain required the Chancellor, too, to concern himself with plans for a central European economic union and envisage their realisation in the event of France's precipitate collapse. Even so, one may well question whether he shared Riezler's romantic faith in the durability of such a new order. He was certainly clear on one point – it could have been put into effect only by the harshest kind of coercion.

The Experts Take Over

Seasoned in the ways of bureaucracy, the Chancellor managed to sidetrack discussion at Headquarters, where it was subject to many unconstitutional and semi-constitutional influences. Insisting that under established procedure the Minister of the Interior had jurisdiction in such matters, he succeeded in turning over the matter of the Memorandum on 9 September to officially detailed bureaucrats for preparation and processing. For reasons of secrecy and in order to avoid the politically irrelevant ballast of purely administrative contributions by lower-echelon officials, he instructed Delbrück to keep to the highest level of officialdom in the major departments. To avoid any political filibusters, Delbrück was also told to shun the vested interests.

Delbrück had a keen sense of jurisdictional privileges and never hesitated to invoke the Chancellor's basic directive of 9 September. He succeeded in outmanœuvring even the Foreign Ministry, allowing it participation in only the verbal consultations, represented usually by Johannes, Head of the Economic Policy Section, occasionally by the Under-Secretary, Zimmermann, who had remained in Berlin. Delbrück secured Bethmann-Hollweg's explicit agreement for this behaviour.

Having succeeded in keeping the policy-making function from the hurly-burly of petty political intrigue by turning the preparatory work over to professional civil servants, the Chancellor now applied his own habits of thoroughness to the task of carefully thinking through and analysing the main issues. He was in constant touch with Delbrück, who fed him the findings of the experts; for Bethmann-Hollweg was by no means insensitive to the problems and solutions enumerated in the Memorandum. On the contrary, he treated the total war situation and the possible peace constellations as matters of the greatest urgency and he was convinced that Germany lacked the military leverage to vanquish Britain and to compel her at the peace table to restore Germany's share in the world market. Hence he felt that even new and unconventional solutions had to be considered with great care and he saw such possibilities in the proposals offered by Rechenberg and Rathenau. Yet he was at pains to rule out any radical speculation and far-fetched planning not based on an overall political concept. A remark in a letter of 12 September 1914, from Riezler to Hamann, however, does reflect the fact that the manifest change in the military situation had given the government temporary relief from the war-aims debate at Headquarters. 'There is less talk of peace terms,' Riezler wrote, 'for the situation in the West is quiescent at the moment, and in Galicia too things are far from settled.'

The Dialogue between Bethmann-Hollweg and Delbrück

It remains to outline in general terms the further course of the discussions between the Chancellor and the executive departments, to illustrate the change that took place in the ensuing months. Although the source material is available, the scope of this essay dictates that we forgo the details of the various estimates of the situation.

A first discussion is reflected in a written exchange

between Bethmann-Hollweg and Delbrück in September. In his campaign against Rathenau's proposal of a customs union with Austria, Delbrück concentrated primarily on the economic aspects. His main argument was that complete abolition of agricultural tariffs would be unacceptable to German farming interests. The advantages accruing to German industry by virtue of its strong position, on the other hand, would seriously threaten the existence of Austrian industry. Under Rathenau's proposal Austria's expected opposition was to be overcome by means of a *coup*, camouflaged as a war measure. As a constitutional Minister and law-abiding administrator Delbrück sharply rejected such a course. He did, however, feel that it was worth considering a customs alliance with lower tariffs among its members and uniform tariffs for other nations. He was nevertheless unwilling to anticipate developments after the war, which was bound to bring about an essential overall shift in Germany's economic situation. This meant that economic relations with Austria would have to be re-examined in the light of overall economic relations rather than settled while the war was on. This did not mean that Delbrück refused on principle to envisage any improvement in the post-war economic situation. 'Unless we annex Luxemburg, Belgium and Holland – and I assume we will not, especially the two latter – we shall have to be intent upon building up their economic relations with us in an appropriate way.'

Bethmann-Hollweg's reply of 16 September was notably concise, in contrast to Delbrück's detailed exposition. He said that the question of an Austro-German customs *rapprochement* would have to be treated in the context of the central European economic union, discussed in his covering letter of 9 September. Further detailed examination would show whether a special status for the two allied Powers within such a union was desirable. The Chancellor was convinced, however, that the creation of *Mitteleuropa* as well as, more narrowly, settlement of Austro-German relations could not be realised 'on the basis of an understanding on common interests, but only in the event of

Germany dictating the peace under force of political superiority'. This hard-headed judgement flew in the face of Rathenau's optimistic expectation that France could be won over to a 'voluntary peace' in the spirit of German peace policy in 1866.

On 13 September, in response to the programme for a central European customs union submitted to him on 9 September, Delbrück abandoned his long-winded manner of argumentation against Rathenau's proposal and mentioned the possible disadvantages of competition from Italian and French wines, Hungarian produce and French textiles in only cursory fashion. He had decided to give loyal allegiance to Bethmann-Hollweg, to get to know the Chancellor's arguments inside out. As a possible argument for such a radical upheaval he pointed out that Germany would be fighting for dominion of the world market rather than the home market. 'Only a Europe comprising a united customs area will be able to face the enormous productive potential of the transatlantic world with the requisite strength. We should thank God that the war gives us occasion and opportunity to abandon an economic system that is about to pass the apex of its success.'

Delbrück, however, did mention the domestic implications of a central European customs union. It could be brought into being only if the agrarian conservatives were outmanœuvred by an anti-rightist liberal majority, and such a majority would not be able to dispense with the Social Democrats. Hence the process of coming to terms with the Social Democrats, which was already under way, must be continued side by side with the development of the *Mitteleuropa* concept, and there must be preparations for a new national policy, to be put into effect, of course, only after the war. Wahnschaffe and Delbrück, with Bethmann-Hollweg's approval, had already agreed on a compromise formula for the duration of the war: the groundwork was to be laid for a great post-war 'national regeneration'.

In his reply of 19 September the Chancellor admitted that 'so radical a reorientation' was bound

to encounter economic and political difficulties. To
bridge the possible disadvantages of total abolition of
tariff barriers in central Europe, he proposed a transitional solution. Without dropping the basic scheme,
tariffs which would at least be uniform were to be fixed
for countries outside the union, for a list of the most important exports, together with low preferential tariffs
for the countries within the union.

As far as the domestic aspects of the problem were
concerned, the Chancellor also pleaded for taking
advantage of an opportunity that might never recur,
to root the Social Democrats firmly in a nationalist
and monarchical spirit. The kind of reorientation
contemplated, he said, meant that the Social Democratic leaders must realise that Germany – and Prussia
in particular – would never surrender the firm foundations on which they had grown. There could be no
loosening of stalwart German nationalism, of the
system the Social Democrats had been so fond of de-
crying as 'militarism'. Let the Social Democrats pay
less attention to 'international understanding' and
more to the need for a strong system of military defence.

Bethmann-Hollweg, in other words, was not prepared to go so far as to concede a parliamentary
system in any domestic reorientation with the Social
Democrats. He appreciated the problems of Germany
as an industrialised nation, but as the 'Squire of
Hohenfinow' he was a conservative Prussian to the
core. The domestic reforms he envisaged were not intended to contribute to weakening the conservative
monarchist foundations of Germany and Prussia but
to strengthening them by binding the Social Democrats to the principles that underlay the State. The
Chancellor's *Mitteleuropa* plans did not include pay-
ing the price of a basic change of system. There was to
be no domestic upheaval to go hand in hand with the
new radical economic policy on the Continent.

Early in October, armed with a briefcase full of
memoranda, Delbrück set out for Charleville and a
further round of talks with the Chancellor on the
issue of a customs union. The upshot of these talks

shows clearly that virtually no political commitments had been made in previous discussion. The situation was still very far from having reached the stage of decision. Delbrück managed to convince Bethmann-Hollweg that the matter had not yet come to a head and that he must be given time to review all the technical details. At the same time, however, Delbrück clearly indicated that resistance to the plan, especially within the higher Prussian government echelons, could be overcome only if the Chancellor himself came out with a clear-cut programme and the unswerving will to put it into effect. What he was doing was to remove himself from the line of fire and to remind the Chancellor of his responsibility. Yet it was precisely such an official commitment that ran counter to Bethmann-Hollweg's inclinations; for the changed military situation and the failure of any French collapse to occur had undermined the very premise of the *Mitteleuropa* project covered in the September Memorandum; and the Chancellor was reluctant to enter into any premature commitment in respect of possible peace negotiations to come, in which Germany was now unlikely to be able to dictate harsh terms. As Delbrück put it in his memoirs, 'work on the project continued to the end of my term of office, but the Chancellor never did issue the policy declaration I wanted'. Interdepartmental committee meetings ran their course, but no longer under the whiplash of Headquarters.

'From the Mildest to the Toughest': The Experts Meet

By mid-October the groundwork for a central European customs union had been developed within the Reich Office of the Interior to the point where discussion of the subject could be usefully continued. In a draft for a general position paper, Delbrück discussed the domestic political situation, especially the state of national minorities within Germany, and the Polish question, and in connection with the latter also the question of a customs union. In the matter of the Polish issue he inclined to the so-called 'Austrian solution' after the war and attacked the separatist policies of the generals in the field, who were working for the restoration of Poland, in concert with the Polish 'Young Turks'. In this connection Delbrück reverted to Rechenberg's idea of territorial compensation which, in the course of the customs union debate, became transformed into 'general political and economic concessions', the original concept dissolving into loosely connected sub-issues within a framework of traditional trade pacts.

On the basis of the work of his staff, Delbrück added a new argument to those he had previously used against a customs union with Austria, a project that had found few new friends beyond Rechenberg and Schönebeck. 'Austria,' he said, 'is so poorly consolidated in political and economic respects, its development potential so unreliable and obscure, that our own political and economic future would be endangered, were we to enter into closer ties with this decaying and disintegrating State.' After a polite disavowal of his ability to judge Austria, since he was not personally familiar with the country, Bethmann-Hollweg's deputy, in a later section of the letter, nevertheless identified himself with the view that the Dual Monarchy's economy was in poor shape and complained of its representatives' arrogance, which was totally inappropriate in view of the country's inefficiency and represented a severe strain on efforts at collaboration.

This was only three months after the July crisis, in which the restoration of Austria as a Great Power had been one of the main goals of German policy – a policy, by the way, that was still finding expression, at least in part, in Rechenberg's sympathies for an Austrian solution of the Polish issue. Basically, Delbrück's verdict meant that a cornerstone of that policy had been thoroughly undermined, lending further urgency to the need for a thoroughgoing overhaul of pre-war political alignments. Even in these early months of the war the problem of bringing about such a realignment became more and more like trying to square the circle, in view of Germany's military and economic dilemma.

Following the line of reasoning in his letter of 13 September, Delbrück presented an argument he described as crucial to the ultimate decision. If Germany had to anticipate that the war would impair her markets, if it were reasonable to assume that Britain would have to abandon her policy of free trade after the war and if it were likely that the British colonies would treat Germany even less favourably than heretofore, in respect of tariffs, then the disadvantages of integration with Austria would have to be accepted as a key to opening up the continental market. Such a decision was probably inescapable since Russia, no matter how she emerged from the war, was bound to become a most dangerous economic rival in the course of time, in view of her manpower and natural resources. The transatlantic world, moreover, possibly allied with Britain, might well turn out an even more potent rival; and against such opposition the countries of central Europe could scarcely prevail, either politically or economically, unless they were firmly united by economic and constitutional bonds.

It is readily seen that Delbrück was using arguments drawn from Rathenau's letter of 7 September. What the two had in common was the goal of a settlement and alliance with France, with which an arrangement over Belgium must be arrived at – the details cannot be elaborated here. Yet overall, as Rathenau summarised it in his diary, the opponents of his views had prevailed, in the wake of growing objections in the interdepartmental meetings during September and October.

Behind Delbrück's thinking about the various possibilities stood a defensive attitude to what was seen as an organised world of enemies that must be fought with its own weapons, if Germany wished to continue to cut any figure at all, in a political and economic sense. In such an embattled world the alternative that three great economic blocs might exist in harmony side by side by a policy of live and let live was not

even considered. Such was the heritage not only of
'Imperialist' thinking but of the war-borne trend towards economic warfare. Throughout the discussions
with the Chancellor, Delbrück refrained from voicing
any decided opinions of his own, assuming instead the
role of a purely non-political, technical and administrative adviser, which was made all the easier, since
there was indeed much disagreement among the various departments. Another interpretation of his reti-
cence, however, would be that it might have stemmed
from his own conservative opposition.

Delbrück invited the departmental chiefs on 21
October to stimulate further work in the direction of
elaborating a range of clear-cut proposals 'from the
mildest to the toughest'. He passed on the different
views to the Chancellor, on the assumption, he said,
that they would be of interest to Bethmann-Hollweg
in preparing for the difficult final decision. Delbrück
was well aware of the immense burden of responsibility that ultimately weighed down on the Chancellor and no one else. He could not make the decision
in Bethmann-Hollweg's place and he had no wish to
do so.

New Hopes of Victory in October 1914

During these October days Bethmann-Hollweg for the
second time faced a major decision, since the military
situation did not exclude the possibility that a decisive strategic success in the West might impend after
all. Both another envelopment in the race to the sea
and a great strategic breakthrough seemed possible.
The capture of Antwerp was accounted a particularly
impressive *coup* to remind the world of Germany's
military power. Churchill was known to have been in
that city until two days before its fall and to have
called for resistance to the last. The fall of Antwerp
thus became a powerful symbol.

On the basis of this estimate of the situation Bethmann-Hollweg asked Pohl, in a talk on 15 October,
for an expression of opinion on the goals Germany
should pursue in peace negotiations. Pohl enumerated

the occupation of Antwerp, Bruges, Ostend and Dunkirk in the West, pushing back the Russians in the East and seizing Alexandretta and Mersina as naval bases in the South. Bethmann-Hollweg did at one point openly demur, admonishing the admiral not to 'talk too big', but as usual when it came to discussing war aims his rhetoric was conciliatory and Pohl thought that he assented. Tirpitz objected to Pohl's war aims on the ground that they contained nothing to indicate victory over Britain and was told in no uncertain terms that here too victory over France and Russia would be crucial. Once again, as in September, the thinking was based on a premise of German victory on the Continent, which was to lay the groundwork for a strategy against Britain.

On 19 October Bethmann-Hollweg invited Tirpitz too for a discussion of possible peace terms; and to that end he once again, on 22 October, asked Delbrück for detailed 'desiderata' against the event of peace negotiations. In style and outward form his directive was related to his covering letter for the September Memorandum. 'Even though there are no such signs so far,' he concluded, 'we must take the possibility into account that one of our enemies might suddenly collapse and we must not be taken by surprise in that event.'

This document supplanted Bethmann-Hollweg's prior directive of 9 September about background research which thus was in force for only six weeks and certainly did not, as Fritz Fischer claims, form the foundation to the end of the war of German war-aims policy. In a technical sense, Bethmann-Hollweg was acting on the interdepartmental discussion about economic policy. The notion of a great central European economic area was not taken up. Instead, the Chancellor limited himself, in the question of future economic policy, to ordering that a substitute must be found, in the French and Russian markets, for the possible losses that might accrue to Germany in the world market for some years after the war. He mentioned the incorporation of the Briey ore region as one measure, precisely something that Delbrück, in

his analysis of 13 September, had described as potentially unnecessary within the framework of a central
European economic union. The Russian market was
to be opened to German exports under a long-term
trade pact that would lower the Russian tariffs of
greatest concern to Germany. Bethmann-Hollweg instructed Delbrück to undertake a preliminary study of
this question, taking into account the modalities that
might arise from the possible establishment of a
customs union with Austria. The accent had sharply
shifted and a customs union with Austria was now
secondary to a trade pact with Russia.

Interest in supranational organisation had been replaced in the directive by traditional forms of trade
agreement, financial war indemnities and colonial
agreements, territorial or in terms of economic policy.
There were added proposals to secure 'freedom of
enterprise abroad without prejudice to the right of
national self-determination'. The most sanguine
eventuality to be explored was victory over Britain,
but it should be understood that this meant compromise on the part of the British after a German
triumph on the Continent rather than the military
defeat of Britain; for possible subjects for negotiation
considered by the Chancellor were patent agreements,
colonial tariff policy and certain measures to make it
more difficult for Britain to move into the protection-
ist camp, which was bound to bring on conscription.

These ideas suggest that Germany hoped for a
status quo with only minor changes. Only the severest
British economic war measures were to be forestalled,
together with too sweeping a revision of pre-war trade
and military policy.

On 23 and 24 October Delbrück gave a major Press
interview on German economic policy. Over and
above wartime needs, he described the revival of trade
and industry as his main concern and expressed his
expectation of co-operation with the neutral countries,
since they, as producers, had an interest in markets.
He tried to show, all in all, that Germany, owing to
her gift for organisation and improvisation and her
considerable degree of self-sufficiency, especially in the

food sector, was able to face the prospect of economic
warfare with confidence.

The War Stagnates: November 1914

On cursory assessment the political situation in
October still seemed to leave a remnant of hope that
the balance might tip in Germany's favour, in that
one of her enemies might suffer sudden collapse; but
during the ensuing weeks the forces shifted more and
more. On 17 October, during preparations for the
offensive in Flanders, Jagow expressed fears that the
war would turn into a morass and slow down to a
walk, from general exhaustion. This prediction came
true in mid-November 1914. The war of position in
the West became irrevocable. The Chief of Staff and
the War Minister confirmed Tirpitz in believing that
there was a complete stalemate in the West.

The inner leading circle – Bethmann-Hollweg, Falkenhayn, Zimmermann, Jagow and not least Tirpitz –
now embarked on a round of talks and written exchanges that amounted to a major stock-taking and
review of the political and military situation. Perhaps
the most significant document for an understanding of
the conclusions drawn from this critical situation was
the 'Raisonnement', as Bethmann-Hollweg called his
basic analysis of 19 November, which he transmitted
to Zimmermann for reaction. It is here referred to
only in respect of the main questions of concern: ending the war with Britain and the ideas relating to that
end.

The issue to be settled – and this found dramatic
expression in the leadership crisis at the turn of the
year – was the shift of political and military emphasis
to Russia, in order to get out of the blind alley into
which Germany had blundered and regain the military initiative, by a combination of strategic success
with efforts at a separate peace. Bethmann-Hollweg
was extremely sceptical that this new effort would
bring success but felt that he could not withstand Falkenhayn's unremitting pressure for a separate under-

standing with Russia because the war in the West had
bogged down and despite every confidence the situation
there had to be described as serious. At the very least,
he remarked, all the possibilities in the East had to be
considered with the greatest care, even though for the
time being there were no signs whatever that Russia
was prepared for negotiations. Hence he reviewed the
alternative that seemed to him most likely:

> Should we fail to split Russia away from the
> Entente, we shall probably not be able to gain mili-
> tary mastery over any one of our enemies. We risk
> the danger that the war will take an unfavourable
> turn for us overall, through the intervention of
> Japan, the sheer manpower of continuing British
> reinforcements, and military reverses, which can
> never be wholly excluded in a war; but even in the
> absence of such an extremity, our only remaining
> chance would be for the war to come to a halt by
> virtue of general exhaustion, without a clear-cut
> military defeat on either side.

He then drew a conclusion that concisely summarised the ideas that have preoccupied us in the
present account:

> In the event of peace we should have Belgium
> and northern France as bargaining counters, to the
> approximate extent that we now occupy those
> regions, while our enemies would be able to put up
> the greater part of Galicia and several of our
> colonies. Britain, in addition, would have the trump
> cards of an unvanquished fleet and unbroken
> dominion over world trade. Of itself this would not
> necessarily mean a situation unfavourable to our
> side, but we should not be able to impose more on
> Russia and France than we could now get from
> them, were either of them ready to conclude a sepa-
> rate peace.

Once again the impossibility of getting the better of
Britain was the point of departure: 'Vis-à-vis Britain

our power would be very slight. Even in the event of peace she would seek to play the role of protector of France, at least, maintaining political sway over that country in any future war with us.' He then outlined the limits of what might be attainable by peace: 'The results for us would be reduced in essence to a demonstration before the world that even the most powerful enemy coalition cannot bring us to our knees. While this might promote peace and further growth, the immediate effect would be that the German people would feel ill-rewarded for the immense hardships they have undergone.'

Following discussion of a number of fortunate contingencies and chances, Bethmann-Hollweg went a step further in his analysis. There could be no absolute confidence that Germany could win complete victory over France and Britain, he explained, even if Russia were split away from the Entente, for with competent leadership the military superiority of the Western Powers was very great and the German navy was probably not in a position to cut off Britain's food supply, not even for a limited period of time. Taking everything into account, the situation had to be described as serious, even with the greatest confidence on the German side. We note that all that was left of the grand plans was the traditional method of territorial bargaining in West and East.

Thus the Chancellor twice over qualified and questioned the political concept of Tirpitz and Falkenhayn, his adversaries and rivals for the Chancellorship. Against the price that the situation in respect of Russia would remain essentially as it had been before the war, they wanted to create one in the West that would be more favourable to Germany, while at the same time eliminating the Triple Entente. Bethmann-Hollweg thought this beyond reach, with or without a separate Russian peace. In his view this was the direction in which the most hard-headed evaluation of Germany's military and political resources pointed.

In analysing the available options in the field of economic policy, we have seen that the basic view was one of a world without peace, a world in which the

Powers were locked in struggle even without war. The
November 'Raisonnement' contains a phrase that reflects perhaps for the first time an alternative view of
the Chancellor, hinting at a first qualification of the
militant spirit inherent in Imperialist thinking. It was
to be openly expressed in Bethmann-Hollweg's letter
to Prince Max of Baden, already mentioned at the
beginning, and in his *Betrachtungen zum Weltkriege*.

'I am not in a Position to Enlighten these Gentlemen on the Military Situation'

Bethmann-Hollweg could imagine that the mere fact
that Germany was able to maintain herself against the
most powerful enemy coalition might promote peace
and further growth; but a keynote also struck in his
Betrachtungen suggests that a policy based so completely on imponderables would have implied, at least
initially, the severest domestic political struggles. He
was aware that he had very little freedom of choice if
he tried to lead a Germany still under the spell of
dreams of power along a road that offered no material
securities and guarantees. Unfortunately this early insight was buried later on. Thus, as long as the situation permitted, he plotted his course along traditional
lines of power politics, an approach to which he was
personally and profoundly dedicated; nor did he relinquish, in so far as possible, his hopes and ambitions
for material guarantees of Germany's political integrity, even though political and military developments
were constantly narrowing his scope for action. He
had some room for manœuvre left, of course, but he
bitterly complained of his restrictions. In a crisis, he
said, his domestic opponents would either have to see
the true military situation for themselves or have to be
briefed on it; but until that time came, he was en-
meshed in a network of intrigue and attacks which
charged him with being weak-kneed and which he refused to meet head-on.

A paradigm of this attitude is seen in his marginal
note on a memorandum submitted by the German

employers' associations in March 1915. Wahnschaffe's comment was that it would become necessary to open the eyes of men who spread such ideas about, to which Bethmann-Hollweg added: 'I am not in a position to enlighten these gentlemen on the military situation. They either accuse me of being weak-kneed or they grow anxious themselves. Neither course is welcome. Enlightenment can come only slowly, from the actual course of military events.'

The bitterness the Chancellor felt over the attitude embodied in this memorandum had been reflected some weeks earlier in a confidential talk he had with Theodor Wolff on 5 February 1915. 'We have been living a lie in both our foreign and domestic policy,' he said. 'Our people have been infected with a spirit of loud-mouthed braggadocio and irresponsible patter.' He had noted this insensate hatred of the enemy only on the home front, he added, much in contrast to the dead seriousness of the troops, which he had witnessed during a recent visit to the front. On this he staked his hopes, as he did later on in 1918, in his letter to Prince Max of Baden. 'It would be dreadful if this brash boastfulness and arrogance were to remain with us when peace comes. A horrifying thought – after the war there will be new men.'

There were immediate developments of which the Chancellor in March 1915 expected a salutary and enlightening effect. The situation grew progressively worse. More and more, during the winter of 1914–15, the preservation of occupied territory for bargaining purposes became a central point of policy, and ultimately this necessity restricted the possible scope of action in the East as well. At the height of the leadership crisis, when the Chancellor was fighting the Chief of Staff for the commitment of reserves in the East, Valentini, Chief of the Imperial Civil Cabinet, who worked closely with Bethmann-Hollweg, warned against endangering the territorial hostages in the West. Britain was the main enemy, he insisted, and a firm grip must be maintained on the occupied territories in the West, as a powerful means of exerting pressure on Britain.

By mid-March these territories seemed in danger. In
a letter to Treutler, the Foreign Ministry representative
at Headquarters, who had the job of maintaining
liaison with the Supreme Command since the Chancellor had returned to Berlin, Bethmann-Hollweg drew a
picture of the situation in the blackest colours, almost
as though he were writing on the eve of Black Friday
in 1918. He said that according to Press dispatches
from Switzerland confidence in victory was sweeping
France. There was a revival of economic life in the
south of France and French military reserves were
promising.

Bethmann-Hollweg saw greater danger that the
enemy, even if he did not succeed in breaking through
the German positions, might slowly push back the
Germans more and more, by virtue of his superior
manpower, artillery and ammunition:

> A German breakthrough, on the other hand,
> would exact tremendous casualties and merely
> bring us a few miles further on to an equally strong
> enemy position. At the present time we hold sub-
> stantial territorial hostages. Our enemies still have
> enough money to ransom them at an acceptable
> price. It seems to me that our situation will grow
> worse with every month the war continues, quite
> apart from the additional billions we shall have to
> raise in that event. Hindenburg and his people con-
> cur in this judgement.

Without the triumphs of August and September to
back them up, the German government once again,
under much more acute pressure, were faced with the
necessity of having to wait for the enemy to consider
further German occupation of the territories in point
as intolerable and on that account forgo fighting the
war to the end, since the only alternative, a protracted
and bloody war of position, might also be found intolerable. Meanwhile, the Germans had to watch idly
as the world made economic arrangements that excluded Germany; and time was against her.

In the face of these developments, discussion of post-war economic policy was concluded for the time being. On 12 April 1915 Delbrück advised the Chancellor of the results of interdepartmental consultations on economic integration with Austria – as anticipated, no agreement had been reached. All the departments more or less rejected a complete customs union, since such close economic integration could not be carried into effect as a 'temporary measure' but was bound to lead to intimate political and military ties; which did not recommend themselves because of scepticism concerning Austria's capacity and durability. There were added problems in the apportionment of customs revenue, reconciliation of agricultural and industrial interests and finding a proper constitutional basis.

As for the second possibility, a looser kind of customs alliance, in which the member States would concede one another preferential tariffs, the main argument against this solution was that it might lead to 'economic isolation', since the principle of reciprocity on which it would be based was incompatible with the basis of existing trade treaties, the most-favoured-nation clause. Apart from the fact that recognition of such an arrangement by the enemy countries could be achieved only through a conclusive victory, its value was extremely dubious, considering the almost certain adverse effect on other markets of great importance.

The ministerial bureaucrats then came to grips with the basic question affecting the economic structure of Germany:

> Our commercial activities are organised in such a way today that unless the most serious interference with our entire economic life is to be risked, we must continue to have access to world markets, notably such major markets as Great Britain, the United States and Russia. It would be against our interests to limit ourself to certain circumscribed markets, even if these were to be expanded. Hence from the viewpoint of German economic policy a proposal to form a customs union with Austria and other central European countries cannot be recommended. A remaining third way would be to con-

tinue the kind of economic policy we have pursued
heretofore, by concluding commercial treaties, preferably with tariff clauses.

Delbrück wished to envisage closer economic integration with Austria only if there were special political reasons that could not be ignored. He conceded that
one such motive might be the imposition of closer political ties with Austria by forcing that country into a
state of economic dependence on Germany, to counteract the possible freezing of wartime alignments even
when peace returned.

Fritz Fischer views the continuity of the *Mitteleuropa* question as an essential link between peacetime and wartime. In my view this ignores the fact
that both before and afterwards the conflict between
an international and a regional marketing orientation
continued to exert its effect undiminished within the
official agencies and among the vested interests. The
idea of a central European customs union was by no
means the only solution, nor even the crucial one.
That was one reason why it came to grief so quickly –
trade pacts were far more amenable to compromise in
the various directions. It is highly significant in this
connection that the German Industrial War Board, in
addition to the joint memorandum from the employers' associations, submitted a commercial treaty
draft based on drastically lowered tariffs. Director
Johannes of the Economic Policy Section of the
Foreign Ministry rejected it:

> Such a standardisation would not be tolerated by
> other countries in the long run and sooner or later
> provide the occasion for a new break. There can be
> no doubt whatever that if the war situation were
> less favourable to us neither Russia nor France
> would dream of accepting such an agreement. Even
> Great Britain could not be coerced into accepting
> the kind of formulation proposed by the Industrial
> War Board.

Delbrück argued along similar lines, adding that
any discrimination against British maritime commerce

by means of special tariffs would redound to the disadvantage of the German merchant navy and thus
gravely prejudice the revival of German overseas exports after the war. He also pointed out the devastating consequences for German agriculture. Even if the
war situation at the time peace was concluded were to
make it possible to impose such agreements on France,
the terms were not desirable.

Conclusion

In conclusion, I append a few remarks that somewhat
transcend the narrow limits of time and method
within which this essay has been held.

Within the framework of the diverse and shifting
estimates of the situation, consideration was given
time and again to a multiplicity of plans and goals,
each expressing some particular political possibility or
concept. They were the subject of official and non-
official discussions seldom ending in any decisions.
They came in ranges 'from the mildest to the toughest', and they were all kept on the shelf, so to speak.
The subjects discussed dealt with the most varied
functions – tactical methods, hostages for bargaining
purposes, forms of indemnity, ways of expanding German power after the war. There was a plethora of
rival aims but never any well-thought-out plan of
victory.

The question is how the government managed it
that these various plans of action, placed at the disposal
of the Cabinet as carefully prepared reserve policies,
and then embalmed in some ministerial file, never
reached a point of no return, never took on any
dangerous political and propaganda momentum of
their own.

There was no such danger so long as these papers
rested in bureaucracy's bosom, under the care of men
of the intellectual rectitude of Delbrück and Solf, who
had a sophisticated sense of self-criticism, and so long
as the politically vulnerable Tirpitz avoided walking

into one of the Chancellor's traps by committing himself to some plan laid down in writing, risking subsequent disavowal because sudden changes in the
situation undermined the premises of the plan.

A man like Solf could ironically speak of 'the game
of border-shifting'. Others, more mindful of aroused
public opinion and annexationist propaganda, had to
fall back on the compromise formula, '... in the event
of a decisive German victory'. Yet one would have to
search long among those responsible and in the know
before finding anyone who really believed in such a
possibility. It was simply a duty to display confidence
in wartime.

A certain protection continued to be afforded by
the flood of memoranda that made it easier to cover
every contingency, even in the political infighting.
Despite all the factors that facilitated control, Bethmann-Hollweg was not blind to the dangers of the war-
aims issue. Secrecy, suppression of Press discussion and
the exclusion of vested interests in the preparatory
work, all were prophylactic measures. Bethmann-
Hollweg knew and feared the constricting pressure of
public opinion; but since he knew the true situation
he was confident of prevailing at the crucial moment,
because of two weighty considerations. The time
might come when out of the deep secrecy of diplomatic
soundings a significant point of contact with the
enemy might emerge, hinting at his willingness to
negotiate. This might be thrown into the balance of
the domestic political struggle over German leadership, placed before the two major political bodies, the
Prussian Cabinet and the unofficial group of Reichstag leaders Bethmann-Hollweg had established.
There the issue could be forged into a decisive and
successful weapon to which the Kaiser could be won
over.

It should be borne in mind how much political
capital the Chancellor was able to make out of the
wretched crumbs in sounding out Russia on a separate
peace, an initiative that came entirely from the German side, without finding any echo, but that did
admirable service in protecting his domestic policy

and in the Polish question. As a last resort there was always publicity and the threat of a storm from the Left. Such eventualities, however, were quite remote at the outset of the war, expressed more as a latent threat in the struggle to preserve the National Unity Front and Social Democratic support, which were indispensable to the pursuit of the war.

In the end the whole question was never settled, right down to the Russian Revolution. Bethmann-Hollweg never had the slightest chance to make peace and was compelled to say so to the party leaders time and again; and so long as there were no discernible and feasible opportunities for peace, all the planning was consigned to the limbo of unreality; and one should guard against stultifying those responsible by suggesting they did not know it. The inner political leadership saw this limbo quite clearly, even though others were blind to it.

Despite the day-to-day struggle over the political truce on the home front, this tended to ease the severity of political conflict considerably for the Chancellor, even as it was probably responsible in part for the stridency of his opponents. Thus he was able to practise the art of 'dilatory compromise' (as a lawyer might put it) to the utmost, side-stepping the danger of losing his place to one of the deluded fanatics and concealing his view of the situation from observers abroad.

If there were any political limitations the Chancellor could not transcend, it was that he was unable to avoid or make up for the loss of German credibility in a world that had ceased to believe that the German government would be willing to compromise. For a long time his faith in Cabinet and secret diplomacy based on hard-headed compromise kept him from taking these limitations as seriously as they deserved. Here too the letter to Prince Max of Baden seems to reflect new insight.

Bethmann-Hollweg, furthermore, agreed with German public opinion and his domestic opponents on one point. He was not prepared to take a first, let alone a public step in offering a modified *status quo*.

He could not bring himself to relinquish in advance the territorial hostages he wanted to use as bargaining counters, if not keep under German sway, at least in part. In retrospect, from the vantage point of Versailles, this might have been Germany's only chance for achieving anything the Chancellor could have described as promoting peace. He thought that even much smaller steps would already signify sweeping admissions of weakness and hints of surrender, which he feared would merely bring on vociferous jubilation and even greater resolution on the part of the enemy.

It is a moot question how much scope he really had in this respect. We know too little about how firm was the Entente's resolution to fight the war to the end. Whatever the conclusions from further research, the question remains of how important German credibility might have been in world opinion – was it perhaps underestimated? Unfortunately, in the age of Imperialism – and perhaps in other ages as well – there was virtually no willingness to accept political risks without material guarantees.

Appendix

Holograph Letter from Bethmann-Hollweg to Prince Max of Baden
(From the papers of Prince Max of Baden, Salem)

Hohenfinow, 17 January 1918

Most gracious Prince,

Your Highness has given me great pleasure with your handwritten letter of 20 December, such as has not come my way for a long time, and I must first of all ask your kind indulgence that my thanks are expressed so late. I have in the meantime found universal confirmation that the speech of Your Highness has made an impression that continues to deepen. The Kaiser, for one, was very much impressed by it. This was related to me by Herr von Valentini, whom I had the privilege of seeing before receiving Your Highness's letter. I am pleased also with the attitude of the

Supreme Command, even though I continue to find its overall political stand obscure and displeasing.

In Your Highness's letter such a wealth of lofty political thoughts are touched upon that I fear my pen will be too feeble to respond to them all. Allow me to reiterate, however, that I gladly follow you in all that you now so handsomely describe as the basis of the 'unwritten law'; and if, in my letter, I mentioned that various methods may flow from that basis, I merely wished to suggest my uncertainty as to whether you find yourself able to approve the ultimate goal I believe I see coming, though I did not identify it at the time.

Ever since I have been no more than a spectator, I am gripped day by day more deeply than before by the awesome grandeur of what we have undergone, by the sublime splendour of man's heroism and the sombre depth of his delusions, through which we are passing. This, the most stupendous revolution ever to shake the globe, cannot end, the nations cannot 'atone' before God and the world for all the horror they have done, unless mankind turns away resolutely from the conditions that conjured up this war and seeks to create something new in their place. I too deeply regretted the phrase in [the reply to] the Papal Note about the coincidence of unfortunate circumstances that caused the war. Not only because it weakens our moral position, but above all because it is untrue.

Imperialism, nationalism and economic materialism, which in broad outline have governed the policies of all the nations during the past generation, set themselves goals that could be pursued by each nation only at the cost of a general collision. It is true that besides these general reasons there were special circumstances that militated in favour of war, including those in which Germany in 1870–1 entered the circle of Great Powers, subsequently achieved world stature and became the object of vengeful envy on the part of the other Great Powers, largely though not entirely by her own fault. Both of these lines, however, the general and the special, are so closely interlinked that

it is impossible to say on which side lay the more
powerful driving force. For myself, I see the general
constellation as the crucial element. How else explain
the senseless and impassioned zeal which allowed
countries like Italy, Rumania and even America, not
originally involved in the war, no rest until they too
had immersed themselves in the bloodbath? Surely
this is the immediate, tangible expression of a general
disposition towards war in the world.

Many had more or less of an inkling of this development; but basically only the Social Democrats
openly pointed towards it, and only they worked
against the war with conviction. The other parties fell
more or less under the spell of Imperialism. In France
and Russia they deliberately set their course for war,
but elsewhere too they ventured more and more on a
slippery slope, allowing the idea of war to gain momentum, often consoling themselves with the thought
that world war was unthinkable and could never come
to pass.

Governments – in France and Russia, for example –
followed the Imperialists, partly from conviction,
partly from an unwillingness to offer resistance.
Where they did not, they soon became too weak to
change course, nor even wished to do so, as in Britain,
which was not steering a direct course towards war,
but also was certainly not thrown into fear and trem-
bling by the idea of it, since in typical British arrogance and selfishness she thought it might promise immediate advantage to her rather than harm. Thus all
efforts to reduce the danger of war by disarmament
and courts of arbitration failed, as did the special
effort to secure the peace by means of an Anglo-
German understanding.

The nations are growing more and more aware of
all this. At the same time the realisation is spreading
that despite Imperialism and nationalism the great
majority of the people at bottom did not want war at
all – or would not have wanted it, had they known its
full horror, as it now stands revealed. It is taken for
granted, therefore, that the governments alone were
responsible for the war breaking out, against the will

of the masses, for Imperialism in all its forms attaining such power, for the fact that Germany has drawn distrust and even hatred upon herself throughout the world; and that it was the fault of the governments that no peaceful way out was found in July 1914. In whatever measure these beliefs and convictions may be justified, they lead with inescapable logic to the conclusion that there should be better government and that government should be in greater agreement with the true will of the people. So great is the force of this challenge, and so widely will the ethical ideas on which it rests spread after this bloodbath, that it is bound to prevail, even against the will of the chauvinists and reactionaries who will survive, though their future power will dwindle in the precise degree of their present savage demeanour. I am utterly convinced that this will happen, the more so since peace is unlikely to come until the war-weary masses will force it in one way or another and since these very masses will discern the full burdens and dimensions of the war only after peace has been concluded.

I know that the thoughts I am here voicing are neither new nor original. In the course of the present cataclysm it has always been my endeavour to isolate those general ideas that will shape the future, so that I might form a correct estimate of their inexorable consequences for Germany.

In this connection there also arises the question of Prussian electoral law, mentioned by Your Highness. My own experience parallels yours. 'Poor Prussia!' I have often told myself, asking whether the move to the general franchise may not destroy our greatest and most tested values, whether the leap we seek to make may not be too big and precipitate. Yet even today I do not for a moment doubt the necessity and propriety of the [Kaiser's] decision [promising introduction of the general franchise in Prussia during the war]. Practically speaking, there is no alternative. In realistic terms it would be impossible to devise a form of popular vote that would avoid sweeping democratisation unless it were based in some way on wealth and privilege. Numberless inquiries have been con-

ducted on this subject, always with the same negative
result; but this is not really what determined me. The
crucial consideration for me was that the only kind of
electoral law in keeping with the just demand for a
regime that would embody the popular will is one
that confers political rights with the same equality
that governs the hardships imposed by the war. This is
no mere theory but an ethical postulate stronger than
any argument – which may not be altogether unjusti-
fied – that the true popular will can never be defined
and that even the universal franchise offers no
guarantee that it will be carried out.

My view of the so-called parliamentary system is
similar. It is at bottom incompatible with our federal
constitution, for it requires firmly organised majority
parties, which we do not have – or do not yet have. It
provides Ministers who are not as well qualified as
under the bureaucratic system. Above all, it harbours
a host of political dangers which we can study in detail in the Romance countries. Yet in the long run the
demand that even the members of the government
should embody the popular will as expressed in the
legislature is a necessary consequence of the war, for
reasons already given, and cannot be denied. Of
course the forms must be adapted to German contingencies, and it must not be overlooked that the
government too increasingly looks for firmer ties with
the legislature, for reasons of their own, at least during such critical times as are likely to be with us long
after the war. Count Hertling's Chancellorship, for
example, would long since have reached its end, had
he not been able to count on a parliamentary
majority, which he was ultimately able to secure only
by including several parliamentarians in the government – although one may well condemn the unseemly
rivalry for these posts that was displayed in the
process.

I think that in judging the overall situation one
should not be deceived by the fact that even the major
liberal parties have acquiesced in the intrusions of the
military into the political sphere. As we know, the
National Liberals have given blanket approval in

advance to all the military requests of the Supreme Command, without even knowing in the least what they were. Complete faith in the military qualifications of the Supreme Command may be amply justified, but one is tempted to view this policy as a symptom that our desire for popular democratic government is coupled with a certain slavishness that seems only the semblance of libertarian government while actually longing for the absolutist leadership of a bureaucratic regime, as was true of the Romans in the Augustan Age. Yet unlike the Romans of that time we are not an ancient people exhausted from civil wars. On the contrary, those sections of our people who have, over the past generation, been our driving force, irksome and even dangerous at times, it is true – the Socialist masses, to speak bluntly – have infused a tremendous dynamism and youthful vigour into our nation. After the war these Germans will not rest content with empty political and economic liberties – they will demand real rights. These masses will simply run the National Liberal fossils into the ground, and topmost among the demands that can then be expected will be the repression of militarism, the more it now conducts itself as a dictatorial form of rule.

These remarks are not at all meant to suggest that the introduction in Germany of a fully formed democratic regime would constitute the ultimate wisdom, especially if it were established on some foreign model; but we should be able to discern the broad outline in which our direction is inscribed in letters of blood; and we should conduct ourselves in such a way as not to be engulfed by the flood.

I am wandering far afield, even though I can touch upon only a small segment of the thoughts and questions that obtrude when one tries to face reality; and even within that segment I see that I have only scratched the surface, only sketchily reviewed a few of many aspects. Perhaps I am exceeding the bounds of propriety in what I have to say and suggest. If so, my only excuse is that the stimulus came from Your Highness's letter.

Your Highness has had the great kindness to speak to me about the question of your Chancellorship, with a frankness for which I am most deeply obliged. Allow me to respond with the same frankness. I have welcomed it that this question has not become acute, since Your Highness is the heir to the throne of Baden. Perhaps it is not the general political attacks to which a Chancellor is exposed that are crucial; but judging from the way things have run throughout the war, came to a head last July and are once again pointing up towards a crisis, I cannot help feeling concern that sharp clashes between the two powers [i.e. the military and the political] will remain the order of the day; and I could wish that Your Highness were spared such conflicts. If it should come to another great crisis, however, in which Your Highness were to be summoned, the situation at home and abroad might be so acute that patriotism might demand that in despite of all conflict Your Highness accept. It goes without saying that I am absolutely convinced, knowing the political views Your Highness entertains, that the affairs of state would be in good hands.

And now I must ask Your Highness's gracious pardon for these importunities. If things were as they used to be and a face-to-face exchange were still possible, I might not have been tempted to impose upon your patience with these written remarks. They are indeed presumptuous in their inadequacy in dealing with great problems as yet probably beyond the power of the human mind. For this reason alone I ask that this letter be taken as a purely personal message. I was, after all, emboldened to write it only on account of the friendly and gracious sentiments Your Highness has always displayed towards me and I sincerely hope will continue to display.

With the greatest respect and gratitude, I remain Your Highness's obedient servant.

                                                BETHMANN-HOLLWEG

6 Gerhard Ritter: A Patriotic Historian's Justification

Karl-Heinz Janssen

Once during the last war Winston Churchill accused the Germans of having involved the world in wars of conquest and aggression five times in the past 125 years because of their hatred of the liberty enjoyed by their neighbours. He was not the only one to think this. In all the great post-war conferences over Germany, all the statesmen from both the East and the West agreed on one thing at least: the wars of 1870–1, 1914–18 and 1939–45 were caused by the Germans alone. Especially in the first years after the German Reich's unconditional surrender in May 1945, in the period of re-education, German as well as foreign historians and writers tried to find historical grounds for the crime of National Socialism. They maintained that there was continuity of political thought and military depravity, stretching from Martin Luther in the Reformation to Frederick the Great of Prussia and to Bismarck, the founder of the Empire, and from Kaiser Wilhelm II to Adolf Hitler, the war criminal.

Professor Gerhard Ritter of Freiburg protested at an early date against this ostensibly plausible but none the less only half-true, superficial and unwarranted interpretation of history. No one of the German historians who had remained in Germany had greater moral right or moral justification than Ritter. He had been freed by the Russians from the hands of the Gestapo in the April of 1945. Ritter, the doyen of German historians until his death in the summer of 1967, considered it his political duty to undertake a sober and fundamental review of the traditional picture of German history, without showing any bias to either side. He did not see Germany's past as nothing

Specially written for this volume.

but shadows: he also found positive and worth-while aspects. He warned his fellow Germans against blind moral grounds, and in doing so he helped restore their self-confidence.

As early as 1948 when there was still a censorship imposed by the American military government, Ritter wrote that it was impossible 'to blame German diplomacy unilaterally and exclusively for the outbreak of the 1914 war and to explain its actions during the July crisis in terms of supposed plans for world conquest – this has been done so often and thoroughly by serious historical research, especially in England, America, Switzerland and Holland, that to repeat it would only be carrying coals to Newcastle'. But when his younger colleague, Fritz Fischer, began to repeat these accusations twelve years later, Gerhard Ritter was forced to react bitterly and indignantly. Twenty years' work, even his life's work, appeared in danger.

To Ritter's disgust the German Press took up and repeated, largely uncritically and even with approval, Fischer's sensational thesis that Germany was solely responsible for the First World War and that the German Reich was aiming at mastery of the world. Ritter looked on this extreme willingness to atone as amounting to political flagellation. He looked on Fischer's book, *Griff nach der Weltmacht*, as a deliberate attempt to obscure the German sense of history, which since the catastrophe of 1945 had taken the place of the earlier self-deification. He considered it a disaster, which caused him sadness and concern, when he thought of the younger generation.

These fears were not entirely unfounded. The young people who applauded Fischer and his assistants at the Congress of the German Historical Association in Berlin in 1964 were not so much interested in the guilt or innocence of their forefathers, as fascinated by the revolutionary element in Fischer's thesis. They were welcoming the rejection of an approach to history which stressed leading figures and pure Cabinet politics and its replacement with an analysis of the composition of the establishment, of social climate and hidden pressure groups, an analysis providing lessons for the present. These young disciples of Fischer believed like the conservative Ritter that Fischer was basically applying a Marxist approach to German history, although not admitting he was a Marxist, as this would have denied him any prospect of success in West Germany from the outset. Although Fischer did not dare to saddle Germany with the sole guilt for the First World War in the first edition of his book, his quotations and evidence were selected, and his exposition organised, in such a way that the reader could really reach no other conclusion. His magic word was 'continuity'.

Fritz Fischer made it rather easy for his most incisive critic, Gerhard Ritter, to cast doubts on his new historical picture. Ritter pointed out with some success how Fischer had made a series of wrong interpretations or reinterpretations of sources. Quite justifiably, he accused Fischer of totally ignoring the environment of the time and of not comparing the different kinds of foreign Imperialism, including that of the United States. He also noted a 'surprising lack of unbiased and genuine historical empathy'. Fischer had fallen into one of the pitfalls of his profession: he had applied contemporary categories, which were based on later experiences, to the past. In places his approach to history had become tendentious literature.

Ritter none the less did not fail to acknowledge the immense amount of research into sources done by his colleague and his service in researching the recent past. He also accepted tacitly Fischer's discovery of the disastrous inter-relation between economics and politics in Wilhelmine Germany. Fischer had had the tremendous advantage of being able to look at those sections of the German archives held in East Germany and closed to Ritter, which included the various war-aims programmes drawn up by the German Ministers and their assistants. Ritter would have agreed with what a younger historian said of Fischer, that he had shifted a gigantic rock into the traditional path of German historical research, which had forced everyone to think about this historical problem completely again.

When Fischer's work appeared Ritter had already
published two volumes of his extremely self-critical
examination of the problem of militarism in Germany. He and his pupils, even before Fischer, had
been looking at the documents relating to the First
World War and using them without regard for the
person or country involved. He had not spared himself nor the interpretation of history he had so far
accepted from scrutiny. In referring to the second
volume of his work, *Staatskunst und Kriegshandwerk*,* he said that he 'had not written the book without being cut to the core; what I describe here is the
pre-war Germany of my own youth. All my life I have
remembered this period as a sunny one, which seemed
only to have been overcast by the outbreak of war in
1914. And now at the end of my life, using the eye of
the researcher, I have been able to see much darker
shadows than were seen by my own generation – let
alone by my own academic teachers.'

Whatever can be said about the theses of Fritz
Fischer and his pupils, Gerhard Ritter's arguments
over the questions of war guilt and war aims are an
indispensable complement. Unlike Fischer, Ritter had
the advantage of living through the period and serving at the front in the First World War. He also had
the necessary maturity and sovereignty of a great historian which allowed him to understand personalities
and the actions of their time and to assess them justly
and critically.

In 1960, that is a year before Fischer's *Griff nach
der Weltmacht* appeared, Ritter had made the following assessment of Germany's role in the July crisis of
1914: 'Furthermore her political and military leaders
were justified in saying that they had not wanted this
catastrophe, and were simply overwhelmed by it; and
we have no right to doubt the genuineness of their
basic desire for peace. No one in a position of authority wanted to bring about a world war; in this sense
the "war-guilt question" no longer exists.'

---

*An English translation of this fundamental work is now pub-
lished by the University of Miami Press, under the title *The
Sword and the Sceptre*.

None of these statements can be maintained today. In fact the contrary must be maintained because of Fischer's research and that stimulated by his work, especially the studies of Egmont Zechlin, Karl Dietrich Erdmann, Fritz Stern and Andreas Hillgruber, and above all because of the knowledge we have of the diary kept at the time by the Imperial Chancellor Bethmann-Hollweg's private secretary, Kurt Riezler. Germany's political and military leaders did not want world war at any cost but they were consciously prepared to risk it. They were not overwhelmed by catastrophe: they made political events develop to the brink of catastrophe.

Two of Bethmann-Hollweg's self-critiques over his own guilt for the First World War were found by one of Ritter's pupils. On 5 February 1915 the Imperial Chancellor told the journalist Theodor Wolff, 'If you are speaking of guilt for this war, we must be honest enough to admit that we also have our own share in it. It would be an understatement to say that I am weighed down by this thought: it never leaves me; I live with it.' And six months after his fall from power he admitted on 24 February 1918 to the Reichstag Deputy, Conrad Haussmann, 'God, in one sense it was a preventive war. But if war was hanging over us, if it would happen two years later more dangerously and inevitably and if the military were saying that it was still possible for us to fight without being defeated but that this would not be the case in two years time....'

Before Fischer put the chief or sole blame for the First World War on Germany, Ritter had been unable to clear the Imperial governments of all responsibility:

There was a certain fatalism, a belief that a great war was inevitable, as well as a belief in strong national prestige and a desire to be accepted in the world, both of which could lead to political blindness. This was certainly not the case in Vienna and Berlin alone, but it was especially disastrous there because of the threat to the Central Powers' posi-

tion. And in the judgement of history political
blindness can also be construed as guilt.

Where Ritter spoke of 'disaster' and 'blindness',
Fischer saw only 'intent' and 'premeditation'. The one
interpreted German policy in the July crisis as defensive, the other as aggressive and even as a logical continuation of pre-1914 Imperial policy. Everything that
Fischer brought forward as evidence, whether from
Press, political or military sources, to prove that Germany was striving for world power, was rejected by
Ritter and interpreted as manifestations of an exaggerated, new German nationalism, which showed itself
to be illiberal, conservative and militarist. He thought
that nothing could be more difficult than to determine
precisely what educated and articulate German
opinion understood by world policy and world power.
Lastly, he thought that the striving for 'a German
world policy' was only an expression of a desire for
considerable political prestige.

Ritter readily acknowledged the threatening and
aggressive tone of the chauvinist Pan-German League,
but 'educated pre-war youth (to which I belonged myself) felt differently'. They followed such liberal
scholars as Max Weber and Hans Delbrück and
'looked hopefully and with real enthusiasm towards a
greater future even though they (like myself) wanted
to have nothing to do with the restricted and exaggerated nationalism of the Pan-Germans'. Ritter wrote
this as defence against Fischer's thesis, although two
years before he had still thought that the unrestrained
demands for political prestige put forward by the
former general and Pan-German military writer,
Bernhardi, and his excessive worship of war, could not
be dismissed 'simply as the ideas of an extreme out-
sider'. He had also noticed a 'militarisation' of the German bourgeoisie which was bound necessarily to exert
strong pressure on a weak Imperial government.

What especially annoyed Ritter was that Fischer
had not taken seriously his analysis of the famous
Schlieffen Plan of 1905 and that he should repeat the
allegation that Schlieffen, the Chief of the General

Staff, had wanted to 'force' France 'out of the Entente' during the first Morocco crisis of 1905–6. In fact Ritter had been able to prove that Schlieffen had never pressed for war, although the opportunity for a defensive strike against France was extremely tempting after Russia's defeat by Japan. The leading figure in German policy at that time, Holstein, was also unable to bring about war because the Kaiser and his Chancellor, Bülow, wanted to maintain peace at almost any price.

The use of power does not necessarily mean the same thing as war and Ritter has shown here that Holstein in 1905 wanted to bark rather than bite, and to blackmail his enemies, in this case France, by brinkmanship. Holstein misjudged the factors of foreign policy, as Bethmann-Hollweg did in 1914, and was convinced that Germany with her temporary military superiority in Europe could risk a great war without actually having to engage in one. But at a critical moment the Kaiser and Bülow left him in the lurch, as they had not the nerve to maintain their position at the Algeciras Conference.

Holstein's policy of bluff and risk aimed at smashing the Entente (just being formed at that time) and at destroying the encirclement threatening Germany. France and Russia were to be forced into a continental alliance with the German Reich, which would finally force Britain to come to an agreement with Germany. In this way he set a precedent which was followed by the Foreign Office and Chancellors in the subsequent crises over Morocco and the Balkans (1909, 1911, 1912–13) and which increased the risk year by year. The intellectual material for this policy, in some ways very similar to the 'brinkmanship' practised by the American Secretary of State, John Foster Dulles, was provided by the same Kurt Riezler, who was both adviser and friend to Bethmann-Hollweg in the July crisis of 1914.

Riezler had realised that a war between the Great Powers in Europe would have disastrous consequences and would shake the European States to their foundations. War, which at that time was still considered by all governments to be the *ultima ratio* of policy, should be replaced by bluff as the 'chief requisite' of diplomacy. Consequently the risks should be calculated very precisely and above all mediation in an international crisis should not be allowed too early before tangible success had been achieved. Riezler did not deny the dangers. 'If a government because of its use of bluff should go further than it originally intended, or if its bluff should be called, then it would probably no longer be able to draw back, even if withdrawal were appropriate. Personal interests, the ambitions of those in power, or the outcry which could be expected from the nationalists, could bring about war, which would never have been justified by the interest involved.'

This is exactly what happened in the July crisis of 1914. On 30 July Bethmann-Hollweg had to admit that every State and nation, even Russia which was so maligned by German propaganda, wanted peace, but 'direction has been lost and the avalanche has begun to move'.

Gerhard Ritter did not accept this risk theory. It must be remembered that in his research he never came across Riezler's diary. In his third volume on the problem of militarism he referred to him in a short sceptical footnote. However, he went to great lengths to argue with two of Fischer's basic arguments, firstly, that Germany wanted a preventive war in 1914, and secondly, that she pressed Austria-Hungary to conduct a timely war of revenge against Serbia so that the balance of power in the Balkans and Near East should be changed to the advantage of the Central Powers.

Ritter knew very well what the German generals had said in favour of a preventive war, but it appeared to him to be far too vague and doubtful. He also did not accept as proof the pretty definite reports of journalists and diplomats in the summer of 1914, although he acknowledged as legitimate the increasing worry of Moltke, the German Chief of Staff, over the dangerous growth of Russian armaments. He was also fond of quoting a letter from the German Secretary of State, Jagow, in which he explained to the

German Ambassador in London, Lichnowsky, that war was inevitable with Russia some day. Ritter interpreted Jagow's words 'I don't want a preventive war, but if war offers itself, we should not run away from it', as 'a depressed fatalism in the face of an apparently inevitable and growing danger, but at the same time a determination to meet it with everything in their power'. When Ritter wrote this he was not to know that a few weeks before the assassination at Sarajevo General Moltke had advised the Secretary of State, Jagow, to undertake a preventive war because Germany now had a good chance of seeing the conflict through to a successful conclusion before Russia's armaments programme was completed. This assessment of the position by Moltke made it somewhat easier for the German government to risk world war in July.

Ritter was also unprepared to accept Fischer's claim that Austria-Hungary was tagging behind German policy in 1914. It appeared after all as though he had turned the whole thing upside down. Ritter had his own theory. He believed that by giving a blank cheque to Austria-Hungary on 5 July – a free hand against Russia's Serbian ally – Germany was letting herself be led by Austria-Hungary. Looking at it from the 1960's he agreed with those critics like the German Ambassador in London, Lichnowsky, who thought at the time that an Austrian war with Serbia was absurd and stupid since it would complicate rather than simplify the problems of the Habsburg multinational empire. He none the less believed that, because of the pressure from nationalist street demonstrations, the German government would have been branded as a traitor to everything German if it had left its Austrian brothers in the lurch. But this idea is hardly convincing, because what Great Power willingly allows itself to be led by another? Also Ritter was basically quite clear himself that the German statesmen had backed the Austrians out of considerations of pure political power, even at the time when the Russians unexpectedly mobilised. We know one reason for it from Riezler's diary: Bethmann-Hollweg wanted to use the

Serbian crisis to break up the Entente, since the Franco–British–Russian bloc would hardly have survived if Russia had backed down once again in the face of German threats of war and sacrificed her vassal.

Ritter mentioned the other reason himself – the need of a Great Power for prestige and the fear of losing her last reliable ally. After the war Bethmann-Hollweg defended his policy by arguing that it would have been possible to back down even after Russia's general mobilisation and to sacrifice Austria-Hungary by referring the matter to the International Court at The Hague, but this would have amounted to 'the abdication of our world position without a fight'. Or as Ritter put it: 'Austria-Hungary could not afford to lose her position as a Great Power by accepting passively the activism of the Serbian nationalists, which had now gone as far as murdering the heir to the throne. And Germany could not afford to lose hers by refusing armed help because of her fear of Russia.'

Although Ritter doubted if it was worth running such an incredible risk to maintain the Danubian Monarchy, he basically had no objection to the decision of Germany's leaders to maintain her real or supposed world position in a world war: 'This drive for power and prestige was so accepted in Europe at that time that it is hardly worth discussing. After all England was not defending her own security from Germany in 1914 but maintaining her own moral and political prestige, her position as a World Power and her maritime supremacy.'

But the basic difference between Germany's attitude and that of the other Great Powers in the July crisis was that her policy was determined to a very great extent, far more than Russia's, by 'considerations of pure military technicalities'. In this respect Ritter was always outspoken. He castigated the disastrous naval policy of Grand Admiral Tirpitz which gave Germany no military advantage but poisoned Anglo-German relations; similarly he castigated the acceptance of the Schlieffen Plan, which entailed a German deployment on one front in the West and a premeditated infringement of Belgium's and Luxemburg's neutrality. He castigated them both as a 'complete surrender of all political reasoning to military planning', since it subordinated the Empire's foreign policy to the pressures of mobilisation and produced the paradox of beginning a war over the Balkans by an attack on France. He condemned Germany's invasion of neutral Belgium as an 'act of force'. He was shocked by the General Staff's demand that France should dishonour herself by agreeing to hand over the forts of Toul and Verdun if she wanted to stay neutral. Nor did he suppress the fantastic figments of the imagination served up by the Army High Command as the basis for the declaration of war against France.

Yet these problems belong to the great complex relationship between politics and war, and in Ritter's eyes were also of secondary importance as far as the question of war guilt was concerned. He maintained that responsible statesmen always have a sphere of freedom of action in spite of everything. He was convinced that if relations between the Army High Command and the Imperial government had been better arranged the war would not have had such an unfortunate start for Germany and hardly such a disastrous end.

Gerhard Ritter could never quite free himself from the comfortable historical view adopted by so many European statesmen and politicians since Lloyd George, that the European nations had 'stumbled' into the First World War. This kind of generalising made the question of responsibility invalid and lifted it out of the emotional sphere, which Fischer's deliberately prejudiced interpretation has brought back again. Very much in the same way as when he discussed the question of war guilt, in discussing war aims Ritter found 'the statesmen more or less helplessly involved in the needs of war and the irresistible pressure from the unleashed emotions of so-called public opinion'.

Ritter's idea of German war aims is diametrically opposed to that of Fischer. According to Fischer Germany's war aims were innately expansionist, aggressive and Imperialist, reflecting the tendencies and forms of political, intellectual, economic and military pressure groups, who were now trying to reach their pre-war aims by force. On the other hand Ritter looked on German war aims similarly to her pre-war foreign policy as essentially defensive, even though not always free from blindness. Its aim was to obtain 'security in the face of a new struggle for existence', that Second Punic War which Germany's ruling élite believed inevitable throughout the whole course of the war, since Britain, 'their main enemy', could not be beaten at the first attempt. Ritter vigorously disputed the concept of a 'striving for world power', Fischer's *Imperium Germanicum* stretching from the Atlantic to the Urals and then from the Near East to Egypt and Central Africa.

If he had been able to prove that the First World War had been in fact a preventive war, Ritter's interpretation might have been more logical. If a power begins a war to forestall an attack threatening it, it will obviously do everything possible to stop a repetition of a similar danger. In our own recent history in the Arab–Israeli conflict, we have seen how a defensive war can turn quite unexpectedly into one of annexation. Annexations caused by fear do not necessarily come from a latent desire to achieve hegemony. If one adopts Ritter's approach and tries to put war aims in a universal framework and discovers similar manifestations in all the countries at war, it is not possible to explain away annexations in the sociological or structural methods employed by Fischer.

From Ritter's work on the question of war aims, six general tendencies and causes can be extracted inherent in the annexionist policies found in modern 'total' war:

(1) The danger myth. In Germany this came primarily from a fear of encirclement, in the other States from a fear of German hegemony.

(2) The moat concept. Despite technological advances in warfare which allowed space and distance to be covered at a much greater rate, the military,

politicians and writers have overestimated the importance of buffer zones. This concept is still adhered to today.

(3) Emotions. One of the legacies of the French Revolution has been that sober considerations of *raison d'état* have often been swept aside by an upsurge of nationalist and militant emotions. Neither the French, Germans, Russians nor Italians were aware that annexations and attempts to limit Powers' sovereignty would not ensure the peace they hoped for but would in fact sabotage it.

(4) The economic profit motive. Patriotic demands were usually accompanied by 'massive material interests'. A good example of this was the German demands for the ore of Lorraine, or French demands for the coal of the Saarland.

(5) The idealising of the power conflict. Everywhere intellectuals were employed in psychological warfare to provide a deeper meaning for the apparently senseless mass slaughter. In Germany numerous phrases were coined, 'idealism versus materialism', 'national unity against collective interests', 'patriotism against pacifism', 'heroism against the barter mentality', 'Western culture against Muscovite barbarism' and so on. Among the Western Powers the slogans ran on the lines of a 'crusade for democracy and liberty against autocracy and militarism'. Ritter felt that all this did not have much political danger but was a necessary stimulant during total war.

(6) The reparations principle. The search for a meaning for the war was supplemented by a search for a price. The people expect some compensation in return for their sacrifice in blood and property, a kind of reward which has been provided since time immemorial by the symbolic cession of booty, tribute or territory.

The shocking extent of German war aims and the strength and breadth of movements in favour of them in Germany has only become known since Fritz

Fischer's book. There is no need to detail them here.
Ritter, however, took away some of their sensational-
ism by continually comparing them with Allied war
aims. His only purpose in doing this was to weaken his
critics' arguments that Germany's unlimited war aims
ruined all hope of a negotiated peace. According to
Ritter the position was the same on the other side.
When Germany explored the possibility of a separate
peace with Russia in the autumn of 1914, Tsar
Nicholas was proposing to Paléologue a plan to break
up Germany and Austria-Hungary. And when the
Central Powers considered offering Russia in the
spring of 1915 free access to the Dardanelles, the
diplomats of Russia and the Entente were agreeing on
a programme which ensured Russian possession of
Constantinople and fortification of the Straits as well
as the division of Turkey in Asia.

Ritter did not fail to point out the discrepancy between the seriousness of her position in the war and
Germany's war aims, but he was able to prove that the
French politicians also, at the end of the extremely
bloody year of 1916, could think of nothing better
than to plan to occupy or neutralise the whole left
bank of the Rhine. The French Prime Minister, Aris-
tide Briand, was following, even at that time, a policy
which anticipated and actually went further than the
Treaty of Versailles in its territorial conditions:
Poland was to be enlarged in such a way that Berlin
would have lost any military cover, while Denmark was
to have all Schleswig and Holland East Friesland. He
believed that these conditions were reasonable and
modest.

Ritter accused Fischer's monumental work of being
out of proportion not only because he had failed to
adopt a comparative approach to the analysis of war
aims. He also accused him of being unable to separate
dreams and hopes from serious aims, and the tactically
qualified ambiguities of the diplomats from the massive naked demands made by the Pan-Germans and
the military.

Ritter's respect for Fischer's piece of work was not
exactly increased when he was able to show up more

than one methodological error and false or even falsifying interpretations of sources. The great historian and masterly biographer's passionate opposition was bound to be provoked by Fischer's attempt to put under the same roof such contradictory characters as the Chancellor, Bethmann-Hollweg, and General Ludendorff, the militarist *par excellence*.

Fischer justifiably replied that it was no good trying to analyse German war aims solely on the basis of the Chancellor's personality. He felt that the power of the military, of heavy industry and of agrarian pressure groups, of the Prussian nobility and the middle-class parties was more important than the futile moderating influence of Bethmann-Hollweg. But, as in all his works, Ritter consciously made the responsible active statesman the centre of his picture. For him the question of war aims was only one aspect of the powerful struggle between politicians and soldiers. He built his description of the first three years of the war on the theme of the 'tragedy of statesmanship', in this case the story of Bethmann-Hollweg's tragic failure.

Seldom in recent German history has a statesman been subject to such contradictory assessments as Bethmann-Hollweg. He was a unique mixture of Prussian official and highly trained intellectual with a Prussian Junker and West German bourgeois ancestry. For decades the picture Germans had of him was that painted by his enemies: weak-willed, an official lacking great political gifts, a deplorable failure, a despicable defeatist, in short a dreamer and philosopher. On the other hand Fischer painted him as a Machiavellian in sheep's clothing, a daring power-conscious politician, who aimed cleverly and ruthlessly at world power despite all opposition.

Neither of these extreme portraits does justice to what his colleague Riezler called this 'peculiar man'. Gerhard Ritter too found it difficult to unravel his puzzling personality. He described him as an honourable statesman with a good character, who 'tried desperately, but never despairingly, to extricate his country from the snare of an overwhelming and fateful war and to find a way out for his people from a hopeless situation'. 'Painstaking and cautious, slow in making up his mind and with no sure political instinct', he was neither a fighter nor a man with an iron will, but was 'free from the degeneracy of the demon of power'.

The apparent contradiction between Bethmann-Hollweg's realistic and unrealistic war aims, his indecisive and uncertain actions and finally his failure, were all explained by Ritter as a product of the complicated constitutional set-up of the Wilhelmine Empire, that peculiar cross between a federal State and a parliamentary democracy.

Unlike his enemies in the West, Bethmann-Hollweg never ruled with the help of parliamentary majorities and so could never feel that he represented the will of the people. The moment when he first attempted it, he fell from power. His only support was the confidence of a fickle ruler who was open to all influences. As Imperial Chancellor and Prime Minister of the largest federal State (Prussia), he was in the middle of a web of contradictory, often competing and mutually exclusive forces. He stood in between the higher ministerial bureaucracies of the larger federal States of the south and central Germany, which expected to be rewarded in the event of a successful end to the war, and a Council of Ministers from the Prussian State, who pursued other interests from those of the leaders of the Empire, above all in the Polish and other eastern questions. He also stood in between the parties in the Reichstag and the Prussian Diet, the great economic pressure groups, and last but not least the military, that force which at least while Germany was winning the war always found it easier than the politicians to obtain the sympathy and the confidence of the masses. Unlike in the Western democracies it was not in a subordinate position but held a position equal with that of the political power. Even the founder of the Empire, Prince Bismarck, found the constitutional set-up and the reality of the Empire so complicated that he was only able to conduct affairs through a balancing act. Bethmann-Hollweg also saw only one way to govern – 'a policy of working along the diagonals'. One cannot understand Bethmann-Hollweg's attitude to Germany's war aims without realising the nature of this makeshift policy. He himself once said of it that 'decisive measures, an open fight over internal questions would be possible and perhaps necessary if peace were secured and the external conflict brought to an end. During the war, however, it was in the national interest to follow the narrow and circumspect path between the emotions, conflicting interests and temptations.' Not without some measure of self-congratulation, he added that 'the diagonal is also a straight path and I believe I have kept to it'.

The government could not allow itself to be tied down by exaggerated war aims because of the Social Democrats, who were much the strongest party in the Empire and committed to fighting a defensive war. From the very first day of the war the Right opposed this collaboration with the Left, and because of the three-class franchise in the largest federal State of Prussia the Right was still the dominant force there. The Conservatives objected to Kaiser Wilhelm's including in his speech from the throne at the beginning of the war a phrase aimed at appeasing the Social Democrats: 'We are not being driven by any lust for conquest.'

The unity of the parties and the 'domestic peace', which was kept with some difficulty, already seemed to be breaking up after only a few months when the parties of the Right demanded a definite declaration in favour of an annexationist peace, while the Left pressed the Chancellor to renounce annexations in public. Bethmann-Hollweg, none the less, believed as always that he could paper over the cracks by patriotic speeches and ominous turns of phrase about 'real guarantees and securities'. Of necessity his observations to the representatives of the different parties and pressure groups were bound to be ambiguous.

None the less even Ritter has to admit that Bethmann-Hollweg did not have the sovereign will-power of a great statesman who, despite the requests and demands presented to him, has a clear, definite and attainable aim, an aim dictated by *raison d'état*. He revised this assessment, however, by adding that not even Bismarck, who has always been praised as a states-man of moderation, could resist the national emotions during the Franco-Prussian War. Unlike Bethmann-Hollweg who suppressed the war-aims propaganda of the Pan-Germans, Bismarck artificially stimulated pub-lic demonstrations in favour of an annexationist peace, and thereby prolonged the war for several months. The annexation of Alsace-Lorraine poisoned relations be-tween the two countries for decades. On the whole it only produces misconceptions if one tries to play off Bismarck against Bethmann-Hollweg. Of course, the founder of the Empire concluded a peace of reconcilia-tion at Nikolsburg after the Austro-Prussian War of 1866, but it is often overlooked that Prussia at the same time annexed more States in north Germany, illegally deposing dynasties, acquiring the Guelphic Fund and ending the liberty of the old Imperial city of Frank-furt.

In the same way as Bismarck directed his war-aims policy from the start in 1870 to the annexation of France's eastern provinces, Bethmann-Hollweg is said to have committed himself during the very first weeks of the World War to a programme which envisaged the 'security of the German Empire in the West and the East for the foreseeable future' on the basis of wide political, military and economic gains. This is the essence of the so-called September Memorandum, which Fischer discovered during his research in the East Berlin archives and which he maintained con-tained the war aims which the leaders of the German Empire were committed to until late in 1918.

Gerhard Ritter was quick to recognise the service performed by Fischer in discovering and editing this Memorandum, but in his own discussion of it there is some disquiet over this remarkable document. He tried to play down its importance, claiming that it was nothing more than a first, provisional and strictly secret draft, more a reflection than a decision. (Riez-ler's diary seems to support this impression, for al-though Riezler had drawn it up he had no word to say about it.) Ritter also believed that it was 'simply incorrect' to consider the September Memorandum as the basis of Bethmann-Hollweg's entire war-aims policy up to his dismissal. But this observation can again be disproved by Riezler's diary. The Chancellor stuck to the essential points of the Memorandum until 1917, although naturally more or less firmly as the military situation changed. Up to this point therefore Fischer's interpretation is correct. But Bethmann-Hollweg was never ready to allow these aims to ruin any chance of a negotiated peace on the basis of the *status quo ante* 1914, if the enemy had been willing for such a peace.

Ritter in his justification did not go as far as Egmont Zechlin, who dismissed the Memorandum as a document produced almost by accident, a virtually unimportant list of the demands of the various government departments, and who considered the plan for a central European federation contained in it as a temporary expedient in the economic war against England. Ritter admitted that Bethmann-Hollweg like other important Germans had abandoned the idea of a purely defensive war because of the tidal wave of German victories in France – the fall of Paris seemed to be only a matter of days at this time – and instead wanted to transform basically the power relationships in central and western Europe and then in the East. Undoubtedly the Memorandum corresponded to the Chancellor's deepest convictions, and if there had been a quick total victory over France he would have looked on it as a sign of great moderation.

It is arguable if this would have been a moderate peace, since France would have been destroyed as a Great Power, her economy turned into a German dependency and put under heavy financial burdens for decades to come, as well as the loss of her richest deposits of iron ore and in certain circumstances the sacrifice of the Channel coast from Dunkirk to Boulogne, which would have been part of the German satellite of Belgium. But the Chancellor's demands were still a long way behind those of the Pan-Germans, who wanted to annex all north-eastern France from Belfort to Toul and up to the mouth of the Somme, to exploit the rest economically and eventually also to divide France into a republic in the north and a Bourbon monarchy in the south, making Toulon a German naval base, as well as expelling all the non-German inhabitants from the annexed lands. (The Kaiser also listened to these fantastic plans.) Consequently one had to take seriously Ritter's contention that Bethmann-Hollweg could only successfully oppose such massive militarist, and even criminal, plans, if he had a counter-programme of his own to offer. 'It would have been unthinkable at that time to meet this programme with a simple demand for the restoration of the *status quo* because of the inflamed desires of the nation for power and conquest.'

Ritter knew of course that it was hardly possible to explain Bethmann-Hollweg's war-aims policy merely as a product of defence against external and domestic enemies. Ritter believed he had found the real motive, which is both surprising and extraordinary: the Chancellor's guilt complex. As Bethmann-Hollweg felt he shared in the guilt for the global catastrophe – there is plenty of evidence for this – 'he had to try to find a "positive" war aim which would help him bury his own worry over the "catastrophe" and look to the future with some hope'. Ritter's own personal experience was also implied, when he added that 'The entire German intellectual world felt much the same desire at that time.'

In other words the Chancellor could justify the war he had risked to his own conscience and the nation if he could show that at the end of it there would be a generally improved situation for the Empire, that the war had not been waged for nothing. (In this remark Ritter unconsciously admitted that the First World War could not possibly have been a defensive enterprise at the very beginning, otherwise Bethmann-Hollweg could have been satisfied with defending Germany's frontiers and the maintenance of Germany's prestige, aims which he was quite prepared to espouse at a later date when the military situation was less favourable than in September 1914.)

What would have really made the war worth while was the creation of a great European common market under German hegemony. Ritter believed that this plan was the 'original and surprising aspect' of Bethmann-Hollweg's war-aims programme. He envisaged a central European economic union which besides Germany would also have included the five members of the present European Economic Community, as well as Austria-Hungary, Poland and Scandinavia. But the members would only have been superficially equal. Ritter was never explicit whether this project was intended to be voluntary or enforced, but consoled himself with the thought that European leadership would have been Germany's in any case if she had won. He drew from Riezler's diary the information that Bethmann-Hollweg, as well as his adviser Riezler, were entirely clear on one point: they considered the new 'central European empire of the German nation' to be the 'European trimmings of our will to power'.

Riezler of course only entrusted such thoughts to his own diary. Officially the Chancellor approved when the nation's expectations turned towards the 'idea of *Mitteleuropa*' in 1915 and 1916, stimulated especially by the book of the liberal Reichstag Deputy, Friedrich Naumann, and the victorious progress of German arms in the Balkans, which had opened up the land route Berlin–Vienna–Constantinople–Baghdad. The German educated middle class were fascinated by Naumann's Utopia of the formation of a central European association with a German–Austrian nucleus surrounded by Hungary, Rumania and the small Slav races, all profiting from the benefits of a large economic union, all united by a federal superstructure. Ritter even took some delight in remembering this: 'At long last appeared a quiet voice of reason and of goodwill, which showed us Germans a "positive" war aim – not merely defence of the country or the rape of foreign peoples, but a fine tempting job of creating a German and European future.' He also felt it a serious tragedy that the Habsburg Monarchy had already decayed so much and that the Slavs considerably distrusted the slogan *Mitteleuropa* as they thought it camouflaged German Imperialist designs. And one would say today that they were justified.

The preparations made by Bethmann-Hollweg for annexing Belgium, Poland and the Baltic States corresponded to his own idea of Europe. Unlike the army he did not want crude annexations but instead wanted to introduce indirect control of their subject neighbours, which would help them to be reconciled with the German Empire. Ritter, far from justifying this policy in retrospect, thought it plausible that almost everyone in Germany at that time wanted to secure the Belgian point of entry into Germany as it was so dangerously near to the Ruhr. Moreover, the German government had some justifiable fear that Belgium after the suffering of the war would give up her neutrality and become a dependant of England. Finally, many Germans looked at this Belgian State, which was not yet a hundred years old, as an artificial creation, whose disappearance need cause no regret. Ritter none the less declared that the Belgian question was 'the curse on the entire German war-aims policy', as it robbed the war of its defensive character, had a disastrous effect on the mood of the German working class and was bound to prolong the war endlessly if Germany could not defeat Britain in the field. In exoneration he cited a sentence of the Chancellor's from November 1914: 'Belgium is a terrible problem. We have to find the least bad solution.'

Bethmann-Hollweg failed to find a solution to that problem, as he also failed to find one to Poland, which he originally envisaged as a German buffer State and where his ideas conflicted with various interests, Russian, Austrian, German, Polish nationalist, Prussian particularist and brutal militarist ones. 'One could call it a belated nemesis of history', Ritter wrote, bearing in mind the partitions of Poland, which the German military wanted to add to by a further fourth partition.

The Chancellor's actions over Belgium and Poland were so unambiguous that Ritter could say very little to defend them; but over the question of the Baltic States, that is the Russian Baltic provinces, his action seemed remarkably contradictory. Bethmann-Hollweg would have had no trouble at all in acting as an annexationist in these lands which used to belong to the Teutonic Order. They still had a considerable German population; public opinion, almost all the politically conscious members of the German Foreign Office, the Prussian Ministers, and above all the popular generals Hindenburg and Ludendorff, who were administering Lithuania and Courland, wanted to 'liberate' this area to protect East Prussia from further Russian invasion and at the same time to open up a new and fertile area for colonisation at the doors of the Empire.

When Bethmann-Hollweg hoped for a separate peace with Russia in September 1915 because of the successful German eastern offensive, he came out decidedly against annexing the Baltic States in a letter to the Chief of Staff, Falkenhayn. He pointed out that strategically they were too exposed, domestically it would not be desirable to acquire a revolutionary-minded Lithuanian population as well as the German ruling class of the area, and diplomatically it would create eternal bitterness between Russia and Germany because it would mean depriving Russia of her few ice-free ports. (Ritter especially blamed Fischer for interpreting this document as proof of Germany's 'striving for world power'!)

In the spring of 1916, because of the pressure of the nationalist journalists, the military and Austrian politicians, who wanted to divert Germany from Poland towards the north, the Chancellor himself decided to incorporate the greater part of Courland and Lithuania into the Empire. He even gave a public statement to the war-aims majority in the Reichstag that Germany could 'not restore voluntarily those peoples she had liberated, whether they were Poles, Lithuanians, Balts or Latvians, to the reactionary Russian regime'.

Ritter and his pupils have proved in great detail, using the example of the Baltic question, that Bethmann-Hollweg never thought for a minute that these demands for annexations would make it impossible to

arrive at a general negotiated peace or to a separate
peace with Russia. Naturally this was only known to a
confidential circle – the Prussian Ministers, the main
committee of the Reichstag and the representatives of
the Greater German federal States. Bethmann-Hollweg came out with a typical remark in the autumn of
1916 when the Central Powers were preparing a peace
initiative, that he was trying to conduct a policy for Germany guided by reason, not by the heart, and that it
would be impossible for him to conduct policy solely
in the interests of the Balts, since what mattered above
all for him was what benefited Germany.

In the spring of 1917 after the Russian February
Revolution when the German government was using
the slogan of self-determination and when the Army
High Command under Hindenburg and Ludendorff
were demanding the annexation of Courland and
Lithuania, the Chancellor produced a compromise
formula – autonomy. It coincided with his old idea of
self-governing buffer States, which would be associated
with the Empire politically, militarily and economically. But the Chancellor also made it clear that 'if this
[the conclusion of peace with Russia] can only be
reached at the price of territorial conquests, then this
should not prevent the conclusion of peace'.

At that time Bethmann-Hollweg's position had
been gravely weakened through his struggle to reform
the Prussian franchise and his continual conflict with
the almost all-powerful army leaders who were
strongly supported by German public opinion. In
these circumstances he was forced to put his signature
to a limitless war-aims programme drawn up by the
generals at the main Army Headquarters at Bad
Kreuznach on 23 April 1917, although his colleagues
dismissed it as 'childish'. Bethmann-Hollweg put
down on record that he had agreed to it on the pre-
condition that 'we will be able to dictate peace'. This
was in fact the position a year later at Brest-Litovsk,
where the September Memorandum, or at least part of
it, was realised, if only temporarily. At that time the
Secretary of State was von Kühlmann, who followed

and continued the peace and war-aims policy of the fallen Bethmann-Hollweg.

This had been preceded by the October Revolution and the complete collapse of the Russian army, whereas in April 1917 Bethmann-Hollweg could not hope for such a favourable end to the war in the East. He therefore added a comment preserved in the records, but which Fischer significantly ignored: 'I have signed the protocol as it would have been ridiculous to resign for the sake of such fantasies. Besides I will naturally not allow myself to be bound by the protocol. However and wherever peace should be possible, I shall follow it up.'

Since Fischer's research it has been popularly alleged that these limitless German war aims *a priori* prevented any chance of a negotiated peace. Ritter examined this allegation and did not find that the English, the French or the Russians (at least not before the October Revolution) were ready for a peace in which there should be no victors or vanquished. All the governments were scared of facing their populations without having won; all wanted to avoid showing signs of weakness in case the enemy raised its price. All put their hope in a war of attrition and all were most anxious to prevent their allies becoming suspicious by negotiating for a separate peace. The German statesmen were justified in having the same fears as well.

In the summer of 1915 Bethmann-Hollweg calculated what Germany might hope to get under the most favourable circumstances if she agreed at that time to an Allied invitation to a general peace negotiation. The result seemed disastrous. What it seemed she could obtain at best would be a strategic improvement of the eastern frontier, a small war indemnity from France (not even therefore the ore basin of Briey), and possibly the Belgian fort of Liège, although the integrity of Belgium would have to be restored. They could only make colonial gains in Africa by the exchange of Togoland and South-West Africa. Even at this favourable time in the war the German Empire would have lost its powerful political and military in-

fluence in Turkey and its economic interests in
Anatolia and Mesopotamia, in the same way that
Austria-Hungary would have had to give up her
dominant position in the Balkans and certain Italian-
speaking areas. The Central Powers had gone to war
because of these interests and power bases, and these
possible small gains would not compensate for their
loss.

Bethmann-Hollweg argued that Germany would
have gained a victory in having maintained herself,
but as the Secretary of State, Jagow, put it, 'we would
have to abandon our world policy for several years'. In
other words she would have lost the war and been reduced to the position of a second-class Power. Taking
the most pessimistic view of what Germany could hope
to gain, she might even have to give up parts of
Alsace-Lorraine, to pay reparations to Belgium and
lose all her colonies. None the less during the peace
initiative of 1916 Bethmann-Hollweg was apparently
ready for such a peace; the war-aims programme of the
moment should not confuse one because it contained
only the maximum demands, which would have been
pared considerably at the conference table. By comparing the aims for conquest being pursued at that
time in Paris, London, St Petersburg and Rome,
Ritter found that Bethmann-Hollweg's demands
amounted 'almost to a total renunciation'.

Germany's attempt at a negotiated peace was
doomed from the outset. A Papal diplomat pointed
out to a German colleague that peace could only be
reached in one way: the Central Powers, at the peak
of their military success, ought to make a general declaration agreeing to re-establish the *status quo* of
France and Belgium as well as restoring Serbia's
sovereignty. This kind of self-denying ordinance
would make a very marked impression both on the
neutrals and on the populations of Germany's enemies
who were already tired of the war. But Ritter was able
to show that the German statesmen could not even
follow this poor chance, although it was presented at
various times, as for instance during the Papal peace
offensive in the summer of 1917 and again before the

start of the German spring offensive of 1918. There
were three main reasons why the German leaders could
not take it up:

(1) Germany could not give up her 'pledges' in Belgium and north-east France, as long as no guarantee was given that the French would evacuate
the areas of Upper Alsace which they had occupied or that the Allies would evacuate the conquered German colonies.

(2) As long as she did not want to risk losing her
alliance with Austria-Hungary, Bulgaria and
Turkey, Germany had to take care of their interests as well as her own and their lost territories
had to be recovered. Germany had moreover
made secret agreements to support her allies in
gaining additional territory.

(3) Germany could not announce a unilateral self-
denying ordinance without running the risk of
the other side's increasing its demands. There
was also the other danger that any government
making such a declaration would be attacked
and brought down by extremist elements within
Germany.

After the fall of Bethmann-Hollweg's government
the course of Germany's war-aims programme was at
last determined by the army, which had always been
keen on annexations, and by the politicians who had
associated themselves with the army's programme as
well as various economic groups.

The most influential person in the Michaelis and
Hertling Cabinets was the Secretary of State, von
Kühlmann, and he was even less in a position than
Bethmann-Hollweg to fight against Ludendorff's pressure. The army and those journalists instigated by it
attacked him as soon as he made any attempt to act
outside the war-aims programme which had been
agreed on internally, as for instance at the start of the
peace negotiations with Bolshevik Russia or during
the Bucharest Peace Conference and in the summer of
1918.

Only on one occasion, owing to his tactical finesse,

was he successful in defeating both the army and the Reichstag – during the Papal peace initiative of the summer of 1917. In agreement with the ruling élite he refused to make the renunciation of Belgium, which the Pope wanted, but he initiated a secret peace mission through the Spanish diplomat, Villalobar, and here he was ready to make even this renunciation if England in return acknowledged the integrity of the German Empire. The mission failed because of the jealousy of the Spanish Foreign Minister. Ritter doubted whether it would have been successful in any case, since Britain would never have acted without her allies' agreement and France would hardly have been able to guarantee Germany's possession of Alsace-Lorraine.

Besides, Ritter believed Kühlmann made a mistake in undertaking this diplomatic intrigue. Germany would have done better to have reacted immediately and positively to the Papal note. The moral success would have improved the German Empire's position. Kühlmann's tragedy was that he was trying to work with the diplomatic weapons of the nineteenth century in a modern, total, popular war of this century.

At the Brest-Litovsk peace conference Kühlmann played an equally dishonest game with the Bolsheviks. Both sides interpreted in their own sense the right of the population on the peripheries of Russia to self-determination, the one from the concept of the class struggle, the other imperialistically. But Kühlmann would have been prepared to accept the *status quo ante* if the Allies had accepted the Bolshevik invitation to the peace conference. The most recent work by Ritter's pupils has shown this beyond doubt.

Kühlmann was not to blame for the developments which led in February 1918 to the *Diktat* Peace of Brest-Litovsk. He had wanted neither the annexation of Livonia and Estonia nor the move into the Ukraine, but he had let things run their course after the Chancellor, Hertling, had let him down in his struggle with the army.

The Treaty of Brest-Litovsk has been generally used as confirmation of the war-aims thesis of the Fischer school. But Ritter, working from different premises, tried to minimise the significance of the peace treaty which was in fact ratified in the Reichstag by a large majority. With some justification he pointed out that this peace could only be a provisional solution and that it would immediately have been brought into question at a general peace conference. But the German conditions and especially their implementation of the Peace in the summer of 1918 cannot simply be explained away in terms of defensive and economic necessity, as Ritter tried to do in defending his hero, Kühlmann. What Ludendorff and some of the economic leaders were pursuing in Russia at the time was Imperialism pure and simple.

Ritter was really shaken to discover that in the Allied countries as well, where the militarists could not get their way as in Germany, the few voices of reason had been stifled by the wave of bellicose feeling so that the suicidal European civil war had to be fought through to the bitter end, to the surrender of one of the parties.

Germany could certainly have had peace in the summer of 1917, provided that she had merely given up those areas annexed in 1871, Alsace-Lorraine, besides Belgium. But, as Ritter once said, 'The German people at all levels of society were never ready to renounce Alsace-Lorraine before final and irrevocable defeat since they had become for the Germans, as for the French (perhaps even more for the Germans!), a national "emblem", the heirloom and symbol of their proudest period of recent history.'

To the end of his life Ritter never fully recovered from the loss of 'German Alsace'. But he also realised the crime against European peace which the German Empire had committed in its first hours of existence, when fully conscious of its power it crossed its set frontiers. This alone should have made Ritter, who was aware of the confused situation in Wilhelmine Germany, of the excessive nationalist feeling, the chauvinist dreams of power and the fatalistic blindness, find a different explanatory expression from that which he used, 'the belated nemesis of history'.

7   Gerhard Ritter and the First World War

Klaus Epstein

*Die Tragödie der Staatskunst: Bethmann-Hollweg als
Kriegskanzler (1914–1917)* is the third volume of
Staatskunst und Kriegshandwerk, the monumental
work produced by Gerhard Ritter on the problem of
militarism in modern German history. The first
volume, covering the years from the accession of
Frederick the Great to the dismissal of Bismarck (1740
–1890), won much praise for the breadth of its scope
and for Ritter's clear-cut stand in favour of the
primacy of *Staatskunst* over *Kriegshandwerk*. (It was,
however, in the opinion of this reviewer, far too
favourable to Bismarck, a point which will be developed later in this essay.) The second volume, covering the Wilhelmine period (1890–1914), was generally
hailed for its forthright condemnation of the anachronistic constitutional structure of the German Empire,
the excessive prestige enjoyed by the military among
the leading strata of German society, the irrational
folly of the Tirpitz naval programme, and the disastrous results wrought by the Schlieffen Plan. The
third volume is far more monographic in character
and encyclopaedic in source foundation than its two
predecessors: although it deals only with the three
years from the outbreak of the First World War
(August 1914) to the fall of the Chancellor, Bethmann-
Hollweg (July 1917), it is longer than the combined
volumes I and II dealing with the 175 years from 1740
to 1914.

Ritter's decision to provide a very full narrative is
due partly to the crowding of important and controversial events into the wartime period; partly to the
vast mass of primary materials available for these

From the *Journal of Contemporary History*, 1 (1966).

years; and partly to Ritter's polemical purpose of de-
molishing what he considers to be the false conceptions of the 'Fritz Fischer school'. The topics covered
by Ritter in separate chapters – each almost monographic in character – are the following: German war
aims, official and unofficial, in 1914; the relationship
between the Chancellor, Bethmann-Hollweg, and the
Chief of Staff, Falkenhayn, during 1914–15; Balkan
policy in the autumn of 1915; plans for *Mitteleuropa*
and for solving the Polish question, 1915–16; America
and the first two submarine crises of 1915–16; the
failure of the Verdun offensive and the fall of Falkenhayn; the Polish Manifesto of 5 November 1916; the
peace move of the Central Powers, the launching of
the submarine war, and the break with America,
December 1916–April 1917; the militarisation of the
German economy, with special reference to the
Auxiliary Service Law and the Belgian deportations
in the winter of 1916–17; Austria's moves towards a
separate peace in the spring of 1917; the Russian
February Revolution and the programme of a 'peace
without annexations and indemnities'; and finally,
the fall of Bethmann-Hollweg in July 1917, which
meant the complete triumph of German militarism.

It will be seen from this summary survey of the
book's contents that Ritter's work comes close to being
a general history of Germany during the three years
1914–17; it falls short of this only because his preoccupation with the relationship between Bethmann-Hollweg and the generals inevitably leads to the comparative neglect of other important topics, though it is in
fact remarkable how much Ritter has to say about
problems not directly connected with the relationship
between *Staatskunst* and *Kriegshandwerk*. The book
is comparatively weak on all aspects of domestic and
socio-economic history; it has little to say on party
politics and the work of the Reichstag; the part played
by economic pressure groups in the shaping of war
aims; the management of Germany's wartime economy;
and the development of public opinion. The bulk of
the work – the definitive analysis of civilian–military
relationships apart – is devoted to a conventional

diplomatic history in the somewhat old-fashioned manner of 'what one diplomat (or statesman) wrote to another'; it should be stressed, however, that it is conventional history written in a magisterial style by a historian who combines critical attention to detail with luminous generalisation and who is deeply concerned with history as a form of art to be appreciated by any interested reader.

Unlike his rival Fritz Fischer, Ritter was unable personally to inspect East German archives, though his pupil Zmarzlik examined some materials for him there. He has, however, explored many archival collections available in West Germany (Bonn, Koblenz, Munich, Stuttgart and Karlsruhe) and in Austria. (The Austrian chapters of the book, while not always germane to the main subject-matter and hence an obstacle to its readability, contain much valuable new information from previously unexplored primary sources. They suffer, however, from too much contempt for the Austrians and an extreme hostility towards General Conrad.) The elaborate footnote apparatus – unhappily placed at the end of the volume, pp. 589–688 – provides a careful documentation of primary sources and gives evidence of the thorough assimilation of secondary sources.

In his footnotes Ritter subjects Fischer's *Griff nach der Weltmacht* to a merciless cross-examination and is successful in demonstrating that Fischer is often deplorably careless in detail and sometimes guilty of *a priori* prejudice in the interpretation of sources. Nothing in Ritter's treatment, however, refutes the *major* aim of Fischer's pioneering work: to show that Germany (or at least nearly all influential people in Germany) succumbed during the First World War to a collective megalomania which expressed itself in utterly unrealistic war aims and a grotesque inability to see the world as it actually was; but Ritter does succeed in the *lesser* task of showing – as have a distinguished group of Fischer's critics which includes men of viewpoints as diverse as Dietrich Mende, K. D. Erdmann, Erwin Hölzle, Hans Herzfeld and Egmont Zechlin – that Fischer tends to exaggerate the pur-

posiveness, continuity and consistency of 'Germany's
drive for world power', and misunderstands the complex figure of the Chancellor, Bethmann-Hollweg.

What of Gerhard Ritter's own point of view? It is very
difficult to characterise it in any single phrase, because
he is – in this respect avoiding Fischer's penchant for
massive generalisation – profoundly impressed by the
multi-dimensional complexity of the problems presented by the war and the men (especially Bethmann-
Hollweg) who dealt with them. Caution is the keynote
of much – not all! – of Ritter's work, a caution which
results from a scholarly ethos which has compelled
him, in the course of a long life, to re-examine continuously the controversial problems of a period he
personally experienced as a young man. He appears
torn at times between the National Liberal outlook of
his early manhood – with its instinctively apologetic
attitude towards criticism directed against Germany's
conduct – and a distinctly post-1945 critical attitude
towards Wilhelmine Germany which yields nothing to
Fischer in the trenchancy of its accusations. The
earlier outlook appears in an occasional relapse into
outmoded nationalist views; an undue stress upon the
defensive character of German intentions and aims;
an obvious desire to relativise whatever was outrageous in German annexationist programmes by
pointing to similar Allied programmes; and the
attempt to build up Bethmann-Hollweg as a 'tragic
hero' who was generally moderate in his views despite
occasional aberrations. The later outlook appears in
his recognition of the problematical character of *all*
German annexationism; his criticism directed against
the anachronistic character of the entire 'power structure' of Wilhelmine society; his extraordinarily – for a
German historian – sympathetic and fair-minded attitude towards Woodrow Wilson and America's policy
in the submarine question; and his contemptuous
characterisation of Ludendorff and the 'militarist
forces' which he represented. Ritter is sometimes inconsistent in his judgements because he is so obviously
torn between the rival poles of old sentiment – ex-

pressed in delightful occasional autobiographical remi-
niscences (pp. 85, 118, 225) – and new insight promoted by his contemplation of the tragic course of
Germany's post-1917 history and by an admirable re-
ceptivity to the fresh outlook of young historians born
after the events described. His assimilation of books
written by non-German experts on the First World
War – for example, Arthur Link, Ernest May, Arno
Mayer and Karl Birnbaum – is a landmark in the de-
provincialisation of German academic history. In the
last years before his retirement in 1955 Ritter himself
trained an unusually able group of German specialists
on the history of the First World War – for example,
Wolfgang Steglich, Karl-Heinz Janssen and Klaus
Schwabe – whose researches have influenced his own
work. It is regrettable, however, that he has not taken
adequate cognisance of the writings of young historians trained by Fritz Fischer – for example,
Imanuel Geiss's valuable monograph on *Der polnische
Grenzstreifen 1914–18* (1960).

A few examples may serve to demonstrate the fact
that Ritter has 'two souls within his breast'. His
residual sympathy with an old-fashioned nationalist
outlook appears most clearly in his first chapter sur-
veying 'The Chancellor and the Dreams of Power
(*Machtträume*) of German Patriots'. To be sure, he
condemns the notorious shift in German public
opinion, following the early military victories, from a
purely defensive outlook to one bent upon conquest
(p. 34); he also recognises the military futility of frontier changes in an age of tanks and aeroplanes, and
their immorality in an age of mass nationalism (p. 35).
He insists, however, that broad allowances must be
made for a nation which sincerely believed itself to be
the innocent victim of foreign encirclement (what
provincialism!) and wanted to escape once and for all
from a situation where it was continuously threatened
by powerful neighbours (as if a country located in
central Europe could *ever* escape permanently from
anything!). Ritter is unduly sympathetic to the
numerous German professors who concocted elaborate
theories on the political, historical and even meta-

physical significance of Germany's war effort, comparing these 'attempts at spiritual self-defence and self-justification' with the Allied 'crusade for democracy and freedom against tyranny' (p. 39). He forgets the world of difference which existed between the parochial–nationalist ideals of German professors and the universalist democratic ideals of the Allied Powers (the fact that the latter may occasionally have been rationalisations for purely nationalist ends is irrelevant in this context). Ritter also betrays some residual Wilhelmine reflexes in his remarkably narrow view of what constitutes a German 'patriot'. He describes with approval the comparatively moderate early war aims of Loebell (Prussian Minister for the Interior) and Solf (Colonial Secretary), both of whom stressed the impossibility (not to say undesirability) of annexations in Europe while desiring the enlargement of Germany's overseas empire. Ritter comments that the demands of the two Ministers are especially interesting because 'they state pretty precisely the minimum of what a patriotic German politician hoped, at the beginning of the war, to achieve from a future peace' (p. 41). The implied corollary to Ritter's statement appears to be that anti-annexationists, i.e. the entire Socialist Party, were *not* patriots.

Ritter goes to considerable pains to stress the defensive character of Germany's war effort and war aims. This constitutes, no doubt, a valuable antidote to Fischer's theme of a Germany rationally and deliberately bent upon realising the offensive goal of the position of a 'World Power', but both historians tend to forget – for opposite reasons – that in the German war-aims movement offensive and defensive elements were inextricably intertwined in the minds of most actors. The term 'offensive' covers motives like greed and the will to power; the term 'defensive', fear and concern about one's ability to cope with future contingencies. Those who insisted upon securing permanent domination of Belgium usually wanted control of Belgian industries (an offensive aim) *and* a better strategic position in the next war (a defensive aim); those who wanted to establish *Mitteleuropa* wanted to

dominate a satellite empire (offensive) and secure protection against anticipated Allied economic discrimination in the post-war era (defensive); those who
wanted vast eastern annexations – however cloaked
under the slogan of 'national autonomy' – wanted
markets (offensive) but were also concerned about the
often cited 'Russian–Asiatic–Mongolian danger' (defensive). What was true of specific war aims was also
true of the general tenor of Germany's diplomatic and
military policy, beginning with her conduct during
the July crisis. Ritter – again in sharp and explicit
opposition to Fischer – insists that Bethmann-Hollweg's policy was essentially defensive and pacific at
that time (pp. 15–20); but he admits that the Chancellor's conduct was influenced by the fatalistic conviction that a showdown with Russia was inevitable
sooner or later. Was it defensive or offensive to force
such a showdown in 1914 in the belief that Russia
might now – but no longer in 1917 – climb down
peacefully and be sufficiently humiliated so that it
could not hope to make new trouble in the foreseeable
future? Are genuine 'preventive wars' – and the German decision to support Austria to the hilt contained
some of the ingredients of a preventive war – offensive
or defensive? They generally look very offensive, but
their ultimate motivation may very well be defensive
in the sense of springing from a feeling of insecurity.
The question is certainly interesting when it comes to
the evaluation of the subjective motives of statesmen,
but it has little objective importance; it has been
raised here only to point out the illegitimacy of
Ritter's exclusive stress upon the defensive motives of
Germany and the obvious apologetic purpose which
this serves.

Ritter is much concerned – in sharp contrast to
Fischer – to relativise the enormity of German
annexationist plans by pointing to the similarly
annexationist aims of Germany's enemies (see Section
II of Chapter VIII: 'The Problem of Peace and the
Allied Governments'). This survey is curiously un-
balanced in devoting half a page to Russia, five pages
to France and fourteen to England – the length of

each discussion stands in inverse proportion to the extent of the annexationist aims championed by the three countries; this appears to be a rare case in which Ritter's treatment was evidently governed by the available secondary literature. He has no difficulty in establishing the fact that Allied statesmen (and the public opinion behind them) were incorrigible annexationists and that they were even less willing than Bethmann-Hollweg to contemplate a 'peace of reconciliation' on the basis of the *status quo ante*. He is on questionable ground, however, in his major contention that there was no qualitative distinction between Allied and German annexationism. Ritter ignores two key facts of the 1914–18 situation: that German annexationism and *only* German annexationism threatened the complete overthrow of the European balance of power; and that *all* German annexationist plans were certain to violate the now fashionable principle of nationality.

Wilhelmine Germany – because of its size, population, geographical location, economic dynamism, cocky militarism, and autocracy under a neurotic Kaiser – was feared by all other Powers as a threat to the European equilibrium; this was an objective fact which Germans should have recognised, irrespective of whether Germany in fact did or did not have intentionally aggressive designs (as affirmed by Fischer and denied by Ritter). Allied annexationist ambitions were, of course, also in many cases morally outrageous, besides being undesirable because they precluded (equally with German annexationism) any negotiated peace; but their realisation did *not* threaten the European equilibrium with the intolerable hegemony of a single Power, whereas the expansion of an already too powerful Germany did. The principle of nationality – increasingly accepted by 'enlightened' public opinion as the most satisfactory basis for international frontiers – was an additional barrier to *any* German expansion. The immediate Allied war aims (for example, France's desire for Alsace-Lorraine, Italy's for Trieste and Serbia's for Bosnia) were substantially in accordance with the wishes of the populations

294 *Klaus Epstein*

affected, whereas *all* German territorial objectives were a violation of the right of self-determination. This is but to say that the bloated German frontiers of 1914 already included a large number of unassimilable and misgoverned Poles, Alsatians and Danes.

Bethmann-Hollweg is the tragic hero of Ritter's book – a man of high intelligence and basic moderation who failed because of a combination of objective circumstances and personal flaws. Ritter's portrait of Bethmann-Hollweg is by all odds the best that we possess – it is certainly truer to life than Fischer's picture of an unbending and inflexible annexationist who consistently adhered to the extreme war-aims Memorandum he had drawn up on 9 September 1914, before he understood the significance of the Marne débâcle. (Fischer, who scored a triumph by discovering this surprising Memorandum in the archives, exaggerates its importance by claiming that Bethmann-Hollweg at heart never deviated from it.) Although Ritter is generally sympathetic to Bethmann-Hollweg, he none the less criticises him on several scores: his extreme annexationism in 1914, his participation in the intrigue which replaced the sober Falkenhayn by the rabid Ludendorff in 1916, his failure to protest against the Belgian deportations of 1916, and his weakness in the crucial debate on submarine warfare. Bethmann-Hollweg's war aims in 1914 were not only fantastic in their ambitiousness but crazy in detail. To give only one example: he wanted to impose a treaty upon England depriving her of the right to levy protective tariffs in the future – a provision which would not only benefit German exporters but so cripple England's finances as to make her incapable of introducing universal military service after the war (thereby perpetuating Germany's military superiority) (p. 44). Ritter says in extenuation of this and other unrealistic plans that they were supported by an overwhelming public opinion – if true, a complete confirmation of Fischer's main theme; that they were subsequently modified or abandoned by Bethmann-Hollweg – a useful corrective of Fischer's

views; and even the great Bismarck made an annexationist mistake in the case of Alsace-Lorraine in 1871.
This last consideration – which could be paraphrased
in the question 'How can you expect Bethmann-Hollweg to be better than Bismarck?' – is surely irrelevant,
and the implication that statesmen cannot learn from
their predecessors' mistakes is not necessarily true and
far from flattering to Bethmann-Hollweg.

We leave it to the reader to follow Ritter in his
major preoccupation of discovering the 'true historical Bethmann-Hollweg'. A concluding observation
should, however, be made on this topic. It appears, at
least to this reviewer, more important to consider
what Bethmann-Hollweg was and what his position
permitted him to be, than what he actually did. There
is general agreement (or will soon be again, once the
revisionist position of Fischer has been revised in
turn) that, compared with Germany's other leaders,
Bethmann-Hollweg was a man of high intelligence
and basic moderation whose views were, to the mis-
fortune of Germany, overridden by Ludendorff in
1916–17. Why were his views overridden so easily by so
incompetent and irresponsible a militarist – a man
without the slightest qualification to rule Germany in
her moment of extreme crisis? Partly because of the
institutional weakness of the Chancellor's office under
the Bismarckian constitution, under which the in-
cumbent was nothing but an Imperial bureaucrat dependent – unless a national hero like Bismarck – upon
Imperial favour; it was considered quite improper for
a Chancellor to base his position upon an appeal to
public opinion or upon a majority in the Reichstag.
That position was bound to be weak in war because
the principle of civilian supremacy over the military
was completely contrary to German traditions. In
Bethmann-Hollweg's case the weakness of the office
was compounded by the weakness of the man. Bethmann-Hollweg lacked charisma and political finesse;
he often radiated a contagious pessimism intolerable
in a war leader; he became unsure of himself when
confronted by the expertise of generals and admirals
in the submarine question; and he lacked Lloyd

George's megalomanic – but invaluable – belief that
he, and he alone, could extricate his country from
its unparalleled difficulties. Bethmann-Hollweg succeeded only rarely in imposing his views upon others,
either by persuasion or intimidation; he shrank from
conflicts with Ludendorff – for example, on the crucial
question of war aims – which he knew he could not
win and believed to be premature, thereby creating a
pattern of acquiescent surrender; and he permitted
his power to be progressively undermined long before
he was finally dismissed at Ludendorff's behest.

Even a stronger Chancellor in a stronger office would
have encountered formidable opposition if he had
sought – as Bethmann-Hollweg did, haltingly and in-
effectively – an early peace based, if necessary, upon
the renunciation of annexations. Ritter spends a great
deal of effort exploring the state of Bethmann-Hollweg's mind and soul – his precise intentions at various
times, his reaction to real and hypothetical events, the
specific circumstances explaining his annexationist
aberrations, etc. This effort certainly yields new insights concerning Bethmann-Hollweg, but it appears
comparatively unimportant for the understanding of
Germany's wartime policy. Ritter admits – though unlike Fischer he does not stress – the fundamental fact
that the ruling élite of Germany – the officer corps,
landowners, industrialists, bureaucrats, professors and
clergymen, plus a majority of the Reichstag until 1917
– ardently favoured an annexationist policy and was
prepared to sweep away any Chancellor who favoured
genuine moderation. It is unfortunate that he pays
such disproportionate attention to Bethmann-Hollweg
as an individual, to the comparative neglect of an
analysis of the basic political, social and economic force
whose constellation reduced any particular personality
– even that of the Chancellor, Bethmann-Hollweg – to
virtual historical insignificance.

Ritter deplores the extreme annexationist outlook of
broad German strata and the fact that this outlook
was sometimes shared, and never effectively opposed,
by Bethmann-Hollweg. He insists, however, that Ger-

man annexationism was not responsible for the needless prolongation of the war (as charged at the time by
the Independent Socialists); one of the main themes of
Ritter's book (pp. 188 ff.) is that a negotiated peace
was an objective impossibility in an age when mass
passions had replaced the calm *Staatsraison* of happier
periods of European history. He argues persuasively
that the Allied Powers were at no time willing to
settle for a negotiated peace based upon the *status
quo ante* – and an undefeated Germany obviously could
not accept terms less favourable than the *status quo
ante*, especially as its armies stood almost everywhere on
enemy soil and its ruling class suffered from a bad case
of collective megalomania. The valid charge against
German annexationism is not that it *prolonged* the war
– since it takes two to negotiate a reasonable peace – but
rather that it handicapped Germany's wartime position by promoting pro-war solidarity in the Allied
countries, preventing Allied–American controversies
about war aims, and embittering substantial sections
of the German people who believed (incorrectly, it
appears) that Germany could have had peace if it had
only renounced annexations. Ritter fully realises (p.
337) that a generous German peace offer – preferably
one explicitly calling for a return to the *status quo
ante* – would have caused tremendous embarrassment
to the Allied governments and strengthened the wan-
ing loyalty of Germany's lower classes to the war
effort. Why, then, did Bethmann-Hollweg – assuming
he was at heart as moderate as Ritter thinks – never
seriously contemplate such an offer? More especially
since its inevitable rejection by the Allies need not
have precluded large annexations in the case of a subsequent German victory? The reasons appear to be:
(i) the refusal of Germany's allies (especially Bulgaria)
to agree to a *status quo ante* peace – hence any peace
move must put strains upon the existing Quadruple
Alliance; (ii) the fear that the Allied will to fight until
total victory would be strengthened by any German
'confession of weakness'; (iii) the belief that annexations would be more difficult to justify, in case of the
subsequent victory, once the goal of a non-annexation-

ist peace had been proclaimed; and – most important
of all – (iv) the intransigent opposition of the
Supreme Command to such a move. The Supreme
Command, in this speaking for the most influential
groups of German society, was bent upon annexations; it even justified these by such preposterous
arguments as the necessity of annexationist goals to
maintain the fighting morale of the army. Bethmann-
Hollweg refused to make a major effort to override
these considerations, partly because he was impressed
by the force of the first three arguments; partly because he never ceased to hope that Germany might
achieve some annexations; but mostly because he
feared a showdown with the Supreme Command
which he believed he could not win. He probably had
the intention of seizing upon any concrete chance of a
negotiated peace if and when such a chance should
come up, and hoped that he could then prevail
against the Supreme Command with the help of the
Kaiser; but such a chance never came, and meanwhile
Germany muffed the great propaganda chance of successfully indicting the Allies for the crime of need-
lessly prolonging the war for purely annexationist
ends. A different Chancellor, of greater personal force
and greater personal prestige, might conceivably have
been strong enough to insist upon a peace offer em-
barrassing to the Allies; but Germany's constitutional
structure (under which soldiers were not subordinated
to civilians), its political power structure (under which
all key positions of German society were held by
annexationists), and its mental condition (already
described as collective megalomania) would have
made difficult any peace move by even a Chancellor of
Bismarckian capacity.

Ritter insists that Bethmann-Hollweg's Peace Note
of 12 December 1916 was sincerely meant, and not just
part of the preparation for launching unrestricted
submarine warfare – an argument which rehabilitates
Bethmann-Hollweg's integrity at the expense of his
intelligence, for the specific terms of the Note were
couched in arrogant and defiant tones which facilitated
rejection. Ritter's two long chapters (V and VIII)

dealing with the submarine question are among the best in the book, and are path-breaking – so far as the German reading public is concerned – in following Ernest May and Arthur Link in their penetrating understanding of Wilson's truly neutral attitude in his peace moves. Ritter's passionate interest in the question arises from his understanding that it (not economic factors or fears for the European balance of power) was primarily responsible for America's entry into the war; and that America's decision was responsible for the defeat of Germany, since the Allied Powers would have been incapable of defeating Germany – especially after the Russian Revolution – without America's active support. Apart from these broad perspectives of world history, the submarine controversy is central in the context of Ritter's theme of the triumph of militarism in Germany during the war. The decision for the submarine war marked the clear-cut victory of military over political considerations; it showed the fatal role played by public opinion in deciding – in a manner unprecedented in German history – a military-diplomatic question upon which the future of Germany depended; and it demonstrated how technical judgements (on, for example, the number and effectiveness of available submarines) could be clouded by nationalist passions. It also reveals Bethmann-Hollweg's deplorable self-doubt in the face of arguments advanced by experts; he made his first error by not preventing the initial launching of the submarine warfare on 1 February 1915, being impressed by the dishonest, bragging claims of the Admiralty; his victories over the Admiralty in both the *Lusitania* and *Sussex* crises never went beyond half-measures, since they never led to the explicit and unconditional renunciation of illegal practices of submarine warfare; he allowed himself to be persuaded that an intermediary policy between unrestricted submarine warfare and total abandonment was impracticable; and he finally acquiesced in the crucial decision for unrestricted warfare – refusing to resign – because he was half persuaded that the navy might be right in its claim that England could be starved out despite America's anticipated entry into the war. Ritter is curiously sympathetic to Bethmann-Hollweg's refusal to oppose the submarine war *à outrance*:

> It is demanding a very unusual (not to say super-human) degree of political instinct and strength of will to expect a man to rely exclusively upon his personal insight (more accurately, his instinct) to take upon his shoulders the terrible responsibility (of vetoing the submarine war) against the advice of all leading soldiers and naval experts, against the will of his monarch, against the majority of the Reichstag, and against the greater part of politically active Germans (extending even into the ranks of the Social Democrats) who expressed themselves on the question (pp. 384–5).

Perhaps so; but this fact throws a glaring light upon the state of German public opinion which confirms the views of Fritz Fischer. It did not require much political instinct, only an elementary understanding of America's strength (as indicated, for example, by readily available statistics on production and financial resources), to convince any rational person that America's entry into the war must be avoided at all costs. Germany's rulers, Bethmann-Hollweg included, were, however, too parochial to understand the real world of 1917. Germany's Chancellor – a man rightly praised for his comparatively sensible views – thought that America's entry into the war would mean nothing more than America's 'delivering food to England, providing some financial help, and sending some aeroplanes and a corps of volunteers' (pp. 384, 657 n. 48). A man so ignorant of the facts supporting his position was helpless when Ludendorff insisted that the launching of unrestricted submarine warfare was the only way in which the war could still be won.

Whereas Chancellor Bethmann-Hollweg is the tragic hero of Ritter's work, General Ludendorff is cast for the role of villain. It is a weakness of the book that there is no elaborate character portrait of this

baneful man; but he emerges from the narrative as
the very stereotype of a militarist in terms of his
brutality, his lack of understanding of political problems, and his insistence upon the paramountcy of
purely military considerations. This was true in his insistence upon submarine warfare, his insistence upon
the Polish Manifesto (5 November 1916) motivated by
the vain desire to recruit Polish soldiers, and his insistence upon the barbarous deportations of Belgian
labourers in the winter of 1916–17 (a policy unfortunately and unaccountably not opposed by Bethmann-
Hollweg). As a foil, Ritter draws a favourable portrait
of Ludendorff's predecessor Falkenhayn (Chapter VI),
who – though he also at times interfered improperly
in political affairs – was a man of sober judgement
whose view of the world was at least as realistic as
Bethmann-Hollweg's, thus providing comparatively few
opportunities for serious quarrels. Why, then, did
Bethmann-Hollweg actively support Falkenhayn's replacement by the Hindenburg–Ludendorff combination in August 1916, a mistake fatal for the rational
conduct of Germany's war effort and Bethmann-Hollweg's retention of the Chancellorship? The reason
seems to be (pp. 248 ff.) that Bethmann-Hollweg did not
like Falkenhayn and did not fear Ludendorff; that he
was impressed by the military criticism directed against
Falkenhayn's Verdun offensive; that he was – as usual
– not insensitive to the clamour of public opinion;
and most of all, that he hoped to use the legendary
prestige of Hindenburg in order to make a 'reasonable
peace' palatable to rabid German public opinion if
such a peace should become feasible. Never was there
so complete a miscalculation. Hindenburg and
Ludendorff became the most intransigent foes of a
reasonable foreign and domestic policy looking towards a 'peace of understanding' and the conciliation
of the German masses through political reforms. They
were, in fact, soon to take the lead in securing Bethmann-Hollweg's dismissal from the Chancellorship the
moment he proposed the democratic franchise for
Prussia and showed his willingness to work with the

anti-annexationist Reichstag majority which emerged
during the crisis of July 1917.

Ritter's account of this crisis (Chapter XII) is one of
the less satisfactory parts of the book. He bemoans the
complete triumph of the Supreme Command, yet refuses to criticise Bethmann-Hollweg's failure to fight
to retain his office. If there was an alternative to
Ludendorff's dictatorship, it consisted of Bethmann-
Hollweg's making a frank and firm alliance with the
left-wing Reichstag majority formed under Erzberger's
guidance at that time. It is true that Erzberger behaved in a thoroughly irresponsible manner in the
latter phase of the crisis by co-operating with the
Supreme Command in bringing down Bethmann-
Hollweg before making sure that there would be a
better replacement; but this should not have deterred
the Chancellor from seeking to retain his position.
Could Ludendorff have insisted upon Bethmann-
Hollweg's dismissal if the latter had mobilised the
Kaiser and the Reichstag majority on his own behalf,
and had not hesitated to expose Ludendorff's primary
responsibility for the submarine fiasco? Ritter has an
inkling of this when he criticises Bethmann-Hollweg
(erroneously) for denying before the Reichstag that
there had been a conflict of opinion between himself
and the Supreme Command on the submarine question:
'he thereby deprived himself in his relations with the
Deputies of a weapon which he might possibly have
used to save both himself and his policy' (p. 561). This
sounds like an accusation of weakness directed against
Bethmann-Hollweg; yet Ritter rather inconsistently
accuses another historian of a 'strange misunderstanding of the general German situation of 1917' for suggesting that Bethmann-Hollweg showed weakness in
not standing up against Ludendorff by mobilising
Reichstag support (p. 688 n. 65). The fact of the
matter is that Bethmann-Hollweg – being the weak
and incompetent man that he was – never seriously
thought of fighting for his position and feared above
all that Ludendorff's dismissal – the alternative to his
own – would lead to a terrible public outcry. So it
would have, but Ludendorff's complete triumph led to

something worse – the disastrous mismanagement of
German affairs by a narrow-minded militarist. If
Bethmann-Hollweg had been convinced of his own
indispensability – as all great statesmen must be – and
had recognised the full measure of Ludendorff's in-
competence – for which overwhelming evidence was
already available in July 1917 – he would have fought
for his position and the fate of Germany might have
turned out more fortunately.

Ritter considers Ludendorff's dismissal of Bethmann-Hollweg the final triumph of German militarism and as such the climax of the story of the relationship between *Staatskunst* and *Kriegshandwerk* in
modern German history. He has, however, promised a
fourth volume which will deal in detail with the final
seventeen months of the First World War and in more
summary fashion with the period 1918 to 1945. It
appears that Ritter exaggerates the importance of the
events of July 1917, for Bethmann-Hollweg had for all
practical purposes been the prisoner of the Supreme
Command long before his fall. It made little difference whether Bethmann-Hollweg did Ludendorff's
bidding reluctantly or Bethmann-Hollweg's successor
Michaelis did it eagerly – the ascendancy of Ludendorff had been established, once and for all, by his victory in the submarine question in January 1917.

The phenomenon of militarism has – in Ritter's
view – three aspects which are usually related to one
another: the inadequate institutional subordination
of soldiers to civilians; the excessive prestige attached
to soldiers, warfare and military ways of thought; and
– as a consequence of both – undue weight being
given, in policy decisions, to technical military factors
at the expense of general political considerations. It
requires stressing that the first two factors were a dis-
tinctive characteristic of Imperial Germany well before 1914; hence there was exceptional danger of the
third when the war broke out. The subordination of
soldiers to civilians was completely contrary to Prussian traditions, although this became explicit (and important) only after the constitutionalisation of Prussia
in 1850, having been previously concealed by the fact

that the monarch was both Head of State and Com-
mander-in-Chief. Moreover, in no country of the
world were 'militarist' attitudes and ways of thought
more prevalent, among soldiers and civilians alike,
than in Imperial Germany. The army enjoyed tremendous prestige: a reserve officer's patent was indispensable for success in many civilian occupations; history books stressed victorious battles even more than
was the case in other countries; the anniversary of
Sedan – the day of the military humiliation of a great
neighbour – was Germany's national holiday; and in
no nation of the world were politics and politicians so
disparaged at the expense of warfare and officers.
These aspects of Germany's institutions and national
outlook all contributed to the inevitable total
triumph of militarism during the First World War.
Ritter, when he comes to explaining the victory of
unbridled and suicidal militarism over statesmanship,
talks altogether too much about fate, destiny and
other metaphysical categories, instead of assigning
specific responsibility to specific forces and figures in
German history. He is right, no doubt, in stressing the
limited alternatives which confronted a man like
Bethmann-Hollweg in view of the institutionalised
power of the German army and the attitude of influential German public opinion. It appears to this re-
veiwer, however, that Ritter accepts the structure of
Wilhelmine society too much as a 'given' and pays in-
sufficient attention to 'how it got to be that way'. The
villain of his volume is Ludendorff, but Ludendorff
was more a symptom than a cause; the real villain remains not only unindicted, but is even one of the
main heroes of Ritter's first volume: Otto Prince
Bismarck.

Needless to say, Bismarck was not a militarist, least
of all in Ritter's definition of the term; he always believed in, and was successful in maintaining, civilian –
that is to say, his own – supremacy over the soldiers.
He generally subordinated narrow military to broad
political considerations, always excepting the unfortunate annexation of Alsace-Lorraine in 1871; and he
was basically a man of moderation who never dreamt

of European hegemony – much less world power – but
wanted only the aggrandisement of Prussia (or a Prus-
sianised Germany) within the framework of the European equilibrium. Yet despite these virtues he must be
considered the foster-father of German militarism in
both the institutional and psychological senses mentioned above. In the Prussian constitutional struggle
of 1861–6 Bismarck was responsible for preserving the
position of the army as *imperium in imperio*; but for
his acceptance of the Prime Ministership at a time
when the King was on the verge of abdication, it is
probable that Parliament – and government dependent upon Parliament in an English-style constitutional
monarchy under the liberal Crown Prince – would
have secured full control over the army and thereby
established civilian supremacy. Bismarck was responsible for perpetuating the anachronistic notion that
the comprehension of military affairs exceeded the
capacity of mere Deputies, and for continuing the institutional arrangements under which the General
Staff and the Military Cabinet were not subordinated
to the Minister of War because the latter, though in
no sense legally responsible to Parliament, might fall
under parliamentary influence because he was compelled to defend the military budget in the Reichstag.
   Worse still was the encouragement given by Bismarck to the militarist mentality. He usually
appeared in uniform when he gave Reichstag
speeches; he declared on occasion that the Prussian
lieutenant was the pillar of the German State ('den
preussischen Leutnant macht uns niemand nach'); he
regretted nostalgically that he had served his King too
much sitting behind his desk instead of standing up
against enemy bullets; and he proclaimed that only
'blood and iron', not speeches and parliamentary
majorities, could solve the great questions of the day.
He was only too happy to bask in the glory of three
successful wars, and he did nothing to teach his
countrymen the simple fact that war had become – at
least in the eyes of enlightened men – a deplorable
anachronism, to be employed only as a last resort, as
an exceptional medicine to cope with exceptional

evils; and that the theoretical glorification of war, and
the practice of sabre-rattling, now offended 'the decent
opinion of mankind'. He did much too little to educ-
ate his countrymen in the requirements resulting from
Germany's extremely precarious position in the centre
of Europe, a situation which could be successfully
mastered only through exceptional political maturity
in the form of moderation in policy and sympathetic
deference to the interests of the other Powers. Instead
Bismarck tolerated, and at times even cultivated, a
mood of narrow chauvinism, blatant arrogance and
self-centred provincialism – all qualities that were to
contribute to the triumph of the militarism which is
the main theme of Ritter's volume. Militarism can be
curbed – if at all – only by the strenuous efforts of a
politically mature nation which is trained, through
the experience of self-government, in the necessity of
civilian supremacy over a potentially irresponsible
group like the officer corps. Bismarck, by perpetuating
the political nonage of the German people, by buttressing the sagging position of the militarist Junker class,
and by emasculating Germany's Parliament, bears a
heavy responsibility for the forces which made militarism victorious. The major weakness of Ritter's volume
is that he does not adequately trace the historical roots
of militarism back into the over-lauded Bismarckian
era, and that he does not stress sufficiently the social
factors behind the triumph of militarism – factors
which are much more important than the condition of
Bethmann-Hollweg's soul. If Ritter had been more
conscious of Bismarck's contribution to the spirit of
militarism in modern Germany, he would have gained
a better perspective for evaluating the forces which
struggled with each other during the crucial years
1914–17; and there would have been less use of categories like 'fate' and 'tragedy' to explain the wellnigh
'inevitable' ascendancy of Ludendorff.

8 1914: The Unspoken Assumptions

James Joll

The crisis of July 1914 is probably better documented than any other in modern history, and because of the political implications of the question of 'war guilt' and the explicit references in the Treaty of Versailles to Germany's responsibility for the war, the literature on the subject, both academic and polemical, is vast. Historians at least have reason to be grateful to the authors of the 'war-guilt' clause in the Treaty, since it prompted the publication of the documents and the opening of the archives. There are admittedly some people who belittle the importance of the First World War and who believe that it will seem to future historians just the first round of a comparatively un-important European civil war when set against the perspective of the changes in Africa, Asia and America during the twentieth century, and there are others who point out that the economic and social changes resulting from the war would have happened in any case, and that the war merely brought about a small acceleration of the pace at which they occurred. Still, for most of us the First World War and its origins remain topics of interest and relevance, while the recent controversy in Germany aroused by the pub-lication of Professor Fritz Fischer's work on Germany's war aims shows that the subject is still one which can arouse deep political passions.

Why does this interest persist, in spite of the fact that there is little more we can hope to obtain in the way of documentary evidence – though it would be interesting to have some more information about exactly what passed between the French President and Prime Minister and their Russian colleagues during

Inaugural professorial lecture delivered at the London School of Economics and Political Science, April 1968.

their visit to St Petersburg from 20 to 24 July? Why
do we still study the coming of the First World War,
even though every incident in the critical days of July
1914 has been scrutinised, analysed and interpreted
again and again? One of the answers lies, I think, in
the discrepancy between the importance of the events
themselves and of their consequences and the ordin-
ariness of most of the politicians and generals making
the key decisions. Luigi Albertini, himself a practising
politician and newspaper editor, whose three vast
volumes on the origins of the war still, in my opinion,
remain the best of the detailed studies, wrote of 'the
disproportion between their intellectual and moral
endowments and the gravity of the problems which
faced them, between their acts and the results thereof'.
And Gavrilo Princip himself, whose assassination of
the Archduke Franz Ferdinand on 28 June 1914 must
in some sense be counted as one of the causes of the
war, when asked by Dr Pappenheim, the psychiatrist
who interviewed him in prison, whether he believed
the assassination was a service, replied that 'he could
not believe that the world war was a consequence of
the assassination; that he could not feel himself responsible for the catastrophe and therefore could not
say if it was a service, but feared he did it in vain'.
Again and again in the July crisis one is confronted
with men who suddenly feel themselves trapped,
caught up in a fate they are unable to control. Bethmann-Hollweg, the German Chancellor, for example,
is reported as saying on 20 July 1914 that he saw 'a
doom (*ein Fatum*) greater than human power hanging
over Europe and our own people'. In some cases this
sense of helplessness is because the politicians' gambles
have gone wrong. In others, lack of understanding of
the technical aspects of war led to the taking of military measures which turned out to be irreversible. 'It
will run away with him, as it ran away with me', the
Kaiser said about Hitler to an English visitor to
Doorn in the 1930s. Did he perhaps have in mind that
moment on the afternoon of 1 August 1914 when, in a
last-minute attempt to limit the war, he asked his
military leaders whether it would not be possible to

give up the idea of attacking France and to concentrate the German armies against Russia, only to be told to his annoyance that it was out of the question to undo the plans elaborated over many years, and that instead of an army ready for war he would have a mass of armed men with no food.

When political leaders are faced with the necessity of taking decisions the outcome of which they cannot foresee, in crises which they do not wholly understand, they fall back on their own instinctive reactions, traditions and modes of behaviour. Each of them has certain beliefs, rules or objectives which are taken for granted; and one of the limitations of documentary evidence is that few people bother to write down, especially in moments of crisis, things which they take for granted. Yet if we are to understand their motives, we must somehow try to find out what, as we say, 'goes without saying'. Even when we have records of what was said, we do not always know the tone of voice in which the words were spoken. What was the inflection with which the Russian Foreign Minister, Sazonov, exclaimed on hearing of the terms of the Austrian ultimatum to Serbia, 'C'est la guerre européenne'? Or what were the overtones in the voice of the old Emperor Franz Josef when he greeted the report of the Serbian rejection of Austria-Hungary's terms with the untranslatable 'Also, doch!'? Did the speakers express pain, regret, relief or surprise? Our judgement of their policies depends in part on the answer; and our answers depend on the picture of their character built up from a number of other sources, so that although we can be certain of the words they used, our interpretation may vary according to our assessment of quite different evidence about their characters.

In moments of crisis, political leaders fall back on unspoken assumptions, and their intentions can often only be judged in the light of what we can discover about those assumptions. It is this that makes it possible for the same document to serve as a basis for totally different interpretations. Let me give an example arising out of Professor Fritz Fischer's work on German war aims and the outbreak of war in 1914.

Professor Fischer found in the archives, and published, a memorandum prepared for the German Chancellor dated 9 September 1914. It is a statement of war aims drawn up at a moment when the effects of the Battle of the Marne were not yet clear and when, therefore, the Germans still had good grounds for expecting a quick victory in the West. This programme is a comprehensive scheme for annexations in France and Belgium and for the establishment of German hegemony in central Europe through the creation of a Mitteleuropa under German leadership. The September Memorandum has strong similarities with a document sent to the Chancellor a few days earlier by the industrialist and financier, Walther Rathenau, the head of the great electricity combine, the A.E.G. We know that Bethmann-Hollweg and Rathenau were neighbours in the country and that they dined together from time to time. What did they talk about on these evenings? Were German gains in a possible war already being discussed before August 1914 round the table in Rathenau's exquisite dining-room in Schloss Freienwalde? If so, how far were these aims in the minds of the German leaders in the critical days of July 1914? It is extremely hard to say; and our assessment of the significance of the September Memorandum of war aims depends on our general view of the mentality, the *Weltanschauung*, of the German leaders as much as on the document itself. Some historians regard the September Memorandum as a hastily contrived plan to meet the immediate situation when Germany was confronted with the prospect of an early and unexpected victory. Others maintain that it is evidence of the sinister nature of Germany's prewar policies and of the views of what we would today call the military–industrial complex which controlled the German government. The links between the general ideas in the air before the war started and the concrete programme produced once war had begun are not in the document but in the minds of Germany's rulers; and it is on one's reconstruction of what was in their minds that our judgement of their actions must be based.

How can historians set about reconstructing the unspoken assumptions of the men they are studying? It
is at this point that we look hopefully for assistance
from other disciplines and turn to the psychologists or
the sociologists or the economists. However, the help
they can give us is limited. Either what they have to
say is too general to fit a particular individual or a
particular situation or – as in the attempts which have
been made to use the techniques of psychoanalysis in
dealing with historical characters – the type of evidence available is too fragmentary to provide the basis
for more than very tentative or rather obvious hypotheses. Even Ambassador Bullitt's enlistment of the
help of Freud in person for his study of Woodrow
Wilson, although it produced a more interesting book
than is generally allowed and gave Freud the chance
of writing an excellent summary of some of his ideas,
throws more light on Woodrow Wilson's personal
relationships and on the psychological causes of his
physical collapse than it does on his actual policies.
Yet there are occasional hints which deserve following
up and flashes of evidence which the amateur psychol-
ogist in each of us cannot help seizing on. Professor
Fritz Stern, for example, has recently drawn attention
to the fact that Bethmann-Hollweg in his memoirs
wrote that for Germany to have followed a different
course in July 1914 would have amounted to *Selbst-
ent mannung* – self-castration – and suggests that the
phrase might be an unconscious allusion to the
charges of civilian effeminacy levelled by the soldiers
at the politicians in Germany.

The historian must seek his explanations where he
can find them, even in unorthodox or unprofessional
places. After all, even L. B. Namier was not ashamed
to use the services of a graphologist in reconstructing
the character of the writer of manuscript documents.
In general, however, other disciplines in the social
sciences can usually only suggest new types of explanation and direct attention to new areas where the
answers may lie. They cannot, that is to say, themselves provide the precise answers to the historians'
questions. To take the most famous and obvious

example, Marx, by drawing attention to the way in
which economic factors produce historical change, has
had an immensely fruitful influence on historical writing. Yet, when one comes to trace the exact effect of
economic factors in, for instance, the crisis of 1914, one
is faced with all sorts of puzzles. If, as I suggested
earlier, some of the German industrialists and bankers
were dreaming of a German economic sphere in
central Europe and possibly envisaging a war as a
means of achieving this, other economic leaders were
pressing in a different direction. Take the case of
Morocco, for example – an important element in the
international tension before 1914. Here it was the
French government which had had to persuade the
bankers to lend money to the Sultan in order to
support French political aims, and not the bankers
who were pressing for political action to further their
economic interests; and German policy in Morocco
between 1909 and 1911 can only be understood when
one realises that the German government and one
group of mining interests wanted to co-operate with
France, while a rival German group was trying to
break this co-operation in their own interests. In the
July crisis of 1914, while some industrialists may have
looked forward to war as an opportunity of extending
their influence and increasing their profits, many of
the financiers and bankers were appalled at the economic chaos which they expected from war. In London, Grey was still, on 31 July, worried about the
financial consequences of being involved in war. 'The
commercial and financial situation was extremely
serious,' he told the French Ambassador, 'there was
danger of a complete collapse that would involve us
and everyone in ruin; and it was possible that our
standing aside might be the only means of preventing
a complete collapse of European credit in which we
should be involved.' And, again on 31 July, the old
Lord Rothschild sent for the financial editor of *The
Times* to try and stop the paper advocating intervention on the side of France and Russia, a suggestion
indignantly refused by its recipient, who returned to
his office white with rage.

Clearly it is extremely important to look at the economic pressures on the governments of Europe in the crisis of 1914, but the pressures will not turn out to have been all in one direction, and no economic explanation will give us the whole reason for the decisions taken. It is certainly true that the financiers and industrialists exercised great influence on the governments of Europe before 1914, but it is not true that the interests of the various economic pressure groups coincided, except that they seem to have agreed in expecting the war to be a short one. This means that it is very hard to determine at any particular moment which of the economic pressure groups was having a decisive influence on the decisions of a particular politician.

General economic or sociological explanations are important in providing us with a broad sense of what is happening in history. It is only rarely that they can give us the precise link between the general and the particular which we need to account for the individual event the historian is trying to explain. The same difficulty confronts us when we try to relate the general climate of ideas and the general ideological background of the time to the particular actions of the politicians and generals who brought Europe into war in 1914. However, I want to suggest one or two areas where we might start to look for clues to help us to reconstruct the unspoken presuppositions of the participants in the drama of 1914. Let us take the case of one of the leading characters, the British Foreign Secretary, Sir Edward Grey. As Foreign Secretary in a Liberal government, most of whose members were more interested in domestic reform than in international affairs, Grey had borne much of the responsibility for the development of British foreign policy between 1905 and 1914. He has been accused both of pursuing a deliberate policy of isolating and encircling Germany and at the same time of contributing to the German decision to go to war in 1914 by hesitating to declare British support for France and Russia in time to deter Germany. I do not think either of these charges is justified, but it is true that Grey was a

puzzling mixture of political shrewdness and political
naïveté. At times his views on international affairs
were of a surprising simplicity: 'It is in German
diplomacy alone,' he wrote to President Theodore
Roosevelt in 1906, 'that one now meets with deliberate attempts to make mischief between other countries
by saying poisoned things to one about the other.'
And there are many other examples of his regarding
relations between States as being comparable to those
between individuals, to be conducted on the same
basis and the same principles as those between English
country gentlemen.

Sir Charles Webster, in his Inaugural Lecture in the
Stevenson Chair, called on historians to study the implications of the term 'guarantee' in international
relations and pointed out the importance of discovering 'what exactly had been in the minds of statesmen
when they undertook such obligations on behalf of
their country'. In the case of Grey, it often seems as
though it was a simple schoolboy sense of honour
which was the criterion by which he judged his own
and other people's political actions. He had already
expressed his dilemma clearly in February 1906, when
a war between France and Germany over Morocco
seemed a possibility. 'If there is war between France
and Germany,' he wrote, 'it will be very difficult for us
to keep out of it. The *Entente* and still more the constant and emphatic demonstrations of affection (official, naval, political, commercial, municipal and in
the Press) have created in France a belief that we shall
support them in war.... If this expectation is disappointed, the French will never forgive us. There
would also I think be a general feeling that we had
behaved badly and left France in the lurch.... As a
minor matter the position of any Foreign Secretary
here, who had made it an object to maintain the
entente with France would become intolerable. On
the other hand the prospect of a European War and of
our being involved in it is horrible.'

In 1914 Grey was thinking in the same terms, and
was constantly remembering his exchange of letters
with the French Ambassador in 1912, in which he had

written: 'I agree that, if either government had grave reason to expect an unprovoked attack by a third Power, or something that threatened the general peace, it should immediately discuss with the other, whether both Governments should act together to prevent aggression and to preserve peace, and if so what measures they would be prepared to take in common. If these measures involved action, the plans of the General Staffs would at once be taken into consideration, and the Governments would then decide what effect should be given to them.' Although Grey had for political reasons to point out that this exchange did not necessarily commit the British government to action, for him there seems no doubt that it was a moral commitment; and it was agonising for him in July 1914 to realise that other members of the government and the Liberal Party did not see things in the same light, and that, while Paul Cambon, the French Ambassador, was playing on the British sense of fair play and asking if the word 'honour' was to be crossed out of the English dictionary, the *Manchester Guardian* was complaining that: 'By some hidden contract England has been technically committed behind her back to the ruinous madness of a share in the violent gamble of a war between two militarist leagues on the Continent.'

All I am trying to say is that it would be a mistake to interpret Grey's policies in too subtle or sophisticated a way or to attribute to him too many long-term deep purposes. His unspoken premises remained the ethical code of a high-principled, slightly priggish Wykehamist, and it is to his school days that we must look for a key to his fundamental attitudes. As he himself wrote later of his boyhood at school at Winchester: 'I was becoming a "Wykehamist". All that is conveyed by this word can only be understood by people who are Wykehamists. The ways of the place, its traditions and the country in which it is set were all getting a hold upon my heart. I had gained something which had become an inseparable part of my affection, which was part of my life's unalterable good....' It is to his education and the education of

the class to which he belonged that we must look for
the key to much of Grey's later political behaviour;
and this suggests that we should in general pay more
attention to the links between educational systems
and foreign policy, between the values and beliefs in-
culcated at school and the presuppositions on which
politicians act later in life. In Grey's case, because he
was a candid man with comparatively simple beliefs,
the links are fairly obvious, but in other cases they
may be harder to trace. Can we, for example, find out
something about French political attitudes by studying the exercises in classical rhetoric to which pupils
in French *lycées* were subjected? And how far did the
Prussian regulations of 1889 which stressed the need
for greater attention to recent German history, in
order to demonstrate 'that the power of the State
alone can protect the individual, his family, his freedom and his rights', condition the attitudes of a whole
generation? Here is a field in which historians should
welcome co-operation with educational sociologists
and social psychologists.

A study of educational systems and their content
may help to explain the actions and unspoken motives
of statesmen and generals in moments of crisis. But
what is even harder for the historian is to re-create the
whole climate of opinion within which political
leaders in the past operated, and to discover what
were the assumptions in the minds of ordinary men
and women faced with the consequences of their
rulers' decisions. In 1914 this is perhaps particularly
difficult. People acted on a number of contradictory
assumptions or half-formulated philosophies of life.
Some of them, when war was imminent, felt themselves caught up in an ineluctable historical process –
an age-old conflict between Germans and Slavs, for instance, which was the view of the younger Moltke,
Chief of the German General Staff at the outbreak of
war. Others felt themselves to be following a course
laid down by an inexplicable God. 'If you see me so
calm,' the Tsar said, once the decision to mobilise the
Russian army had been taken, 'it is because I have a
firm and resolute faith that the fate of Russia, of my-

self and of my family is in the hands of God who has placed me where I am. Whatever happens, I shall bow to His will conscious of having had no other thought than that of serving the country He has entrusted to me.' Others simply could not accept the collapse of years of liberal hopes of international conciliation and international solidarity. Many people felt that the fabric of international life had been too tightly and intricately woven for it to be broken by war. As the Belgian Socialist leader Émile Vandervelde said in 1911: 'There are in Europe at present too many pacifist forces, starting with the Jewish capitalists who give financial support to many governments, through to the socialists who are firmly resolved to prevent mobilisation of the natións and in the event of defeat to spring at the throats of their rulers.' If the positive force of international co-operation was not enough, then the fear of chaos and revolution ought to serve to prevent war. For many people all over Europe, it was impossible not to be optimistic and not to hope for the best. As Jean Jaurès remarked a day or two before he was assassinated by a nationalist fanatic, 'Les choses ne peuvent ne pas s'arranger' – 'Things must turn out all right.'

It was Jaurès nevertheless who had seen most clearly where a European war might lead. In 1905, when for the first time for years war between France and Germany seemed a real possibility, he had written: 'From a European war a revolution may spring up and the ruling classes would do well to think of this. But it may also result, over a long period, in a crisis of counter-revolution, of furious reaction, of exasperated nationalism, of stifling dictatorship, of monstrous militarism, a long chain of retrograde violence. . . .' Fear of revolution, however, could work both ways; while it might sometimes prevent governments from risking a war, more often war seemed a way of averting revolution by an appeal to deeper national loyalties. Certainly, both in France and Germany the fact that, when war came, the Socialists gave it their positive support was an important element in the sense of relief which many people experienced once war had begun.

In a very few cases – that of Austria-Hungary is the clearest – the idea of war as a means of escape from insoluble internal difficulties played a positive and conscious part in the decisions of July 1914. But in nearly all the belligerent countries the outbreak of war meant a temporary cessation of domestic politics and the establishment of an *Union Sacrée*, of a *Burgfriede*. Even in Britain, as the crisis became more serious, Asquith, the Prime Minister, wrote – correctly – 'It is the most dangerous situation of the last fifty years. It may incidentally have the effect of throwing into the background the lurid pictures of civil war in Ulster.'

In general, it could perhaps be said that for every man who foresaw a black future in July and August 1914, there were, in each belligerent country, at least as many who saw in the war a release from public and private tensions. The enthusiasm which greeted the war, however, went beyond a sense of relief at the diversion or postponement of political disputes. Nor was it limited to militarists like the German Crown Prince with his notorious summons 'Auf zu einem frisch-fröhlichen Krieg' – in itself, incidentally, perhaps no worse than Secretary John Hay's description of the Spanish–American War of 1898 as 'a splendid little war'. The great historian Friedrich Meinecke declared that August 1914 was 'one of the great moments of my life which suddenly filled my soul with the deepest confidence in our people and the profoundest joy'. And in England there were young writers who felt much the same thing:

> Honour has come back, as a king, to earth
> And paid his subjects with a royal wage;
> And nobleness walks in our ways again;
> And we have come into our heritage.

How can we explain these different reactions to the coming of war? And can we link the attitudes that underlie them to the specific decisions of politicians, diplomats or generals? Or, in other words, what is the connection between the history of ideas and the his-

tory of international politics? Is there any point in
trying to find one? It is tempting, for instance, to see
whether there are links between the art of a society
and its political attitudes and to follow the suggestion
of Sir Joshua Reynolds, who held that the character of
a nation is, perhaps, more strongly marked by their
taste in painting than in any other pursuit although
more considerable; as you may easier find which way
the wind sits by throwing a straw in the air than any
heavier substance. One would like to be able to relate,
for example, the passionate desperation of Alban
Berg's *Three Orchestral Pieces*, Opus 6, on which he
was working in August 1914, to the European crisis, or
to be able to say that the fragmentation of the image
introduced into European painting by Picasso and
Braque after 1907 somehow reflects the break-up of
bourgeois society. I am sceptical about the possibility
of talking in this way with any degree of precision,
and, in the case of Berg, his despair seems to have
been the result of a quarrel with his master, Schön-
berg, rather than of public events towards which,
indeed, he took a conventional Austrian patriotic
attitude. It is interesting to note, however, that so distinguished a historian as Sir Llewellyn Woodward
takes the view that there is a direct historical connection between art and society. In the introduction to
his recent work on *Great Britain and the War of 1914–
1918*, where he writes of his own youth before the First
World War, he says: 'I neither understood nor sympathised with the new fashion in imaginative writing. I
continued to think of the barbarians infiltrating into
and finally overthrowing the high civilisation of the
western Roman Empire. . . . When I looked at the
latest modes in painting I thought of the curious forecast made by the Abbé Lamennais over a century ago
about an atheist society falling into ruin in spite of its
immense material achievements: "Reason will decay
before men's eyes. The simplest truths will appear
strange and remarkable and will scarcely be en-
dured." ' Historians of a younger generation mostly
now take for granted and even admit to enjoying the
literary and artistic developments which Sir Llewellyn

deplores, but there are no doubt some among them –
of whom I am definitely not one – who are equally
ready to see in the advanced artistic manifestations of
the 1960s the same signs of decay as Sir Llewellyn re-
calls noting half a century ago. One is tempted to say
that from Plato onwards it has been conservatives who
have been readiest to look to the arts for signs of
decadence in society, until one remembers the discussions in socialist and communist circles about social
realism, and is forced to conclude that philistinism is
not the prerogative of any one political movement.

In an ideal syllabus for a course in International
History there would certainly be provision for the
study of international artistic movements as well as of
the history of international politics, but in our present
attempt to discover the unspoken assumptions of the
ruling classes and political leaders in Europe in 1914,
I do not think that a study of the best art and literature of the time will get us very far; and the historian
would certainly be hard put to it to trace any significant links between Berg and Berchtold or between
Picasso and President Poincaré. The truth is that if we
want to reconstruct the intellectual climate of an age, it
is not to the newest or most original writers and artists
to whom we must turn. We can see now, for instance,
that Freud or Einstein were among the most interesting and important figures of the years immediately before 1914, but it is only after several decades that
popularised versions of their ideas have entered into
the *Weltanschauung* of the ordinary man and affected
the general climate of opinion, just as it has taken
many years for the pictorial discoveries of, say, a Klee
or a Mondrian to influence the images with which the
mass media surround us. Although Arthur Balfour or
R. B. Haldane might claim some knowledge of German philosophy, or Clemenceau be on friendly terms
with Monet and Debussy, most of the members of the
ruling classes of Europe before 1914 were acting on
ideas and assumptions formulated twenty or thirty
years before, and took little interest in advanced ideas
or artistic developments.

If we want to understand the presuppositions of the

men of 1914, to reconstruct, so to speak, their ideological furniture, it is to the ideas of a generation earlier, as filtered through vulgarisers and popularisers, that we must look. Let me give one or two examples. It is a commonplace that Darwinian ideas had a great influence on the ideology of Imperialism at the end of the nineteenth century, but it is important to realise how literally the doctrine of the struggle for existence and of the survival of the fittest – a doctrine that owes as much to T. H. Huxley as to Darwin – was taken by many European leaders just before the First World War. Here is a passage, for instance, from the memoirs of the Austrian Chief of the General Staff, Franz Baron Conrad von Hötzendorf: 'Philanthropic religions,' he wrote, 'moral teachings and philosophical doctrines may certainly sometimes serve to weaken mankind's struggle for existence in its crudest form, but they will *never* succeed in removing it as a driving motive in the world. . . . It is in accordance with this great principle that the catastrophe of the World War came about inevitably and irresistibly as the result of the motive forces in the lives of States and peoples, like a thunderstorm which must by its nature discharge itself.' Seen against this sort of ideological background, Conrad's continuous insistence on the need for a preventive war in order to preserve the Austro-Hungarian Monarchy is much more comprehensible.

The doctrine of a perpetual struggle for survival and of a permanent potential war of all against all is one with natural attractions for soldiers, who are failing in their duty if they are not actively preparing for just such a clash. But the pseudo-Darwinian view of international society extended to civilians as well. Kurt Riezler, for example, the personal assistant and confidant of the German Chancellor, Bethmann-Hollweg, was a highly sophisticated and intelligent writer about international affairs – and his book on *Principles of World Policy* published under a pseudonym just before the First World War foreshadows some of our own thinking about peace and war today. But underlying Riezler's cool analysis and realistic

appraisal of forces and events is a firm conviction that
States are living organisms, driven by their inner
nature into conflicts with each other, conflicts which
may be postponed by diplomacy, or delayed as long as
there is enough unallocated living-space in the world
to allow for peaceful competition, but which may
easily take the form of total war. The view of international society which Riezler implicitly accepts himself,
after examining alternative conceptions, is stated by
him as follows: 'Eternal and absolute enmity is
fundamentally inherent in relations between peoples;
and the hostility which we observe everywhere and
which refuses to disappear from political life, however
much the pacifists may speak or struggle against it, is
not the result of a perversion of human nature but of
the essence of the world and the source of life itself. It
is not accidental, temporary and removable, but a
necessity which may perhaps be put off for centuries
and fall into the background, but which will break
out again and claim its place as long as there are men
and nations.' This kind of thinking in the intimate
circle of the German Chancellor perhaps explains
Bethmann-Hollweg's fatalistic acceptance of the risk
of war inherent in his policy, and of the ultimate inevitability of armed conflict. In this connection it is
worth noting, as Dr Imanuel Geiss has pointed out,
that it is possibly from another essay by Riezler that
Bethmann-Hollweg took the notorious phrase 'a scrap
of paper' with which he described the treaty guaran-
teeing Belgium. 'We make treaties of arbitration,'
Riezler had written, 'and we develop a new international law, but events constantly prove how easily
international paper is torn up. . . . In a struggle in
which all are involved and consideration for the
onlooker abandoned, all conventions will be in vain.'

One could produce many more examples of this
kind of thinking from other countries as well as from
Germany and Austria-Hungary. When Lord Milner
died, for example, a *Credo* was found among his
papers containing the significant phrase 'A Nationalist believes that this is the law of human progress, that
the competition between nations each seeking its

maximum development, is the Divine Order of the World, the law of life and progress.' I only want to suggest that one cannot understand the outlook on international relations of the generation of 1914 without taking into account the pseudo-Darwinian element in their ideas. Many historians have recognised this, but it would be valuable to have a systematic study of the dissemination and perversion of Darwin's ideas in the fifty-five years between the publication of *The Origin of Species* and the outbreak of the First World War.

The other thinker who is all-important for the understanding of the moral and intellectual climate of 1914 is, of course, Friedrich Nietzsche, and here again it would be valuable to have a study of the translation and dissemination of his works and of the writings about him on the lines of Geneviève Bianquis's book, *Nietzsche en France*, written some forty years ago, and the recent work by Gonzalo Sobejano on *Nietzsche en España*. When Nietzsche finally collapsed into madness in 1889, he was little read; by the time of his death in 1900 he was already a figure of European importance whose teachings were being quoted, misquoted and interpreted in a number of different ways, and in the years before 1914 no one with any intellectual pretensions was ignorant of his work. During the war itself, in 1917, 140,000 copies were sold of the pocket edition of *Also sprach Zarathustra*, and in England at least, as Desmond MacCarthy pointed out in 1914, he was somehow already vaguely held responsible for the war. Certainly, his ideas, often misunderstood, taken out of context or perverted, contributed to the acceptance of the idea of war not just as a lamentable episode in international relations but as an experience desirable and salutary in itself. 'There will be wars as never before on earth,' Nietzsche had written. 'With me begins on earth High Politics.' ('Erst von mir an gibt es auf Erden Grosse Politik.') Nietzsche's ideas contributed to the fulfilment of his own prophecies.

But, of course, while some members of the governing élite in Germany and some nationalist thinkers in

France were affected by Nietzsche's teaching in one
form or another, these ideas were even more important to those who were preparing to overthrow the
existing social order. The impact of ideas is always
greater on revolutionaries than on supporters of the
established system, and, before 1914, in some parts of
Europe at least, students, as now, were eager for fresh
ideas which would justify their restless desire for
action and for new forms of thought and expression. If
politicians and bureaucrats are influenced by the doctrines of a generation earlier, student rebels seize
eagerly on any ideas which are in the air and which
seem to be the most advanced, and Nietzsche, although much of his writing had appeared some thirty
years before, was still thought of as the inspirer of the
avant-garde. The fascinating investigation which Dr
Vladimir Dedijer has conducted into the background,
beliefs and origins of the Young Bosnia movement,
from which the assassins of the Archduke Franz Ferdinand came, has shown how, for these Serb students,
half-understood philosophical principles were quickly
transformed into action, and how advanced ideas
about politics and art, literaure and life were inextricably confused and contributed to a passionate
sense of excitement and commitment. As one of the
intellectual inspirers of the southern Slav radicals
wrote: 'Thought, free thought, is the greatest and
bravest ruler of the universe. It has huge space wings
of the freest and most audacious bird, for which fear
and danger do not exist. Its wild flight goes to infinity
and eternity. It destroys today what was created
yesterday. It destroys every dogma, every norm, every
authority. It has no other faith but the faith in its
power. It creates critics, subversives, rebels and
wreckers.' These ideas, with their echoes of the Nietzschean 'reversal of all values', were what inspired the
young men who murdered the Archduke and his wife
and precipitated the crisis of 1914; and it is no surprise to learn that Princip, the actual assassin, was
fond of reciting Nietzsche's short poem *Ecce Homo*,
with its lines 'Insatiable as flame, I burn and consume
myself'.

Again, the café intellectuals who supported Musso-
lini, himself an eager reader of Nietzsche, when, in the
early months of the war, he left the Italian Socialist
Party to become one of the main agitators in favour of
intervention, and who took as one of their slogans
'Guerra, sola igiene del mondo' (War, the only hygiene
for the world), were voicing ideas which they thought
they had found in Nietzsche. Even the poet Rainer
Maria Rilke – not usually a writer to whom one turns
for echoes of contemporary political or public events –
combines Nietzschean language, to which he was
always responsive, with a sense of the prevailing
excitement on the outbreak of war, in his *Fünf
Gesänge*:

> Andere sind wir, ins Gleiche geänderte: jedem
> sprang in die plötzlich
> nicht mehr seinige Brust meteorisch ein Herz.
> Heiss ein eisernes Herz aus eisernem Weltall.

('We are different beings transformed into the same:
suddenly like a meteor a heart leapt into the breast no
more one's own. Hot, an iron heart in an iron universe.')

Ideas and images of this kind contributed, it seems
to me, to a climate in which the fact of war was not
just regretfully accepted but, by many people, positively welcomed. Walther Rathenau was not the only
one to find August 1914, in his own words: 'Great and
unforgettable. It was the ringing opening chord for an
immortal song of sacrifice, loyalty and heroism.' And
even a man who was already pessimistic about the
situation, such as General von Falkenhayn, the Prussian War Minister who was soon to become Chief of
the General Staff, was sufficiently impressed by the
grandeur of events to exclaim on 4 August, 'Even if we
end in ruin, it was beautiful.'

The sense of inevitability and the sense of relief, as
the crisis mounted and as war came, were partly due,
as I suggested earlier, to the technical sequence of
mobilisation plans and to the fact that politicians,
even if they wanted to, could not stop the military

machine once it was in motion, and partly to the fact that many of Europe's leaders saw in the international crisis a distraction from internal problems. But it is also due, I suggest, to the fact that by 1914 the ideas both of Darwin and of Nietzsche had become widely assimilated, so that there were many people in Europe, both among rulers and ruled, who thought of life in terms of the struggle for survival, or who were looking for an opportunity to transcend the limitations of their ordinary lives and to find a new set of values in what they believed would be a new and enriching experience.

Lloyd George made the somewhat pedestrian point in his *War Memoirs* that 'War has always been fatal to liberalism. Peace, Retrenchment and Reform have no meaning in war.' If one stands back from the details of the crisis of 1914 and thinks about some of the ideas prevalent in Europe at the time, the outbreak of the First World War can be seen as a defeat for those in all the belligerent countries who believed in the application of reason to the settlement of disputes, who believed that all problems have solutions, and that international goodwill and co-operation would suffice to prevent war. This is the attitude, for all their differences, both of the socialist leaders assembled in Brussels on 29 and 30 July 1914, planning to organise an international congress for the following week to discuss the measures to be taken against war, and of Sir Edward Grey, interrupting his Sunday's fishing to authorise, from his cottage at Itchen Abbas, the dispatch of a telegram suggesting a Conference of Ambassadors in London 'in order to find an issue to present complications'.

If we are to understand the conflicting beliefs which lie behind the actions of statesmen and the reactions of their followers, we must look at a number of ideas, attitudes and assumptions which are not always to be found in the archives. And one could of course suggest many other lines of approach in addition to the rather obvious ones I have proposed. These might be philosophical: how much, if anything, for example, did the doctrine of the offensive adopted by French military leaders before 1914 owe to a misunderstanding of Bergson's ideas about *élan vital*? Or they might be historical: in what way does the concept of a vital national interest arise or an idea such as that of the 'balance of power' develop? 'Great revolutions,' Hegel wrote, 'which strike the eye at a glance must have been preceded by a still and silent revolution in the spirit of the age, a revolution not visible to every eye, especially imperceptible to contemporaries and hard to discern or to describe in words. It is lack of acquaintance with this spiritual revolution which makes the resulting changes astonishing.' It is as important for the historian of international relations to understand these changes in what Hegel calls the spirit of the age as it is for him to understand changes in the structure of the economy or developments in military technology.

Sir Charles Webster called his Inaugural Lecture in the Stevenson Chair 'The Study of International History'; and Professor Medlicott's was entitled 'The Scope and Study of International History'. I am afraid that by giving this lecture a more specific title I may have implied that I was going to talk about something different, instead of trying to suggest ways of extending the scope and deepening the study of International History. But the crisis of 1914 owes its continuing interest to the fact that it provides an opportunity of trying many different approaches and offering many different types of historical explanation. It is an example of the extent to which what we call International History must in fact embrace all kinds of history, and it suggests that any attempt to insist on a too rigid departmental division of historical studies into economic history, diplomatic history, military history, art history, and so on, must lead to an impoverishment of our historical understanding. Specialists in each branch as well as specialists in other disciplines must help each other if we are to succeed in reconstructing the thought and action of the past. 'Since wars begin in the minds of men,' the Charter of UNESCO lays down, 'it is in the minds of men that the defences of peace must be constructed'. This is certainly an aim which Sir Daniel Stevenson would have appreciated. The study of the minds of the men of 1914 – whether they deliberately made the war or, as Lloyd George claimed to believe, stumbled into it – is of obvious intrinsic historical interest, but I also believe that by studying the origins of a particular war we may contribute to the understanding of situations likely to cause other wars and to the understanding of the causes of war in general. But, in any case, it is only by studying the minds of men that we shall understand the causes of anything.

9 Social Darwinism as a Factor in the 'New Imperialism'

H. W. Koch

In spite of general recognition, particularly because of the massive documentation in the works of Fritz Fischer and Imanuel Geiss, their critics have frequently been sceptical over their methodology and conclusions. Thus the *Journal of Modern History* noted in Geiss's work a preconceived thesis which is noticeable both in his arrangement and selection of documents. 'Can we be certain,' asked the reviewer of *The Times Literary Supplement*, 'that Bethmann-Hollweg and his colleagues were so different from other European statesmen in their almost unconscious assumption of the Darwinian necessity and empirical morality of war?' He explicitly warned against an interpretation of Germany's attitude during the July crisis which was made in isolation from the general 'European fever'. Professor Butterfield, too, warned against confusing the existence of military plans with the foreign policy of a particular country and of considering plans which emerged after the outbreak of war as historical sources for pre-war policy. Particularly in this connection, Butterfield argued, great care should be taken with the conclusions drawn from the material submitted by Fritz Fischer; and he urged caution against overestimating Pan-German propaganda before comparative studies on the Pan-Slav agitation or militaristic agitators in Great Britain and France were available.

Fritz Fischer and his pupils frequently speak of a specifically German Imperialism, of a specifically German brand of Darwinian thought, which inevitably

From *Zeitschrift für Politik* (Hochschule für Politische Wissenschaften, Munich), XVII (1970).

produces the impression that the German brand of
Imperialism and Social Darwinism are fundamentally
different from similar manifestations in Great Britain
and the United States. Undoubtedly the diaries of
Kurt Riezler, his book *Grundzüge der Weltpolitik in
der Gegenwart*, the writings of Bernhardi or the
memorandum of the Pan-German agitator General
Gebsattel to Crown Prince Wilhelm are all evidence
for the existence of Imperialist and Social Darwinian
modes of thought. However, the question arises
whether Social Darwinism in particular represents a
specifically German mode of thought. Unfortunately,
historical research in Europe (if one excludes the
tentative beginnings in an article by Hans-Günther
Zmarzlik and some of the early writings of Jacques
Barzun) has produced no significant comparative
study over the role of Social Darwinism in the political thought of the European Great Powers. There
exists no analogous essay to that of Richard Hofstadter's *Social Darwinism in American Thought*. As
long as the scholar lacks a work of this kind and high
quality, and as long as the abundantly available
source material has not been touched, let alone fully
exploited, it is a little too early to agree with general-
isations based on nothing more than the opinions of
Riezler and other prominent German politicians. We
simply lack an additional dimension which would
enable us to recognise and judge the influential intellectual 'unspoken assumptions' – or prejudices – with
which many politicians approached problems at the
turn of the century.

Every analysis of intellectual movements, such as
those represented by the influence of Darwinian ideas,
is inevitably bound to run the inherent risk of artificially isolating an intellectual movement. After all one
must not forget that the stock of Darwinian ideas was
inextricably interwoven with other intellectual movements. One may also object that few read Darwin or
Spencer; but with equal justification one could ask
how many National Socialists had actually read *Mein
Kampf*, how many Socialists *Das Kapital*? These questions can be countered with the same reply which

Georg Lukács has given in connection with the influence of the works of Nietzsche. One need not have read any of these authors in order to be ideologically influenced by them. Secondary works, periodicals and newspapers frequently manage to simplify the essential core of an elaborate thesis, and at a popular level spread the content of many ideologies. This process of popularisation of systems of ideas can at a particular point in time become socially and therefore by implication politically significant.

The object of this essay is precisely to outline this process of the popularisation of the ideas of Charles Darwin, their effect in breadth as well as in depth, those ideas which in the last quarter of the nineteenth and during the pre-war period of the twentieth century apparently justified the urge towards Imperialism and which caused that mass psychosis, whose hysteria we find best illustrated by the outbreak of war in 1914 which was greeted by the masses with relief in the capitals of Europe.

Not without justification has the nineteenth century, in so far as we limit ourselves to central and western Europe as well as the United States, been called an age of liberalism, a liberalism which was a reaction to the centralising tendencies of absolutism, and whose principles we find expressed by Locke or in the American Declaration of Independence. The principles of liberalism represented the essence of all those ideals whose realisation was hoped and worked for in central and western Europe during the nineteenth century in order to spread them finally across the entire globe for the benefit of mankind. These principles included, of course, personal liberty, liberty of political expression, the pursuit of happiness and the sanctity of private property. At the same time it was recognised how important it was to control political institutions and the executive through a well-informed public opinion. Generally speaking, liberal politicians proceeded from the premise that personal and political liberties were part and parcel of natural law, the core of which in turn was based on the assumption that the ultimate objective of all human

striving lay in the full satisfaction and realisation of
the positive capacities of man.

However, already at an earlier stage, but particularly in reaction to the French Revolution, a tendency
emerged, though initially in no way attempting to
touch the foundations of the liberal creed, under the
impact of growing industrialisation and developing
technology, for the natural sciences to move towards
empiricism, away from the *a priori* assumptions of
natural law theories. The liberal movement, however
different it may have been in character, influence and
political tactics in the various regions of central and
western Europe, brought on to the political stage a
commercial and industrial middle class whose liberal
ideology changed – initially almost imperceptibly – as
it gained economic and political power. During much
of the nineteenth century this class was the spearhead
and pathfinder of liberal reforms, and the growth of
trade and industry made its growing hold upon
political power and the spread of liberal principles
seemingly inevitable. But the Industrial Revolution
in Europe had not only created a new middle class,
but also a growing urban proletariat, which in time
began to formulate its own political and social demands. Vis-à-vis this new working class, liberals now
began to defend the political and social *status quo*
and consequently were bound to appear as conservatives and reactionaries.

Political positions changed; liberalism transformed
itself from a middle-class reform movement to a
bastion of defence of the existing political, economic
and social order. Under the circumstances it was
hardly an asset that 'liberalism' lacked a systematically
developed and formulated theory. As an effective
political movement it frequently combined basically
different elements, co-operating for specific ends and
purposes; it was devoid of a clearly defined and
common ideological basis. In Great Britain, for instance, Nonconformists managed to work hand in
hand with Jeremy Bentham, well known for his radical atheism.

In view of the growing complexity of social prob-

lems, themselves an inevitable consequence of the
Industrial Revolution, 'liberalism', the political expression of a commercial and industrial middle class,
ought to have become the movement of the entire
national community for promoting the interests of all
classes – a necessity which, for instance, Max Weber
and Friedrich Naumann realised – if 'liberalism' was
to remain a politically active force. The individualism
of its early period ought to have fused with the social
realities of an expanding modern industrial society.
To continue as an important political force, 'liberalism' ought to have acted both as the protector of individual rights as well as the protector of those
threatened by unrestrained individualism.

The failure to achieve a transformation of this kind
is one of the root causes of the decay of the politically
organised 'liberal' movement in Europe. This is not to
say that liberal principles themselves decayed, but
simply that the cause of social reform came to rest in
the hands of political movements which hardly described themselves as 'liberal'.

A modern industrial society which demanded social
reforms in the name of the happiness of the greatest
number found itself confronted by the archaic nature
of the liberal concept of the State, according to which
the latter should exercise only a 'night-watchman'
function, to protect private property. The rest could
be regulated by private contract. It is here that one
meets the dilemma of nineteenth-century liberalism:
should it jettison its economic philosophy of *laissez-
faire* by subjecting the economic and social affairs to
state control, or should it accept the risks inherent in
the consequences of an unregulated industrialism,
such as the threat to the social and political *status
quo*? To resolve this dilemma would have required a
fundamental revision of liberal premises.

At this point of confrontation with an apparently
insoluble dilemma began the path leading away from
natural law theories towards the natural sciences,
supported and substantiated by the measurable scientific experiment. Of course, all did not come as
suddenly as it might appear. One need only think of

Ricardo or Malthus in the early nineteenth century, let alone the scientists of preceding centuries. What is new, however, is the impact of this change of direction, both in breadth as well as in depth.

The first important example that comes to mind is Herbert Spencer's social philosophy. Although derived from the ethical and political ideals of Utilitarianism and as yet not made logically dependent on the natural sciences, particularly on biology and biological evolution, the centre of Spencer's philosophy was occupied by a new concept of organic development. He postulated that nature progresses on a constant straight line, from energy to life, from life to intellectual activity, from that to the formation of society and from thence towards civilisation. Nature progresses from simple forms of society to more complex, more differentiated and more integrated civilisations. He argues that human society provided a good example for the observation of those critieria which differentiated lower from higher stages of development, the obsolete from the useful new, the able from the unable, and by implication, therefore, good from evil.

Logically Spencer's argument should lead to the conclusion that State and society were becoming more and more complex as well as integrated. But Spencer – and this highlights the liberal dilemma and paradox – 'liberal' that he was, endeavoured to prove that a society of growing complexity was actually upholding a State which in practice through the growing reductions of its functions would simplify itself to the extent that in the end there would be no rational reason any more for its continued existence. To meet this paradox Spencer maintained that the origins of the State lay in a society organised primarily for war. A growing industrial society was making wars superfluous and the centralising functions of the State as well. As long as industry and society were left to themselves, the evolutionary process would assure the survival of the ablest, and all legislation would become obsolete the moment when this process had brought about the perfect integration of the individual and society. Consequently, Spencer was a fanatical oppo-

nent of all forms of state interference in industrial
and social problems. The net result of his philosophy
implied the giving up of the principle of the happiness of the greatest possible number in favour of the
principle of selection through the survival of the
ablest.

Spencer, in the context of this essay, represents a
random example to demonstrate how liberal principles were virtually appended to the progress of the
natural sciences. Spencer's influence, however, seen
from a European perspective, should not be exaggerated. The situation which Spencer believed he saw in
the British Isles was described on the European mainland at different levels, to take Comte, his pupils and
Positivism as simply one example. What it is important to realise, though, is that older natural rights
theories as well as religious revelation were pushed
aside by the march of progress. In an age of industry
and the ascendancy of the natural sciences they lost
any influence or general relevance.

The merit (a term which used in the context does
not include qualitative value) of having underpinned
the 'liberal' principle of *laissez-faire* in all spheres of
life with the natural sciences and of giving it not only
a local but a global impact belongs to Charles Darwin.
He developed his evolutionary theories for the first
time in *The Origin of Species*, in which he attempted
to contradict the traditional belief of the separate
creation of all species of plants and animals. In his
second main work, *The Descent of Man and Selection
in Relation to Sex*, he went a step further and submitted all the evidence he had collected to prove that
man, like all living creatures, had developed through
a process of natural selection from simpler, more
primitive forms. While Spencer had developed his
ideas without any direct logical dependence on the
natural sciences, Darwin created the important link
between the natural sciences on the one hand and
social and political sciences on the other. He had hit
upon a simple principle of movement and development
which helped the better understanding of the entire
history of mankind. Like Marxism, whose founder and

early representatives frequently expressed their affinity
with the thought of Darwin, Darwin's hypothesis was
revolutionary because it destroyed the foundation of
all ideas hitherto accepted about the nature of man
and human life, and caused fundamental re-thinking
of much that had so far been taken for granted and as
self-evident. Much as Marx believed he had found the
key to social change in the class struggle, Darwin believed he had found it in natural selection through
struggle and the survival of the fittest. The coincidence that Darwin's theory came at a moment when
rapid progress was being made in the other natural
sciences and at the same time as new States were emerg-
ing in central and southern Europe, or successfully
asserting their existence, as in the United States, can be
assumed to have greatly assisted the rapid spread of
his teachings. Moreover, in order to gauge Darwin's
influence relatively accurately we must not ignore the
general spread of literacy. True enough, Darwin had
his precursors like Lamarck; even Leibniz had occupied himself with evolutionary theories. But their
discussions never moved beyond the relatively small
circle of scientists or those interested in science. The
immense spread of periodicals beginning about a
century and a half ago, written for the specialist as
well as for the layman, supplemented during the last
quarter of the nineteenth century by the quick growth
of newspapers, particularly in Anglo-Saxon countries,
increased the readers' forum. Scientific articles and
their hypotheses found their own vulgarised 'version'
for the 'wider public' in the daily papers. In other
words, there was now not only a new scientific theory,
but also a popular Press and an educated or semi-
educated public to absorb it.

To begin with, Darwin had not the slightest intention of applying his biological revelation to a field
other than biology. But – and he realised that himself
– his theory responded to the call of the *Zeitgeist*: it
supplied a perfect principle of causality, a principle
which many of his contemporaries elevated to a creed
in the natural sciences, a creed which was quickly torn
from its biological context and applied to a social and

political environment. The theory of evolution, the concept of the selection of the fittest through the struggle for existence, revolutionised therefore not only biology but a society whose character became pronouncedly industrial. This variation of Darwinism has generally become familiar under the term 'Social Darwinism'. The impact of the vulgarisation of Darwin's ideas and their popularity, and their application in many areas of political, economic and social life, resulted to a certain degree in the progressive eclipse of liberal principles, especially in the field of international relations.

Two variations of Social Darwinism dominated; the first had a dynamic, the second a static nature. Social Darwinism was dynamic in the sense that in international relations it served as a motive power as well as justification for expansionist policies; in practice this meant territorial aggrandisement, acquisition or further expansion of colonies and naturally the kind of armaments necessary to secure new gains. The alternative was considered to be stagnation and decay – a belief in change through territorial, economic and military expansion.

The static variety applied (mainly in parts of western Europe and the United States) to the field of domestic politics, especially social policy in the debate over which, in the words of Richard Hofstadter:

> Social Darwinism was seized upon as a welcome addition, perhaps the most powerful of all, to the store of ideas to which solid and conservative men appealed when they wished to reconcile their fellows to some of the hardships of life and to prevail upon them not to support hasty and ill-considered reforms. ... It was those who wished to defend the political *status quo*, above all the *laissez-faire* conservatives, who were the first to pick up the instruments of social argument that were forged out of Darwinian concepts.

In order to analyse as well as illustrate Social Darwinism, we should first of all examine its impact upon international relations. This requires a minor digression, a sketch of international relations in Europe during the nineteenth century. The Congress system of European diplomacy after the fall of Napoleon I has been described very accurately by F. E. Hinsley as a coalition of States, organised for the purpose of defence of commonly accepted values and agreements. This meant no unilateral change of existing treaties or of the territorial *status quo* without the consent of the other signatory Powers. The basis of this system was the defence of the principle of monarchic legitimacy and the existing social order by governments which, under the impact of the French Revolution, had combined against the majority of elements contained in their social structures making for change.

But because of continuing and fresh conflicts of interest among the European Great Powers, the Congress system was short-lived. But this did not mean that the Powers abandoned a platform with planks of commonly accepted agreements. In place of the Congress system was put the so-called 'Concert of the European Powers', which could be upheld as long as monarchic legitimacy and the social *status quo* were to be defended and while on the other hand the physical strength and the economic growth rate of the Powers remained relatively stagnant.

On various occasions the Concert seemed near to disintegration, for instance when there was an attempt to extend it to the Ottoman Empire, over the Italian question in 1859 and 1864 and over the German question in 1866 and 1870. But – to stay with Hinsley's argument – a closer look shows that the visible events had been preceded by a slower but remarkable change in the relative distribution of power, which had made the political premises of 1815 obsolete in so far as they concerned Italy and Germany. The real distribution of economic power was no longer in accord with that of 1815. The real significance of this process lies in the fact that these changes took place within the existing framework of power and of the power structure. Consequently, in spite of change the principles of the Concert of the European Powers survived even though they were suspended on occasions.

Between 1871 and 1890 the territorial *status quo* was still generally accepted, but from 1890 onwards until 1914 it slowly decayed and for the first time since the *ancien régime* the Powers of Europe were compelled to rely upon a balance of power among themselves and the means generally associated with this – alliances and armaments.

The reasons for the decay of the European Concert are as manifold as they are debatable. Firstly, the Concert had developed within a European framework, but it was now increasingly subjected to pressures originating from areas outside Europe, pressures which the European Concert simply was not strong enough to cope with. The problems of the Straits and of the Egyptian question are but two illustrations. Secondly, one notices the awareness of the growth of a power vacuum outside Europe, which increasingly touched upon the older traditional interests of the European Powers. International stability depended no longer simply on the distribution of power in Europe, but on the distribution of power in a global sense.

Thirdly, the growth of the democratic universal franchise, the entire process of democratisation, brought the emotion of the masses as a logical consequence into the spectrum of all those factors upon whose correct assessment a stable European policy was based. The growth of democracy brought forth the age of mass politics and its emotionally rather than rationally formulated appeals to the masses, and thus unintentionally and unconsciously produced a new concept of the State with a vastly greater range of functions. In 1815 the respective governments were confronted by their respective societies. Although the conflicts between society and State had not been fully resolved, in 1914, temporarily at least, behind every government in western and central Europe stood the solid, though class-conscious, phalanx of a national community. The criteria of power were no longer the degree of political stability, maturity and geographical advantages, but they were of an industrial, economic and organisational nature.

Every State (irrespective of whether it was orientated along the rational or the romantic concept of the nation) had acquired a specific identity, had become a specific organism, subject to the natural laws of life and death, growth and decay. And Social Darwinism provided a plausible theory, which apparently confirmed all these assumptions scientifically. Suddenly there existed a consciousness of and a differentiation between satisfied and unsatisfied, between old and young nations – everything apparently supported by proofs produced by the natural sciences, by the adaptation of Darwin's theories.

The renewed discussion over the 'responsibility' for the outbreak of the First World War has placed particular emphasis upon the German representatives of Social Darwinism. Less well known are their Western colleagues. In Great Britain none other than Walter Bagehot adopted the Social Darwinian gospel. 'Conquest,' he wrote, 'is the premium given by nature to those national characters which their national customs have made most fit to win in war, and in most material respects those winning characters are really the best characters. The characters which do win in war are the characters which we should wish to win in war.' One has to bear in mind that Bagehot was a highly sophisticated political theorist. The form in which these arguments were reproduced in the daily Press, and in popular and service journals, are considerably cruder.

The *leitmotif* of liberalism in the nineteenth century had been the belief in continuous human progress, a progress apparently verified by the advances of the natural sciences which finally produced the concept of human progress through the struggle for existence and the selection of the fittest through it. When this concept was applied to a social and political environment, to individuals and to nations, it was bound to deepen the existing cleavages between the peoples, particularly in an age of strong economic competition, in an age in which social unrest – it was assumed – had to be directed into 'harmless channels', an age of new and young nations filled by a sense of

mission, whose specific nature had not been closely
defined and was therefore not fully articulated. The
search for purpose and a sense of national existence
led into many directions. Nietzsche finally condemned
the Christian religion; he drew the ultimate logical
consequence from the principle of the survival of the
fittest, namely that existing moral categories and
values stood in the way of this kind of selection. His
alternative was a race of supermen, produced and
selected through the right of the stronger.

On a broader, more popular level a general interest
in evolutionary theories was naturally generated
which at that level turned into a vulgar propagation
of brutal strength and the worship of martial qualities. Charles Pearson in his book *National Life from
the Standpoint of Science* wrote: 'The path of progress is strewn with the wrecks of nations; traces are
everywhere to be seen of the hecatombs of inferior
races, and of victims who found not the narrow way to
perfection. Yet these dead people are, in very truth,
the stepping stones on which mankind has arisen to
the higher intellectual and deeper emotional life of
today.'

The elder Moltke made his own logical conclusion
when he equated the Darwinian portrait of nature
with the battlefield, expressing the spirit of the times
with the words that 'war is an element of the order of
the world established by God, without which the
world would stagnate and lose itself in materialism'.

Here perhaps we can see the expression of and the
connection of Social Darwinism with cultural pessimism, which, quite contrary to the thesis put forward by
Fritz Stern, was a much more far-reaching phenomenon than a purely German one. It can be recognised
in most nations in the throes of industrialisation at a
particular point in time. One should think, for instance, of Thomas Hardy's *Far from the Madding
Crowd* or the brothers Henry and Brooks Adams,
especially the latter's book *The Law of Civilisation
and Decay*. The growth of an industrial society, the
dislocations in the traditional social structure caused
the change categorised by David Riesmann from the

'inner-' and 'tradition-directed' man to the 'outer-
directed' man, a type whose system of values is no
longer determined by religion or tradition but by an
environment in which he has no roots, where his
values are determined by his 'peer-groups': all these
disturbances were bound to cause deep psychological
dislocations from the perspective in which everything
new was also abnormal. Because of the Industrial
Revolution an old and proud middle class found itself
displaced or in the process of being displaced by a
class of *nouveaux riches*. Representatives of that older
class, like Henry Adams, looked back to a supposedly
Golden Age. They considered war inevitable; only an
act of God could cleanse the world from the abomina-
tions and excesses of the selfish materialism of the new
Industrial Age. This view emerges clearly from the
changes in attitude noticeable in the range of Adams's
works from his *History of the United States 1801–1817*
to *The Education of Henry Adams*. He had hoped by
using the methodologies of the natural and the still
infant social sciences to come nearer to historical
truth. He had at first added Social Darwinism to a
universe determined by Newton; the sum proved false
through the discovery of a radioactive substance and
the Second Law of Thermodynamics. 'There is a
universal tendency to the dissipation of mechanical
energy any restoration of which is impossible ... within a finite time ... the earth must ... be unfit for the
habitation of man.'

On the one hand evolution led from protozoa to
man; on the other hand, however, entropy led from
heat to cold. Adams's final conclusion therefore was
that the solar system would be reduced to chaos
through the cooling of the sun and end in death by
heat emitted and spent by the sun. The march of
liberal progress through the natural sciences here
found its antithesis as well.

The growing modernity of industrial society appeared to Henry Adams as sufficient evidence for
the waste of energy, as in the examples of the motor-
car and the aeroplane. By comparison with the eternity of Christian universalism as symbolised by the

cathedrals of Mont-Saint-Michel and Chartres, with the age in which all bent their knees before the 'one God', man was confronted by a multiplicity of ties on the one hand, depersonalisation on the other; in fact man was standing in the antechamber of chaos. Adams was not sure whether man would step through the last door. Still, in a letter in 1905 he expressed his opinion that if we maintain the rate of progress which we set in 1600, then we will hardly need another century and a half until our entire intellectual foundations are turned upside down. In that case, he argued, law as theory as well as an *a priori* principle would make way for brute strength. Morality would become the police and explosive materials would attain global effectiveness in their destructive power. Disintegration would overwhelm integration.

Ample evidence for similar expressions can be found in the published materials in central and western Europe of the period. The well-known articles of the *Saturday Review* between 1896/97 have been often – too often – quoted. This journal was not by any means the only one which poisoned the international climate with its Social Darwinism. Shortly before the First World War the well-known monthly, *Nineteenth Century*, published an article entitled 'God's Test by War'. It is worth quoting at some length :

> Amidst the chaos of domestic politics and the wave-like surge of contending social desires the biological law of competition still rules the destinies of nations as of individual men. And as the ethical essence of competition is sacrifice, as each generation of plants or of animals perishes in the one case, or toils and dares in the other, that its offspring may survive, so with nations the future of the next generation is determined by the self-sacrifice of that which precedes it.

This sacrificial impulse, the author says, 'is the root source of all human morality and finds its crown in patriotism'. And he goes on to ask:

What of England? Is the heart that once was hers still strong to dare and to resolve and to endure? How shall we know? By the test. That which God has given for the trial of peoples, the test of war.

Of course, says the author, one has to be prepared, and the implication of this is:

that victory is the result of efficiency, and efficiency is the result of spiritual quality. Thus then efficiency in war, or rather efficiency for war is God's test of a nation's soul. By that test it stands, or by that test it falls. This is the ethical content of competition. This is the determining factor of human history. This is the justification of war.

Victory in war is the method by which, in the economy of God's providence, the sound nation supersedes the unsound, because in our time victory is the direct offspring of a higher efficiency, and the higher efficiency is the logical outcome of the higher morale.

Hence it follows that if the dream of short-sighted and superficial sentimentalists could be fulfilled – if war could be rendered impossible on earth – the machinery by which national corruption is punished and national virtue rewarded would be ungeared. The higher would cease to supersede the lower, and the course of human evolution would suffer arrest.

And coming back to victory the author emphasises that:

victory is the crown of moral quality, and therefore while nations wage war upon one another the survival of the fittest means the survival of the physically best.

The real court, the only court in which nations' issues can and will be tried is the court of God, which is war. This Twentieth Century will see that trial, and in the issue which may be long in balance, whichever people shall win it the greater soul of righteousness will be the victor.

The shadow of conflict and of displacement greater than any which mankind has known since Attila and his Huns were stayed at Châlons is visibly impending over the world. Almost can the ear of imagination hear the gathering of the legions for the fiery trial of people, a sound vast as the trumpet of the Lord of Hosts. . . .

A prophecy indeed: One may say that this is at best an illustration of the use of Darwinian concepts by a crackpot. But this is contradicted by any careful scrutiny of the newspapers and periodicals of the period, especially between 1890 and 1914. They offer more than ample examples of Social Darwinian currents of thought in Germany, Britain and the Empire, the United States and France.

Particularly in France agitation with Social Darwinian undertones was consciously supported and partly even guided by the government and the army. As a result of the aftermath of the Dreyfus affair not only French public confidence in the army but also morale within the army had been seriously shaken. While in 1897 the number of officer cadets at Saint-Cyr was 1,920, by 1911 the figure had declined to 871. After the fall of the Combes Cabinet reaction set in, aiming at restoring both confidence and morale. The publicity offensive conducted with Social Darwinian arguments opened up old sores and became once again the propaganda of revanchism. That Germany's foreign policy was added grist to the mill of French foreign policy requires no further elaboration.

But journalists and writers were not the only ones who spread the poison contained in Social Darwinism. Statesmen, like Lord Salisbury, Joseph Chamberlain, Bethmann-Hollweg, Delcassé and Theodore Roosevelt, did so in the same measure. Of the so-called 'case studies' there are many in which Social Darwinian agitation occupied the centre of the public stage, from the Spanish–American War to the Boer War. 'We are a conquering race,' maintained Senator Albert J. Beveridge. 'We must obey our blood and occupy new markets and, if necessary, new lands.' That in the course of the 'pacification' of the Philippines orders like that of General Jake Smith were issued – 'I wish you to kill and burn; the more you burn and kill the better it will please me' – seems no more than a logical corollary.

An important example of European significance is represented by the Anglo-German naval rivalry. Whatever reasons there were for and against, the acrimonious public debate which accompanied it was marked by an excess of extreme Social Darwinian argumentation. A nation expands or it decays, the indicators of expansion being the number and value of actual colonial possessions. To protect them and itself a nation required a strong navy, even if only conceived as a 'risk fleet'. Those lessons had been driven home well enough by the most influential naval writer of the period, Captain Thayer Mahan. In view of the psychological climate the build-up of strong naval forces not only in Germany but in the United States and Japan appears not natural but logical. The literary advocates of navalism made themselves heard with their consensus aptly summarised in the opinion 'that lasting good is only evolved in this world through strife and bloodshed. While injustice and unrighteousness exist in the world, the sword, the rifled breech-loader and the torpedo boat become part of the world's evolutionary machinery, consecrated like any other part of it.' The German arguments were not one iota better.

Purely within the context of Anglo-German relations and their occasional difficulties, even the naval rivalry would probably have been responsible for some ups and downs in the relations between the two countries, but they alone could hardly have caused the systematic deterioration of feeling and sentiments at all levels of both respective societies. The responsibility for this seems to lie primarily with the psychological climate in which the differences between the two countries grew. In such an atmosphere that amorphous body called 'public opinion', whether in the form of Navy League or the *Flottenverein*, could be mobilised at an instant's notice and relied upon to support any crazy armaments scheme, for in the end everything turned on the question of survival of the fittest. Social Darwinism largely eliminated rational public discussion on a broader level and replaced it by emotional outbursts which – on both sides – saw in any of the opponent's suggestions or arguments a mere stratagem and further confirmation that the slightest concession would be a step towards defeat in the struggle for existence.

Even here history is not without its own irony. At about the same time as the first ironclads sank the Turkish fleet off Sinop, a Bavarian artillery sergeant had fired the first underwater shot and members of the Russian court were treated to a performance of a Mozart quartet in an underwater diving-boat off Kronstadt. The weapon of the future was experiencing its birth-pangs and outdating – even before they were built – all those products of steel and sweat in which Anglo-Saxon and Teuton sailed forth for battle in 'the struggle for existence', called upon 'to fear God and dread nought'. Both nations survived, but in the shadow of super-Powers in whose armoury battleships are mere scrap-metal. Ironically, what has survived is the underwater boat.

While the dynamic variation of Social Darwinism was characterised by the doctrine of progress through the elimination of unfit nations, the second variation, static in nature, was marked by the elimination of unfit individuals. For the first time a prominent British review spoke up in favour of a nationally directed policy of euthanasia as a means of 'racial' selection.

That is not to say that because of this the nineteenth century loses its claim to have been 'the Age of Reform'; it merely qualifies this claim. Moreover, it must not be forgotten that social reform varied in its intensity from country to country, from continent to continent. From this point of view the United States was the most backward nation, the German Empire the most progressive. But in Germany the entire social question had been subordinated to the interest of the State and its stability, while social reform in western Europe was based on different foundations. There, in the classic home of liberalism, the liberal reform movement had carried the banner of reform as far as the middle class which it represented allowed. From then it passed into the hands of the Socialists.

In an age of the growing emancipation of the masses and the expansion of the suffrage, in an age of improving living standards, rudimentary political wisdom forbade the propagation of the concept of the elimination of unfit individuals. This would hardly have been conducive to the settling of the unruly spirits of the working classes. Hence the rise of racialist theories represented a welcome element to supplement Social Darwinism and to provide a common denominator for the otherwise strictly segregated class structure of a nation. It was a common denominator which helped to integrate all classes in the age of the 'New Imperialism'; even the lowest social strata now had a yardstick with which to measure those below their own miserable existence.

Racialism was not dissimilar to the role played by slavery in the southern states of the United States. Less than 10 per cent of their population were plantation-owners with more than fifty slaves, 6 per cent held up to fifty slaves, 8 per cent had only one or two slaves. That is to say, if slavery was really the cause of the American Civil War, 76 per cent of all Southerners fought for an institution in which they had no material share – except its symbolism.

Much the same is the case with racially influenced Social Darwinism. The racial theories which were rampant in Europe and the United States were in reality antidotes to potential social revolution. 'Race' became a symbol, elevated to the equivalent of 'nation'. As long as the masses, even for a limited time, could be made to forget the injustices and the exploitation of the society within which they lived, there was more chance of reducing dangerous stresses arising within the nation. Nationalism, perverted into race hatred, pushed the class struggle into the background for a short time.

The so-called 'scientific elaboration' of racial theory had preceded Darwin. Gobineau had laid its foundations in his essay on *The Inequalities of the Human Races*, an essay which inspired the history of the Aryans and laid the basis for comparison and classification of political institutions. Influenced by the results of the comparative method in philology and mythology, it was suddenly believed that signs of unity had been found in the primitive institutions of the Aryans, especially their most famous branches, the Greeks, Romans and Teutons. This product of doubtful scholarship was quickly taken up by the popular media of communication and injected into the mental fabric of the nations. There the famous branches were soon narrowed down to a respective nation, namely to the one which one was a member of.

For the British the burden of Empire presupposed the existence of a divine power which had selected them for a divine mission through the evolutionary process, through the survival of the fittest. Or as Cecil Rhodes put it, 'I contend that we are the first race in the world and the more of the world we inhabit the better it is for the human race.' As the word spread in the Anglo-Saxon world of the superiority of the race and its world mission, Germans quickly noted the change from previously held theories of the 'common Teuton stock' to the more selective Anglo-Saxon base and replied to it with Germany's mission to bring *Kultur* to the world in general and to the 'uncivilised Slavs' in particular. 'We are the salt of the earth,' said Kaiser Wilhelm II. With each nation discovering its own mission, its own specific racial superiority, if not hatred at least dislike and suspicion of the foreigner and his evil designs began to prevail over more serious domestic issues. In Europe national exuberance, already on the verge of excess, gathered further force.

Furthermore, the nations of Europe, especially Germany, Austria and France, experienced the process of industrialisation which was much more genuinely a 'revolution' than that which had taken place in Great Britain. In central Europe, the German Empire and Austria-Hungary, this process displaced large parts of the population from their place on the 'status ladder', especially artisans, small traders and farmers, and re-

duced them to proletarian status and dependence. A
new industrial middle class stepped into their place,
marked by the slogan current in all Western languages,
the 'money power of capitalism'. Money power, capital
interest, etc., had ever since the beginning of Christian
religious instruction, intuitively rather than reasonably,
been associated with one race – the Jews. The association of capital and Jewry, existing in some cases, but
mainly based on a series of unproven assumptions,
resulted in a further association, that of Jewry and the
age of industrial modernity. The smoking stacks of
factory chimneys, money power, the preference for
'community' before 'society' provided a fresh impulse
to a tendency latent throughout European society –
anti-Semitism. Anti-Semitism in particular, racism in
general, came together with the popular desire of the
age of the natural sciences to discover the elements of
nature in human life, a discovery which, so it was
thought, would provide the chance of cultivating them
in the interest of the race of European–Aryan civilisation. In an age of growing depersonalisation, the disintegration of traditional ties, race became the last
bulwark in the defence of national individuality.

Social Darwinism and, closely connected with it,
racism, the reaction of many levels of the population
to the materialism of an industrial age, created that
psychological climate in which political decisions were
made, 'national interests' interpreted. They provided
some of the 'unspoken assumptions' of the era. In the
popular reaction to the outbreak of the First World
War, as well as in the fatalism of some of the leading
statesmen, was expressed the often never admitted
conviction that war was inevitable: it was the Lord's
sword which was sweeping away evil, furthering good,
to discard the rotten to make way for the healthy, to
replace, as Germans believed, 'materialist civilisation'
with the '*Kultur* of the spirit'.

Typical examples of men who represented the *Zeitgeist* have already been mentioned, but none of them
went as far as to carry these 'principles' to their logical
conclusion. This role was preserved for a man who was
only one among thousands on Munich's Odeonsplatz

in August 1914 listening to the proclamation of war and who subsequently volunteered for military service. However, the years in which his *Weltanschauung* was shaped were those of the turn of the century and the first decade and a half of the twentieth century. His 'ideology' was hardened by the years of front-line experience and that of the short-lived Soviet Republic in Bavaria. To dismiss Hitler's ideological tenets as 'the product of the doss-house' is an inadmissible simplification of complex events – quite apart from the fact that Hitler was never in the economic circumstances which would have compelled him to seek refuge in a 'doss-house', except for a very specific purpose.

It is a simplification which totally ignores the intellectual currents of the turn of the century, those currents, coming second- or third-hand, which influenced the young Hitler. In *Mein Kampf* he remarks that at an early stage he had learnt to look at history from a specific point of view. 'To study history and to learn from it means to look for those driving forces and to find them, which represent the causes of the results, which before our own eyes are historical events.' As it has been correctly remarked, the emphasis of this sentence lies on the principle of causality, a sentence which amounts almost to a creed in the natural sciences. It outlines clearly how Hitler approached problems: from his point of view clear, cool, emotionally detached, or 'ice-cold' as he would have called it. From this perspective he observed the world, as it appeared to him in Vienna. The existing social realities were unimportant when compared with the question of their origins and the circumstances which had brought them about. The search for a causal principle pushed social reality into the background; his 'scientific method' preserved him from becoming 'sentimental'. Every reform impulse was bound to fail, unless the root of all evil had been discovered, until the roots of national society had been freed from poisonous weeds. The logical conclusion therefore was to eliminate all those forces which polluted nation and race, the extermination of that

which in his judgement was destructive to life or un-
worthy of living. As Marx and Lenin postulated an
economic determinism, so Hitler postulated a biological determinism.

Any assessment of Hitler's views has to bear in mind
that he looked at realities as the product of certain
laws. He considered his task to find these laws; once
they were found, they formed a *Weltanschauung*
whose precepts would direct action. The essentially
self-taught Hitler believed he was acting methodologically like a natural scientist.

The 'laws' which Hitler believed he had discovered
derived directly from a rampant Social Darwinism
and racism; their radicalisation in his anti-Semitism
came from the economic and social upheaval of central Europe and the specific conditions of the Habsburg Empire, the hothouse of most of the ideas which
were to dominate central Europe during the following
decades. Freud, Wittgenstein and Mahler are only
three examples of many; even only a first reading of
Karl Kraus's *The Last Days of Mankind* makes it
apparent how in that environment that kind of *Angst*
psychosis could originate which was instrumental in
giving Hitler – for lack of a better term – the courage
to pursue his principles to their criminal logical end
and to take the step from theory to practice.

Hitler's so-called 'scientific method' had shown him
the 'Jew' as the solvent of any national order, as the
prime element of decomposition of a society in the
throes of industrialisation. 'Rootless Jewry' was for
him the destroyer of racial and national (that race and
nation could be mutually exclusive he did not realise
at this early stage) individuality, the agents of materialist industrial depersonalisation. In other words, like
many of his contemporaries in the Western world, he
analysed political and social problems with the aid of
medical–biological categories, and the inevitable consequence of the discovery of an allegedly harmful
germ is the attempt to exterminate it.

The Social Darwinian component of his thought is
best expressed in his concept of 'living-space', or in the
brutal words formulated before his S.S. Guard at

Christmas 1940: 'Bird, you eat or you die.' From his point of view the war which broke out in 1939 was neither necessary nor useful. In view of the Russo-German pact Poland could not defend herself anyway, hence the 'dictates of reason' commanded Poland to accept the German demands, particularly since neither Britain nor France could assist their ally. That Poland did not give in, that Britain and France continued the war, was in Hitler's view contrary to all reason. Consequently an explanation was required which consisted in turning the 'un-understandable' into a 'conspiracy of world Jewry' and from there to proceed to the final step – genocide. References to such a possibility are contained in Reichstag speeches of 1939, and to the actual execution in his speech of 8 November 1942.

Hitler adhered to these lunatic principles to the last minute of his life. In his political testament, the largest part of which consists in blaming 'world Jewry' for having caused the war, he placed great emphasis upon drawing a clear distinction between the 'humane' means he had deployed to solve the 'Jewish problem' and those means used by the Allied air forces to annihilate 'innocent women and children'.

To a man locked away in his Headquarters in East Prussia or in the bunker of the Reich Chancellery in Berlin, a man who had never entered Auschwitz or Treblinka, the technically 'perfect' system of mass murder in the gas chambers was bound to appear more 'humane' than the death of parts of Germany's civilian population by napalm and phosphor.

It would be absurd to attempt to deny that Hitler was a demon and a phenomenon, but his *Weltan-schauung* is explicable (this must not be confused with 'excusable') in terms of the intellectual environment of the turn of the century; as a political and 'ideological' phenomenon he is explicable in terms of the specifically German and Austro-German conditions which first helped to shape him and under a specific set of circumstances made him acceptable to the German people as their leader. No doubt, Hitler in many respects represents the German intellectual and political tradition, magnified and distorted to a perverted degree – but he represents no less ideas and systems of ideas once popular and even respectable in Europe as a whole.

However thin and tenuous it may be, the connection exists between the liberal belief in progress, the march of science and Auschwitz.

Notes on Contributors

KLAUS EPSTEIN, until his death Professor of History at Brown University, Providence, R.I. Author of *Erzberger and the Dilemma of Germany Democracy* (1959) and *The Genesis of German Conservatism* (1966).

FRITZ FISCHER, Professor of Medieval and Modern History at the University of Hamburg. Author of *Griff nach der Weltmacht* (1961) and *Krieg der Illusionen* (1969).

IMANUEL GEISS, Lecturer in History at the University of Hamburg. Author of *Der polnische Grenzstreifen 1914–1918* (1960) and editor of *Julikrise und Kriegsausbruch 1914* (1963–4).

P. H. S. HATTON, Lecturer in History, Westfield College, University of London.

KARL-HEINZ JANSSEN, Political Editor of *Die Zeit*. Author of *Macht und Verblendung, Kriegszielpolitik der deutschen Bundesstaaten 1914–1918* (1962) and *Der Kanzler und der General: Die Führungskrise um Bethmann-Hollweg und Falkenhayn 1914–1918* (1967).

JAMES JOLL, Professor of International Relations at the London School of Economics and Political Science. Author of *The Second International* (1955) and *Intellectuals in Politics* (1960).

H. W. KOCH, Lecturer in History at the University of York. Author of *Hitler Youth* (1972) and Editorial Consultant of the American edition of Gerhard Ritter's work *Staatskunst und Kriegshandwerk*.

EGMONT ZECHLIN, Professor of Medieval and Modern History at the University of Hamburg. Author of *Die deutsche Politik und die Juden im ersten Weltkrieg* (1970) and *Kriegsausbruch 1914 und Kriegszielproblem in der internationalen Politik* (1972).

Bibliography

The literature concerning the outbreak of the First
World War as well as that on German war aims has
become so vast that it is virtually impossible even to
list a representative cross-section. Readers are referred
to the bibliographies contained in the works of
Albertini, Langer, Taylor and Schmitt.

ALBERTINI, LUIGI, *The Origins of the War of 1914*, 3
vols (Oxford, 1952–7).

BARNES, HARRY ELMER, *The Genesis of the World War:
An Introduction to the Problem of War Guilt* (New
York, 1927).

BASLER, WERNER, *Deutschlands Annexionspolitik in
Polen und im Baltikum 1914–1918* (Berlin, 1962).

BAUMGART, W., *Deutsche Ostpolitik 1918* (Munich,
1966).

BESTUSZHEV, IGOR W., *Bórba v Rossii po voprosam
vnésnei politiki 1906–1916* (Moscow, 1961).

——, 'Russian Foreign Policy February–June 1914',
Journal of Contemporary History, I 3 (1966).

BIRKE, ERNST, 'Die französische Osteuropapolitik 1914–
1918', *Zeitschrift für Ostforschung*, III (1954) 321 ff.

BIRNBAUM, K. E., *Peace Moves and U-Boat Warfare: A
Study of Imperial Germany's Policy towards the
United States April 18, 1916–January 9, 1917* (Stock-
holm, 1958).

BOVYKIN, V. Y., *Istorii vosniknoveniya pervoi mirovoi
voiny: otnospheniya Rossii i Frantsii v 1912–1914*
(Moscow, 1961).

BURCHARDT, LOTHAR, *Friedenswirtschaft und Kriegs-
vorsorge. Deutschlands wirtschaftliche Rüstungs-
bestrebungen vor 1914* (Boppard, 1968).

BUTTERFIELD, HERBERT, 'Sir Edward Grey in July 1914',
Historical Studies V, Papers Read to the Sixth Irish

Conference of Historians, ed. J. L. McCracken (London, 1965) 1 ff.

CARLGREN, W. M., *Neutralität oder Allianz. Deutschlands Beziehungen zu Schweden in den Anfangsjahren des Ersten Weltkrieges* (Stockholm, 1962).

CONZE, WERNER, *Polnische Nation und deutsche Politik im Ersten Weltkrieg* (Cologne–Graz, 1958).

DALLIN, ALEXANDER, *et al.*, *Russian Diplomacy and Eastern Europe 1914–1917* (New York, 1963).

DEDIJER, VLADIMIR, *The Road to Sarajevo* (New York, 1966).

DEHIO, LUDWIG, *Deutschland und die Weltpolitik im 20. Jahrhundert*, 2nd ed. (Frankfurt, 1961).

DROZ, JACQUES, 'Die politischen Kräfte in Frankreich während des Ersten Weltkrieges', *Geschichte in Wissenschaft und Unterricht*, XVII (1966) 159 ff.

ENGEL-JANOSI, FRIEDRICH, *Österreich und der Vatikan 1846–1918*, 2 vols (Graz–Vienna, 1958–60).

ERDMANN, KARL-DIETRICH, 'Zur Beurteilung Bethmann Hollwegs', *Geschichte in Wissenschaft und Unterricht*, XV (1964) 525 ff.

FAY, SIDNEY BRADSHAW, *The Origins of the World War*, 2 vols (New York, 1928).

FELDMANN, GERALD D., *Army, Industry and Labor in Germany 1914–1918* (Princeton, N.J., 1966).

FELLNER, FRITZ, *Der Dreibund. Europäische Diplomatie vor dem Ersten Weltkrieg* (Munich, 1960).

——, 'Zur Kontroverse über Fritz Fischers Buch *Griff nach der Weltmacht*', *Mitteilungen des Instituts für österreichische Geschichtsforschung*, LXXII (1964) 507 ff.

FISCHER, FRITZ, 'Deutsche Kriegsziele. Revolutionierung und Separatfrieden im Osten 1914 bis 1918', *Historische Zeitschrift*, CLXXXVIII (1959) 249 ff.

——, 'Kontinuität des Irrtums. Zum Problem der deutschen Kriegszielpolitik im ersten Weltkrieg', *Historische Zeitschrift*, CXCI (1960) 83 ff.

——, *Griff nach der Weltmacht. Die Kriegszielpolitik des kaiserlichen Deutschlands 1914–18* (Düsseldorf, 1961), 2nd ed., 1962; 3rd ed., 1964; special ed., 1967. (English translation: *Germany's Aims in the First World War*, London, 1966.)

——, 'Weltpolitik, Weltmachtstreben und deutsche Kriegsziele', *Historische Zeitschrift*, cxcix (1964) 265 ff.

——, *Weltmacht oder Niedergang. Deutschland im Ersten Weltkrieg* (Frankfurt, 1965) (Hamburger Studien zur neueren Geschichte, Bd. 1).

——, 'Vom Zaun gebrochen – nicht hineingeschlittert. Deutschlands Schuld am Ausbruch des Ersten Weltkriegs', *Die Zeit*, no. 36 (3 Sep. 1965).

——, *Krieg der Illusionen* (Düsseldorf, 1969).

GALANTAR, JOSZEF, 'Stefan Tisza und der Erste Weltkrieg', *Österreich in Geschichte und Literatur*, no. 10 (1964).

——, 'Die Kriegszielpolitik der Tisza-Regierung 1913–1917', *Nouvelles études historiques*, ii (Budapest, 1965) 201 ff.

GATZKE, HANS WILHELM, *Germany's Drive to the West: A Study of Germany's Western War Aims during the First World War* (Baltimore, 1950).

GEISS, IMANUEL, *Der polnische Grenzstreifen 1914–1918. Ein Beitrag zur deutschen Kriegszielpolitik im Ersten Weltkrieg* (Lübeck–Hamburg, 1960) (Eberings Historische Studien, Heft 398).

——, 'Zur Beurteilung der deutschen Reichspolitik im Ersten Weltkrieg. Kritische Bemerkungen zur Interpretation des Riezler-Tagebuchs', in H. Pogge von Strandmann and Imanuel Geiss, *Die Erforderlichkeit des Unmöglichen. Deutschland am Vorabend des Ersten Weltkrieges* (Frankfurt, 1965) (Hamburger Studien zur neueren Geschichte, Bd. 2).

—— (ed.), *Julikrise und Kriegsausbruch 1914. Eine Dokumentensammlung*, 2 vols (Hanover, 1963–4).

—— (ed.), *Juli 1914. Die europäische Krise und der Ausbruch des Ersten Weltkrieges* (Munich, 1965).

GOTTLIEB, WOLFRAM WILLIAM, *Studies in Secret Diplomacy during the First World War* (London, 1957).

GROH, DIETER, 'The "Unpatriotic Socialists" and the State', *Journal of Contemporary History*, ii 4 (1966) 151 ff.

GUINN, PAUL, *British Strategy and Politics 1914 to 1918* (Oxford, 1965).

GUTSCHE, WILLIBALD, 'Erst Europa, dann die Welt',

Zeitschrift für Geschichtswissenschaft (1964) 745 ff.

———, 'Bethmann Hollweg und die Politik der "Neu-orientierung". Zur innenpolitischen Strategie und Taktik der deutschen Reichsregierung während des Ersten Weltkriegs', *Zeitschrift für Geschichtswissenschaft* (1965) 209 ff.

HALLGARTEN, GEORG WOLFGANG FELIX, *Imperialismus vor 1914. Die soziologischen Grundlagen der Aussenpolitik europäischer Grossmächte vor dem Ersten Weltkrieg*, 2 vols, 2nd ed. (Munich, 1963).

HANTSCH, HUGO, *Leopold Graf Berchtold. Grandseigneur und Staatsmann*, 2 vols. (Graz–Vienna, 1963).

HATTON, P. H. S., 'Harcourt and Solf: The Search for an Anglo-German Understanding through Africa 1912–1914', *European Studies Review*, 1 (April 1971).

HELMREICH, E. C., *The Diplomacy of the Balkan Wars 1912–1913* (Cambridge, Mass., 1938).

HERZFELD, HANS, 'Die deutsche Kriegszielpolitik im Ersten Weltkrieg', *Vierteljahrshefte für Zeitgeschichte* (1963) 224 ff.

———, 'Zur deutschen Politik im Ersten Weltkrieg. Kontinuität oder permanente Krise?', *Historische Zeitschrift*, CXCI (1960) 67 ff.

HILLGRUBER, ANDREAS, 'Riezlers Theorie des kalkulierten Risikos und Bethmann Hollwegs politisches Kalkül in der Julikrise 1914', *Historische Zeitschrift*, CCII (1966) 24 ff.

———, *Deutschlands Rolle in der Vorgeschichte der beiden Weltkriege* (Göttingen, 1967).

HÖLZLE, ERWIN, 'Das Experiment des Friedens im Ersten Weltkrieg', *Geschichte in Wissenschaft und Unterricht*, XIII (1962) 465 ff.

HUBATSCH, WALTHER, 'Ursachen und Anlass des Weltkrieges 1914', in *1914–1939–1945. Schicksalsjahre deutscher Geschichte* (Boppard, 1964).

———, *Die Ära Tirpitz. Studien zur deutschen Marinepolitik 1890–1918* (Göttingen, 1955).

JABLONOWSKI, HORST, 'Die Stellungnahme der russischen Parteien zur Aussenpolitik der Regierung von der russisch-englischen Verständigung bis zum Ersten Weltkrieg', *Forschungen zur osteuropäischen Geschichte*, V (1957) 60 ff.

JANSSEN, KARL-HEINZ, *Macht und Verblendung. Kriegs-
    zielpolitik der deutschen Bundesstaaten 1914–1918*
    (Göttingen, 1962).
——, *Der Kanzler und der General. Die Führungskrise
    um Bethmann Hollweg und Falkenhayn (1914–1916)*
    (Göttingen, 1967).
KANTOROWICZ, HERMANN, *Gutachten zur Kriegsschuld-
    frage 1914*, from the papers edited by Imanuel Geiss
    (Frankfurt, 1963).
KEHR, E., *Der Primat der Innenpolitik*, ed. H.-U.
    Wehler (Berlin, 1965).
KOCH, H. W., 'The Anglo-German Alliance Negoti-
    ations: Missed Opportunity or Myth', *History*, LIV
    182 (1969) 378–92.
LAFORE, LAURENCE, *The Long Fuse: An Interpretation
    of the Origins of World War I* (London, 1966).
LANGER, W. L., *The Diplomacy of Imperialism 1890–
    1901* (New York, 1951, reprinted 1956).
LEE, DWIGHT ERWIN (ed.), *The Outbreak of the First
    World War: Who Was Responsible?* (Boston, 1958).
LINK, ARTHUR S., *Wilson: The Struggle for Neutrality
    1914–1915* (Princeton, N.J., 1960).
LYNAR, ERNST W., Graf von (ed.), *Deutsche Kriegsziele
    1914–1918* (Darmstadt, 1964).
MAMATEY, VICTOR S., *The United States and East Cen-
    tral Europe 1914–1918* (Princeton, N.J., 1956).
MARDER, A. J., *The Anatomy of British Sea Power:
    A History of British Naval Politics in the Pre-Dread-
    nought Era 1880–1905* (London, 1964).
——, *From the Dreadnought to Scapa Flow*, vols. I–IV
    (London, 1961–70).
MARKERT, WERNER, 'Die deutsch-russischen Beziehung-
    en am Vorabend des Ersten Weltkriegs', *Osteuropa
    und die abendländische Welt* (Göttingen, 1966) 166
    ff.
MAY, ERNEST R., *The World War and American Isola-
    tion 1914–1917* (Cambridge, 1959).
MOMMSEN, WOLFGANG J., 'Der italienische Kriegsein-
    tritt und die Krise der Politik Bethmann Hollwegs
    im Frühjahr 1915', *Quellen und Forschungen aus
    italienischen Archiven und Bibliotheken*, XLVIII
    (1968) 282 ff.

MONTICONE, ALBERTO, 'La missione a Roma del principe von Bülow 1914–15', *Quellen und Forschungen
aus italienischen Archiven und Bibliotheken*, XLVIII
(1968) 309 ff.

——, 'Salandra e Sonnino verso la decisione dell'intervento', *Rivista di studi politici internazionali*, XXIV
(1957) 66 ff.

NECK, RUDOLF, *Arbeiterschaft und Staat im Ersten
Weltkrieg 1914–1918*, I (Vienna, 1964).

——, *Österreich-Ungarn in der Weltpolitik 1900–1918*
(Berlin, 1965).

PAPST, KLAUS, *Eupen-Malmedy in der belgischen
Regierungs- und Parteienpolitik 1914 bis 1940*
(Aachen, 1964).

PETZOLD, JOACHIM, 'Zu den Kriegszielen der deutschen
Monopolkapitalisten im Ersten Weltkrieg', *Zeitschrift für Geschichtswissenschaft*, VIII (1960) 1396 ff.

PIKART, EBERHARD, 'Der deutsche Reichstag und der
Ausbruch des Ersten Weltkrieges', *Der Staat*, V (1966)
47 ff.

POLETIKA, N. P., *Vosnikovenie pervoi mirovoi voiny
(Yulskii krisis, 1914)* (Moscow, 1964).

——, *Politik im Krieg. Studien zur Politik der deutschen herrschenden Klassen im Ersten Weltkrieg
1914–1918* (Berlin, 1964).

RATHMANN, LOTHAR, *Stossrichtung Nahost 1914–1918.
Zur Expansionspolitik des deutschen Imperialismus
im Ersten Weltkrieg* (Berlin, 1963).

RAUCH, GEORG VON, 'Neue sowjetische Literatur zur
Vorgeschichte des Ersten Weltkrieges', *Jahrbücher
für die Geschichte Osteuropas*, n.s., XII (1964) 572 ff.

RENOUVIN, P., *Les origines immédiates de la guerre*,
2nd ed. (Paris, 1927).

——, *La première guerre mondiale* (Paris, 1965).

——, 'Les buts de guerre du gouvernement français',
Revue historique, CCXXXV (1) (1966) 1 ff.

RICH, N., *Friedrich von Holstein*, 2 vols (Cambridge,
1965).

RITTER, GERHARD, *Staatskunst und Kriegshandwerk.
Das Problem des 'Militarismus' in Deutschland*; vol.
II: *Die Hauptmächte Europas und das Wilhelminische Reich (1890 bis 1914)* (Munich, 1960); vol.

III: *Die Tragödie der Staatskunst. Bethmann Hollweg als Kriegskanzler (1914–1917)* (Munich, 1964);
vol. IV: *Die Herrschaft des deutschen Militarismus
und die Katastrophe in 1918* (Munich, 1968).

——, *Der Erste Weltkrieg. Studien zum deutschen
Geschichtsbild* (Bonn, 1964) (Schriftenreihe der
Bundeszentrale für politische Bildung, Heft 65).

——, 'Die politische Rolle Bethmann Hollwegs während des Ersten Weltkrieges', *Rapports,* IV: *Méthod-
ologie et Histoire contemporaine,* edited for the
Comité International des Sciences Historiques
(Vienna, 1965).

ROCHAT, GIORGIO, 'L'esercito italiano nell'estate 1914',
Nuova Rivista Storica, XLV (1961) 295 ff.

ROHLFES, JOACHIM, 'Französische und deutsche His-
toriker über die Kriegsziele', *Geschichte in Wissenschaft und Unterricht,* XVII (1966) 168 ff.

ROSEN, EDGAR R., 'Italiens Kriegseintritt im Jahre 1915
als innenpolitisches Problem der Giolitti-Ära', *His-
toriche Zeitschrift,* CLXXXVII (1959) 289 ff.

SCHIEDEL, WOLFGANG, 'Italien und Deutschland 1914–
15', *Quellen und Forschungen aus italienischen Archiven und Bibliotheken,* XLVIII (1968) 244 ff.

SCHLÖRER, ALFRED, *Krieg–Staat–Monopol 1914–1918.
Die Zusammenhänge von imperialistischer Kriegs-
wirtschaft, Militarisierung der Volkswirtschaft und
staatsmonopolistischem Kapitalismus in Deutschland
während des Ersten Weltkrieges* (Berlin, 1965).

SCHMITT, BERNADOTTE E., *The Coming of the War 1914,*
2 vols. (New York–London, 1930).

——, *The Origins of the First World War* (London,
1958).

SCHUDDEKOPF, OTTO-ERNST, 'Politik und Kriegsführung.
Die Kriegszielpolitik der Mittelmächte während des
Ersten Weltkriegs', *Neue Politische Literatur,* X
(1965) 247 ff.

SCHWABE, KLAUS, 'Zur politischen Haltung der
deutschen Professoren im Ersten Weltkrieg', *Historische Zeitschrift,* CXCIII (1961) 601 ff.

SMITH, JAY C., *The Russian Struggle for Power 1914–
1917: A Study of Russian Foreign Policy during the
First World War* (New York, 1956).

Steinberg, J., *Yesterday's Deterrent: Tirpitz and the Birth of the German Battle Fleet* (London, 1965).

Stern, Fritz, *Bethmann Hollweg und der Krieg. Die Grenzen der Verantwortung* (Tübingen, 1968).

Stone, Norman, 'Army and Society in the Habsburg Monarchy 1900–1914', *Past and Present*, no. 33 (1966) 95 ff.

Taylor, A. J. P., *The Struggle for Mastery in Europe, 1848–1918* (Oxford, 1954).

——, 'The War Aims of the Allies in the First World War', in *Essays Presented to Sir Lewis Namier* (London–New York, 1956) 475 ff.

——, *Politics in Wartime* (London, 1964).

Ternovsky, R. N., *Sovietskaya istoriografiya Rossiiskovo Imperialisma* (Moscow, 1964).

Thayer, John A., *Italy and the Great War: Politics and Culture, 1870–1915* (Madison, 1964).

Übersberger, Hans, *Österreich zwischen Russland und Serbien. Zur südslawischen Frage und der Entstehung des Ersten Weltkrieges* (Cologne–Graz, 1955).

Valiani, Leo, La *dissoluzione dell'Austria-Ungheria* (Milan, 1966).

——, 'Le origini della guerra del 1914 e dell'intervento italiana nelle ricerche e nelle pubblicazioni dell' ultimo ventennio', *Rivista Storica Italiana*, LXXVIII (1966).

——, *Il partito socialista italiano nel periodo della neutralità 1914–1915* (Milan, 1963).

Vigezzi, Brunello, *L'Italia di fronte alla prima guerra mondiale*, vol. 1: *L'Italia neutrale* (Milan–Naples, 1966).

Wegerer, Alfred von, *Der Ausbruch des Weltkrieges,* 2 vols (Hamburg, 1939; 2nd ed., 1943).

Wernecke, Klaus, *Der Wille zur Weltgattung* (Düsseldorf, 1970).

Zechlin, Egmont, 'Friedensbestrebungen und Revolutionierungsversuche', *Beilage zur Wochenzeitung 'Das Parlament'*, nos. 20 (1961), 24 (1961), 25 (1961), 20 (1963), 22 (1963).

——, 'Das "schlesische Angebot" und die italienische Kriegsgefahr', *Geschichte in Wissenschaft und Unterricht*, XIV (1963) 533 ff.

——, 'Deutschland zwischen Kabinettskrieg und Wirtschaftskrieg. Politik und Kriegsführung in den ersten Monaten des Weltkrieges 1914', *Historische Zeitschrift*, CXCIX (1964) 347 ff.

——, 'Die Illusion vom begrenzten Krieg', *Die Zeit*, no. 38 (17 Sep. 1965).

——, 'Probleme des Kriegskalküls und der Kriegsbeendigung im Ersten Weltkrieg', *Geschichte in Wissenschaft und Unterricht*, XVI (1965) 69 ff.

——, 'Bethmann Hollweg, Kriegsrisiko und S.P.D.', *Der Monat*, Heft 208 (Jan. 1966) 17 ff.

——, 'Motive und Taktik der Reichsleitung 1914. Ein Nachtrag', *Der Monat*, Heft 209 (Feb. 1966) 91 ff.

——, *Die Deutsche Politik und die Juden im Ersten Weltkrieg* (Göttingen, 1970).

——, *Kriegsausbruch 1914 und Kriegszielproblem in der internationalen Politik* (Göttingen, 1972).

ZMARZLIK, HANS-GÜNTHER, *Bethmann Hollweg als Reichskanzler 1909–1914* (Düsseldorf, 1957).

Index